W9-DEI-063

Geographical Perspectives on Inequality

David M. Smith

Professor of Geography, Queen Mary College, London

BARNES & NOBLE BOOKS   NEW YORK

(a division of Harper & Row Publishers, Inc.)

© 1979 David M. Smith
Published in USA by
HARPER & ROW PUBLISHERS INC.
BARNES & NOBLE IMPORT DIVISION

Library of Congress Cataloging in Publication Data

Smith, David Marshall, 1936-
   Geographical perspectives on inequality.

   Bibliography: p.
   Includes index.
   1. Economic history — 20th century. 2. Income
distribution. 3. Equality. 4. Geography, Economic.
I. Title.
HC59.S5576   330.9'04   79-11818
ISBN 0-06-496380-2

To my Mother
and to the memory of my Father –
J. Marshall Smith, 1899–1977

Printed and bound in Great Britain

Contents

Contents

Between one country and another, one province and another and even one locality and another there will always exist a *certain* inequality in the conditions of life, which it will be possible to reduce to a minimum but never entirely remove. Alpine dwellers will always have different conditions of life from those of people living on plains.

FRIEDRICH ENGELS, 1875
(K. Marx and F. Engels, *Selected Correspondence*)

Preface

Inequality, in its various forms, is one of the most serious problems facing the contemporary world. Most of us are aware of the contrast between the 'haves' and 'have-nots' of our own society, and we also know something of differences in living standards among peoples elsewhere. There is widespread agreement that such gross inequalities as exist today are unjust, and that we should work towards a more equal world. But slums still survive, depressed regions remain so, and the 'development gap' between the rich and poor nations seems not to be narrowing significantly. How does inequality arise, why does it persist, and what can be done to reduce or eliminate it?

This book offers a geographical perspective on inequality. It seeks to reveal the nature and extent of place-to-place variations in living standards at different geographical scales: among nations, among regions and cities within nations, and within individual cities. It explores the role of the organization of human activity in geographical space as a factor making for inequality. The analysis offers no dramatic new solutions, but it should provide the basis for a better understanding of the origins of inequality as a geographical condition and of the difficulties in the way of plans to promote greater equality in human life chances.

While the book is aimed primarily at sixth formers and undergraduates studying geography, it has been written very much with the general reader in mind. At times the content extends well beyond the conventional bounds of geography as an academic field. The abstractions, formulae and jargon of contemporary human geography have been avoided for the most part, in favour of an approach that allows the facts to speak for themselves. There is far less mystery about inequality and the reasons for it than might be supposed from some of the tortuous treatments in modern social science. References in

11

the text have been kept to the minimum consistent with identifying sources of information, statistics and quotations. The bibliography should provide ample guidance for readers who wish to take matters further.

The approach adopted in this book relies heavily on generalization from case studies. The cases have been chosen so as to exemplify problems of inequality in different kinds of societies: advanced capitalist nations, Third World countries and socialist systems. They are based largely on the author's own research. The individual case studies build up into a final synthesis, to provide some general understanding of inequality in geographical space. While each nation, region and city has its own distinctive pattern of inequality reflecting local conditions, the forces making for differentiation of living standards have a much broader origin in the prevailing structure of society, its political institutions and its economic base. The geographical perspective is thus an integral part of contemporary political economy, rooted in the reality of the human life experience.

Acknowledgements

The many years of research on which this book is based have been facilitated by the support of a number of different institutions. My interest in regional-development problems in Britain emerged at the University of Manchester in 1963–6, and its continuation while at Southern Illinois University from 1966 to 1970 was made possible by grants from the American Philosophical Society. The broadening of this research into work on the geography of social well-being in the United States was assisted by a grant from the Social Sciences Council, University of Florida, in 1971. First-hand experience of Peru was provided by the opportunity to participate in a research project funded by the Organization of American States and directed by Joshua C. Dickinson, in 1976. Visits to the Soviet Union were made possible by support from Queen Mary College, University of London (1976), and the British Academy (1978). References to South Africa and Australia incorporate observations made while a visiting member of staff at the Universities of Natal, the Witwatersrand and New England (Armidale, NSW) in 1972–3.

The colleagues in various parts of the world who have in some way contributed to my understanding (such as it is) are too numerous to name. Some of them will recognize their work or data, duly acknowledged by citations, though they will not necessarily approve of the use to which I have put it or the interpretations placed upon it. I hope that I have always been as fair and objective as possible in references to their particular country; this has certainly been my aim. The friendship, consideration and hospitality of so many people have enabled me to feel at home almost everywhere that I have lived, even if the grass seemed greener in some places than others.

The Department of Geography at Queen Mary College has provided a congenial and stimulating intellectual environment in which to write this book, thanks to Eric Rawstron and my other colleagues. Excellent technical services have been provided by Mr P. Newman and his staff. In Linda Agombar I have a superb secretary. Fiona Rees helped in various ways as research assistant. Peter Goodyear read the proofs.

13

Acknowledgements

As always, my family deserve more thanks than I can possibly convey, for their support and practical assistance. Margaret got me through the darkest days and gave advice when it mattered most. Michael did some calculations. Tracey helped with the bibliography. All share my process of discovery, making it so much richer.

David Smith
Loughton, Essex, December 1977

1 Introducing Inequality: Who Gets What Where

Ever since man began to explore the world around him, differences among peoples and their ways of living have aroused deep curiosity. To the Caucasians of temperate western Europe, the inhabitants of the newly discovered lands of South America, the 'dark continent' of Africa and the 'mystic orient' must have seemed as strange as the flora and fauna. Similarly, to the indigenous peoples confronted for the first time by the appearance, culture and technology of the white man, what they saw might well have been manifestations of a deity or creatures from another planet. On such visually conspicuous differences was built the subject of human geography, as the study of the peoples of the world and how they live.

Many of these differences are now a thing of the past, of course. With European colonization, empire-building and the development of an integrated world economy, there has emerged almost an international cultural ubiquity. Patterns of consumption (or at least aspiration) differ little between the well-to-do classes of Europe, America, Asia and Africa. The world's poor share a misery that changes little with national borders. The major cities of different lands appear increasingly similar: voracious acres of concrete-and-glass office blocks, modern factories, apartment complexes and expansive suburbs of single-family homes. People with black (yellow or white) skins are a familiar sight to most of us, as part of the passing crowd and sometimes as neighbours, colleagues and friends; in any case miscegenation has blurred inter-racial boundaries in many parts of the world. Perception of differences among peoples and places is being replaced by a growing awareness that all do not experience to the same extent some common conception of the 'good life' that modern science, technology and industry have made possible. Curiosity about *differences* is being replaced by concern about *inequality*.

15

Where the Grass is Greener

We live in an unequal world. This is part of our day-to-day experience, as we travel to work through neighbourhoods inferior to our own, buy goods that others cannot afford, stay at home for a holiday while thousands flock abroad, see contemporaries achieve pay awards greater than ours. In so many different respects we are able to compare our circumstances with those of others. Indeed, we are positively encouraged to do this by advertising that shows people enjoying a life in some respects superior because of the things that they possess. The modern materialist culture of the so-called advanced industrial world involves the conspicuous differentiation of the successful, through competitive displays of finely furnished homes, electronic gadgets, powerful cars, access to expensive hotels and restaurants, and so on. The advantages enjoyed by such people are there for all to see. Similarly, the penalties of being at the other end of the socio-economic scale are obvious to anyone who cares to examine conditions in the city slums, or what planners now delicately call areas of 'multiple deprivation'.

Our awareness of inequality is increasingly being extended outside our own environs, often well beyond the country in which we live. This is a result of two important aspects of modern life: growing personal mobility and more sophisticated means of communication – along with the resources and leisure to take advantage of them. Longer holiday trips enable us to see something of the life-style of people that we may not encounter at home, whether they be the poor farmers of southern Europe or the set who gravitate towards the yacht basin, casino and couturier. As the mass media open up glimpses of parts of the world that we cannot experience first-hand we see evidence of the conditions of the poor in Africa, Latin America and South-East Asia, for whom simply keeping alive is a struggle with uncertain outcome. Television brings us face to face with some of the harsh reality of famine, the disrupted lives of refugees from the latest war and the squalor of the squatter settlements in the cities of the underdeveloped world. This growing awareness also works the other way, as the mass of the world's poor become more informed, through the growth of literacy and the proliferation of the transistor radio. They see their own situation in relation to that of other people in other places, and increasingly question the inevitability of their position of disadvantage.

Inequality in living standards is one of the most serious problems facing the contemporary world. Properly managed, the resources and technology are available to provide a tolerable if modest existence for everyone, even with the world's population reaching 4,000,000,000. But the resources are unevenly distributed, the technology unevenly developed and the produce of farms and factories unevenly consumed. Far from being satisfied with existing levels of affluence, the people of the industrialized countries are perpetually striving for more, as new products and sophisticated services are made available. Resources that might have been used to provide a decent diet and basic medical care for the poor are absorbed in the production of trimmings for the rich – and of the weapons with which to protect their way of life. The gap between the 'haves' and 'have-nots' thus grows, and with it the potential for conflict. Questions of control over resources and appropriation of the benefits generated by their use are at the root of most contemporary political issues, whether they be trading relationships between advanced nations and the Third World, race conflict in Southern Africa or arguments about a redevelopment proposal in an English city. As long as we live in a world of scarcity in which it is impossible for all of everyone's wants to be met, who gets what will be a matter of contention.

The Geographical Perspective

The question of who gets what is a focus for inquiry in a number of academic disciplines. For example, the American political scientist Harold Lasswell some years ago entitled a book on his subject *Who Gets What When, How*. Paul Samuelson, whose textbook *Economics* is probably known to millions of students, sees his field as concerned with the questions of 'what, how and for whom'. The geographer has a perspective that distinguishes this subject from others concerned with inequality, and it is important to understand this before we proceed any further.

17

Where the Grass is Greener

The geographical perspective may be summarized as a concern with who gets what *where*, and how. The stress on *where* underlines the geographer's preoccupation with spatial or areal inequality – with differences in living standards according to place of residence. These variations may be examined at different geographical scales, to focus on inequality among national populations, regions, neighbourhoods and so on. The geographer thus places primary emphasis on where people live as a contributor to differential life experience. The basic descriptive task is to identify these place-to-place variations, which are often overlooked by economists, sociologists and others who are more interested in inequality among classes, races or other groups in society.

The spatial perspective embraces the process of distribution as well as the facts of spatial inequality. If standards of living vary according to where people live, then geographical space and the organization of life in this space may have a bearing on who gets what. While other social scientists may stress the role of political power, class structure, group conflict or the organization of production and distribution as contributors to inequality, the geographer stresses the way in which the *spatial* structure of the economy and society may work to the advantage of some people in some places and to the disadvantage of others. For example, it might be shown that the tendency towards spatial concentration of economic activity penalizes people living away from major cities or service centres, or those whose freedom of movement is restricted so that they cannot fully participate in city life.

But before adopting a geographical perspective as a distinctive or separate approach to understanding inequality, a note of caution is needed. No single discipline holds the key to such a complex problem as how the benefits and penalties of life come to be so unevenly distributed. The geographical viewpoint will inevitably stress certain facts and relationships, some of which tend to be neglected by economists, sociologists and political scientists. But there is a risk of over-emphasizing the importance of *spatial* variation in living standards and the role of *spatial* organization in the process of unequal distribution. As we try to show what can be learned from a geographical approach, we will have frequent cause to consider how

18

this relates to the broader structure of society. This inevitably introduces matters conventionally viewed as 'economic', 'political' or 'sociological', as opposed to 'geographical'. The discussion of *spatial* inequality and *spatial* contributions to the process of unequal distribution thus necessarily develops into a broader discussion of political economy. What this book seeks to show is that such a broad, multi-disciplinary perspective requires explicit recognition of the role of space in the organization of production, and of spatial elements in distributive processes and outcomes. But on its own, the geographical perspective sheds very limited light on the world, and may obscure more than it reveals.

What is Distributed

If the phrase 'who gets what where' encapsulates the basic issue of spatial distribution, then the question of *what* is distributed is of critical importance. We are accustomed to thinking of inequality very much in terms of money, whether at the personal level of differences in wages and salaries or at the wider level of national variations in per capita income. But there is more to life, and thus to standard of living, than monetary income. It is a truism that money cannot buy happiness, however useful it may be as a means of access to so many things from which happiness is supposed to be derived. Thus the discussion of inequality must range far beyond income, in the conventional sense of the term.

Economists are in the habit of making a distinction between the *flow* of income to an individual (or group of people) and the *stock* of wealth. Consideration of wealth adds an important dimension to the study of inequality. Ownership of wealth, in the form of money, land or other assets, provides direct access to some of the good things in life by virtue of providing purchasing power or social status. Wealth is also capable itself of generating income without the discomfort of earning it through work, i.e. dividends from capital investment and rent from land or other property. To focus attention on income may obscure the fact that wealth, and the power that it provides, may be a more important source of inequality in society.

19

Where the Grass is Greener

Private ownership of property, and especially of the means of production, is a fundamental contributor to inequality in capitalist societies – though inequality is not an exclusively capitalist phenomenon, as we shall see in subsequent discussions.

But for a more complete conception of inequality we should seek a much broader definition of both income and wealth than those generally adopted. We might define income as comprising flows not only of money but also of various other things on which standard of living depends, such as health, education, security and recreation. Some of these may be acquired through the expenditure of money income, but others come independent of income as social services or simply as attributes of the particular environments occupied by different people. We might define wealth as the stock of all things that can be drawn on to enhance level of living, such as job skills, influence on others, political power, or physical access to shops and other sources of need satisfaction.

The past decade has seen a general emergence of interest in non-monetary aspects of human well-being. It is becoming increasingly apparent that conventional measures of 'development' or 'progress', such as growth of per capita income and gross national product (GNP), are far from satisfactory as real guides to whether life is getting better or worse. For one thing, rising affluence by such measures may be accompanied by rising crime, alcoholism, drug abuse and alienation of youth. For another, such aggregate statistics as *average* personal income or *total* value of goods and services produced may hide the fact that great inequality still exists: even if there is more money and more goods and services to distribute, some people may remain poor and even become worse off than before. The growing appreciation of this forms part of a contemporary questioning of economic growth and physical production in general as the be-all and end-all of our existence. Preoccupation with materialistic objectives has diverted attention from some of the more apparently intangible aspects of life, such as environmental quality and tranquillity of mind, which may more likely deteriorate than improve with further economic growth.

Something of the range and complexity of human needs is

20

expressed in the following view of the family by an American sociologist, Marvin Sussman (1972, p. 133):

> Family objectives and needs include achieving a livelihood, thus meeting basic and derived needs for shelter, clothing, satisfaction of hunger, conditions under which procreation and sexual gratification can occur and socialization take place. Social interaction implies relationships with others in order to satisfy the need for emotional response, warmth, and affection. The shelter that houses the family unit, the food provided for its members, the clothing that protects individual members from the elements, and protection of family members against outside aggressors are necessary to meet physical maintenance objectives and needs.
>
> Mental well-being has been an increasingly recognized need in societies of high complexity. Here the objectives of family socialization include the development of capabilities to handle frustrations that emanate from conflicting demands within and outside the family, competition over scarce rewards, and frustrations stemming from failure of reciprocal expectations in inter-personal relationships. The family provides the psychological and physical territory in which one can be emotional, express one's feelings, and give and receive affective response.

The stress on mental well-being is, of course, a reflection of the extent that more fundamental needs relating to physical survival are met in countries like America, if not in the underdeveloped world.

Part of the contemporary reaction to materialism and economic-growth mania has been an increasing interest in the concepts of *social* well-being and the quality of life. There have been attempts to develop social indicators to supplement conventional economic indicators of progress, as exemplified by Britain's annual *Social Trends* (HMSO) and the United States' *Social Indicators* (US Office of Management and Budget). The development of measures of social well-being or ill-being is a major preoccupation of the social sciences, and some survey research institutions are attempting to monitor individual attitudes to life quality. The implicit assumption is that the quality of life is subject to scientific analysis, and to improvements planned with rational deliberation.

A major problem in this approach is, of course, how we define social well-being or the quality of life. Even if we restrict ourselves to

21

the perhaps more familiar concept of standard of living, the same question arises. In fact, it is difficult to make a distinction between such concepts. All refer to the satisfaction of human needs – physical and mental – so it seems best to view them as synonymous. Thus, for the purpose of further discussion in this book, we will not complicate matters by seeking subtle distinctions between such terms as standard of living, social well-being and quality of life. They will take on a specific meaning by virtue of the conditions used to measure them, but in all cases the objective is to establish the extent to which individual or social needs are met.

The question of definition still remains, however. Clearly, the constituents of the good life are personal to each individual. Some of us find our satisfaction in a new car or colour television, some in the pleasures of the concert hall or discotheque, some in relationships with other people. Some things will be more important to a society than others. We must try to generalize or find a level at which some consensus can be recognized, if inter-personal and inter-areal comparisons are to be made. There have been many attempts to do this in recent years; some will appear in later chapters of this book.

For the immediate purpose of clarifying the meaning of living standards or social well-being, we may look briefly at alternative criteria suggested by four different authorities (see Table 1.1). The first is from an early report by the United Nations, listing what was described as an 'acceptable international catalogue' of the components of level of living. The second summarizes the constituents of a level-of-living index proposed by Jan Drewnowski, Professor of Economic and Social Planning at the Institute of Social Studies, The Hague, as an extension of research originally undertaken at the United Nations Research Institute for Social Development in Geneva. The third shows the major 'areas of social concern' identified by the Organization for Economic Co-operation and Development (OECD) as a basis for compiling sets of social indicators. The fourth lists major criteria of social well-being used to guide the selection of data in an early geographical application of social indicators in the United States, some of the results of which will be presented in Chapter 3. There is considerable overlap between the lists, suggesting a large measure of agreement among the research workers

Table 1.1. Alternative criteria of human well-being

---

1. *UN components of level of living*
    Health, including demographic conditions
    Food and nutrition
    Education, including literacy and skills
    Conditions of work
    Employment situation
    Aggregate consumption and savings
    Transportation
    Housing, including household facilities
    Clothing
    Recreation and entertainment
    Social security
    Human freedom

2. *Composition of Drewnowski's level-of-living index*
    Nutrition
    Clothing
    Shelter
    Health
    Education
    Leisure
    Security
    Social environment
    Physical environment

3. *OECD areas of social concern*
    Health
    Individual development through learning
    Employment and the quality of working life
    Time and leisure
    Personal economic situation
    Physical environment
    The social environment
    Personal safety and the administration of justice
    Social opportunity and participation
    Accessibility

4. *Criteria of social well-being in the United States*
    Income, wealth and employment
    The living environment
    Health
    Education
    Social order
    Social belonging
    Recreation and leisure

Sources: UNO, 1954; Drewnowski, 1974; OECD, 1976; D. M. Smith, 1973.

concerned. While such conceptions of standard of living would not meet universal approval, they seem general enough to capture the essence of the 'what' that is distributed differentially within most societies.

Ideally, the study of inequality should embrace differential experience with respect to the full range of conditions of the type suggested in Table 1.1. Anything less risks missing important aspects of life, which in practice is likely to lead to an over-emphasis on more tangible and easily measured material conditions. But this is not to say that we must seek some comprehensive measure of human well-being before we can find out anything worth while about inequality. Much can be learned from limited information – for example on health or housing quality – as we shall see in subsequent chapters.

Before we leave the subject of what is distributed, a warning is needed about the danger of confusing means for ends. All too often in contemporary discussions of inequality the focus is on income and its expenditure, as we have suggested, with the implicit assumption that human well-being will increase in direct proportion. Thus in health care, for example, an equal distribution (e.g. by regions) could imply equal expenditure on health services. But there are two important reasons why this may not be so. First, if we begin with unequal (regional) levels of health it may require an unequal allocation of resources to attain equality in results, with more money being spent on the least healthy or most needy. We shall learn more of this in Chapter 5, in an examination of resource allocation in Britain's National Health Service. A second and related difficulty is that producing the same result (e.g. a given reduction in the mortality rate) may require more effort or expenditure in some places than others. Just as it costs more to produce a bushel of wheat on poor land than where it is fertile, so it can take more doctors and supporting services to improve health in city slums than in suburbs with a clean environment and sanitary housing. Similarly, it takes more doctors to care for a scattered rural population than to provide the same level of service in a city.

The precise relationship between expenditure ('inputs') and results ('outputs') is a difficult technical matter, beyond the scope of the present discussion. The point to grasp here is that inequality should, as far as possible, be judged in terms of results. If the ultimate end is human happiness or fulfilment, the significance of inequality observed on the basis of other criteria may appear conjectural, in the absence of clear evidence that this has a bearing on people's happiness. However, this should not prevent us proceeding on the common-sense assumption that good health, nourishing food, shelter from the elements, personal security and so on are far more likely to bring satisfaction than sorrow and that they are indeed necessary for the perpetuation of society itself.

Measuring Inequality

If we are to say anything precise about inequality, we need methods of measuring the conditions of concern. This requires not only accurate information on what is being distributed – income, health, security or whatever, but also ways of identifying the degree of inequality actually experienced. Putting meaningful numbers to economic and social conditions is a problem common to all approaches to the study of inequality, and indeed to many other aspects of social inquiry. We will leave this aside for the time being, to reappear in some of the cases in later chapters. The concern here is with the measurement of inequality itself.

As a simple illustration, we may consider the value of goods and services produced, as distributed among major world regions (Table 1.2). The largest shares are accounted for by North America and Western Europe, and the smallest by Oceania (the Pacific countries) and the Middle East. But these figures – the first column in the table – have little meaning in themselves: they must be related to population if they are to tell us anything about comparative standards of living. Calculating GNP on a per capita basis shows North America still first, but second place is taken by Oceania where Australia and New Zealand pull the per capita figure above that for Western Europe. Asia produces more than Latin America and the Middle East, but the size of its population pushes per capita GNP below that of the other regions.

The per capita figures in Table 1.2 offer a rough indication of the

25

Table 1.2. The distribution of world production in relation to population

Major region	GNP (1000 M $US)	Population (millions)	GNP per capita ($US)
North America	1259	231	5450
Western Europe	1057	397	2662
Eastern Europe	748	352	2125
Asia	572	2003	286
Latin America	181	294	616
Africa	78	322	242
Oceania	52	16	3250
Middle East	48	101	475
Total	3995	3716	1075

Source of data: Business International, 4 December 1973.
Note: GNP = Gross National Product, i.e. the value of goods and services produced for final consumption or investment including net income from overseas. The figures refer to the year 1972.

degree of inequality among major world regions. The range from $5450 in North America to $242 in Africa gives a ratio of 22·5:1 between the richest and poorest region. In other words, the average African produces only one dollar's worth of goods and services for every $22·5 produced by the average North American. As GNP is identical to national income, this ratio is also representative of differences in consumption possibilities at a given level of prices. Another indication of the magnitude of inequality is provided by deviations of the regional figures from the total world per capita rate of $1075. The average difference between the regional GNP per capita and the world figure is as much as $813. Looking at the individual figures, three regions record more than twice the world average (North America, Oceania and Western Europe), with Eastern Europe almost as high; three regions show half the world figure (Asia, Africa and the Middle East), with Latin America almost as low. Thus there is a clear division between the two worlds of the rich and the poor, on this broad continental scale.

Various descriptive statistics can be used to measure inequality more precisely. How the simplest of these can be calculated is shown in Table 1.3. Here the data from Table 1.2 are first converted into percentage distributions showing each region's proportionate share

Table 1.3. The percentage distribution of world production and population, and data for the Lorenz curve

| Major region | Percentage distribution | | | Coefficient of | Cumulative percentages | |
	GNP	popn	Differences	advantage	GNP	popn
North America	31·5	6·2	25·3	5·08	31·5	6·2
Oceania	1·3	0·4	0·9	3·25	32·8	6·6
Western Europe	26·5	10·7	15·8	2·48	59·3	17·3
Eastern Europe	18·7	9·5	9·2	1·97	78·0	26·8
Latin America	4·5	7·9	3·4	0·57	82·5	34·7
Middle East	1·2	2·7	1·5	0·44	83·7	37·4
Asia	14·3	53·9	39·6	0·27	98·0	91·3
Africa	2·0	8·7	6·7	0·23	100·0	100·0
Total	100·0	100·0	102·4			

Source of data: see Table 1.2.

of world production and population respectively, so that they can be compared directly. If production was equally distributed according to population, then these two columns of percentages would be identical, e.g. North America would account for 6·2 per cent of production instead of the 31·5 per cent shown. The greater the differences between these figures, the greater the degree of inequality. The differences are listed in the third column of the table. Summing them gives us the figure of 102·4; dividing by the number of regions (8) gives the *mean deviation* of 12·8. Taking half the sum of the differences produces a *concentration index* from 0 to 100, where 0 indicates perfect equality (i.e. no differences) and 100 indicates all GNP, or whatever is being distributed, going to one region, i.e. the extreme of inequality. The result of 51·2 shows very considerable inequality on the 0 to 100 scale.

Another way of showing the difference between two distributions is provided by a graphic device known as the *Lorenz curve*. To draw this for the relationship between regional production and population, we have to place the regions in order according to their *coefficient of advantage*. This is simply the ratio between the regional share of the two attributes concerned, i.e. for North America it is 31·5÷6·2, or 5·08. A coefficient greater than 1·0 shows that the region has more of the world's production than its share of population; less than 1·0 indicates the reverse. The regions are in fact listed in order of the coefficient of advantage in Table 1.3 (see fourth column). Now, the two distributions must be expressed as cumulative percentages, i.e. the first figure is for North America alone, the second is the proportion in North America and Oceania, and so on. These are shown in the last two columns of the table.

To draw the Lorenz curve, we plot the two sets of cumulative percentages against each other. The result is shown in Figure 1.1. Reading along the curve from the bottom left, the first dot is 31·5 GNP and 6·2 population (North America), the second is 32·8 and 6·6, and so on until the curve reaches 100 and 100 in the top right. If both sets of percentages had been the same, the 'curve' would have been the diagonal line representing equal shares. The degree of inequality in distribution is shown by how far the Lorenz curve departs from the diagonal. The proportion of the total area below the diagonal that is above the Lorenz curve (shaded in Figure 1.1) is measured by a device known as the *Gini coefficient*, which is 62 (%) in the present case. The Gini coefficient is the most common general measure of inequality in distribution (see Appendix, p. 364).

Regions of the size of those used in this illustration are, of course, far too large for the serious study of inequality. They contain much internal variation: indeed, some people living in the poorest parts of the world are better off than the poor in richer areas. To get a clearer picture we must look at smaller areas in which there is less internal differentiation. As a further illustration of the measurement of inequality we will examine briefly a single city in the United States.

San Diego, California, has a population of about three quarters of a million. For the purpose of examining inequality, it is divided into the six areas shown in Figure 1.2. Although variations in life experience do exist, of course, these areas are relatively homogeneous in their general socio-economic character. The Coastal, Kearny Mesa and newly developed North San Diego areas tend to be the more affluent, while Central, Eastern and South San Diego have the largest proportions of people with low incomes. Figures 1.2a, b and c show the incidence of three conditions of social concern, each

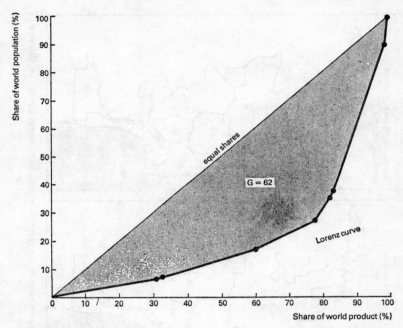

Figure 1.1. Lorenz curve showing inequality in the distribution of world production in relation to population, by major regions. (Source of data: Tables 1.1 and 1.2.)

expressed as a proportion of persons 'at risk'. Inequality is evident in each of the maps, otherwise all six areas would have the same figure. But how do the three conditions compare? This can be shown by the respective Gini (G) coefficients and Lorenz curves, as explained above. Figure 1.3 reveals that persons on public assistance (i.e. recognized to be in poverty) are most unequally distributed, or most highly concentrated geographically. Infant deaths are most evenly distributed. In passing, it should be noted that the three patterns tend to correspond, so that the areas with most people in poverty also have the highest infant mortality and the lowest proportions of children graduating from high school: one kind of disadvantage is apparently compounded by others. The significance

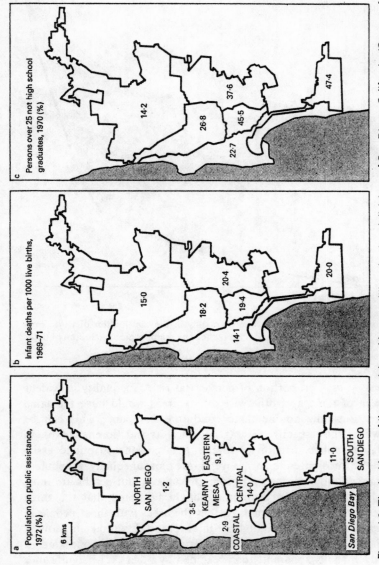

a Population on public assistance, 1972 (%)

6 kms

NORTH SAN DIEGO
1·2

KEARNY MESA
3·5

EASTERN
9·1

COASTAL
2·9

CENTRAL
14·0

SOUTH SAN DIEGO
11·0

San Diego Bay

b Infant deaths per 1000 live births, 1969–71

15·0

18·2

20·4

14·1

19·4

20·0

c Persons over 25 not high school graduates, 1970 (%)

14·2

26·8

37·6

22·7

45·5

47·4

Figure 1.2. The incidence of three social-problem conditions in six subdivisions of San Diego, California. (Source of data: Ontell, 1973.)

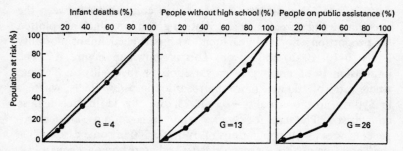

Figure 1.3. Lorenz curves for three social problems in San Diego, California. (Source of data: Ontell, 1973.)

of the differences in degree of inequality is that certain municipal health and education services make for levelling out of infant mortality and (to a lesser extent) high-school graduation rates, whereas there is no similar programme to reduce the highly localized incidence of poverty other than the palliative of public assistance.

The measurement of inequality enables us to identify change over time as well as the existing situation. Thus the Gini coefficient for infant mortality in San Diego 1969–71 is lower than that calculated for 1960–62, indicating a reduction in inequality of distribution among the six areas of the city. But such judgements must be made with caution, because the value of G is sensitive to ways in which the territory under review is split up. Thus the same calculation performed on data for thirty-four smaller subdivisions of the city shows virtually no change: $G = 11·5$ for 1960–62 and 11·4 for 1969–71. Smaller areas reveal more of the local extremes – hence the higher G values – and suggest that at this spatial scale there has been no appreciable reduction in the unequal distribution of infant deaths.

The problem of sensitivity of inequality measures operates in other ways. Suppose that we wished to compare the spatial incidence of infant mortality in an American city with an Australian city. For the purpose of illustration, we will take Tampa in Florida and Sydney in New South Wales. The County Health Department covering Tampa compiles data on infant mortality for census tracts, while the State of New South Wales uses municipalities. Without resorting to the Gini coefficient we can make a rough comparison between the two cities using a frequency distribution graph, on which are plotted the proportion of areas in each city with particular infant mortality levels: 0–10, 10–20 and so on. This is shown in Figure 1.4. The impression is of much greater variation or inequality in Tampa, where rates of 100 and more are recorded in a few tracts, whereas in Sydney no municipality exceeds 25. But this is, in fact, a false comparison. The data for Sydney relate to large and quite heterogeneous areas with populations of over 100,000 in some cases, while the Tampa figures are for much smaller and more homogeneous areas. So the way in which the data are compiled will reveal more of the local extremes in Tampa. Tampa does have a higher general level of infant mortality (25 per 1000 live births compared with 18 in Sydney), and probably greater inequality, but the differences in geographical distribution are certainly not as pronounced as the graph suggests.

The necessary, if regrettable, conclusion from this is that it is extraordinarily difficult to make precise comparisons of the degree of

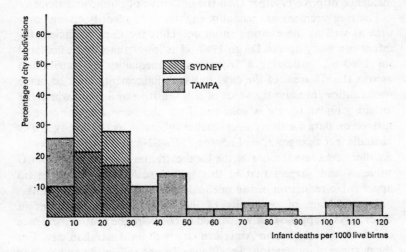

Figure 1.4. Comparison of the frequency distribution of infant mortality rates by areal subdivisions, for the city of Tampa, Florida, and the Sydney metropolitan area. (Source of data: Hillsborough County Health Department and State of New South Wales.)

inequality experienced in different parts of the world. We can take a particular set of subdivisions of one nation or city and measure inequality in the distribution of a whole range of conditions if data are available. But unless a closely similar set of subdivisions exists in another nation or city we cannot make valid comparisons. The problem is less serious in undertaking comparisons within the same country – for example between Tampa and other American cities, where data by tracts are available. It is the wider and perhaps more interesting questions, such as how American cities compare with those in Australia, the USSR and elsewhere, that the measurement problem makes it so difficult to answer. As we attempt comparisons in subsequent chapters, it is important to bear in mind these technical difficulties, that predispose the student of inequality to extreme caution. We must always beware of asking more of our data than its accuracy and the techniques at our disposal can legitimately yield.

Patterns of Inequality

Now that we have explored something of the possibilities and limitations of measuring inequality among areas, let us look at some actual patterns at different spatial scales. We will do this by continuing the discussion of infant mortality. There is no more vivid indicator of human 'life chances' than infant mortality, which tells us the probability of a newly born child surviving the most danger-ous year of its life. Babies are especially vulnerable to disease, and their capacity for survival is influenced by the mother's state of health and her ability to sustain another life. Infant mortality is thus widely accepted as a sensitive indicator of the general level of health in a society, especially for those not in an advanced stage of economic development. Even in more affluent industrial nations high local rates of infant mortality can be quite accurate reflections of other conditions in a community, such as low economic status of the population, poor standards of sanitation and limited availability of medical services.

A comprehensive world picture of infant mortality is impossible because reliable figures do not exist for many countries. And those that are available may refer to different times. However, some impression of the variation among nations is provided by Table 1.4, which lists sixty-five countries for which there are satisfactory data. The range is enormous – from one child in five dying during its first year in Ethiopia to little more than one in a hundred in Sweden. Looking down the columns of figures reveals a clear geographical pattern, with most of the high values in Africa and South-East Asia, Latin American countries prominent between 100 and 60, and most of Europe at low levels but with the rate falling from south to north. The USA, Canada, Australia and New Zealand all have low rates, as do certain economically advanced enclaves in South-East Asia, i.e. Singapore, Hong Kong and Japan.

Infant mortality is also subject to substantial variation within nations – something hidden by aggregate statistics. As an example, white rates in the USA by states are mapped in Figure 1.5. These

Table 1.4. Infant deaths per 1000 live births, 1970

Ethiopia	200·0	Mexico	68·5	West Germany	23·6
Tanzania	160·0	Lebanon	67·3	Israel	22·9
Liberia	159·0	El Salvador	66·6	Czechoslovakia	22·1
Turkey	153·0	Argentina	63·3	Belgium	20·5
Haiti	146·9	Costa Rica	61·5	Singapore	20·5
Sudan	145·0	Portugal	58·0	USA	19·8
Algeria	140·0	Yugoslavia	55·5	Hong Kong	19·6
India	140·0	Sri Lanka	53·0	Republic of Ireland	19·5
Indonesia	137·0	Romania	49·4	Canada	18·8
Pakistan	128·4	Uruguay	42·6	East Germany	18·5
Tunisia	125·0	South Korea	41·0	UK	18·5
Ghana	122·0	Panama	40·5	France	18·2
Uganda	120·0	Hungary	35·9	Australia	17·9
Kenya	119·0	Poland	33·2	New Zealand	16·7
Honduras	117·0	Jamaica	32·2	Switzerland	15·1
Egypt	116·3	Greece	29·6	Denmark	14·2
Iraq	104·0	Italy	29·6	Finland	13·2
Philippines	96·9	Puerto Rico	28·6	Japan	13·1
Guatemala	87·1	Spain	28·0	Netherlands	12·7
Colombia	80·6	Bulgaria	27·3	Norway	12·7
Chile	79·2	Austria	25·9	Sweden	11·0
Ecuador	76·6	USSR	24·4		

Source: United Nations Research Institute for Social Development, 1976.

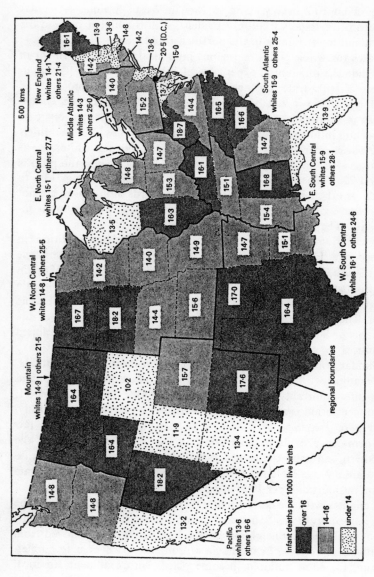

Figure 1.5. Variations in infant mortality in the United States, by states and major regions, 1974. (Source of data: *Statistical Abstract of the United States*, USGPO.)

New England
whites 14·1
others 21·4

Middle Atlantic
whites 14·3
others 26·0

E. North Central
whites 15·1   others 27·7

South Atlantic
whites 15·9   others 25·4

E. South Central
whites 15·9
others 28·1

W. North Central
whites 14·8 | others 25·5

Mountain
whites 14·9   others 21·5

W. South Central
whites 16·1   others 24·6

Pacific
whites 13·6
others 16·6

500 kms

Infant deaths per 1000 live births

over 16

14–16

under 14

regional boundaries

13·9
13·6
14·8
14·2
13·6
20·5 (D.C.)
15·0
13·7

16·1
14·2
14·0
15·2
14·4
16·5
16·6
14·7

18·7
14·7
15·3
16·1
15·1
16·8
14·8
16·3
15·4
15·1
13·5
14·9
14·7
15·1
14·0
16·7
14·2
14·4
15·6
17·0
16·4
18·2
15·7
17·6
16·4
16·4
11·9
18·2
10·2
13·4
14·8
14·8
13·2

35

range from 10·2 in Wyoming to 18·7 in West Virginia. A regular pattern of regional variation is evident, with the higher rates in the south and lower figures in the north-east and west.

Rates for whole states or regions hide local variations. They can also hide the differential experience of sub-groups within the population. To illustrate this, we show rates for whites and 'others' (mainly blacks) in the nine major regions into which the United States is subdivided for official statistical purposes. In every case non-white infant mortality is higher than for whites. But the difference varies markedly with region: in some the non-white rate is almost twice that for whites, while in the Pacific region the ratio is only 1·22:1. The range of regional rates for whites is from 13·6 to 16·1; for others it is 16·6 to 28·1. In other words, non-whites are not only worse off in general but also subject to greater regional inequality. The same is true at the state level.

International comparisons help to put these kinds of conditions in perspective. For example, the non-white infant mortality rate in the East South Central region (1974) compares closely with that of Spain in 1970 (see Table 1.4). The 1970 figure for Mississippi blacks – little short of 50 – was not much better than that for Sri Lanka at the same date. The black child's chances of a first birthday in parts of the American South are no greater than in some underdeveloped countries.

Similar comparisons help to shed light on more local variations, for example within a city. In Figure 1.6 we return to San Diego, and map infant mortality rates by neighbourhoods for the period 1966–71. A longer period is needed here than the three years used previously, in Figure 1.2, because otherwise the smaller areas have too few incidents to provide reliable rates. In this illustration most of the northern and southern extensions of the city are excluded because data are not available for 1966–8. For each neighbourhood, the rate of infant mortality per 1000 live births is given and also the name of the country with the closest figure in Table 1.4. As we pass from the high-mortality areas south and east of the city centre to the low areas of the coastal neighbourhoods, it is as if we have moved from southern Europe to Scandinavia within the space of a few miles. Again, for some children in some places within affluent America,

36

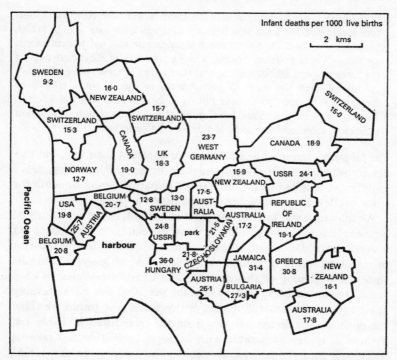

Figure 1.6. Variations in infant mortality in San Diego, California, 1966–71, compared with selected national rates, 1970. (Source of data: Ontell, 1973, and Table 1.4.)

survival prospects resemble those of much poorer countries; for others adequate medical attention, nutrition and protection from disease are virtually assured and the only dangers are those posed by genetic malfraction or accidents.

A similar view of another American city, Detroit, is provided by William Bunge. He shows infant mortality rates in the rich suburbs (exemplified by Grosse Pointe) similar to those of the better-off Western European nations, falling to figures comparable with those of Trinidad and Guyana in the inner-city slums of the East Side. This microcosm of our unequal world is vividly described by Bunge (1974, pp. 51–2) as follows:

37

We have in Detroit, absolutely the entire world. The New Black Bottom Region on the East Side has an infant mortality rate as high as San Salvador and there Detroiters are in alliance with San Salvadorès people as Third World starving people. The Grosse Pointe Region is part of the International Jet Set Region and they are in alliance, geographically connected, with the other Grosse Pointes of this world. Going from New Black Bottom to Grosse Pointe is going from San Salvador to Buckingham Palace. You have gone across the latitudes of infant mortality, from one antipode of this world to another.

The 'alliances' referred to may be more apparent than real, but this description does help to emphasize the geographical interdependence of different peoples in a city (and world) where ill health or death for some is often the price of better conditions for others elsewhere.

We may turn this kind of comparison around, to see something of how the less advantaged nations look in relation to the advanced industrial world in a historical perspective. Figure 1.7 shows changes in infant mortality in London and the USA, at ten-year intervals since the beginning of this century. The trends are similar, with a steady reduction from over 170 deaths per 1000 live births seventy years ago to just under 20 today. Between the two graphs we show the position of selected nations, from the rates listed in Table 1.4. To find a figure comparable with Ethiopia in 1970 would take us well back into the nineteenth century in London or the USA. Tanzania's infant mortality is at the level of the first decade of the twentieth century in London and the USA. Given the rate of improvement over time in the advanced industrial world, it would take Tanzania almost seventy years to get down to a figure of 20. It would take India almost as long. The other countries listed, like the underdeveloped world as a whole, are decades behind the advanced nations by the comparison shown here.

Of course, progress may be faster in the underdeveloped world, as innovations in medical care, nutrition and personal hygiene diffuse from the more advanced nations. But great inequalities are likely to persist on a world scale. And within the underdeveloped nations the improvements may be selective, affecting conditions of some people in some places but leaving others untouched. Thus the élite of the cities and the rich country landowners may enjoy levels of medical

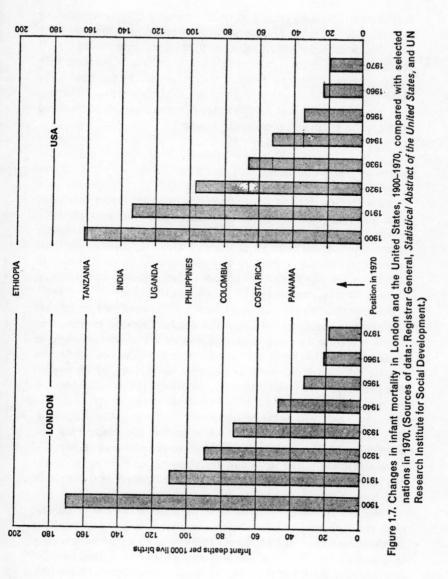

Figure 1.7. Changes in infant mortality in London and the United States, 1900–1970, compared with selected nations in 1970. (Sources of data: Registrar General, *Statistical Abstract of the United States*, and UN Research Institute for Social Development.)

care comparable with people of similar status in North America or Western Europe, while for the mass of the urban and rural poor the new clinics and their staff may be fighting an ever losing battle against endemic diseases, malnutrition and inadequate housing, with the prospects of serious famine always in the background. For children born in some places even today, as these words are written, the chance of seeing that first birthday is virtually nil. And for those who do, there will be no cake and candle.

Inequality and Social Justice

Faced with facts such as these, questions of social justice inevitably arise. The relationship between inequality and social justice is not a simple one, however. An unequal distribution is not necessarily unjust, whether we refer to chances of child survival, educational opportunity, money income, or any other condition contributing to human well-being. Understanding this is vital to the interpretation of inequality, its origins and its possible justification.

An important distinction must be made between two terms that can easily be confused: *equality* and *equity*. Equality means every person receiving the same treatment irrespective of who *or where* he or she may be. Equity means fairness or, in the words of the *Oxford English Dictionary*, 'recourse to principles of justice', which implies that people may be given differential treatment if this is deemed fair or just. This is similar to the distinction made by Aristotle two thousand years ago between *arithmetic* and *proportional* equality, the former meaning that everyone is treated the same while the latter requires that people receive things in proportion to desert, i.e. equal treatment in the same circumstances where the circumstances can vary among individuals and groups. Some people in some places may be recognized as more deserving than others.

The basis on which differentiation is made is critical in judging observed inequality as equitable or inequitable, just or unjust. What are the criteria that might be applied? These can vary with the society in question, but the most obvious and widely recognized basis of desert is *contribution to the common good*. Thus people who are able to contribute the most valuable services to society generally get the greatest rewards. Part of the ideology or set of beliefs prevailing in capitalist societies is that the level of wages, salaries or profits generated by competitive market forces reflects the relative contributions of the workers, managers and businessmen who are responsible for the production of goods and services. The extent to which the market provides a true reflection of the relative worth of a day's labour on the shop floor as opposed to the board room (for example) is a matter of controversy, however. There are reasons for some scepticism regarding the labour market as a just mechanism for income distribution. Most societies recognize market imperfections, whereby some people get more or less than they deserve by other criteria. This can be redressed by income redistribution, for example via heavier taxation on the rich, and social services to assist the poor, though recognition of imperfections is no guarantee that they will be rectified. There is also the more fundamental objection that ownership of the means of production gives employers more power in the labour market than workers, thus biasing the distribution of income in favour of the capitalist and landowning class – an argument vehemently denied by those who see organized labour in the form of trade unions as unduly powerful. Socialist societies, such as the USSR, have replaced the market-place by central planning and collective decision-making as a means of deciding who deserves what in recognition of societal contribution, though the outcome is not necessarily very much more equalitarian than in advanced capitalist societies. We shall return to these issues in later chapters.

Another common basis for differentiation is *merit*. This can mean recognition of special claims by those who have had to overcome more-than-usual difficulties in order to make their societal contribution. Examples would be professions involving long periods of training (such as medicine and higher education) or particularly unpleasant and dangerous work. Merit can also be used to justify privileged treatment for people with special status that marks them out as more deserving for a variety of reasons. Race in South Africa is a case in point: although the inferior treatment of black people is often justified on the grounds of their smaller contribution to society (they work predominantly in unskilled manual jobs), it is

41

also held by some that simply being white is sufficiently meritorious to warrant higher pay. Thus whites can get paid more than blacks for doing the same job, as is the case, for example, in vehicle repair or university teaching. Other countries have equally idiosyncratic merit criteria: in Britain, for example, simply inheriting a peerage brings a seat in the 'upper' legislative chamber without the inconvenience of submitting to the scrutiny of an electorate, as well as opportunities for lucrative directorships and other posts not open to people of greater ability who lack a title. Criteria such as these have wider implications than the personal advantage of the individuals concerned, for they contribute to the perpetuation of a privileged class and a way of life that generates much broader social inequalities.

The extent of existing inequalities is increasingly focusing attention on another possible distributive criterion – *need*. It was Karl Marx who popularized the phrase: 'From each according to his ability, to each according to his needs!' But this was viewed as being the ultimate aim of a communist society, not something that could be implemented immediately following the overthrow of capitalism. In the transitional socialist society incentives are still required and payment for work is in accordance with its quantity and quality, so that some get more than others, irrespective of need. Special needs are recognized, however, in both socialist and capitalist societies. This is usually accomplished through the provision of free social services, income supplements, subsidized housing and other benefits. The practical difficulty here is determining just what people's needs are and which should be met as a guaranteed right. Certain physical needs for food, clothing, shelter and security must be met in order for people to survive – and only in the more advanced industrial nations can these be largely assured for most citizens. How far people's felt 'needs' for a well-furnished home, a television and forty cigarettes a day should be met, irrespective of ability or inclination to contribute to society through work, is a more controversial question.

How do these generalities about social justice relate to inequality as a geographical condition? In what circumstances might we be able to see justice in an unequal areal distribution of income, infant mortality or whatever? Taking our cue from the three basic criteria discussed above, such circumstances could include: better conditions in areas making greater contributions to the common good, e.g. places manufacturing things most in demand or producing with high levels of efficiency; better conditions in areas where special merit is recognized, such as areas with a harsh environment to be overcome (like Siberia in the USSR where wage supplements are paid), or with a special status, such as the capital city; compensation in areas of particular need, e.g. investment incentives and greater public expenditure in depressed regions or the funding of social programmes in city slums. Thus spatial inequality cannot necessarily be regarded as unjust. It may be justified by various criteria enshrined in the prevailing ideology or code of morality that guides the operation of the society, economy and polity. As in any other kind of analysis of inequality, there is no ultimate moral sanction for uneven distribution: what is considered just is a product of society in action.

But there may still be many situations of unjust areal differentiation, in relation to widely accepted criteria of distributional equity. These we may recognize as cases of *spatial discrimination*. Strictly speaking, 'discrimination' simply means making a distinction, which may be done justly as well as unjustly. But the term generally carries with it connotations of unfairness when applied to differential treatment, racial discrimination being an obvious case in point. Thus spatial discrimination implies a process with an unfair outcome, i.e. *spatial injustice*, as opposed to spatial differentiation to which no conception of equity or moral judgement has been applied – negative or positive. While we are accustomed to the idea of discrimination according to race, colour, religion and (more recently) sex, the idea of spatial discrimination is less familiar. Yet where people live can easily result in unfairly disadvantageous treatment.

Differential life experience is part and parcel of the way in which human activity is organized in geographical space. And spatial organization is itself very much a reflection of how society is organized around the production of goods and services. With every residential location there goes a set of advantages and disadvantages. Some people live in the shadows of factories, breathing foul air and disturbed by noise; others inhabit attractive suburbs, with tree-lined boulevards not yet discovered by commuters' cars and juggernaut trucks. Some live close to work while others must spend hours a day on the roads or railways. Some people have convenient access to shops, banks, schools, doctors' surgeries, and other necessary services; others must travel long distances to satisfy essential demands of modern living. People in the countryside are increasingly disadvantaged, as societies become ever more strongly focused on the major metropolitan areas. Yet even within the city some neighbourhoods are much more poorly serviced than others: intra-city differences in life chances can in fact be far greater than those between the average urbanite and country-dweller.

Let us look at an extreme example of what might be considered geographical or spatial discrimination. In many American towns and cities the residential areas occupied by black people are conspicuously inferior to those of whites. This is especially so in the rural South, where almost every town has its segregated black community, which often lives in shacks of mainly timber construction, lining unmade streets, and which has only poor municipal services. Such a town is Shaw, Mississippi. Shaw has a population of about 2500, of whom 1500 are blacks and 1000 whites. Residential segregation by race is virtually complete; all but a handful of the 450 or so houses occupied by blacks at the end of the 1960s were in exclusively black neighbourhoods. Shaw achieved some notoriety a decade ago, when a group of blacks brought a court action against the town, alleging discrimination with respect to the provision of various services. Some of the facts revealed by the case were as follows: almost 98 per cent of all houses fronting on to unpaved streets were occupied by blacks; 97 per cent of houses not served by sanitary sewers were in black neighbourhoods; street lighting and drainage in black neighbourhoods were inferior; there were disparities in the provision of water mains, fire hydrants and traffic signs. Figure 1.8 illustrates the degrees of residential segregation, and discrimination with respect to street paving. The black residential areas tend to be on the periphery of the town. The position of the two schools and cemeteries symbolizes the segregation of the 'old South' – literally, from the cradle to the grave.

The issue at stake in the court action was whether discrimination

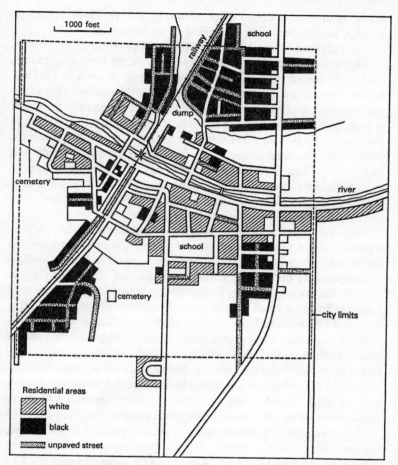

Figure 1.8. Race-space discrimination in Shaw, Mississippi. (Source: Salih, 1972, Fig. 1; based on a survey by Yale Rabin, 1969.)

in municipal services breached the 14th Amendment of the United States Constitution, which guarantees American citizens 'equal protection of the law'. Although the case was lost in the local District Court, this verdict was overturned on appeal. It was accepted that differential treatment of black and white neighbourhoods in

Shaw constituted a denial of equal protection. In short, discrimination in service provision was found to be unjustified.

But what kind of injustice is this? It clearly has a spatial expression, as Figure 1.8 shows. Most municipal services, by their very nature, cannot be denied to individuals scattered about a town at random: entire streets or tracts of territory are necessarily involved. But is this really *spatial* discrimination? The origin of the differential treatment is race, not space, and to see the process as exclusively spatial is to risk confusing surface manifestations for root causes. And even the rather obvious racial origin of the discrimination may be only part of the story. Race discrimination often has an economic dimension to it, such as the maintenance of a cheap and perhaps disenfranchised labour force. Such was the case in the American South until very recently. Such is still the case in South Africa.

There are, however, situations in which location and distance play a more positive role in the process of discrimination. Two instances are shown in Figures 1.9 and 1.10. The first is a case familiar to medical geographers as one of the earliest examples of a map helping to identify the cause of disease. In September 1854 over 500 people died from cholera in a small area of the Soho district of London. A map prepared by Dr John Snow showed that these deaths were concentrated around the location of a water pump on what was then Broad Street, while there was no similar grouping around other local pumps. It was then discovered that seepage from a cesspool or drain had contaminated the well below the Broad Street pump. A cholera epidemic was the result. People living closer to this pump and more likely to consume its water were more likely to contract cholera and die.

The second case is one of more topical interest – airport noise. Figure 1.10 shows the spread of noise from Boston's international airport, as estimated for 1975. The 'noise exposure forecast' (NEF) contours reflect volume of traffic, types of aircraft and the frequency and pattern of operations throughout the day. The area of 'extreme noise', within the 40 NEF contour, covers the immediate vicinity of the airport, extending along the flight paths. The outer (30 NEF) contour, representing 'objectionable noise', incorporates substantial parts of the Boston metropolis. Something of the extent of noise nuisance from international airports in other American cities is

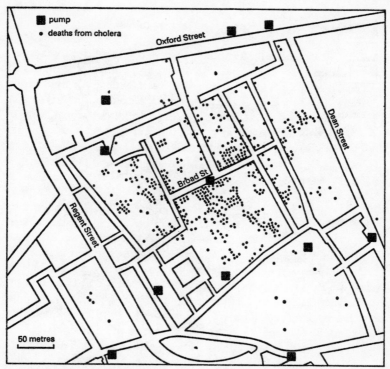

Figure 1.9. Cholera deaths in Soho, London, September 1854. (Source: Howe, 1972, Fig. 52.)

indicated by the following figures: an estimated 432,000 people within the 30 NEF ('objectionable noise') area around O'Hare Airport in Chicago in 1975, and no less than 1·7 million people similarly affected by Kennedy Airport in New York (Stevenson, 1972, p. 214).

Airport noise is a case of spatial discrimination that raises an obvious issue of social justice. How much people suffer from this growing nuisance depends largely on where they live, which may have no bearing on how much they benefit from the operation of the airport. Indeed, those people who can afford to fly most often may also be most able to choose their place of residence so as to avoid

47

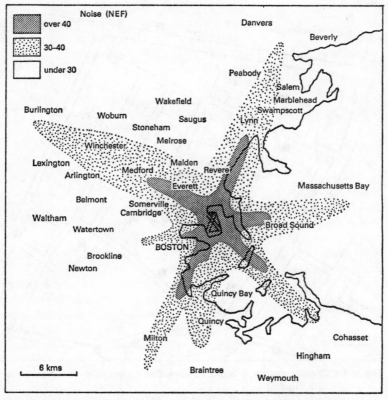

Figure 1.10. Estimated noise from Logan International Airport, Boston, Mass., 1975. (Source: Stevenson, 1972, Fig. 8.12.)

airport noise. Thus a substantial part of the real cost of travelling by air is being met by people who fly infrequently, if at all. Despite such possible palliatives as grants towards double glazing (and perhaps ear plugs), there is no effective way of ensuring that those who gain compensate those who lose in this kind of situation. The supersonic airliner Concorde is an extreme case in point. Quicker travel for a very small minority of rich people or businessmen is being produced at the cost of assaulting the eardrums of millions of

48

people who in no way benefit – hence the popular demonstrations against landing rights for Concorde in New York. Passengers, aviation journalists and others ecstatic about this great technological achievement (opposition to which is tantamount almost to lack of patriotism) might feel differently if they lived beneath a flight path to Kennedy or Heathrow Airport.

While the spread of cholera from an infected well and noise from an airport may appear indisputable cases of a *spatial* process of discrimination, we must not overlook the fact that these processes themselves exist in a broader historical and societal context. The incidence of a cholera epidemic reflects the state of medical science at that time. The people who are exposed to the dangers of poor water supply may reflect social structure; the poor are generally at greater risk than those who can afford to live in more salubrious environments or install refinements such as piped water. That noise from jet airliners is a nuisance at all is a function of the state of modern technology – of the existence of airliners and failure to make their engines quiet. It also reflects the fact that our resources and ingenuity are expended on personal mobility for the affluent rather than, for example, on basic medical care in the Third World or in parts of American cities with Third World infant mortality rates. This, in its turn, stems from a prevailing set of attitudes and values, but at the root of it all are the imperatives of an economic system driven on by the fostering of material consumption rather than by the satisfaction of more basic human needs.

A critical question that arises in any discussion of spatial inequality or discrimination is thus how far this can really be attributed to geographical circumstances. It could be argued that certain places appear disadvantaged simply because of the kind of people that live there. The slums are such because they are disproportionately occupied by people unable to earn what is needed for decent living and bringing up a family, not because they occupy particular positions in the city. Similarly, the smart suburbs are such because well-to-do people live there, not because of some intrinsic quality of place. The distinction is sometimes made between 'people poverty' and 'place poverty': to stress limitation on life chances as a characteristic of place risks missing the possibility that it is particular classes

49

of people that are the subject of discrimination rather than the places in which they live. Poor people live in certain places, largely because their choice is limited; their poverty is the outcome of the operation of the economy rather than of conditions in the slums, though a deteriorating physical environment and inferior services may contribute to their misery.

This question has an important bearing on how we view the process of distribution, from which inequality arises. It is also highly relevant to discussion of policies that might be implemented to reduce spatial inequalities deemed to be unjust. We will reserve further comment until later, save for two observations that must be kept in mind as we explore the cases presented in later chapters. The first is that the geographical perspective, as a partial view of reality, carries with it the risk of placing too great an emphasis on spatial variations and on the role of spatial organization – a point made earlier in this chapter. For a full comprehension of the processes at work we must get beneath our distribution maps, into how the society actually operates. The second observation is that location in space *is* a relevant consideration in the differentiation of human life chances. However much the general features of inequality may be traced to the prevailing social formation within which production is organized, the surplus appropriated and rewards disbursed, geographical space is part of the reality within which life is lived. Every decision to build or invest, whether private or public, is in the end a locational decision, for what is to be done must be done some*where*. And where it is done – where the factory is set up, the motorway constructed or the hospital built – has a bearing on the differentiation of human life chances. Every location decision has the capacity to benefit some people and penalize others. If the facility in question is some source of need satisfaction, physical accessibility to it will be differentially distributed according to where potential users live. If it is a source of nuisance, some people will be hurt more than others by virtue of physical proximity. On a broader scale, there may be distinctively spatial tendencies within an economic, . social or political system that have a bearing on inequality not itself expressed geographically: metropolitan concentration is a case in point, as we shall see in a later chapter.

It may often prove difficult to make a clear distinction between geographical aspects of a problem and other contributory factors. Sometimes it is unhelpful even to attempt what may be a false distinction, arising more from our unquestioning acceptance of such categories as 'geographical', 'economic', 'political' and 'social' than from the reality we try to understand. But what should be clear in the chapters which follow is that a geographical perspective must necessarily contribute to the analysis of an issue so broad and significant as inequality in human well-being.

2 Inequality among Nations: Development and Underdevelopment

In this chapter we will look at various aspects of inequality on a world-wide scale. Beginning with national differences in productive output and income, we will then consider purchasing power, security and other conditions that might be regarded as contributing to level of living or development. While the emphasis is for the most part on the extent of existing inequalities, our analysis will also begin to reveal some of the forces making for differences in human life chances, not only among nations but also within them.

Production and Income

The satisfaction of human needs requires the production of goods and services. These may be consumed directly, as in the case of a can of beer or a haircut, for example, or they may contribute to other stages in the production process in the form of such things as materials, components, machines and consultancy services. A distinction is sometimes made between the 'productive' activities of industry and the 'non-productive' service sector. However, it is important to recognize that services can also contribute to the creation of wealth as well as to final need satisfaction: education helps in the formation of a more skilled and intelligent labour force and health services keep people fit, both thus enhancing productivity. Even public expenditure on culture and the arts may have an effect on productivity if it makes people more content with life, though its real justification lies elsewhere – in the capacity of such forms of recreation to satisfy fundamental human needs. The total value of goods and services produced is thus an obvious first measure of national differences in levels of living.

52

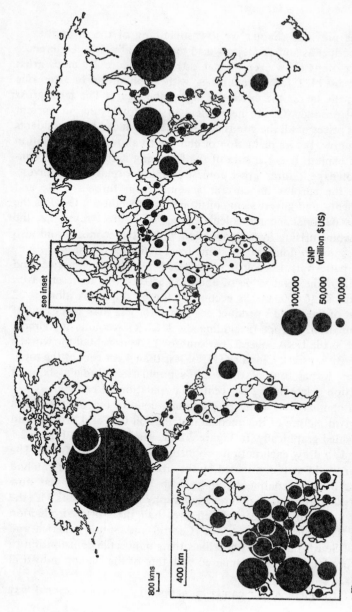

Figure 2.1. The distribution of world product or income: GNP by nations, 1972 (Source of data: *World Bank Atlas*, 1974; the figures are GNP at market prices, for countries with populations of one million or more.)

GNP (million $US)

100,000

50,000

10,000

800 kms

400 km

see inset

53

In the previous chapter we saw something of the disparities in gross product as among major world regions (Table 1.2). Differences among nations show even greater extremes. Figure 2.1 maps gross product in 1972 for all countries with populations of over one million: the larger the circle the higher the figure. The term gross national product (GNP) here refers to the total value at current markets prices of all the goods and services produced by all residents of a country, before deduction of charges to allow for depreciation of fixed capital. It is the sum of the following items: personal consumption expenditures, gross domestic capital formation (i.e. investments), the surplus on current account from foreign trade and investments, and government consumption expenditure. GNP is the same as national income calculated net of indirect taxes, i.e. the total income arising from production within the economy and also that accruing to domestic residents from activities overseas.

The pattern is of course dominated by North America and Europe. Of the total value of about \$3,650,000,000 represented on the map, \$1,167,000,000 is accounted for by the USA alone – 32 per cent of the world's product or income for less than 6 per cent of its population. Europe (excluding the USSR) accounts for almost as much as the USA: over 27 per cent for 13·5 per cent of the world's people. By contrast, China's GNP is less than 4 per cent of the total, for over 20 per cent of the world's population; India's share of production is less than 2 per cent, its population 15 per cent.

Such comparisons could be continued country by country. But a more vivid picture of the unequal distribution of world product can be provided graphically. In Figure 2.2 the same data as in Figure 2.1 are used to draw each nation proportional in size to its GNP. The familiar world map dominated by the size of the Asian, African and South American continents, along with North America, has now been replaced by a quite different geography. The six nations with the largest GNP in fact occupy well over half the world 'production space'. The small size of Africa, Central and South America and most of South-East Asia underlines their minuscule contribution to world production when compared with that of the leading industrial nations.

GNP (or income) per capita is mapped in the conventional way

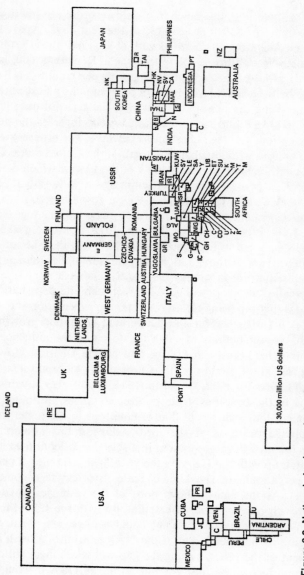

Figure 2.2. National size by product – the countries of the world drawn proportional to their total GNP. (Source of data: as for Figure 2.1; map by courtesy of John Fagg.)

55

in Figure 2.3. Nations are shown in classes according to fractions of the USA figure of $5590 per capita for the year 1972. Apart from Canada and Australia, all countries with at least half the USA figure are in North-West Europe. (Note that the UK, with $2600, is not one of this group). The second group, with per capita GNP of a quarter to half the USA level, is again predominantly European but now emphasizing the relative prosperity of Eastern Europe; it also includes the USSR and Japan. The third group includes the poorer European nations and the richest ones elsewhere. The lowest category covers all nations with less than one-tenth of the United States GNP per capita and includes no less than 79 of the 124 for which data are available. This poorest group itself embraces a wide range – from $550 in Saudi Arabia down to only $60 in Rwanda (i.e. not much more than 1 per cent of the US figure). Fifteen nations register less than $100 GNP per capita for the year 1972. Something like half the world's population live in countries with less than about $200 per capita per year. Although today's figures are higher than in 1972, the overall pattern of inequality has hardly changed.

The so-called 'development gap' between rich and poor nations is clear. But is this gap being closed? A common expectation is that the process of industrialization and accelerated economic growth will enable the poorer nations to catch up, to enjoy the affluence now largely taken for granted in Europe and North America. However, the facts cast grave doubt on this. Comparing per capita income in 1970 with figures for 1949, Atkinson (1975, p. 239) sees 'a worsening over time in the position of the poorest countries, although some improvement has occurred in that of countries in the upper middle range relative to those at the top'. Atkinson has attempted to calculate the growth rates required in a selection of countries if they are to catch up with the USA by the year 2000, assuming 2 per cent growth per annum in the United States' per capita income (see Table 2.1). As the figures show, none of the countries listed have actual growth rates capable of catching up with the USA: in fact, only two (Singapore and Zambia) could achieve one third of the USA figure by A.D. 2000. And if the USA continues growth at the 3·2 per cent of the 1960s, closing the gap will take longer still. Even if per capita income did not grow at all in the USA it would take

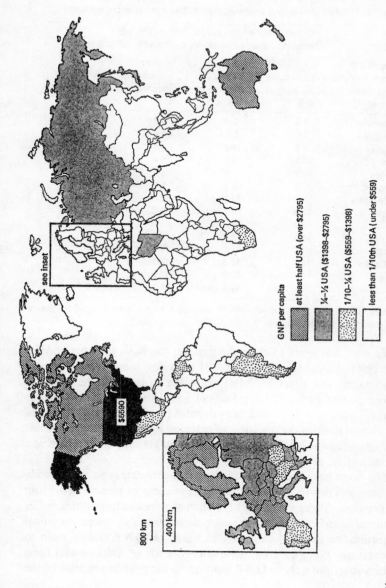

GNP per capita

at least half USA (over $2795)

¼–½ USA ($1398–$2795)

1/10–¼ USA ($559–$1398)

less than 1/10th USA (under $559)

$5590

see inset

800 km

400 km

Figure 2.3. GNP per capita by nations, 1972. (Source of data: as for Figure 2.1.)

57

Table 2.1. *Growth targets and achievements 1960–70 for selected nations*

Countries (in descending order of per capita income)	Growth rate of per capita income (% per annum) required to reach by the year 2000:			Actual growth rate 1960–70
	per capita income of US	half per capita income of US	a third of per capita income of US	
Venezuela	7·3	5·0	3·6	2·3
Singapore	7·5	5·1	3·8	5·2
Mexico	8·5	6·2	4·8	3·7
Brazil	10·1	7·8	6·4	2·4
Zambia	10·3	7·9	6·6	7·1
Malaysia	10·4	8·1	6·8	3·1
Philippines	12·4	10·1	8·8	2·9
Egypt	12·4	10·1	8·8	1·7
Thailand	12·6	10·3	8·9	4·9
Kenya	13·5	11·2	9·8	3·6
Nigeria	14·3	12·0	10·6	0·1
Sri Lanka	14·6	12·3	10·9	1·5
India	14·6	12·3	10·9	1·2
Tanzania	14·9	12·6	11·2	3·6

Source: Atkinson, 1975, p. 244; see this source for an explanation of the basis
   for the calculations.

India over 200 years to close the gap, on the basis of experience in the 1960s. Donaldson (1973, p. 14) provides some even gloomier predictions: 494 years for Malaysia to catch up with the USA at recent growth rates, 727 for Malawi and 1960 years for Pakistan. And for poor countries with growth rates persistently below those of the richest nations the question of catching up simply does not arise. The implications of this for world political stability (not to mention social justice) are serious, to say the least.

The point has already been made that the monetary value of goods and services produced is an imperfect indicator of human well-being or progress. There is more to life than the transactions captured in national economic accounts. But there are also more technical objections to national comparisons based on GNP and its ratio to population. First, data for some countries are of dubious accuracy, with respect not only to GNP but also to the population base of the per capita figure. Secondly, national income accounts do not include the value of goods and services produced for the consumer himself or herself, which can be substantial in a largely subsistence economy. Thirdly, the exchange rates used to convert values to a common currency (e.g. $US, as in the figures presented above) may not be an accurate reflection of purchasing power – a matter to be explored below. These considerations tend to depress the relative position of poorer nations, thus somewhat exaggerating the gap separating them from the rich. Other complications include the distinctive accounting systems used in socialist countries, which means that differences in living standards compared with the advanced capitalist world may not be accurately reflected by GNP or income per capita.

National aggregate data of course hide internal variations among both people and places, as was pointed out in the previous chapter. The wage or salary received by the individual worker will vary with occupation, and very often with location. To get a little closer to the lives of real people, Table 2.2 lists annual earnings in four occupations as they vary among thirty-seven of the world's major cities, from information compiled by the Union Bank of Switzerland. The differences shown are broadly consistent with the continental and national disparities in income per capita to which attention has already been drawn. But there are differences in relativities. For example, the New York primary-school teacher earns 25 times the salary of someone in the same occupation in Bombay, yet USA per capita GNP is 50 times the figure for India. The bus driver in London gets twice what he would in Mexico City, yet the UK's GNP per capita is $3\frac{1}{2}$ times that of Mexico. Income differences for the same work may be much less than national aggregate per capita figures might suggest. Low per capita income in a country is partly a reflection of the occupational structure: if everyone got equal pay for equal work throughout the world, some countries would be poorer than others simply because they have more people in low-paid jobs. The same is true of regions, cities and neighbourhoods within nations.

There are many interesting comparisons that could be made in Table 2.2. For example, the figures for Johannesburg, reflecting

Where the Grass is Greener

Table 2.2. Gross annual earnings ($1000) in selected occupations for major world cities, 1973

City	Primary teachers	Bus drivers	Bank tellers	Secretaries
Europe				
Amsterdam	8·0	7·7	9·4	5·8
Athens	3·2	3·0	3·7	3·0
Brussels	6·6	6·1	9·3	7·1
Copenhagen	9·5	9·6	8·8	8·2
Düsseldorf	10·7	8·5	10·2	8·5
Geneva	11·9	9·7	11·4	7·9
Helsinki	6·9	6·5	4·8	5·5
Istanbul	2·2	2·0	2·3	3·3
Lisbon	3·7	2·8	4·8	4·3
London	5·8	5·6	5·4	5·4
Luxemburg	10·5	8·6	10·0	6·4
Madrid	5·8	3·1	4·8	3·6
Milan	4·4	5·9	9·7	5·1
Oslo	8·0	7·5	9·1	7·5
Paris	6·5	6·3	6·9	6·0
Rome	4·1	7·0	9·4	4·3
Stockholm	11·1	9·7	9·6	7·8
Vienna	4·8	5·2	6·6	5·7
Zurich	12·3	9·8	12·0	8·0
North America and Australia				
Chicago	16·6	8·3	7·4	8·1
Montreal	11·5	8·5	6·9	6·4
New York	18·0	11·5	9·9	9·4
San Francisco	12·2	11·1	6·9	9·6
Sydney	10·1	6·5	8·7	7·2
Central and South America				
Bogotá	1·4	1·1	1·4	3·3
Buenos Aires	1·5	nd	4·0	3·4
Caracas	3·3	2·8	7·0	5·0
Mexico City	3·5	2·8	4·4	3·4
Rio de Janeiro	1·6	2·2	1·4	6·1
São Paulo	2·1	1·2	3·2	6·5
Africa, Middle East and Asia				
Beirut	2·9	3·1	4·5	4·3
Bombay	0·7	0·8	1·1	0·8
Hong Kong	4·8	2·3	3·6	5·6
Johannesburg	7·8	6·5	5·8	5·3
Singapore	4·3	1·8	3·7	3·3
Tel Aviv	3·4	5·7	5·2	4·0
Tokyo	6·5	7·0	9·5	4·7

Source: Union Bank of Switzerland, 1974.   nd = no data

predominantly 'white' occupations, emphasize the privileged economic position of South Africa's whites in a poor continent. Tokyo wages can be higher than in London. More than half the European cities listed pay their secretaries more than in London. And so on. There are also differences among occupational relativities. In Caracas, bank tellers earn more than twice as much as teachers but only half as much in New York; secretaries are better paid than bus drivers in all the Central and South American cities listed, whereas in North America the reverse is the case. What the workers of the world get depends very much on what they do *where*.

Purchasing Power and Consumption

If living standards have to do with the satisfaction of human needs and wants, then income is obviously important. It provides the wherewithal to make purchases, and also offers access to social status, prestige and power. But the same income can sustain different consumption levels in different places. There may be differences in how much of the nominal (gross) wage reaches the pay packet after taxation, social-security payments and so on. There will be differences in the prices asked for comparable goods and services. There may also be differences in the effort needed to earn the same wage, the most obvious being variations in the length of the working day or week. It is the purchasing power of work performed that matters to the individual, rather than some grand abstraction like per capita national income.

Applying purchasing power data to international comparisons can reduce the size of the difference between rich and poor. For example, one study suggests that the true gap between the USA and other countries is only four ninths of that indicated by exchange-rate conversions, where the gap is defined as the difference in per capita incomes as a proportion of the income of the other country concerned. This would reduce the gap between the USA and Uganda, for example, from 36 to 17 (Atkinson, 1975, p. 241). However, there are technical difficulties involved in this kind of comparison at such a broad national level.

61

Table 2.3. Hours of work needed to earn the price of the same basket of goods in selected occupations for major world cities, 1973

City	Primary teachers	Bus drivers	Bank tellers	Secretaries
Europe				
Amsterdam	12	nd	18	31
Athens	25	43	30	42
Brussels	19	24	15	20
Copenhagen	25	28	27	31
Düsseldorf	15	26	22	30
Geneva	11	21	18	28
Helsinki	17	26	33	34
Istanbul	36	64	46	39
Lisbon	14	42	18	22
London	18	20	18	20
Luxemburg	10	16	14	25
Madrid	13	38	24	34
Milan	22	23	13	27
Oslo	18	22	21	27
Paris	15	21	20	26
Rome	25	20	15	32
Stockholm	18	25	24	32
Vienna	19	26	22	30
Zurich	11	21	18	26
North America and Australia				
Chicago	6	15	16	15
Montreal	8	13	15	16
New York	7	13	12	15
San Francisco	11	13	20	16
Sydney	9	17	13	14
Central and South America				
Bogotá	38	70	49	29
Buenos Aires	18	nd	13	16
Caracas	29	38	14	19
Mexico City	22	36	23	31
Rio de Janeiro	30	48	46	17
São Paulo	31	115	35	21
Africa, Middle East and Asia				
Beirut	23	39	20	26
Bombay	110	118	76	99
Hong Kong	20	63	38	26
Johannesburg	7	12	12	13
Singapore	26	83	37	43
Tel Aviv	25	25	24	32
Tokyo	26	28	17	30

Source: Calculated from data from Union Bank of Switzerland, 1974.
nd = no data

Table 2.3a. Composition of the shopping basket

1 kilo white bread	500 g coffee beans	1 kilo rumpsteak (beef)
1 kilo rye bread	100 g instant Nescafé	1 kilo veal cutlets
1 kilo white flour	250 g Indian tea	1 kilo pork chops
1 kilo spaghetti	850 g green beans (canned)	1 kilo pork roast
1 kilo rice (long grain)	850 g fruit salad (canned)	1 kilo lamb chops
1 kilo sugar	1 kilo potatoes	1 kilo frying chicken
1 kilo salt	2 kilo most commonly	(frozen)
1 litre cooking oil	purchased seasonal	2 kilo ocean fish (2 kinds,
1 kilo butter (best quality)	vegetable (2 kinds,	1 kilo each)
1 kilo margarine	1 kilo each)	70 cl table wine, medium
1 litre milk (pasteurized)	1 kilo apples	quality
1 kilo hard cheese	2 kilo most commonly	33 cl can of beer (light)
12 eggs (fresh, large,	purchased fruit (2 kinds,	33 cl can of Coca-Cola
domestic)	1 kilo each)	1 litre mineral water

Some indication of differences in purchasing power or *real* income can be provided by making adjustments to the data for occupational earnings in world cities in Table 2.2 (see Table 2.3). First, the gross earnings have been converted into figures net of taxes and social security contributions. This is an important adjustment; in the case of teachers, for example, the deductions vary from nil in Bombay to almost 40 per cent of gross salary in Helsinki. However, it must be remembered that although such deductions reduce take-home pay they do support a range of social services that is far greater in cities like Helsinki than in the Bombays of this world. Next, allowance has to be made for hours worked, taking into account the length of the working week and the amount of holiday each year. Again, the differences among cities can be substantial: a bus driver's week ranges from 39½ hours in Milan to 48½ in Tokyo, while working days per year taken for holiday range from 14 in Singapore to 32 in Stockholm. Having made these two adjustments, net earnings per hour worked can be calculated. But to relate this to what can actually be purchased requires information on prices of goods and services. For the purpose of such a comparison, the Union Bank of Switzerland specified a representative 'shopping basket' of groceries, including bread, milk, cheese, vegetables, meat, beverages and other foodstuffs (see list in Table 2.3a). The cost of these goods was found from supermarket prices: the range for the basket as a whole was from $24·95 in Buenos Aires to $78·98 in Düsseldorf. Our final calculation is how long people in the selected occupations must work to earn the goods in question.

The results are listed in Table 2.3. The variation among cities is clear, and requires little elaboration. People in Central and South American cities and those listed in Asia and the Middle East have to work longer for the shopping basket than those in North America and most European cities. People in southern Europe have to work longer than those in the north and west. But the differentials are generally less than is suggested by the earnings figures in Table 2.2. For example, if we take our school teacher earning 25 times as much in New York as Bombay, he or she has to work about 16 times as long in Bombay as in New York to earn the same basket of goods. The bus driver in Mexico City works 22 hours compared with 18 in London, though the wages in Mexico City are only half those in London. The main reason for these and other similar differences is that people in the world's poorer cities tend to retain more of their earnings (but get less by way of social services) and pay lower prices for food. And it must be remembered that the shopping basket on which these calculations are based is not representative of what people in Third World cities will actually buy: the Bogotá bus driver is very unlikely to eat rumpsteak washed down with wine. Actual expenditure on food may thus be substantially less than for the kind of goods in this typically advanced-Western-world shopping basket, though the diet that results may be less sustaining. Nevertheless, the figures in Table 2.3 do stress the extent of a highly personal aspect of inequality: putting food on the family table demands much greater work effort in some places than others, even for people in the same occupation.

As another example of this kind of purchasing power comparison, we have worked out how long it would take to earn two single consumer goods – a car (Volkswagen 1300) and a packet of cigarettes (20 Marlboro). Two occupations are taken, representative respectively of manual workers (an automobile mechanic) and management (a personnel manager). Figure 2.4 charts the results, with the cities shown in descending order according to the lengthening work effort required of the mechanic to buy the car. Brief reference to the top and bottom cities is enough to illustrate the range of opportunity revealed. In San Francisco the auto mechanic can earn the price of the car in less than 14 weeks (assuming no other expenditure); in Bogotá he

VOLKSWAGEN 1300

1 working year

□ 1 working week

A PACKET OF 20 MARLBORO CIGARETTES

1 working hour

□ 1 working minute

San Francisco
New York
Chicago
Johannesburg
Montreal
Zurich
Geneva
Düsseldorf
Luxemburg
Sydney
Tokyo
Paris
London
Milan
Amsterdam
Vienna
Stockholm
Brussels
Mexico City
Copenhagen
Oslo
Lisbon
Rome
São Paulo
Caracas
Helsinki
Buenos Aires
Tel Aviv
Rio de Janeiro
Hong Kong
Beirut
Singapore
Madrid
Athens
Bombay
Istanbul   no data
Bogatá

Figure 2.4. Time taken to earn the price of a car and a packet of cigarettes, for auto mechanics (black) and personnel managers (white) in major world cities. (Source of data: Union Bank of Switzerland, 1974.)

65

needs almost 14 years. The personnel manager in San Francisco can earn the Volkswagen 1300 in under 6 weeks; his counterpart in Bogotá will take over 40 weeks. The nearest a mechanic in most Third World cities will ever come to a new Volkswagen is repairing the one owned by the manager. As for cigarettes, the packet of twenty with its evocation of Marlboro country will cost the San Francisco mechanic 5 minutes 36 seconds of labour and the manager 2 minutes 18 seconds; in Bogotá the times are 70 minutes and 4 minutes respectively. The diagram as a whole shows the poorer cities at a greater disadvantage with respect to earning a car than in the case of the basket of food. This is because the international price differentials now work the other way; for example the Volkswagen 1300 costs most in the Third World cities – $11,071 in Bogotá compared with $2596 in San Francisco.

In passing, it might be pointed out that, in regarding cars and cigarettes as, literally, 'goods', we are adopting a widely if not universally held value judgement. Whether the consumption of these two targets of acquisitive desire is really good for people other than those who make their livings producing them is a questionable matter. Cigarettes cause illness and death, which imposes costs on individual smokers and their families and also on the community that pays the price of medical care. They also cause annoyance to others, along with the pleasures of consumption. Shortage of cars may be a conventional indicator of underdevelopment, but part of the price of the mobility they bring is death on the roads, environmental degradation and air pollution. The relative absence of motor traffic makes at least one major European city (Moscow) an unusually agreeable place for pedestrians, rather like a no-smoking compartment for people who hate cigarettes. These comments are simply a reminder that any discussion of consumption raises questions of values: what seems good for some people may not be so good for others or, on balance, for society at large.

Comparisons of levels of consumption tend to avoid such issues, by focusing on relatively non-controversial criteria. Hence the stress on income: high income is better than low income to almost everyone, especially those at the lower end of the scale. Similarly, almost everyone would accept that much education is better than little, that the more healthy a population the better, that it is better to live in a well-constructed home with modern services than in a city slum or village hovel. We may argue about the relative worth of an additional year at school as opposed to more infant welfare centres, of an increase in the national level of literacy compared with a reduction in the infant mortality rate. But in doing so we are debating degrees of goodness rather than good or bad. Eventually, a point may be reached when we ask whether further expenditure of resources on education or health care, for example, really improves people's education or health, but such speculation is a luxury reserved for the rich nations where people are assured of standards still far off in most of the rest of the world.

Before leaving the question of the purchasing power of work, something must be said about differences between capitalist and socialist countries. Information of the kind compiled by the Union Bank of Switzerland is confined to the non-socialist world, and to make comparisons with Eastern Europe or the USSR, for example, is much more difficult. This is in part because of shortage of data. But it also arises from the fact that socialist countries operate on a different set of assumptions as to what comprises individual as opposed to collective consumption from that prevailing in the capitalist world. We shall return to this point, after an illustration similar to those already presented.

Some indication of differences in work time required to earn the money for certain consumer goods in West and East Europe is provided by Table 2.4. Here we compare a typical West German worker with one in Czechoslovakia – a country relatively advanced economically in the context of East Europe as a whole. The Czechoslovak worker needs from 2 to almost 10 times the time of the West German at work, depending on the item in question. And the Czechoslovak will be spending a higher proportion of income on 'basics', especially food, than his German counterpart, leaving a smaller surplus for other things. Nevertheless, ownership of consumer durables in Czechoslovakia is quite high: 150 radios per 100 households in 1971, 80 TV sets, 80 washing machines and 50 refrigerators (Mieczkowski, 1975, p. 287). Of course, these figures say nothing about the quality of the goods in question: they are often less reliable in the East than

67

Table 2.4. *Time required for workers in West Germany and Czechoslovakia to earn the price of selected consumer goods (hours of work)*

	West Germany	Czechoslovakia	Ratio (Cz ÷ W G)
Television set	133	470	3·5
Sewing machine	88	287	3·3
Portable typewriter	32	129	4·0
Transistor radio	12	117	9·8
Pair of shoes	6	17	2·8
Pairs of ladies' stockings	0·8	5·8	7·3
17·5 kg assorted meat	27·4	53·9	2·0
1 kg chocolate	1·5	10·5	7·0
Can of crab meat	0·7	1·4	2·0
Can of Nescafé	0·5	4·2	8·4
Frankfurters (canned)	0·4	1·6	4·0
Can of strawberries	0·3	1·2	4·0

Source: Mieczkowski, 1975, p. 288; following Sik, 1972, p. 86.

in the West, and more difficult to get repaired when they go wrong.

Unfortunately, no comprehensive figures are available to compare the USSR with the USA or UK, for example. Ownership of some consumer durables in the Soviet Union is certainly reaching Western levels, e.g. 71 per cent of homes with television and 56 per cent with refrigerators in 1974 (compared with 24 and 11 per cent, respectively, in 1965). Frank Giles of the *Sunday Times* (23 October 1977) reports a price of 5500 roubles for the cheapest Soviet-built Fiat car, the equivalent of about 36 months' wages for the average industrial worker. If this can be equated roughly with the Volkswagen 1300, then, of the cities featured in Figure 2.4, only in Bombay, Instanbul and Bogotá would a mechanic have to work longer for his car than the Soviet industrial employee. In 1976, this writer observed men's clothing in a shop in Irkutsk, Siberia, priced at 50 roubles for a suit, mackintosh or light overcoat and 100 roubles for a heavy overcoat or 125 roubles for one with a fur collar. The average industrial worker earns about 150 roubles a month, to which should be added the supplement of 40 per cent or so paid in Siberia. So an Irkutsk worker might need two weeks to earn the money for a heavy overcoat; an article of comparable quality could be purchased out of an average British worker's weekly wage, with some money left over.

Whether a result of careful research or of casual personal observation, these kind of comparisons can be misleading as general readings on relative living standards, however. As was pointed out above, different attitudes to consumption prevail. For example, rent (or mortgage repayment) is a major item of expenditure for most British families; in the USSR the charge made for accommodation is purely nominal, just a few roubles a month in most cases. The American worker may be able to earn the price of a car or a colour TV in a much shorter time than his Soviet counterpart, but may eventually lose a life's savings paying for medical care which would be free in Eastern Europe (not to mention welfare states in the West). Again, we are in the realm of societal values. In some countries, the consumer durables symbolic of the affluent society are a struggle to obtain, but a wide range of services are provided collectively via taxation and without a direct user charge. In others, material goods flow in abundance but serious illness can bring financial ruin. In still others, of course, there is neither material well-being nor social security – only the question of which should come first, and for whom, when the magic process of development finally gets under way.

Level of Living

To fill out our picture of variations among nations in levels of consumption we could now look at a wide range of economic and social conditions. But however interesting these patterns might prove to be individually, we would soon find the exercise repetitive. The poorer countries by the criterion of GNP or income per capita tend also to be poor with respect to health, education, housing quality and so on, as well as in the sphere of material consumption. This can be confirmed in the field of health by looking at the infant mortality figures in Table 1.4 in the previous chapter: going down the table is very much like going up the GNP per capita scale. If many conditions tell basically the same story about national variations, and if we are reluctant to measure level of living simply by product or income per capita, could we perhaps combine data on a number of critical conditions into a more general indicator?

This question has occupied the attention of a number of scholars and research institutions concerned with the measurement of level of living, development and human well-being. Of special interest is the work undertaken at the United Nations Research Institute for Social Development (McGranahan, 1970). They derived a composite 'development index' for fifty-eight nations based on 1960 data on eighteen social and economic conditions. These included measures of health, education, housing occupancy and the consumption of telephones, newspapers and radios, as well as more conventional economic indicators. Other well-known attempts to place nations on a composite development scale using advanced statistical methods include those of Berry (1960) and Adelman and Morris (1967).

For the present purpose we shall use a simpler composite index, based on information for six conditions. These have been selected to represent three broad dimensions of living standards: physical well-being, mental well-being and material well-being. The physical state of the population is measured by life expectancy and animal protein consumption (as an indicator of quality of diet). Mental development is measured by the number of people in primary and secondary education and by newspaper circulation (an indicator of literacy). Material conditions are measured by two common indicators of affluence: telephone and car consumption, the latter accepted with some reservations in view of the doubts already expressed as to the general desirability of mass car-ownership. Despite the fact that only six conditions are used, they should provide a reasonably accurate general indication of level of development or living standards. Five of them are, in fact, among those found by McGranahan (1970) to be most closely related to a much wider range of conditions considered relevant to level of living. GNP or income per capita is deliberately excluded, as we shall wish to see how a composite level-of-living index compares with the more conventional economic indicator. Table 2.5 lists the six conditions in full, together with the average, maximum and minimum values relating to the fifty-four countries for which data are available.

Each of the conditions is measured in its own units and on its own

70

Table 2.5. Conditions included in a composite index of level of living or development for fifty-four countries

Condition	Average	Maximum	Minimum
Physical well-being			
1. Expectation of life at birth (years)	61·8	74.9	38·1
2. Animal protein consumption (per capita per day)	33·6	73·8	4·2
Mental well-being			
3. Primary and secondary educational enrolment (% of popn aged 5 to 19)	56·9	87·8	8·6
4. Daily general-interest newspaper circulation (per 1000 popn)	139·3	538·0	0·1
Material well-being			
5. Telephones (per 1000 popn)	111·3	586·8	90·0
6. Passenger cars (per 1000 popn)	79·5	433·6	1·0

Source: United Nations Research Institute for Social Development, 1976.

scale, of course. This raises the question of how the six sets of data can be combined into a composite index. There are various ways of doing this, described fully in books on social indicators and numerical methods (e.g. D. M. Smith, 1973, 1975). The method adopted here is to convert each set of figures into 'standard scores' (sometimes called standard deviates), where the average for all countries is set at zero and the standard deviation (a measure of spread about the average) is set at unity. With these two summary characteristics standardized for each of the six conditions (i.e. in each case the mean = 0 and standard deviation 1·0) the standard scores can simply be summed for each country. This gives a set of composite scores in which each of the six conditions contributes equally overall. We shall use this technique again in the next chapter. A fuller account of the mathematics involved is given in the Appendix (p. 365), along with a simple worked example.

The results of this calculation are set down in Table 2.6. The fifty-four nations are listed in order of their performance on the composite index. Note that a score of exactly 0 would be equivalent to an average performance on all six conditions; worse than this is indicated by a minus sign for the composite index. The relative positions of the various countries cause no surprise. We move down the list from

Table 2.6. Performance of fifty-four nations on a composite index of level of living or development, 1970

1. USA	11·6	19. Argentina	2·1	37. El Salvador	—3·6
2. Sweden	11·0	20. Poland	1·7	38. Turkey	—3·8
3. New Zealand	10·2	21. Greece	1·5	39. Tunisia	—4·1
4. Netherlands	9·9	22. Spain	1·4	40. Thailand	—4·3
5. Canada	9·1	23. Hungary	1·3	41. Honduras	—4·6
6. Australia	8·7	24. Portugal	—0·1	42. Guatemala	—5·2
7. Denmark	7·8	25. Yugoslavia	—0·9	43. Kenya	—5·3
8. Norway	7·3	26. Jamaica	—0·9	44. Iran	—5·3
9. W. Germany	6·5	27. Panama	—0·9	45. Zambia	—5·4
10. France	5·9	28. Costa Rica	—1·1	46. Morocco	—5·6
11. Belgium	5·9	29. Chile	—1·1	47. India	—5·7
12. Japan	5·3	30. Venezuela	—1·2	48. Uganda	—6·6
13. Austria	5·0	31. Cuba	—1·4	49. Senegal	—6·6
14. Ireland	4·1	32. S. Korea	—2·4	50. Liberia	—6·9
15. Italy	3·5	33. Colombia	—2·6	51. Tanzania	—7·0
16. Czechoslovakia	3·0	34. Sri Lanka	—2·7	52. Sudan	—7·6
17. Israel	2·6	35. Ecuador	—3·4	53. Burundi	—7·9
18. Uruguay	2·4	36. Philippines	—3·4	54. Ethiopia	—8·0

Source of data: see Table 2.5.

North America, the Antipodes and the Scandinavian countries, through Western Europe (with Japan) to Eastern and Southern Europe and the better-off South American countries. Then, as we enter the minus scores, more South American and South-East Asian countries appear, leading to the solidly-African bottom end of the table. The pattern should be familiar from our examination of GNP per capita.

But how far are the level-of-living scores really predictable on the basis of GNP? Is the level of living merely a reflection of a nation's per capita product? To answer this, the scores in Table 2.6 have been plotted against GNP per capita in Figure 2.5. The close alignment of the dots on the graph shows that the two conditions are very closely associated. As GNP per capita goes up, so does the level-of-living index, in a highly predictable fashion. The coefficient of correlation (r) between the two conditions is 0·93.*

*The product moment correlation coefficient (indicated by the symbol r) measures the degree of linear association between two variables. The coefficient is on a scale from 1·0 to —1·0, where 1·0 indicates perfect positive association, —1·0 perfect negative association and 0·0 a random association.

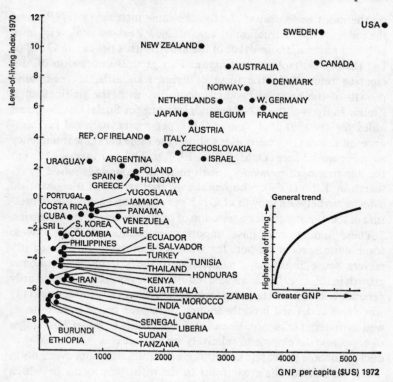

Figure 2.5. The relationship between a composite level-of-living index and GNP per capita, for fifty-four nations. (Sources of data: UN Research Institute for Social Development and World Bank.)

The relationship between our level-of-living index and GNP per capita is not as straightforward as might appear at first sight, however. There is a distinct tendency for the scatter of dots on the graph to climb steeply at first and then level out, as summarized in the general trend curve in Figure 2.5. This indicates that level of living rises rapidly with relatively small increments in GNP per capita at low levels of development, but that in richer countries level of living increases less. Thus at the bottom end of the scale an increase in GNP of, say, $200 per capita raises level of living by about 2 points

73

on the index 'scale. But at the top the same increase in GNP raises the index by only a fraction of a point. New Zealand achieves a level of living not much below that of the USA, with a per capita GNP of less than half the American figure. This general impression of 'decreasing returns', in the form of living standards, to continuing growth of the national product, conforms with the findings of a similar analysis of the UN Research Institute for Social Development index for 1960. Plotted against GNP per capita, national performance on the development index shows the same curvilinear tendency as in Figure 2.5 here (D. M. Smith, 1977, p. 220). Further doubt as to the importance of *economic* growth to *social* progress is raised by research by King (1974), who has shown that there is little statistical association between growth of GNP per capita and a composite measure of social progress, for a selection of relatively developed countries.

These findings may have important implications. They provide some quite specific support for what an increasing number of observers sense intuitively, namely, that the continuing economic growth in the so-called advanced industrial world does not necessarily generate commensurate increases in general living standard, especially when this is defined broadly enough to include social conditions as well as material affluence. However, for countries in the earliest stages of economic development, relatively small increases in national product or income per capita can bring very substantial improvements in living standards. The reason has to do with the process by which improvements are made in specific spheres of human life. It is generally the case that returns on investment or resources devoted to satisfying human needs conform to the same kind of curve as is shown in Figure 2.5. In other words, at a low level of attainment a little investment can produce substantial improvement whereas at higher levels the same improvement requires much greater effort or resources. Take infant mortality, for example: the rate in a poor African country can probably be halved (say, from 150 per 1000 live births to 75) simply by the provision of basic and relatively inexpensive ante- and postnatal care, but to halve the rate in an advanced country (e.g. from 20 to 10) would require much more sophisticated and expensive methods. Similarly, life expectation at first increases rapidly with nutrition level (measured by calorific content of diet), but the curve flattens out at higher levels (see Meadows, 1972, pp. 104–6).

This kind of analysis clearly suggests that the transfer of resources from rich nations to poor could greatly improve life in the latter, at relatively little cost to the former. The same may apply within nations, as we shall see later, in the case of health care (Chapter 5). Perhaps, in the advanced Western world, we are approaching a condition of over-abundance, judging by some of the social strains in the archetypal affluent society of the contemporary United States. Perhaps we would be better off, in a broad human sense, with no more economic growth, in which case transfer of our own growth capacity to the underdeveloped world does not even require an altruistic motive.

Before reaching such specific conclusions, some reservations about the analysis presented above must be made, however. As has already been said, data at the national level are subject to errors which make comparisons difficult. Level of living is defined on the basis of six specific conditions; the inclusion of others could change the index and the national relativities in performance. The relationship shown in Figure 2.5 is based on less than half the world's nations with populations of over one million, and excludes countries like the UK and USSR for which data are incomplete. A fuller set of accurate data could show a different result, though it seems likely that the general form of the curvilinear relationship would still appear. Finally, we cannot assume a direct *causal* relationship between GNP per capita and level of living, such that growth in the former inevitably generates improvements in the latter, of a magnitude broadly predictable from the graph. What actually happens – who gets what where from the process of economic development – depends very much on the nature of the society concerned. We shall return to this theme in later discussions.

Before leaving this cross-national comparison one further point must be made, about qualitative aspects of level of living. The composite index derived above hides the fact that nations with similar overall performance (i.e. similar index scores) may rate quite differently on individual contributors to living standards. A nation with a

Where the Grass is Greener

high composite score may show up relatively unfavourably on one or two conditions. The standard score calculation explained above enables us to prepare profiles of living standards for individual nations, distinguishing their performance on each of the six conditions included. These help to reveal something of the structure of consumption as it varies among nations.

Examples of level-of-living profiles are shown in Figure 2.6. The vertical scale represents standard scores, or units of departure from the average of all fifty-four nations (i.e. 0). The numerals 1 to 6 refer to the six conditions listed in Table 2.5. The higher a column in the positive direction, the better off a nation is on the condition in question; the lower in the negative direction, the worse off. The profile for the USA shows that its high total index score is very much dependent on high *material* living standards, as indicated by telephone and car consumption; on life expectation and the two measures of mental development, the USA is less well off than a number of European countries. The Netherlands shows a much more balanced standard of living. Czechoslovakia reveals a poor comparative performance on personal material consumption, typical of

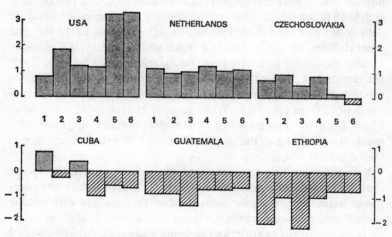

Figure 2.6. Level-of-living profiles for selected nations. (Source of data: see Table 2.5.)

communist countries, where greater relative stress is placed on social consumption and well-being. Cuba somewhat resembles Czechoslovakia, but at a lower overall level; the post-revolutionary stress on health and education shows up in the profile. Guatemala is badly off to a similar degree on all but the education measure. Ethiopia, with the lowest total index score, suffers particularly from a bad performance on life expectation and children in school. Such profiles are suggestive of fundamental differences in national life. For example, an uneven development in favour of material consumption of such items as motor cars to the neglect of health and education probably reflects an unequal society, with a privileged section of the population enjoying standards much greater than the rest. The contrast between Ethiopia and Cuba is instructive in this respect: the former was (at the time of these data) a highly élitist society, while Cuba is run on strongly equalitarian lines.

This discussion of qualitative aspects of development raises again the question of the relative importance of different conditions. The six adopted here have been weighted equally in the composite index. But might we be justified in giving more weight to life expectation than car ownership, for example? If so, the USA index score would suffer, perhaps bringing it down below the level of some European countries with higher life expectation than in the USA but fewer cars. The level of living or development depends not only on what is included but also on how we judge the relative desirability of the different attributes. In the next chapter we will discuss a case in which these kinds of value judgements are taken into account in the measurement of living standards.

Security, Freedom and Happiness

Let us now turn to some rather more abstract aspects of life. We are quite well informed as to variations among nations in income, material consumption and some social conditions, because these are relatively easily measured (though not always very accurately). We know less about such general conditions as security, freedom and happiness, yet these occupy important places in the rhetoric that embodies many national ideals. The problem is one of meaning as well as measurement, of course. Security, freedom and happiness mean quite different things to different individuals and groups. We will examine these concepts briefly, again in the context of cross-national comparison.

Security implies safety. The *Oxford English Dictionary* suggests the kind of meanings evoked by the word secure: untroubled by danger or apprehension, safe against attack, reliable, having sure prospect. The concept of security relates to the predictability of life – to how sure people can be of their existing situation. At one extreme, security could in practice mean safety from the prospect of premature death through accident, calamity or arbitrary execution. At the other, it might mean the ability to continue to live in material comfort even if deprived of employment, i.e. economic or social as opposed to physical security. How does the level of personal security vary among nations?

Figure 2.7 illustrates the incidence of two rather dramatic threats to personal survival: famine and domestic violence. These are probably the most important single causes of premature death in the modern world. Cigarettes and motor vehicles may run them close, but there is more deliberation concerning the prevalence of lung cancer, road accidents and death from air pollution, in that they appear to be part of the price of material progress collectively accepted, if not necessarily condoned by everyone.

The map identifies the world's hunger belt, where famine has reached what may reasonably be termed crisis proportions and where nutritional levels are well below those needed to maintain healthy life. Famine is rampant over large parts of the areas shown. In others, a poor harvest could make the difference between survival and starvation for many people. Deaths from starvation in parts of Africa in recent years are in the hundreds of thousands. Some famines are publicized, as an intrepid Western reporter or TV camera team find their way to one of these crisis areas. Others occur virtually unnoticed by the well-fed population of the advanced industrial world. Every so often an international gathering, such as the World Food Conference of 1974, draws attention to the plight of the world's 'starving millions'; pious expressions of concern are made, proposals

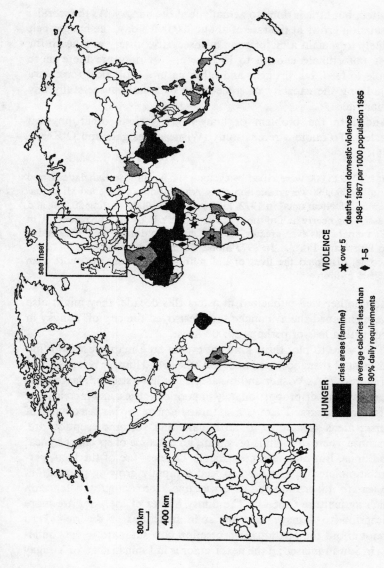

Figure 2.7. Where life is threatened: the world's hunger belt and major incidences of domestic violence. (Sources: *Time*, 11 Nov. 1974; Taylor and Hudson, 1972, Table 3.4.)

HUNGER

crisis areas (famine)

average calories less than 90% daily requirements

VIOLENCE

★ over 5

◆ 1–5

deaths from domestic violence 1948–1967 per 1000 population 1965

see inset

800 km

400 km

79

debated, but little is done to actually feed the hungry. As the world's population grows at the rate of about 200,000 a day, the hunger belt is likely to remain a major zone of insecurity, misery and death for those unfortunate enough to live there. Not only are there more people to feed, but drought and other natural ecological forces are prejudicing the capacity of some areas to sustain successfully any human life.

Added to the problem of hunger are various other physical disasters. To quote a recent study (Wisner, Westgate and O'Keefe, 1976):

> In 1970, 225,000 were killed by cyclone and flooding in Bangladesh, and another 600,000 were made homeless. An earthquake flattened Managua, capital of Nicaragua, in 1972, killing at least 6000, injuring 20,000, and destroying nearly half of the sprawling town's housing. The recent toll in Guatemala was even greater. At least 8000 Hondurans died in 1974 due to Hurricane Fifi . . . In 1973 alone, 25 major disasters killed 110,000 people, disrupted the lives of 215 million more, and cost more than [£]500 million.

Among other well-publicized disasters this decade, they might also have mentioned the avalanche that destroyed the city of Yungay in Peru, with a loss of perhaps 20,000 lives.

If we were to plot these kinds of events on a map, we would find that most of them occurred in or near the broad hunger belt identified in Figure 2.7. As Wisner and his associates have stressed, large-scale disasters occur disproportionately in poor countries, and increasingly so in recent years. There is a natural element in this selectivity, of course: areas vulnerable to earthquake and volcanic eruption are, like those where drought is prevalent, an outcome of specific physical conditions. But man also contributes. Careless use of the land, perhaps stimulated by the need to feed a rapidly growing population, can lead to soil erosion and otherwise upset the ecological balance on which agriculture depends. The flimsy homes of the poor are more susceptible to damage than the solid structures of the rich. Peru cannot afford the earthquake protection now standard in new buildings in San Francisco; if the next tremor is in Lima instead of Yungay the death toll will be enormous. Rich countries can make their people more physically secure; the poor remain vulnerable. Even famine resulting from drought can hardly be viewed as a 'natural' disaster, when food production is a human activity organized within a particular social formation, not an instinctive animal reaction to immediate need. Many of the countries in which millions of people are inadequately fed, if not permanently hungry, have a 'modern' agricultural economy in which large plantations supply the advanced industrial nations with food and raw materials. Any explanation of the geographical incidence of hunger must take into consideration the forces operating within the world economy that allocate land in poor countries to production for the rich.

The other aspect of insecurity featured in Figure 2.7 is death from domestic violence. A careful tabulation by research workers in the United States estimates how many people were killed in events of domestic political conflict between 1948 and 1967. The total is over one million. The largest absolute numbers are 615,000 in Indonesia and 177,000 in South Vietnam; and these figures refer to the period before the escalation of the Vietnam war and the conflicts in neighbouring Laos and Cambodia. The map identifies two scales of domestic violence. In the largest, at least five persons in 1000 of the total population (in about 1965) died – and even this may be an underestimate. The greatest proportional death toll was in Rwanda, where strife in the mid 1960s cost the lives of almost one in 100 of the population. As with famine and other disasters, the major incidents of domestic violence are concentrated in the world's poverty belt. The only European cases of the magnitude of one death for every thousand people are in Greece in the late 1940s and in the Hungarian uprising of 1956–7. Clearly, the accuracy of some of these figures can be doubted in the absence of systematic and unbiased 'body counts'. But the fact remains that people in poorer parts of the world are most vulnerable to domestic violence arising from political instability – itself in part a function of poverty.

One possible way of looking at security is to regard it as a kind of freedom – freedom from fear, worry, or arbitrary acts of nature and one's fellow men. To many people, freedom is release from some

81

specific evil, whether it be slavery, racial domination, communism, capitalist exploitation, sex discrimination or government interference with 'free' enterprise. But freedom is also thought of in a more positive way. Resorting to the dictionary again, freedom denotes personal liberty, independence, power of self-determination. These notions are subject to varied and conflicting interpretations, so that any attempt to define and map the degree of people's freedom is bound to be highly controversial. But it is worth at least an illustration, to raise some of the more specific issues involved.

In Figure 2.8 we show two possible classifications of the nations of the world, from different ideological perspectives. Let us consider first an American view of freedom as conveyed by Freedom House Inc. of New York, who describe themselves as an 'organization dedicated to strengthening democratic institutions'. In 1973 Freedom House published a comparative world survey of freedom. Dr Raymond Gastil, a prominent social scientist, was commissioned to devise 'objective' criteria to judge the current state of political and civil liberty in every nation of the world. Civil rights are taken to be the rights of the individual against the state, such as free expression and a fair trial. Political rights are legal rights to play a part in determining who governs or what the laws of the community are. The specific conditions considered are freedom of the press, whether political institutions and governments change by an orderly process, the presence of two or more political parties, and constitutional guarantees in law and in practice to assure individual rights. The analysis does not take into account degree of economic equality or presence and absence of social distinctions, except in so far as these are regarded as directly related to liberty. Various sources of information were used, to place each nation on scales of 1 to 7 for political and civil liberty respectively. A score of 1 indicates a very high level of liberty and 7 very low.

The map shows countries considered 'free' on these scales. For the most part, these countries rate 1 or 2 on both criteria. Countries with 1 on both are identified as having the highest levels of freedom – the advanced Western democracies of North America, North-West Europe and Australia/New Zealand. The other 'free' countries include

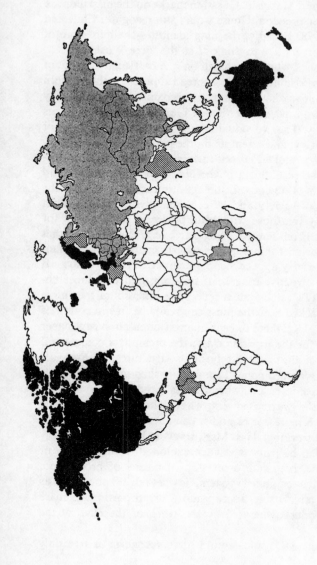

An American view of freedom

■ highest levels of freedom

▨ other free countries

An alternative view

▨ socialist or communist countries

800 km

Figure 2.8. Alternative views of the 'free world'. (Source: American view from *Freedom at Issue*, *Freedom* House, New York, No. 17, Jan.–Feb. 1973.)

(surprisingly, perhaps) the Dominican Republic, three Central American nations and Malaysia. Question marks on the map indicate doubt as to whether Freedom House would still recognize Chile and India as free in 1978. Broadly, the map identifies the hard core of what Western observers like to think of as the 'Free World'.

This classification is, of course, based on one particular concept of freedom. It might command quite widespread approval in the Western capitalist/democratic world, but it must be recognized as ideologically based. It stems from a particular view of life that places great stress on *individual* liberty. The individual is seen very much as master of his or her own destiny, and attempts on the part of the state to constrain the pursuit of individual self-interest are regarded with disapproval, unless the curtailment of the liberty of others that would occur without them is obvious. Little attention is given to how the broader structure of society and its economic system may restrict freedom, especially for those with little power in the markets for goods and labour. From another perspective (e.g. the Marxism that underpins much socialist thinking) the criteria considered important by Freedom House may appear inconsequential. It might be argued that there are no objective criteria of freedom, and that those enshrined in a society's value system reflect the interests of the ruling class. It might be asked how the press can really be free in countries like the USA and UK, where there is no mass-circulation newspaper published by and for the working class: the press, as a commercial concern, is part of the capitalist business structure and exercises editorial selectivity accordingly. It might be asked what an orderly change of government matters, when the real need is for revolutionary overthrow of the existing powers; what a choice between parties matters, when both represent capitalist or bourgeois interests rather than those of the working class. Marxists would also ask how any man or woman can be truly free when exploited in the employ of another. The right to private ownership of means of production, fundamental to the capitalist system, is viewed by socialists as enabling a small minority to appropriate a disproportionate share of the surplus product generated by the work of the mass of the people.

This alternative view would require us to recognize as free only those nations where a socialist system of production prevails.* Only here is no man exploited by another, the argument would run. Only here is there true economic freedom, because control is vested in the people themselves. Nations that can be considered socialist or communist are identified in Figure 2.8. These do not include the Western 'social democracies' with socialist-style or labour governments, because the prevailing mode of production remains capitalist. The map stresses the spatially contiguous nature of the 'communist block', except for Cuba and the southern African nations of Tanzania, Angola and Mozambique (where the precise form of socialism to be followed is still not clear). Needless to say, most of the countries shown fall into the 'not free' category according to Freedom House.

A comparison between Figures 2.8 and 2.7 shows the position of the major world hunger and poverty belt in relation to the alternative 'free' worlds of capitalism and socialism. For the most part, the poor nations fall into neither the communist block nor the 'free' part of the capitalist world. It is in this 'Third World' that the ideological struggle between capitalism and socialism is being waged, of course. But there is one perhaps more immediate consequence for the poor Third World nations, especially for those very substantial sections of their populations living highly vulnerable lives. They enjoy the benefits of neither the comprehensive social services available in a socialist–communist state nor the relatively well-developed material affluence and social security or welfare programmes of the advanced capitalist nations. In looking at the models provided by capitalism and socialism they may aspire to the best of both worlds; in reality they get neither. Which of the alternatives may offer a poor, underdeveloped nation the best prospect of enhancing the well-being of its population is a question to which we shall return later.

The notion of alternative conceptions of security and freedom is closely related to the current concern with 'human rights'. Almost daily, we (in the West) learn of affronts to human rights in the communist world, particularly threats to the freedom of speech of so-

*The term 'socialist' is used throughout this book to denote countries with a predominantly publicly-owned and centrally-planned economy. Most of these countries are considered to be 'communist' in the West, their fortunes being guided by the Communist Party. It is debatable whether any of them have achieved true communism.

called dissidents in the USSR. Such reporting usually carries with it the unstated assumption that human rights, like freedom, can be defined in some absolute sense, clearly understood and upheld in the 'free world' but denied by the communists. The reality, of course, is that different societies believe in different sets of rights. Both the major 'superpowers' have written constitutions incorporating rights supposedly guaranteed their citizens. It is instructive to compare them. The Bill of Rights, comprising the first ten Amendments to the Constitution of the United States, provides for such things as: freedom of religion, speech, the Press and peaceable assembly; the right to keep and bear arms; security in the home; procedures to ensure fair treatment in criminal prosecution and protection of private property (see M. R. Smith and D. M. Smith, 1973, p. 39). The emphasis is very much on the liberty and protection of the individual against the power of the state. The new Soviet constitution published in June 1977 (see *The Times*, 6 June 1977) provides for the rights to work, rest and leisure, health protection, maintenance in old age and disability, housing, education, and to use the achievements of culture, as well as to more individualistic rights similar to those of the US Constitution. Of course, there are questions as to how far such rights are upheld in practice. But the basic point should be clear – that in the USSR certain rights are recognized that relate to collectively organized production and consumption, the maintenance of which is felt to justify some curtailment of more individual liberties such as freedom of speech. In the USA, there is more stress on individual freedom, especially in the sphere of economic activity, part of the price of which is that no one can be guaranteed work and some related aspects of social security. Which conception of human rights is 'best' is a matter of personal preference and experience rather than something on which an absolute moral judgement can be made. We must therefore beware of judging other societies by our own standards. It may be better to judge the USSR or USA by the extent to which their own espoused ideals are upheld in practice.

It now remains to discuss the concept of happiness. This is, if anything, even more elusive than security or freedom. To some people happiness is found in material possessions – the latest car, a colour TV and so on; to others, it comes from excursions to what remains of the unspoilt countryside, or from relationships with other people. To some, happiness derives from a visit to the concert hall, an exciting book or a gourmet meal; others are content with a day when there is something to eat and the perpetual threat to security has been avoided. Happiness is a highly personal thing. It is very much related to our own life experience, to the bounds of expectation derived from the life we know and the nature of the society in which we live. The more we know of the lives of other people in other places, the wider the basis on which we may judge the quality of our own lives.

To measure happiness may seem quite inconsistent with the nature of the concept itself. However, the idea of placing people's happiness on a numerical scale appeals to contemporary social science, with its stress on quantitative precision and objectivity. But it is extraordinarily difficult to devise a way of measuring happiness to compare merely two individuals, never mind the population of nations. If I claim to be happier than you and you believe yourself happier than I, what possible objective arbitration procedure could there be? The technique commonly adopted by social scientists interested in subjective or psychological well-being is survey research, whereby a sample of the population are asked to place themselves on a scale recognizing different degrees of happiness or satisfaction with life. Then some average can be calculated for the inhabitants of particular places. Experiments of this kind have been conducted by leading research institutes, such as the Social Science Research Council's former survey research unit in London, the University of Michigan's Institute for Social Research in the USA and the Research Group for Comparative Sociology at the University of Helsinki in Finland.

A cross-national survey of this type has been undertaken by Gallup International Research Institutes. More than 10,000 people were interviewed, in nearly seventy countries, answering various questions as to their feelings about life. A summary of some of the results is shown in Table 2.7, where different parts of the world are listed in order of their GNP per capita. The figures indicate that satisfaction with life is quite closely related to the general level of economic development; there is a striking difference between sub-Saharan Africa, the Far East and India on the one hand and the economically advanced nations on the other. But happiness is not a

Table 2.7. *Happiness, life satisfaction and concern in different parts of the world, based on a Gallup poll*

Area	Very or fairly happy personally	Highly satisfied: with life in own nation	with job	with standard of living	Concerned over finances all or most of the time
United States	90	34	49	46	26
Scandinavia	96	52	55	65	17
France	88	15	25	22	22
West Germany	74	55	44	44	10
Australia	94	46	30	57	12
British Isles	92	23	49	38	22
Japan	66	18	24	27	41
Italy	68	9	33	26	29
Africa sub-Sahara	68	18	7	5	69
Far East	48	12	7	8	68
India	37	5	4	4	75

Source: *Reader's Digest*, October 1976; based on data from Gallup International Research Institutes.

Note: the figures are estimates of the percentage of total population, derived from sample surveys; the range of error is plus or minus six percentage points.

direct function of national product per capita. People in Britain are happier than in some wealthier nations – a finding greeted with delight (and not a little incredulity) by the popular press, as the pound sterling experienced its latest crisis amidst warnings of impending economic doom in September 1976, when the Gallup Survey was published. Sub-Saharan Africans appear as happy as the beneficiaries of Japan's affluent society. West Germany's 'economic miracle' seems to create a relatively high level of satisfaction with the three aspects of life shown, but fewer Germans are very or fairly happy than in any of the other parts of the advanced industrial world shown (excluding Japan and Italy).

The final column in the table offers a reading on people's sense of economic security. Again, the disadvantaged position of the poorer parts of the world is clear. But there are also variations among the richer countries. The United States may have the highest GNP per capita, but a quarter of the population surveyed admitted to being concerned about finances all or most of the time. This may well reflect the continuing pressure to consume yet more new products and to replace those that go wrong, stimulated by advertising and the desire to emulate others. Also relevant is the persistence of a substantial number of people in poverty (perhaps 25 million according to a recent official estimate) and the absence of effective social-security programmes. Japan occupies a position between the rich and poor world, with respect to money problems.

While such findings as these must be treated with caution, they do tend to support the proposition that economic growth and prosperity is important, but is not the only influence on happiness. In the poorer parts of the world growth of physical output and incomes is a necessary condition for the better satisfaction of human needs. But in the richer nations people's perception of their own life quality may derive largely from other conditions, once a reasonable income and basic social security is assured. The pursuit of economic growth and its attendant hedonistic materialism may ultimately be more destructive than supportive of human happiness and personal fulfilment.

Development and Inequality

Human life chances or prospects for happiness vary from country to country. They also vary within nations. Place-to-place variations within nations is the subject of the next two chapters. But before leaving broad cross-national comparisons, some comments are required on the general question of inequality in distribution. A high degree of internal inequality is characteristic of particular types of societies and particular stages of development.

Cross-national comparisons of inequality are made especially difficult by the kind of measurement problems referred to earlier in this book. The basis on which figures are compiled in different nations often makes them incompatible. However, Taylor and Hudson (1972) were able to assemble sufficient data to calculate Gini coefficients for the distribution of income and land in about fifty nations, mainly in Central and South America, South-East Asia and Europe. If these figures are compared we find that those three world regions are

89

characterized by different types of inequality (D. M. Smith, 1977, pp. 226–31). The Central and South American countries generally have a very high degree of inequality in the distribution of land and also marked inequality in income distribution. At the extreme are Peru ($G = 93\cdot3$ for land, $39\cdot8$ for income) and Guatemala ($86\cdot0$ for land and $48\cdot8$ for income). South-East Asian countries have a much more equal distribution of land but considerable variations in income inequality (the range is from $G = 43\cdot0$ in Thailand to $14\cdot9$ in Japan). In Europe, the reverse is the case, with low levels of income inequality but a tendency towards high inequality in land ownership: for example the UK has the most equal distribution of income ($G = 5\cdot0$) but a figure as high as $G = 72\cdot3$ for land.

These geographical variations reflect important differences in economic and social structure. Most of the Central and South American countries have a small, wealthy élite of landowners and capitalists, running large ranches or plantations and also gaining most of the wealth generated by industrial activity. South-East Asia has much more intensive agriculture, with smaller holdings of land more evenly distributed among the farming population, but there may still be rich rajahs, princes, merchants and others, along with large inequalities in income as between town and country or skilled and unskilled occupations. In Europe, the concentration of land-ownership is a relic of the pre-industrial era and its feudal aristocracy; economic development and the growing power of organized labour have brought a much more even distribution of income.

Inequality in national income distribution is most easily measured from data on sector shares, i.e. how much goes to agriculture, mining, manufacturing and so on compared with their shares of total employment. This is the basis of the Taylor and Hudson figures referred to above. But we can also compare earnings in specific occupations representing different socio-economic groups. This can be illustrated by returning to the world cities featured earlier in this chapter in the discussion of purchasing power. Figure 2.4 showed graphically how long personnel managers and auto mechanics would have to work to earn the price of a car and a packet of cigarettes. The respective size of the bars indicates something of the degree of inequality between these two occupations. To be more precise, the ratios of their earnings, gross and net (i.e. after tax and social security deductions), have been calculated in Table 2.8. Again, there is some geographical pattern. The largest ratios, or greatest inequality, are in Central and South America; the lowest are in North-West Europe and North America. The final column indicates the degree of income redistribution effected through the deductions from gross earnings: the higher the figure the greater the relative shift in favour of the mechanics. In some cities in richer countries the relativities do not change, or there is a slight move in favour of the managers (figures of less than 1).

This table, and the data on land and income distribution summarized above, suggests a relationship between inequality and level of development. The degree of inequality appears to fall as we move from poor to rich nations. Such a generalization has featured quite prominently in the literature of economic development (e.g. Williamson, 1965; Adelman and Morris, 1973), with the added refinement that at the lowest level of economic development what little income there is tends of necessity to be relatively evenly distributed. In other words, inequality *rises* in early stages of development, as industrialization and commercial agriculture begin to transform a 'traditional' society, but falls after a critical level of economic advance has been achieved. Thus, if some measure of inequality is plotted on a graph against GNP per capita, the relationship should approximate to the form of an inverted U (i.e. ∩).

Figure 2.9 shows that there is some truth to this assertion. Inequality in sixty-six countries is measured by the ratio of income shares of the richest 20 per cent of the population and the poorest 40 per cent. The higher the ratio, the greater the inequality. These figures are plotted against GNP per capita (on a logarithmic scale, so that the situation in the poorer countries can be shown clearly). At the bottom (left-hand) end of the scale are such nations as India and Chad, with low aggregate incomes relatively evenly distributed. At the other end are rich nations such as the USA and the UK, again with fairly even distribution by world standards. But in the middle part of the graph, where GNP ranges from about $200 to 1500 per capita, great differences in distribution are apparent. At the top, with a highly unequal distribution, are certain ex-colonial

91

Where the Grass is Greener

Table 2.8. Ratios of earnings of personnel managers and automobile mechanics in major cities, 1973

City	Gross pay	Net pay	Gross÷net
Europe			
Amsterdam	1·94	2·03	0·96
Athens	4·60	4·12	1·12
Brussels	3·10	2·80	1·11
Copenhagen	3·08	2·61	1·18
Düsseldorf	4·57	4·26	1·07
Geneva	2·29	2·29	1·00
Helsinki	2·45	2·25	1·09
Istanbul	2·20	1·81	1·22
Lisbon	3·64	3·30	1·10
London	2·11	2·12	0·99
Luxemburg	3·41	3·32	1·03
Madrid	10·47	9·14	1·15
Milan	3·15	2·97	1·06
Oslo	2·50	2·47	1·01
Paris	3·12	3·12	1·00
Rome	4·72	4·32	1·09
Stockholm	2·37	1·93	1·23
Vienna	3·85	3·57	1·08
Zurich	2·38	2·19	1·09
North America and Australia			
Chicago	3·21	2·93	1·10
Montreal	2·04	1·88	1·09
New York	2·82	2·68	1·05
San Francisco	2·53	2·28	1·06
Sydney	2·32	1·94	1·20
Central and South America			
Bogotá	25·62	17·49	1·46
Buenos Aires	3·50	3·37	1·04
Caracas	5·45	5·34	1·02
Mexico City	4·46	4·00	1·12
Rio de Janeiro	8·75	7·32	1·20
São Paulo	6·58	5·53	1·19
Africa, Middle East and Asia			
Beirut	10·00	9·76	1·02
Bombay	4·45	4·21	1·06
Hong Kong	4·75	4·55	1·04
Johannesburg	1·54	1·60	0·96
Singapore	5·60	4·98	1·12
Tel Aviv	1·36	1·30	1·05
Tokyo	2·88	2·89	0·99

Source: Calculated from data from Union Bank of Switzerland, 1974.

Note: gross earnings per year include all supplementary payments but exclude overtime pay; *net* earnings are gross earnings minus income tax and social service contributions for retirement, disability and health insurance. The ratios are managers' earnings divided by mechanics' earnings, for gross and net earnings respectively.

Inequality among Nations: Development and Underdevelopment

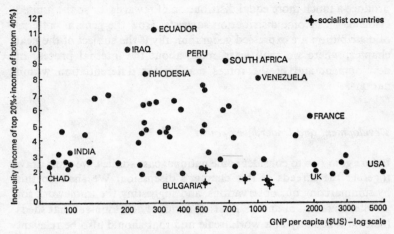

Figure 2.9. The relationship between income inequality and GNP per capita by nations. (Source: D. M. Smith, 1977, Figure 8.7; data from Ahluwalia, 1974.)

territories (South Africa and Rhodesia) and other countries in which effective control is exercised by a small élite, often backed by some kind of military regime. At the bottom are countries where the income of the bottom 40 per cent approaches that of the top 20 per cent. Included here are the five socialist countries in Eastern Europe for which data are available: there is no personal income from capital investment to skew the distribution in these countries, though differences in wages between sectors of the economy and workers with different skills make for some income inequality.

Clearly, the degree of inequality in income distribution is not a simple function of economic development. There are different paths to development. The path controlled by an expatriate or indigenous capitalist élite of the kind to be found in many colonial and Latin American countries is likely to lead to great inequalities – to a highly uneven pattern of development, with some people (and places) severely disadvantaged while others enjoy great affluence. A development strategy pursued under socialism, while perhaps no less 'élistist' in the sense of the degree of concentration of control, appears to

93

produce a much more equal distribution of rewards, or so the limited evidence on income distribution suggests. How the general patterns of distribution are expressed geographically is the subject of the next chapter, where we shall learn more about the internal process of development and of the forces making for differentiation within nations.

Development and Underdevelopment

Before going on to consider some national case studies, we must draw together the threads of this chapter's discussion. We shall do this by summarizing our observations, and suggesting the framework for an interpretation of uneven levels of national development that sheds light on inequality at a world scale and that should also be relevant to the understanding of differences within nations. The case studies that follow will enable us to refine and perhaps modify what may be thought of as a skeletal theory of spatial inequality or uneven development.

We have seen that the world's wealth is very unevenly distributed among nations. Differences in GNP as between the industrially advanced nations and those of the underdeveloped world are enormous, and the gap appears not to be narrowing significantly. A few oil-rich states are emerging as deviant cases, with high per capita income but otherwise sharing many of the attributes of underdevelopment: widespread poverty, ignorance, ill-health and a highly skewed income distribution. But otherwise the countries of the so-called Third World have been fortunate to see much of an improvement in their position relative to that of North America, Europe and the few 'advanced' nations elsewhere. When income is viewed in 'real' terms as purchasing power, the gap between rich and poor nations is reduced somewhat, but very considerable differences still remain.

Variations among nations in per capita income or product are reflected in many other conditions that contribute to standard of living or human well-being. These include health, education, environmental quality and aspects of economic or social security, as well as access to material goods. There is some evidence that standard of living defined broadly enough to include aspects of social well-being is subject to decreasing returns to economic growth, such that further advances in GNP per capita generate a less-than-proportional increase in general human well-being or life quality, especially in the richer nations. But this is of little relevance for the mass of the world's people at the poor end of the scale, who depend very much on greater income from production for the development of basic services that are taken for granted in most of the industrially advanced nations.

Living standards or level of development are multi-faceted conditions. Their structure, in the form of the final outputs of goods and services, varies from country to country. With the same general level of income or GNP, some societies will stress material production while others will devote more resources to social services, the preservation of the environment and so on. Such differences can be important indicators of the values and priorities of societies (or of those who rule). There is a general tendency for social objectives to gain importance as advanced stages of economic development are reached. But there are significant differences among nations even at the top end of the affluence scale, as exemplified by the greater materialistic preoccupation of American society when compared to the 'welfare states' of Western Europe. Eastern Europe and the USSR have their own special blend of materialism and social security.

Broadening our views of inequality at a world scale, we observed that areas of high personal vulnerability tend to correspond with the underdeveloped countries. This is where the greatest threats from hunger, natural disaster and domestic violence occur. It is also in these countries that there is perhaps greatest curtailment of individual freedom. Many Third World countries have neither the personal liberty that figures so prominently in the ideals of liberal Western democracies nor the freedom from exploitation in the labour market to which socialists attach so much importance. While the struggle to survive is a major constraint on freedom in poor countries, a more fundamental factor is the highly unequal distribution of wealth, income and political power. This is itself an important attribute of the condition of underdevelopment.

95

Where the Grass is Greener

In seeking explanation for the world pattern of uneven development, the traditional geographical perspective tends to stress environmental conditions. Obviously, areas with climates unable to sustain a reliable level of food production will be prone to famine if alternative supplies from elsewhere are unobtainable in times of need. Certain environments may also carry a predisposition towards diseases of various kinds. Environments prone to natural disasters such as earthquakes, volcanic eruptions and floods make the struggle for existence that bit harder. The climatic extremes found in parts of the tropical world make some types of agriculture difficult. It is also argued that the underdeveloped countries lack the material resource base of minerals and sources of energy required to sustain industrialization on a European or North American scale.

While none of these considerations may be dismissed out of hand, they have certainly been exaggerated, not least by geographers unduly influenced by the environmental determinism that pervaded this subject until quite recently. Now it is being increasingly understood that problems of food supply, health care and so on are essentially human problems, stemming from a failure of economic and social organization. People can live well in quite 'difficult' environments with severe climatic extremes, if the necessary resources and technology can be mustered in an appropriate organizational structure. Advanced economic development is taking place outside the tropics in areas of great environmental difficulty – Siberia, for example. In any event, the underdeveloped countries contain large areas with quite temperate conditions, which themselves show that advanced agricultural and industrial development in the Western sense is possible. As to the limitation of natural resources, many underdeveloped countries have very considerable deposits of important minerals; the question is more one of how they are exploited – by whom and for whose benefit.

Other more traditional explanations for underdevelopment focus on certain qualitative characteristics of the population of poor countries. At the extreme, these degenerate into quite unsubstantiated claims of racial inferiority. More often, it is suggested that social custom (and perhaps climate) predispose people to a relaxed (even 'lazy') attitude to life, inconsistent with the motivation and work

96

ethic required for a modern economy. Again, there is an element of truth in such arguments, to the extent that some cultures do indeed place priority on certain attributes of life that may conflict with the regulation of human behaviour needed to run a complex organization. Attitudes to time and leisure are a case in point: lack of punctuality and a tendency to use work as a means of social intercourse are familiar to anyone who has worked with government departments in Third World countries. But such was (and to some extent still is) the case in the 'advanced' world: Europe's peasants did not become regular clock-punching factory workers overnight, and many a contemporary London typist probably covers as little paper as her counterpart in Lima. And how many 'business' lunches are strictly business? As to entrepreneurial or business skills, supposedly so limited in the Third World, there appears to be no shortage of businessmen when the opportunity arises, whether it be an Arabian sheikh wheeling and dealing with a Western nation in some arms-for-oil bargain or speculative urban development in a Latin American city. There is also the question of whether the aggressive, competitive ethics so revered in the West are really as essential to the development of a modern economy as is often supposed. In some respects the co-operative spirit of group solidarity found in pre-industrial societies might offer a superior basis for the development of an economy truly responsive to human needs, given the resources and technology to do the job.

Explanations based on environmental difficulty and the personal shortcomings of inhabitants of poor countries are thus of very limited assistance to us. Recognizing this, emphasis has shifted in recent years to the process of development. At this point we must be clear as to what is meant by economic activity and what conditions must necessarily be fulfilled for output to expand, or for growth to occur. Production involves the transformation of natural resources into things (goods and services) that satisfy human needs or wants. Given the resources of the land and its minerals, the level of output will be governed by the efficiency of the transformation process. This, in its turn, depends on the level of development of the productive forces, or the labour skills and technology available. A relatively unskilled workforce with little mechanization at its disposal will require much greater time and effort to attain the same output as will skilled workers with sophisticated plants, or will produce less in the time that they have. To make production more efficient, and thus expand output, requires investment in the training of labour and the creation of superior technology. A precondition for economic growth is thus capital accumulation, or a surplus product over and above that required to sustain and reproduce the labour force. The fundamental economic problem facing most poor nations is the low level of development of the productive forces, and the difficulty of mobilizing what surplus product exists. This is compounded by relatively high rates of population increase that require 2–3 per cent economic growth per year simply to maintain the existing level of production per capita.

Such observations form the basis of the 'vicious circle' explanation for underdevelopment. Low levels of output generate low incomes, which sustain low levels of demand and savings to stimulate and sustain new investment and thus increase the level of output. The development problem is viewed as how to break out of this cycle of self-perpetuating poverty. In the terminology of Rostow's influential book *The Stages of Economic Growth* (1960), it is the question of how a 'traditional society' makes the transition to the 'take-off' stage of rapid industrial growth, driven on by fast capital accumulation and reinvestment. This question has been the subject of much debate on the part of economists and others interested in the design of economic development strategy. Our concern here is not so much with how development might be induced but with why the process has been frustrated or retarded in so much of the world. If rapid and self-sustaining economic growth has been achieved elsewhere (as is the case) and if environment and population are no absolute barrier (as appears to be the case), why have so many nations not truly broken out of the cycle, to take-off into the era of prosperity and mass consumption?

Until very recently, answers to this question have tended to stress the difficulties of 'modernizing' traditional societies. Modernization involves not only the application of science and technology to enhance productive efficiency but also changes in social structure and values thought necessary to sustain a more sophisticated organization of production. Most Western writers assume that economic development will be implemented under a capitalist mode of production, albeit guided or facilitated by government planning. The societal transformations that promote take-off are thus seen very much in the context of capitalist institutions and ethics, stressing market relations, the private profit motive and technical aspects of productive efficiency. One general drawback of this approach is that it tends to overlook the experiences of development under socialism, and the possibility that some alternative path may be more suited than capitalism to the reality of an underdeveloped country. The very nature of the capitalist system and its social relationships may itself constitute a barrier to development, or introduce distorting factors in the process of economic advance. For example, the tendency for so much of the early fruits of economic expansion to accrue to the existing élite can exacerbate income inequality, and it is the distribution of income that largely determines the structure of production for the home market, i.e. whether the output is predominantly basic commodities for the masses or luxuries for the rich. The conventional view also gives insufficient attention to two fundamental *geographical* aspects of the development process that have an important bearing on the level of development achieved by individual nations. The first of these deficiencies arises from the tendency to view nations as homogeneous entities in which all the people will gain from development. The reality is that the impact of Western-style capitalist development can be uneven spatially, so that some people in some places may lose rather than gain (a matter to which we shall return in the next chapter). The second deficiency is that the nations themselves are too often viewed in isolation, whereas their level of development can only be understood in the context of external relations with other countries.

Responding to these deficiencies, a broader approach has been emerging during the past few years. It stresses the feature of *interdependence* in development. In a non-geographical sense, interdependence refers to the fact that development involves a complex set of interrelated changes: economic, social, cultural and political, not merely growth of productive output – a theme introduced earlier in this chapter. The interdependence approach applied geographically stresses that level of development in one country (or region) is dependent on place in a wider, interconnected economic – social – political system. Very simply, underdevelopment in some places may be a consequence of development in other places, just as the disadvantage of some groups in society may be attributed to the more favourable status of others. This interdependence view of the process of development and underdevelopment is reflected in recent geographical literature (e.g. de Souza and Porter, 1974; Brookfield, 1975; D. M. Smith, 1977, ch. 8).

Much of the inspiration for what has almost become a new orthodoxy in development theory stems from Marx and from the writings of Lenin and Rosa Luxemburg on imperialism. A major feature of this approach is recognition of the process of expansion of capitalism from its bases in Europe and (later) North America, in search of raw materials, labour, markets for its products and opportunities for capital investment. The initial stage of plunder and forced subjugation of people in colonial territories leads to the setting up of enclaves of capitalist production and trading. These are extended as plantations are set up, mines developed and some manufacturing initiated. Gradually, the capitalist system penetrates and ultimately breaks down the indigenous mode of production. Labour is 'released' for the further expansion of the modern capitalist sector while the traditional agricultural and handicraft activities decline. Frank (1969) gave a specifically spatial expression to the relationship thus established, seeing the 'metropoles' (cores) of the world capitalist system dominating a series of dependent satellites (the periphery) from which an economic surplus is extracted and transferred back to the metropole. The advanced capitalist nations thus exploit those of the Third World. Instead of developing an economic structure and spatial organization appropriate to their domestic needs, the underdeveloped countries have become largely food and raw-material exporters and importers of manufactured goods. Their trading position, at best precarious because of reliance on a narrow range of primary products for export, has tended to deteriorate in recent years because of a shift in terms of trade which means that the price of manufactured goods from the advanced nations has risen faster than that of primary goods.

This external economic dependency has been perpetuated under what is sometimes termed neo-colonialism. Despite political independence, the economy of most ex-colonial countries remains dominated by foreign capital, and geared to the requirements of Europe and North America rather than to the needs of the local people. This is true of the recently independent countries of Africa (Davidson, 1975) and also of much of Latin America where *de facto* control of major sectors of the economy is exercised from the USA. The interests of overseas capital are protected by the support of indigenous regimes of 'moderate' (or reactionary) political persuasion, sympathetic to foreign business and duly rewarded by financial aid, arms and bribes. In some cases 'left-wing' governments have actually been replaced by regimes more supportive of American interests, as happened in Chile, Guatemala and the Dominican Republic. The active role of the US Government, via the Central Intelligence Agency, in overthrowing governments in other countries is fully explained in recent exposés (e.g. Agee, 1975).

Some Marxist writers on development problems emphasize that the 'nation exploits nation' view is an oversimplification, hiding the true class nature of the exploitation process. The role of the indigenous bourgeois élite is indeed very important in the underdeveloped countries. These people are those who gain most from the activities of foreign companies, as employees, agents, subcontractors and suppliers of professional services, or simply as recipients of bribes for some favour effected by access to or participation in the process of government. The indigenous élite also include military leaders, whose prestige is much enhanced by sophisticated weaponry from overseas. In terms of lifestyle, the élite of many underdeveloped countries closely resemble the more affluent members of society in North America and Europe: they are part of the same international bourgeois class. As recipients of most of the social surplus not syphoned back to investors in the developed nations, the indigenous élite perform a critical role in determining the pace of internal investment, which can be reduced by high expenditure on luxury consumption. Another aspect that cuts across national divisions is the emergence of the trans-national corporations which increasingly control the world capitalist economy. This is an incipient international ruling class, into which the élites of the underdeveloped world have been co-opted, that runs the world capitalist system in the interests of the rich. Among those who gain are the working class of many advanced countries, whose high living standards are to some extent dependent on exploitation of the masses in Third-World countries.

But, might not the underdeveloped countries be even more underdeveloped without their capitalist enclaves and overseas investments? The answer to this depends on what type of development would otherwise have taken place. Without the initial push from outside, many underdeveloped countries might have remained 'backward' in a conventional (Western) sense, with low levels of material existence. Indigenous capital accumulation might have sparked off some modern industry but the pattern of development could have been even more unequal than under dependent capitalism, if controlled by a local capitalist élite in its own interests. What might have been (or might yet be) achieved under socialism, with public ownership and control of the means of production, is difficult to say. The few experiences of this strategy in the underdeveloped world are still too young to evaluate. As we shall see in subsequent chapters, socialism itself is no guarantee of even development and the elimination of spatial inequality within nations. And, at the international level, there is a distinct possibility that the actual practice (as opposed to the theory) of socialism may have its own imperialist tendencies that work to the disadvantage of peripheral or satellite countries.

All we have been able to do here is to sketch out the broad features of a contemporary theory of underdevelopment that stresses interdependence. Set in context, as the latest stage in evolving thought concerning uneven development at the international scale, it is in some respects more distinctively geographical than earlier interpretations. Certainly, it recognizes the role of the spatial organization and of interconnectedness of economic activity, in addition to the traditional concern with the uneven distribution of resources. It also recognizes the reality of continuing inequality between the rich and poor nations, and advances explanations with, at least, strong intuitive appeal. The actual mechanism of surplus extraction in the Third World and its concentration has not been identified, nor have the details of how the capitalist mode of production interacts with indigenous modes in so-called dualistic societies. These are still matters of contention among Marxist scholars and others examining these approaches. In the chapters that follow we will hope to add some flesh to the theory, and perhaps some modifications, in the light of specific case studies, while at the same time seeing more of the phenomenon of spatial inequality itself. In so doing, we will leave the international arena for the regional and urban level within individual nations, for our aim is a view of the process of uneven development that transcends particular subdivisions of geographical space.

3 Inequality within Nations: Regional Variations

Inequality in living standards within nations can be observed at different spatial scales. There may be variations at a very broad regional level, as, for example, between a relatively rich and well-serviced metropolitan district focused on the capital city and the poorer peripheral parts of the country. There may be a more intricate pattern, in which regions are found to occupy a number of different levels: prosperous places in the periphery may compare quite favourably with parts of the core region. There may be differences among cities, in accordance with such features as size and function as well as geographical situation. Within regions, there may be systematic variations between town and country, and also some differences among rural areas. Finally, there may be marked variations within the urban areas themselves, especially the larger cities.

We cannot possibly do justice here to all these different dimensions of intra-national inequality. This chapter will concentrate on fairly broad patterns, as displayed by data for major administrative or statistical subdivisions. Four cases have been selected to explain various facets of the problem of uneven regional development. The first two, dealing with the United States and Great Britain, continue the discussion of certain technical aspects of the identification of spatial variations in living standards initiated in the previous two chapters, but they also begin to suggest some of the causal factors at work. The third case takes Peru as representative of the underdeveloped world, and focuses more directly on the forces promoting regional inequality. Finally, some observations are offered on spatial inequality in socialist countries at the regional level, to show that differentiation in living standards is by no means confined to capitalism.

These four cases are continued into the next chapter, where urban inequality is examined against the broader background set out here.

The United States: Inter-state Inequality

The United States is perhaps the most appropriate case with which to begin our exploration of inequality within nations. It is a vast country, with a variety of peoples and environments and with rich resources unevenly distributed. Thus considerable variations in living standards might be anticipated, in the absence of some powerful national policy making for the equalization of human life chances. The American way of life presents a sharp contrast between the rhetoric of liberty, freedom and justice, with its equalitarian overtones, and the reality of a relatively unconstrained capitalist economy which inevitably generates inequality. The fact that contemporary American society is often taken as a model for national development elsewhere is an added reason to understand the extent to which inequality and poverty still exist in the epitome of the affluent society.

In addition to its intrinsic interest, the USA has the advantage of well-developed sources of information. Government departments collect and publish statistics on a wide variety of conditions, social as well as economic, and these can be supplemented by data from special research organizations and from the proliferation of academic literature. The United States thus offers the best prospect in any nation for measuring the various facets of living standards or life quality that the breadth of these concepts requires. In the account that follows we will be able to compare a number of independent attempts to identify inter-state variations, so as to see how far different approaches reveal the same geographical patterns. But before proceeding, it is important to recognize that even in the USA data on certain aspects of life are still lacking or unreliable. The concepts of living standards actually adopted may thus appear somewhat biased in the direction of the more easily measured materialistic criteria. And, as at the national level, we must bear in mind that average figures for territorial units as large as states will hide local inequalities that may in fact represent the greatest extremes in human life chances (a matter to which we shall return in Chapter 4 when intra-city variations are considered).

We may begin with a general picture of variations among the nine major regions defined for the compilation of census statistics and certain other figures from official sources. Table 3.1 shows how the regions rate on five selected indicators. Income per capita varies from almost $6500 a year in the Pacific Region (states of California, Washington and Oregon) to $4560 in the East South Central Region (including the 'deep South' states of Louisiana and Mississippi) – a difference of roughly $1900. As a measure of housing quality, median value of owner-occupied houses shows the better-off regions of New England and the Pacific coast having almost twice the figure of the East South Central and West South Central Regions. Proportion of

Table 3.1. Regional performance on various economic and social indicators in the United States

Region	Income: per capita income ($) 1975	Housing: median value ($) 1970	Education: high school graduates (%) 1970	Health: infant mortality* 1974	Crime: robberies (per 100,000 popn) 1975
New England	6086	20,700	56·5	14·1	155
Middle Atlantic	6377	18,900	51·9	14·3	348
East North Central	6131	17,500	53·1	15·1	240
West North Central	5715	14,500	55·3	14·8	126
South Atlantic	5404	15,100	46·2	15·1	203
East South Central	4560	12,200	40·7	28·1	120
West South Central	5115	12,000	46·3	24·6	145
Mountain	5375	16,300	61·3	21·5	137
Pacific	6462	21,900	62·6	16·6	244
USA	5834	17,000	52·3	14·8	218

Source: *Statistical Abstract of the United States*, USGPO.

* Per 1000 live births, white population only.

people graduating from high school ranges from over 60 per cent in the two western regions (Mountain and Pacific) to barely 40 per cent in the East South Central Region. Infant mortality follows a similar pattern, as was observed in Chapter 1 (Figure 1.5). Although the chosen measures of income, housing, education and health reveal some differences in the ordering of the regions, they convey the same basic pattern, with the worst conditions in the south and the best in the north-east and on the west coast.

The final condition listed in Table 3.1 shows a different pattern, however. The robbery rate, taken to represent the incidence of crime, is highest in two of the regions which look best on the other indicators, i.e. Middle Atlantic and Pacific. It is lowest in the East South Central Region, which is bottom of the list for the other four conditions. Care must be taken in interpreting crime figures, for the robbery rate may be high in richer areas simply because there is more to steal. In addition, the FBI, who compile the figures, have some dubious statistical practices (D. M. Smith, 1974). But even if not entirely accurate as a measure of the general level of criminal activity, these figures do suggest that the apparently better-off parts of the country may not be so in all respects. Part of the price of living in a more affluent region may be a greater risk of theft. We shall return to the question of conflict between different aspects of life quality later in this discussion.

Variations among the nine census regions can provide only a broad impression of geographical inequality. For more details we must look at smaller territorial units. Though by no means ideal, the forty-eight contiguous states provide the most convenient level for further analysis. That there is greater inequality at this scale is shown in Figure 3.1, which maps per capita income by states along with the regional figures from Table 3.1. The range is now from $6854 in Connecticut to barely $4000 in Mississippi. Seven states have a per capita annual income of over $6500; three have less than $4500. Some of the variation is compensated for by lower costs of living in low-income states, but there are still substantial differences in the real income of the average person in the richer states when compared to the poorer (generally southern) states.

Figure 3.1 reveals a clear geographical pattern. The South shows

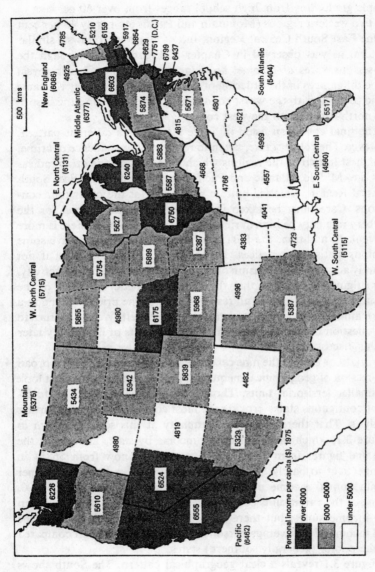

Figure 3.1. Variations in per capita income 1975 in the United States, by states and Census regions. (Source of data: *Statistical Abstract of the United States*, USGPO.)

New England (6086)

Middle Atlantic (6377)

E. North Central (6131)

W. North Central (5715)

Mountain (5376)

Pacific (6462)

South Atlantic (5404)

E. South Central (4560)

W. South Central (5115)

Personal Income per capita ($), 1975

over 6000

5000–6000

under 5000

500 kms

4785
5210
6159
5917
6854
6629
7751 (D.C.)
6799
6437
4925
6603
5874
5671
4801
4521
4969
5517
4815
5883
4668
4766
4557
6240
5587
6750
4041
5627
5387
4383
4729
5754
5899
5968
5855
4980
6175
4996
5387
5942
5839
5434
4819
4482
4980
5329
6226
5610
6524
6555

108

up as the major low-income region, with other low-income states to the north in New England, the Rockies and Great Plains. The 'major manufacturing belt' of the textbooks, extending from Boston and New York in the east to Chicago in the west, comprises a relatively high-income region, extending somewhat into the middle part of the Great Plains. In the west California and Nevada show up as a second high-income region.

How far is this pattern reflected in more general standards of living? To answer this question, we will first look at the results of a study designed to measure inter-state variations in social well-being. For the purpose of this investigation, social well-being was taken to refer to seven major aspects of life, to which reference was made in Chapter 1 (Table 1.1). These are as follows:

1. Income, wealth and employment
2. The living environment
3. Health
4. Education
5. Social order
6. Social belonging
7. Recreation and leisure

(Item 7 was, in fact, omitted, as impossible to measure by states.) The choice of these criteria, and their subsequent definition, was made on the basis of an examination of the content of a selection of books on social problems, to reveal what may be regarded as major concerns of contemporary American society.

Almost fifty different conditions were taken to measure these major criteria of social well-being (see D. M. Smith, 1973, ch. 7 and 1977, ch. 10). For example, income, wealth and employment was represented by data on per capita income, bank deposits, income supplement ('welfare') payments and so on. The environment was measured by housing quality. Health was broken down into physical and mental components, along with measures of access to medical care. Education included achievement, duration and level of service. Social order was measured by such conditions as alcoholism, narcotics addiction, incidence of venereal diseases, family breakdown and the crime rate. Social belonging covered electoral participation (voting rates), aspects of criminal justice and racial segregation. Reservations can of course be made about some of the conditions chosen and the way in which they are measured. But the data assembled provide a satisfactory if not perfect basis for the development of a general state indicator capturing a wide variety of aspects of life.

A composite index was derived in exactly the same way as the development indicator described in the previous chapter (see Appendix, p. 365). Instead of the six measures used in the cross-national comparison there are forty-seven for the American states. The results of summing the standard scores are mapped in Figure 3.2. The figures shown are the summations converted into standard scores themselves, with the decimal points omitted for simplicity. Thus a score of 0 would represent the average for all forty-eight states, 100 would be one standard deviation above the mean and −100 would be one standard deviation below it (a standard score of −1·0).

As with the pattern of income variations, Figure 3.2 displays clear geographical regularity. Of special interest is the fact that a line separating above-average and below-average states runs quite neatly east to west, the only exception being the New England state of Maine which falls just below zero. The bottom ten states comprise a contiguous block corresponding with the so-called old South, i.e. the former cotton belt of geography textbooks. This may now be thought of as America's major region of economic and social deprivation. The top ten states are more scattered, but are clearly separated from the bottom ten by an east–west belt of states at intermediate levels of well-being.

The correspondence of this pattern with that of per capita income is close, but by no means perfect. For example, California has one of the highest per capita income figures but performs only moderately on the social well-being index. Nevada is an even more deviant case, with per capita income comparable with California but a negative score on social well-being. Two of the top states in Figure 3.2, Utah and Iowa, have only moderate levels of per capita income. Clearly, something other than income and conditions closely reflecting income is pulling some states up and others down in the composite indicator of social well-being. As the summary figures by region in

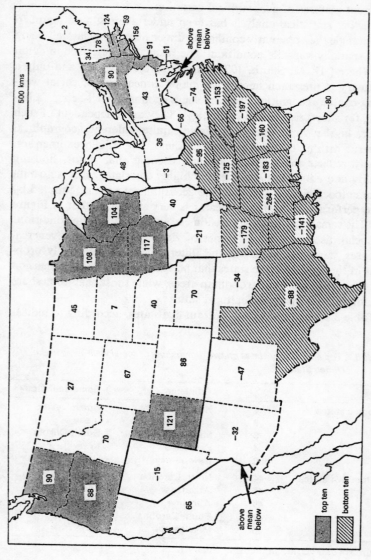

Figure 3.2. State scores on a composite indicator of social well-being. (Source of data: D. M. Smith, 1973, Table 7.2.)

111

Where the Grass is Greener

Table 3.1 suggested, different aspects of living standards are giving different pictures of geographical variation.

Further statistical analysis has been undertaken in an attempt to disentangle the apparently conflicting dimensions of social well-being as a spatially variable condition. The results are described in detail elsewhere (D. M. Smith, 1973, ch. 7 and 1977, ch. 10) and only a summary is presented here. Two major dimensions of social well-being can be recognized: 'general socio-economic well-being' (affluence, for short) and 'social pathology'. They are independent of each other, in the sense that they display quite different geographical patterns with no correlation between them. The affluence dimension largely reflects measures of income, occupational status, housing quality and education levels, and is highly correlated with per capita income (coefficient r of 0·86). The geographical pattern adopted by state performance on this indicator is very similar to that in Figure 3.1. The social pathology dimension closely reflects certain conditions of social disorder such as crimes of violence, incidence of venereal diseases, narcotics addiction and illiteracy. These are largely problems of the big cities; the states that perform worst on this dimension are those with major metropolitan areas, while those that do best are predominantly rural, agricultural states.

Table 3.2 lists the top and bottom five states, according to indica-

Table 3.2. Top and bottom states on two dimensions of social well-being in the United States

		Affluence	Social pathology
Top five states	1	New York	North Dakota
	2	Connecticut	Idaho
	3	Massachusetts	South Dakota
	4	California	Iowa
	5	New Jersey	Utah
Bottom five states	44	North Carolina	Illinois
	45	Arkansas	Louisiana
	46	Alabama	Maryland
	47	South Carolina	California
	48	Mississippi	New York

Source of data: D. M. Smith, 1973, Table 7.7.

tors of performance on these two dimensions of social well-being. The most remarkable difference is shown by New York State, which is top of the affluence table but bottom on social pathology. It has a high *average* level of affluence, but also the deep pits of poverty and social degradation in the slums of Harlem and other parts of the New York metropolis; in other words, there is very considerable variation in human life chances within the state. California achieves almost as dramatic a shift, with the slums of Watts in Los Angeles and the poorer parts of other cities bringing its social pathology score down. The poor performance on social pathology of the other three bottom states reflect conditions in Baltimore (Maryland), New Orleans (Louisiana) and Chicago and East St Louis (Illinois). Some relatively low-affluence states perform very well on social pathology because of the absence of high crime, drug abuse and other city problems. The poor states of the South do better on social pathology, but most of them still fall well below the average for all states, especially those with substantial cities; the poor urban social environments of the South are as bad as anywhere in the country.

Returning to the general pattern of social well-being on the composite indicator mapped in Figure 3.2, we may now ask how closely this agrees with the results of other similar studies. The most comprehensive attempt to develop general social indicators for American states is by Liu (1973), working at the Midwest Research Institute in Kansas City, Missouri. The major conditions guiding Liu's approach are based on criteria developed by former President Eisenhower's Commission on National Goals, and may be summarized as follows:

1. Individual status (opportunity for self-support, development of individual capabilities and widening choice).
2. Individual equality (race and sex differences, social-economic discrimination)
3. Living conditions (general economic conditions, facilities available, social and environmental conditions)
4. Agriculture (farm incomes, mechanization, value of product, etc.)
5. Technology (promotion and encouragement of technological progress, scientific manpower)

6. Economic status (income, employment, manufacturing activity, etc.)

7. Education (school enrolment, attainment and resources committed)

8. Health and welfare (medical services, levels of health and welfare programmes)

9. State and local government (citizen information and participation, professionalism and performance of administration).

Data on over a hundred conditions were compiled to measure these criteria, and a composite score was derived in exactly the same way as described above (the summation of standard scores). The Liu study was an updating of an earlier attempt by J. O. Wilson (1969) to derive a quality-of-life indicator from eighty-five measures of the same nine criteria from the Eisenhower report on national goals.

Table 3.3 lists the ranking of the forty-eight contiguous states according to the Liu and Wilson studies, alongside those from the study summarized above in Figure 3.2 (D. M. Smith, 1973). The three sets of results are very similar. Liu (1974) has calculated a coefficient of rank correlation between his scores and the other two: it is 0·84 with the Smith rankings and 0·78 with Wilson. Where there are major differences in the rankings of individual states (e.g. those by Smith on California and Nevada) this can largely be accounted for by the greater emphasis on the social-problem conditions that appear in the social pathology dimensions in the Smith study.

Whatever the differences between the three sets of ranks, there is close agreement on which are the best and worst states. This is shown in Figure 3.3. Eight states in the South fall into the bottom ten on all three rankings; three others do so on two. The top ten show less agreement, with only four states appearing in this category on all three rankings. The worst states are highly concentrated geographically. The best ten on the three sets of rankings show more of a scatter, though they appear regularly in the west, upper midwest and north-east.

Liu (1974) points out that the rank order of the lowest states is highly correlated with their ranks according to per capita income, but that this is not so with the highest states. In other words, per

Table 3.3. Alternative rankings of American states according to criteria of social well-being or the quality of life

State	Smith	Wilson	Liu
Alabama	46	46	47
Arizona	33	22	11
Arkansas	45	47	41
California	16	1	1
Colorado	11	6	2
Connecticut	1	3	3
Delaware	18	12	16
Florida	38	29	35
Georgia	44	42	38
Idaho	13·5	27	24
Illinois	22·5	11	28
Indiana	30	24	33
Iowa	4	10	20
Kansas	13·5	25	21
Kentucky	40	44	45
Louisiana	42	43	43
Maine	29	38	36
Maryland	28	21	27
Massachusetts	2	4	7
Michigan	19	15	23
Minnesota	5	2	13
Mississippi	48	48	46
Missouri	32	39	37
Montana	26	30	9
Nebraska	22·5	31	14
Nevada	31	19	17
New Hampshire	12	28	31
New Jersey	7	13	18
New Mexico	35	36	22
New York	8·5	7	12
North Carolina	43	38	44
North Dakota	20	18	26
Ohio	24	16·5	32
Oklahoma	34	32	30
Oregon	10	8	5
Pennsylvania	21	20	15
Rhode Island	17	14	10
South Carolina	47	47	48
South Dakota	27	35	29
Tennessee	41	40	39
Texas	39	34	34
Utah	3	16·5	8
Vermont	25	26	25
Virginia	37	33	40
Washington	8·5	5	4
West Virginia	36	41	42
Wisconsin	6	9	19
Wyoming	15	23	6

Sources: D. M. Smith, 1973; J. O. Wilson, 1969; Liu, 1973.

Note: ranks with 0·5 indicate tied scores.

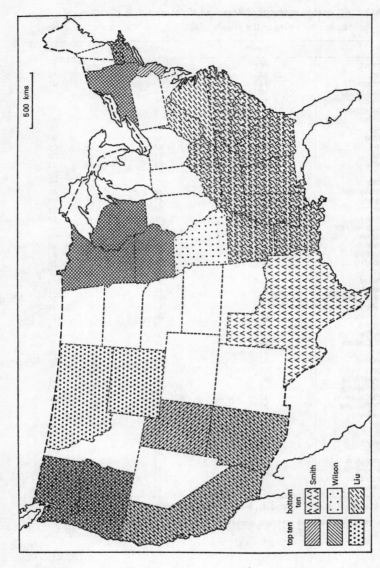

Figure 3.3. Top and bottom ten states according to three different studies of socia. well-being or quality of life in the U S A. Sources: Liu, 1973; D. M. Smith, 1973; Wilson, 1969.)

capita income is a much better predictor of state performance on social well-being or quality of life at the lower end of the scale than at the upper end. This echoes our finding in the previous chapter (Figure 2.5), where it was shown that level of living appears to be more closely associated with GNP per capita in the underdeveloped world than for the economically advanced nations. As Liu (1974, p. 141) concludes:

> States with very low levels of per capita income also tend to rank low in all measures of quality of life. Economic improvements seem to be necessary conditions for the Southern states to strengthen the quality of life in those states. After the low economic positions in the South have been changed relative to other states, however, economic enhancement becomes neither a sufficient nor a necessary condition for a better quality of life.

Indeed, the extremes of affluence may bring their own problems of social pathology, including high rates of property crime, alcoholism, drug addiction, divorce and stress-induced illness. These have their highest incidence in the richer states, especially California.

The broad pattern of geographical variation in living standards revealed in three different studies is also confirmed by analyses at the inter-city level. Various attempts to rate the major cities or metropolitan areas on some kind of quality-of-life scale show a similar concentration of the 'worst' cities in the South, with a fairly regular pattern of improvement northwards and westwards (D. M. Smith, 1973, chs. 3 and 8). The most recent research along these lines is summarized in the next chapter, as an introduction to inequality in the American city.

An obvious question raised by this kind of analysis is whether people in apparently deprived regions really feel worse-off than people elsewhere. In other words, do people's subjective views of their own level of well-being or life satisfaction correspond with the picture revealed by supposedly more objective measures, of the kind used in the studies referred to above? Some evidence emerging from a large-scale survey of 'psychological well-being' undertaken at the University of Michigan's Institute for Social Research suggests significant differences between subjective and objective measures.

For example, white people in the South are revealed as feeling more positive about their lives than people in the rest of the country (Andrews and Withey, 1976). However, Gould (1969) has compared a measure of perception of the residential desirability of American states with the general social indicator derived from the J. O. Wilson (1969) study referred to above, and revealed a high positive correlation ($r = 0.78$). Liu (1975a) has found his quality-of-life indexes to be quite accurate predictors of inter-state migration rates: people appear to be moving to particular states in close proportion to the quality of life there, as measured by Liu's 'objective' data. More research is needed before we can resolve the possible conflict between objective and subjective measures, in the light of people's apparent preferences as they 'vote with their feet' in deciding where to live.

Before leaving the American states, some general observations on the forces making for such a regular pattern of regional inequality are in order. We have already observed an urbanization effect, with the major industrial areas having relatively high general levels of affluence but accompanied by the social problems of the large city slums. As we shall see in the next chapter, the operation of the American economy and the inadequacy of certain social services produces pockets of severe poverty, and it is the conditions of these people that create the apparent paradox of high *average* levels of social pathology in affluent states. The states provide too coarse-grained a spatial framework to reveal the more local coincidence of low income, material deprivation and social disorganization typical of the inner-city slums.

The richer regions owe their high standards of living to a fortunate combination of raw materials, markets and labour skills, and to industrial organizations and service infrastructures highly conducive to efficiency in production. Such is the case in the manufacturing belt of the north-east and on the west coast – the latter having the added attraction of a climate that greatly enhances the quality of life for many workers and employers. The South stands out as the nation's great anomaly, with an environment capable of sustaining extensive production of such industrial materials as cotton and timber as well as a heavy industrial base. The region also has a climate that makes it in many respects as attractive as the Pacific coast for people seeking their place in the sun, in a literal sense as well as with respect to economic opportunity. The relative disadvantage of the South with respect to actual living standards must be explained in the light of both regional and national conditions. The South has a distinctive economic and social history, the early stages of which were dominated by the plantation agriculture of the cotton belt, based on cheap slave labour. Developed as a colonial dependency of Britain, the South remained in a position of economic subservience after independence – but now dominated by the 'Yankee' North. Conflict between North and South eventually led to the Civil War, the defeat of the South, and a subsequent failure to achieve the level of industrialization experienced in the major manufacturing belt, and later on the west coast. What industry did develop in the South (e.g. textiles and footware) was predominantly labour-intensive and paid low wages. The relatively low per capita income of the southern states can still be explained in part by the industrial structure and predominance of low-wage activities. The modern era of industrial migration to favoured locations in the South has not helped all parts of the region. The city slums and rural poverty remain largely untouched.

A major feature of the social geography of the South that contributes to its relative deprivation is the concentration of Negroes or blacks. The more blacks in a state's population, the lower its general level of living (the correlation between the state scores in Figure 3.2 and proportion of population white is 0·81). The era of slavery, followed by a century of discrimination in which blacks were denied the same level of services and economic opportunity as whites, has left this segment of the population in a disadvantaged position. The deliberately unequal and discriminatory society that developed in the South also has wider implications for the quality of life. For example, it appears to encourage a general disdain and lack of concern for society's weaker brethren, as indicated in the relatively low levels of 'welfare' benefits and the absence of other mechanisms for the redistribution of income and resources from rich to poor. Not only is there greater inequality *within* southern states than elsewhere in the USA, but there is also less redistribution via public expenditure (see Williamson, 1965; Booms and Halldorson, 1973; D. M.

119

Smith, 1977, ch. 10). The poor are thus not only poorer relatively as well as absolutely, but also more vulnerable in the South.

Some attempts are made by the Federal (central) Government to upgrade levels of living in poor states, via new social and economic programmes. But in a federal nation these can be resisted by the state and city governments. Thus the economic advance of the South, on which its social development appears to depend, is left largely to the market forces, political manoeuvring, and whims of businessmen that bring investment in the form of, for example, new plants and government defence contracts. But those who benefit from the new employment opportunities are not necessarily the hard-core poor who are most in need, as we shall see in the discussion of the American city in the next chapter.

Regional inequality is clearly an endemic feature of the American economy. Trends over the past century show a reduction of income differences (D. M. Smith, 1977, p. 290), but the better-off regions today are substantially the same as they were decades ago. This would not be so remarkable a finding, if it were not for the fact that the free-market economics upon which American capitalism is founded predicts otherwise. In theory, the productive factors of capital and labour will flow to areas offering relatively high returns and wages respectively. As poor regions with cheap labour attract capital and rich regions with high potential earnings attract workers from elsewhere, a state of balance or equilibrium is achieved, whereby regional levels of income (or more generally, social well-being) tend to be equalized – or so the theory of perfect competition has it.

The persistence of regional inequality or 'imbalance' in the USA clearly casts doubt on the equalizing capacity of a free-market economy. The perfect mobility of factors of production postulated in theory simply does not work in practice: distance can be a barrier to the dissemination of knowledge concerning investment and employment opportunities, as well as imposing costs on the movement of labour and commodities. The automatic adjustment of capital and labour to changing economic circumstances is inconsistent with the demands of the geographical space in which productive activity is actually conducted, a dimension of the real world largely ignored in conventional economic theory.

Some of the implications of this for the American economy can be explained briefly, with reference to the South. On the labour side, there has certainly been large-scale outward migration in recent years, particularly of blacks. But many people have remained unemployed in pockets of poverty in the old cotton belt or Appalachian mining valleys, perhaps preferring the devil they know to the uncertainties of a new environment. And large numbers of those who have left have been unable to find work in the cities of the north, despite the fact that migrants tend to be the more enterprising people with somewhat better education and skills. What the black from the South can offer in the labour market of New York or Washington, D.C., for example, may not be what industry there is seeking by way of new employees. So many of the South's poor have merely gone to swell the ranks of those 'on welfare' in cities elsewhere. The unemployment problem has not been solved: it has merely changed its location.

On the capital side, the belief that investors will seek out pockets of cheap labour in poor regions is not quite consistent with the actual practice of plant location in contemporary America. The South has certainly attracted new industry seeking to economize on labour costs. But the region has not gained much in modern industries such as electronics – high-wage, capital-intensive activities – that could make important contributions towards improving the South's income levels, despite the fact that parts of the South appear at first sight to be highly favourable for electronics manufacturing. However, traditional location theory, in which businessmen choose least-cost locations for their factories, does not work in the US electronics industry (D. M. Smith, 1971, pp. 374–87). This is partly because what matters most to a modern industrial corporation may be linkages with other related firms, suppliers of components and sources of scientific or technological development, which tend to point to a northern or west-coast location. It is also because leading US companies are going multi*national* rather than multi-regional, locating more investment and employment abroad (e.g. in Europe) than in Appalachia or the deep South (Holland, 1976b, p. 100). The United States is part of a world-wide economic system.

Regional inequalities in levels of living in the USA must be understood as a consequence of how a capitalist economy actually operates. Initial regional advantage tends to be compounded by further advantage; regional economic decline has a similar cumulative momentum. The 'natural' tendency is thus for the perpetuation of inequality. As Holland (1976b, pp. 102–10) points out, the trend towards regional convergence in per capita income in the USA depends on unique historical factors and the role of government, rather than on the workings of the free market.

We shall return to the question of the adequacy of conventional economic theory as a guide to understanding uneven development, in the final chapter of this book, armed with the experience of a number of other cases.

Great Britain: Value Judgements in Regional Variations

Attempts to use some kind of scale of living standard or quality of life in geographical description inevitably involve value judgements. But this is also true of *any* exercise in areal differentiation based on human criteria. Any areal classification or regional subdivision requires judgements as to the relevant or proper conditions to be included, or judgements as to what really matters to man. It is therefore a fallacy that 'pure description' in human geography can be value free.

The lists of criteria and the conditions chosen to measure them in the studies of the United States summarized above comprise value judgements as to the meaning of social well-being, quality of life or whatever the guiding concept happened to be. They may legitimately claim to represent the views of wide segments of expert or popular opinion, but they are still value judgements with no ultimate scientific or moral authority as the *correct* criteria.

While selectivity was applied in the compilation of the lists, no attempt was made to discriminate among the particular conditions included, with respect to their relative importance. As we have pointed out, the composite social indicators derived by the summation of standard scores implicitly assumed equal weighting of all the con-

122

ditions included. How could we accommodate the fact that some conditions may be more or less important than others, in the general 'equation' of living standards or human life quality? The case study that follows explains a method of deriving group value judgements to generate weightings in the calculation of composite social indicators.

The problem posed is how to identify broad regional variations in the quality of life in Britain, incorporating value judgements as to the relative importance of different conditions. The areal units are the eight so-called standard regions of England, together with Wales and Scotland. Northern Ireland is not included because of the lack of comparable data. As with the American states, the ten British regions are large areas with heterogeneous populations, so it must again be borne in mind that measures of average life experience will hide a great deal of intra-regional variation or inequality.

Twenty-five conditions were chosen initially, as possible measures of life quality (Table 3.4). They were selected to represent as closely as possible the concept guiding the study of social well-being in the USA discussed above. Reliance on the most easily available sources of regional statistics meant that there is no measure of some conditions that it would have been desirable to include, such as crime, delinquency, alcoholism, mental health, electoral participation, access to social services and leisure facilities. Data on most of these conditions are not available by standard regions; the term 'standard' is still largely a misnomer in this context, in so far as the compilation of official statistics in Britain is concerned.

Brief comments on the conditions listed in Table 3.4 should help to clarify the concept of life quality that is implied. Numbers 1 to 8 relate to levels of production, income and employment; inequality of earnings is captured by numbers 5 and 6. Conditions 9 to 15 reflect different aspects of home environment and consumption, mainly housing and its contents but also including time lost in commuting (9). Illegitimacy is the only measure of social disorganization, a general criterion under-represented in the list because of shortage of data. Three health conditions come next, followed by three on education and one measure (23) of sex inequality. Finally, two physical-environmental conditions are included, with obvious

123

Table 3.4. *Some possible measures of the quality of life in British regions*

Condition	Sign*
1. Gross domestic product per head (£) 1971	+
2. Average weekly household income (£) 1970–71	+
3. Households with weekly income £40 or more (%) 1970–71	+
4. Median weekly earnings of full-time male employees (£) 1972	+
5. Male earnings inequality (upper quartile ÷ lower quartile) 1972	−
6. Male: female earnings ratio (male median ÷ female median) 1972	−
7. Unemployment rate (%) 1972	−
8. Hours worked by manual male employees (average per week) 1972	−
9. Median journey time to work (minutes) 1972	−
10. Weekly family expenditure on food, clothing and shelter (% of total) 1970–71	−
11. Households with one or more car (%) 1971	+
12. Households with telephone (%) 1971	+
13. Households with fixed bath (%) 1966	+
14. Dwellings owner-occupied (%) 1972	+
15. Dwellings built since First World War (%) 1972	+
16. Illegitimate births (%) 1972	−
17. Infant mortality (deaths under 1 year per 1000 live births) 1972	−
18. Persons with long-standing illness (per 1000 popn) 1972	−
19. Incapacity through sickness (days per male at risk) 1970–71	−
20. Seventeen-year-olds in school (% of 13-year-olds 1968) 1972	+
21. Pupils per teacher in all schools 1972	−
22. Students in further education (% of student-age popn) 1971	+
23. Male: female student ratio (males ÷ females) 1971	−
24. Mean daily temperature (°C) 1969–72	+
25. Mean annual rainfall (mm) 1969–72	−

*+means high scores are 'good' and low 'bad'
—means high scores are 'bad' and low 'good'

reservations about the validity of data for areas as large as standard regions – reservations that must also apply to most economic and social conditions, as we have already recognized.

Each condition in the table has a sign: + or − . These indicate the normative or judgemental interpretations to be built into the final quality-of-life indicator (the data for the USA in the cases above were treated in exactly the same way, though the full lists of conditions are not presented). For example, the plus sign for condition 2 shows that we judge high household incomes as 'good'; the minus sign for condition 16 says that high illegitimacy is 'bad'. These judgements can be supported as representing a broad societal consensus as to what is desirable or undesirable, but they are still purely value judgements with which some people may disagree. It might be noted in passing that such a list should not include structural economic or social conditions like proportion employed in services or degree of urbanization. While sometimes taken to be indicators of 'development', the normative interpretation of such conditions is by no means as clear-cut as might be supposed.

Having compiled data on the twenty-five conditions of concern, these are then transformed into standard scores.* Following what should by now be familiar practice, the summations provide an initial composite quality-of-life score for each region, as shown in Table 3.5. The result will be of no surprise to people accustomed to thinking in terms of south–north differentials. The South-East region (including Greater London) is clear leader, followed by the other southern and midland regions, with scores in the northern regions, Wales and Scotland increasing negatively in that order.

The next step is to recalculate the composite index, incorporating a set of value judgements as to the relative importance of the conditions included. As an illustration, we will use the findings of some surveys conducted on first-year students of human geography at Queen Mary College, University of London. Each student was asked to indicate which five of the twenty-five measures as listed in Table 3.4 best represented the quality of life to her or him. The number of times each measure was chosen was then transformed to a scale of 0 to 1·0 by dividing by the total number of students: thus 1·0 would indicate chosen by everyone, 0·5 chosen by half the class and 0 would mean chosen by none.

Table 3.6 lists the results, as obtained from four different years of students. There is a strong degree of agreement among the years as to the relative importance of different conditions. Unemployment comes first each time. The second and third conditions as chosen in 1976 – expenditure on basics and weekly household incomes – show

---

*Note that conditions with a minus sign in Table 3.4 have their signs reversed in the standard scores, so that in Table 3.5 high positive values are 'good' for every condition and high negative values are 'bad'.

Table 3.5. Standard scores on quality-of-life conditions, with a composite regional indicator

No.	North	Yorks–Humber	East Mids	East Anglia	South–East	South–West	West Mids	North–West	Wales	Scotland
1.	-1·14	-0·21	0·03	-0·14	2·58	-0·50	0·87	-0·17	-0·78	-0·53
2.	-0·53	-0·84	-0·50	-0·17	2·42	-0·82	1·00	0·55	-0·85	-0·26
3.	-0·48	-0·75	-0·56	-0·25	2·24	-0·60	1·26	0·52	-1·21	-0·14
4.	-0·09	-0·71	-0·36	-1·47	1·85	-0·99	1·43	0·11	0·67	-0·43
5.	0·49	0·78	1·66	-0·09	-1·83	-0·67	0·78	-0·38	0·49	-1·25
6.	-0·35	-0·63	-0·07	1·20	1·90	0·63	-1·76	-0·21	-0·92	0·21
7.	-1·59	0·00	0·79	0·94	1·45	0·58	0·44	-0·50	-0·50	-1·65
8.	0·78	-1·35	0·07	-1·71	-1·00	0·25	1·67	0·25	0·78	0·25
9.	0·75	0·12	0·12	1·37	-2·37	1·06	-0·18	-0·18	-0·81	0·12
10.	1·15	0·38	0·38	1·81	0·05	-0·49	-0·27	-0·05	-1·92	-1·04
11.	-1·59	-0·69	0·12	1·63	0·82	0·88	0·86	-0·15	-0·52	-1·34
12.	-1·17	0·36	-0·80	0·66	2·17	-0·35	0·26	0·09	-1·52	0·30
13.	0·21	-0·26	0·21	-1·06	1·66	1·48	0·59	-0·30	-1·40	-1·13
14.	-0·99	-0·07	0·31	0·31	0·44	1·09	0·18	0·70	0·57	-2·55
15.	0·49	-0·02	0·75	-0·02	0·75	-0·28	1·01	-0·54	-2·63	-0·49
16.	-0·32	-1·18	-0·32	1·90	-0·44	0·91	0·54	-1·67	0·79	-0·19
17.	-0·97	-0·97	-0·27	1·11	1·81	0·41	-0·27	-0·97	1·11	-0·97
18.	-1·72	-0·84	0·41	-0·74	1·68	0·12	1·00	0·12	-0·94	-0·90
19.	-0·94	-0·37	0·53	-1·16	1·31	0·39	0·71	-0·38	-2·16	-0·27
20.	-0·68	-0·20	-0·68	-1·09	1·49	0·00	-0·68	-0·98	1·66	1·18
21.	-0·89	-0·28	-0·89	-0·53	2·16	1·14	-0·48	-1·30	0·12	-0·08
22.	0·08	1·15	0·28	-0·42	-0·83	-0·42	-0·14	0·81	1·56	-2·09
23.	-0·06	-0·06	0·99	1·83	-0·48	0·78	-0·59	0·15	-0·48	-2·06
24.	-1·86	0·01	-0·47	0·55	0·99	0·91	-0·34	-0·22	1·60	-1·20
25.	-0·26	0·54	1·04	1·17	0·92	-0·29	0·54	-0·26	-1·85	-1·55
Sum of all scores	-11·68	-6·09	2·77	9·01	21·74	5·22	8·43	-4·96	-9·14	-15·28
Rank of region	9	7	5	2	1	4	3	6	8	10

Sources of data: Abstract of Regional Statistics and Social Trends.

Table 3.6. Preference weightings for regional quality-of-life measures,
derived from a survey of first-year university students

Condition (see Table 3.4 for full description)	1974 (62)*	1975 (70)*	1976 (65)*	1977 (73)*
1. Gross domestic product	0·306	0·243	0·369	0·342
2. Weekly household income	0·500	0·714	0·754	0·562
3. High-income households	0·145	0·171	0·215	0·288
4. Weekly earnings	0·032	0·043	0·015	0·082
5. Male earnings inequality	0·113	0·071	0·015	0·192
6. Male : female earnings ratio	0·048	0·029	0·030	0·096
7. Unemployment	0·725	0·843	0·846	0·877
8. Hours worked	0·081	0·157	0·108	0·151
9. Journey to work	0·032	0·029	0·046	0·027
10. Expenditure on basics	0·597	0·700	0·769	0·644
11. Car ownership	0·113	0·043	0·030	0·068
12. Telephones	0	0	0	0·014
13. Fixed baths	0·117	0·114	0·169	0·164
14. Dwellings owner-occupied	0·387	0·357	0·308	0·192
15. Dwellings post First War	0·194	0·186	0·169	0·192
16. Illegitimacy	0·081	0·029	0·030	0·055
17. Infant mortality	0·516	0·157	0·277	0·452
18. Long-standing illness	0·065	0·071	0·115	0·068
19. Incapacity	0·081	0·114	0·085	0·110
20. School attendance	0·097	0·114	0·077	0·082
21. Pupils per teacher	0·435	0·586	0·323	0·233
22. Further education	0·258	0·214	0·231	0·082
23. Male : female student ratio	0·016	0·014	0·015	0
24. Temperature	0	0	0	0·027
25. Rainfall	0	0	0	0

* Number of students.

a steady popularity over the four years; with the importance assigned to unemployment, this may reflect perception of the economic nature of the 'crisis' in contemporary Britain. However, too much should not be made of these comparisons, as the survey technique is not refined enough to produce definitive conclusions. It must also be remembered that student opinion is not necessarily representative of the populace at large.

These group value judgements may be applied as weights in a composite indicator simply by multiplying each region's standard score (Table 3.5) on each condition by the appropriate figure from Table 3.6. The results are listed in Table 3.7, where a comparison can

127

Table 3.7. Regional performance on a composite quality-of-life indicator with data weighted by student-group values

Year		North	Yorks-Humber	East Mids	East Anglia	South-East	South-West	West Mids	North-West	Wales	Scotland
1974	sum	−2·61	−1·07	0·52	2·37	5·87	0·73	1·46	−1·14	−1·87	−4·47
	rank	9	7	5	2	1	4	3	6	8	10
1975	sum	−2·39	−1·03	0·40	2·09	6·08	0·61	1·73	−0·83	−2·63	−4·04
	rank	8	7	5	2	1	4	3	6	9	10
1976	sum	−3·22	−1·08	0·47	2·23	6·28	0·29	1·89	−0·57	−3·02	−4·20
	rank	9	7	4	2	1	5	3	6	8	10
1977	sum	−2·46	−1·37	0·73	2·23	6·18	0·30	2·04	−1·04	−2·72	−4·91
	rank	8	7	4	2	1	5	3	6	9	10

Source: Based on responses of students in first-year human geography class at Queen Mary College, University of London.

be made between the regional scores derived from the attitudes of each of the four years of students. The 1974 figures rank the regions just the same as in the unweighted scores in Table 3.5. But in 1975 Wales and the North change places: there is a substantial deterioration in the score for Wales (i.e. it is larger negatively), mainly because of a lower weighting for infant mortality on which Wales performs relatively well. In 1976 the East Midlands and South-West change places, while Wales and the North resume their 1974 positions, only to change again in 1977. The conditions included and their regional scores are the same in each year: only the value judgements as to their importance have changed, to alter relative regional performance.

Different sets of weights produce different regional scores, as Table 3.7 shows. But an important finding from this study is that the application of group value judgements makes little difference when compared with a composite indicator in which all conditions contribute equally. The same was found in a similar experiment with the United States data by states described earlier in this chapter: applying weights from a student survey changed the state rankings only slightly (D. M. Smith, 1973, p. 41). The reason for this is that most of the conditions included differentiate between the territories in a similar manner; for example, in the British case the South-East does well on most conditions and Scotland badly. Thus it does not matter much which specific conditions are included and emphasized in a composite index. Only if great weight is given to conditions out of line with the general trend, with atypical patterns of regional variation, will a weighted composite index differentiate territories in a manner that departs markedly from an indicator incorporating equal weightings.

The actual pattern revealed by the weighted index (from the 1977 students) is mapped in Figure 3.4. Quality of life is shown to fall steadily away from the metropolitan core of South-East England to the periphery of Wales, the North and Scotland. A line separating the above-average and below-average regions cuts the country neatly in half, rather as it did with the USA (Figure 3.2 above). Again, we find a regular pattern of geographical variation. Such a pattern is obviously very much a simplification of reality, based as it is on such a coarse areal subdivision. Data for smaller units would doubtless reveal local peaks and troughs in each region's quality-of-life

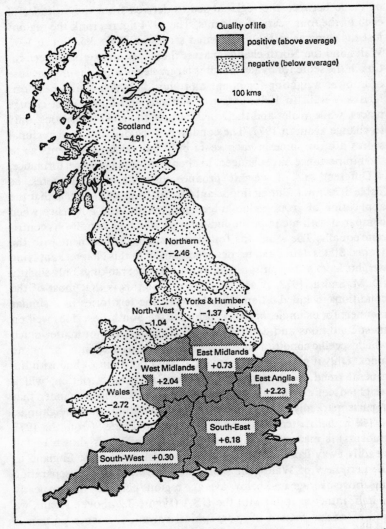

Figure 3.4. A weighted quality-of-life indicator for British regions. (Source of data: see text.)

topography. But the general picture of core to periphery deterioration in quality of life, living standards, or whatever we choose to call the concept, is supported by the evidence in more detailed studies of a similar nature (e.g. Coates and Rawstron, 1971; Knox, 1974).

Differences between what may broadly be termed 'north' and 'south' have been a matter for concern in Britain for most of the past three decades. Like regional variations in the USA, they trace their origins back into the country's economic history. The northern industrial-growth regions of the nineteenth century suffered severely in the depression of the 1930s, and the post-war years have seen the continuing decline of the activities on which much of the original prosperity of these regions was based. For example, the contraction and reorganization of the Lancashire textile industry has cost half a million jobs since the Second World War. Successive governments have committed steadily increasing resources to 'industrial-location' or 'regional' policy, to encourage the development of new employment opportunities in the peripheral regions. Some replacement industries have grown quite successfully, diversifying the previously narrow economic structure of the peripheral industrial districts centred on South Wales, Manchester, Tyneside and the Clyde. But unemployment remains high in the periphery relative to the Midlands and south. And there are still marked regional differences in living standards, as the analysis above reveals.

In a 'mixed' economy, such as prevails in Britain, there are limits to the extent to which governments may constrain the economic forces driven on by competitive market mechanisms. Thus if consumers at home and abroad are willing to buy electronic goods made in London but not textiles made in Lancashire, at prevailing price levels, the government may be both unwilling and unable to subsidize textile production or protect the domestic market from cheaper foreign goods. And to invest in new industry in the north on a scale sufficient to maintain a growth rate comparable with the south may be impracticable, by virtue of limitations on both public resources and the persuasive power of government with respect to private business decisions. In any event, massive industrial investment in what may be relatively high-cost locations can prejudice the efficiency

131

of the entire economy. Similarly, public resources used to upgrade such conditions as the quality of services and the environment in declining regions can be made available only at the expense of other more prosperous regions where investment in infrastructure is required to sustain industrial expansion.

At the root of the so-called regional problem in Britain is the contemporary tendency towards a spatial concentration or 'polarization' of economic activity. This may well be a natural state towards which a capitalist or market economy moves. The process of rapid urbanization focused on gigantic 'primate' cities in various parts of the world suggests that this polarization is by no means confined to the advanced capitalist nations. Indeed, it is most pronounced in underdeveloped countries (see the case of Peru below). An important element in this process is the growing concentration of ownership of the means of production, as expressed in the emergence of transnational corporations and conglomerates. Generally, these organizations have their main base in a capital city or centre of the world money market, such as London. Thus situated, such organizations exercise a much more impersonal and (literally) remote control over branch plants in other more peripheral locations. They may close a factory in a northern city simply because it does not fit into the new corporate structure or identity, however profitable it may be. It is significant that the so-called rationalization of the Lancashire textile industry which brought the final phase of mill closure was organized largely by London-based groups.

Some of the implications of the emerging centralization of business in Britain have been examined by Westaway (1974a and 1974b). As control or managerial functions become steadily more focused on London (and, to a lesser extent, the major provincial cities), the occupational structure becomes more unbalanced. Opportunities for career advances and access to positions of influence and power are limited away from London. This is paralleled by inequalities in, for example, material rewards, housing, education and health. Hence the persistence of inter-regional differences in levels of living, despite official policies aimed at more 'balanced' development.

British society is only gradually becoming aware of the deeper ramifications of the problem of regional inequality. Something of a growing sense of the need for more local control is reflected in the devolution movement, involving the decentralization of *public* administrative functions and limited self-government for Wales and Scotland. But this leaves untouched the concentration of *private* control in the corporation offices and finance houses of London and overseas business centres. It is in these places that the real power over life in the British regions is exercised. And increasingly, this is a matter beyond *British* control, never mind some embryonic regional or provincial government.

There is a clear connection between this view and something that we said earlier about recent American experience. Increasingly, control over the investment decisions that generate jobs and income in particular places is in the hands of multinational multi-plant firms, free to put their capital into an attractive location overseas rather than in a depressed Lancashire mill town or an Appalachian mining community. To these firms, the financial incentives offered by governments at home under regional-development policy may be irrelevant to the overall corporation policy of investment, pricing and so on. And such firms may be able to overcome disincentives designed to prevent development in prosperous or congested areas, by virtue of their size, power and political influence. As Holland (1976b, p. 43) argues, 'indirect incentives and disincentives no longer bite effectively on the leader firms in manufacturing and some modern services whose geographical mobility has been demonstrated by their world-wide location of plant and offices', yet it is 'precisely those firms whose over-all size, market position, professional management and multi-plant structure makes them most suitable as instruments of regional development'. Holland goes on to cite evidence of the minimal significance of British regional-development incentives to such major concerns as Unilever, Cadbury-Schweppes, GKN and Tube Investments. Similarly with policy directed towards improvements in regional infrastructure or the creation of external economies in planned growth points: the modern highly integrated corporation may be able to provide these conditions for itself wherever it operates.

The extent to which ownership of the British economy is in foreign hands is clearly an important matter. Since the Second World War we have become accustomed to American investment and take-overs,

133

but the emerging economic power of Japan and the Arab countries now raises the spectre of a broader loss of sovereignty over what we think of as British assets. As overseas control grows, then the term 'British economy' itself becomes a misnomer. The proportion of assets of UK manufacturing industry owned by foreign multi-nationals was about 16 per cent in 1970 and has been rising by just over half a percentage point each year (McDonald, 1977, p. 68). If this trend continues, a quarter of the manufacturing sector will be foreign-controlled by the mid 1980s. The United States accounts for about two thirds of the total overseas stake in UK industry.

The impact of foreign investment has been geographically selective, and this has an important bearing on differential regional development (Dicken and Lloyd, 1976; Dicken, 1977; McDermott, 1977). Initially, there was a high degree of concentration in the South-East, which accounted for half the total employment in foreign-owned manufacturing concerns in the early 1960s. More recently, the tendency has been for dispersal into the peripheral regions, especially Scotland and Northern Ireland. Dunning (1972, p. 12) has estimated that upwards of 150,000 jobs have thus been created, directly or indirectly, in the Development Areas, greatly strengthening their economies. But *control* is much more concentrated in London and the South-East than is productive capacity. The more important the control function, the less likely it is to be exercised in the peripheral regions. McDonald (1977, p. 78) summarizes recent findings as follows:

This kind of regional distribution coupled with the corporate policies of multinational enterprise sharpens regional disparities. These companies tend to use their professional services, located at head office or in specialist divisions, rather than local labour near the factory, to hire maintenance labour from within the company, and to centre purchasing decisions about capital equipment and raw materials at head office, making it unlikely that such purchases will take place at the local factory. These policies tend in turn to reduce local spending through a decline in the regional wage packet, leading to a decline in regional consumption. Further, providing specialist facilities on a national basis may increase the level of regional imports. Altogether, such corporate policies lead to a fall in the level of local income.

The important point to grasp is that, when a large corporation sets up a branch, in a Development Area or elsewhere, it does so in pursuit of its own commercial interests. These are not necessarily consistent with the aims of regional-development policy, especially with respect to employment practices. An example is provided by Ford in the 1960s at Halewood on Merseyside, where there was a highly selective recruitment policy directed towards attracting the cream of the local labour force; preference was given to 'stable' men with family commitments, while those in the greatest need of a new job – the young, former dockers and the unemployed – were discouraged. The state of the labour market on Merseyside enabled Ford to get its workers at lower rates than prevailed at the company's plants at Dagenham and in the Midlands. As Benyon (1973, p. 65) remarks, 'the reasons which influenced the Ford Motor Company's move to Halewood were the same as led it to establish a plant at Genk in the underdeveloped region of Belgium. Unemployment means low wages and a vulnerable labour force.' If conditions conducive to low-cost operation do not exist in Britain's depressed areas, the capital investment goes elsewhere in the corporation's international operating system.

Who gains from the transfer overseas of capital that might otherwise have built factories in Britain's declining regions? Some of the investment goes to already prosperous parts of the emerging industrial heartland of the EEC countries, to add to polarized growth on a European scale. (The whole of Britain except for the south-eastern corner with the London metropolis may eventually form part of the poor periphery of the prosperous continental core of western Europe, North Sea oil notwithstanding.) But capital is also attracted to the underdeveloped world, where cheap labour can provide an enormous saving on costs compared with those in Britain's 'problem' regions. Here, perhaps, lies the solution to the international development gap, referred to in the previous chapter, with the multinational corporation acting as a beneficial instrument of income redistribution. It is to the underdeveloped world that we must now turn, to trace some of the wider implications of what we have observed in advanced industrial nations. The critical issues are how the process of development takes place and the degree of central-government control required.

135

Where the Grass is Greener

Peru: Underdevelopment and Regional Inequality

The United States and Britain exhibit characteristics of the general condition of uneven development, as revealed in regional inequalities in level of living. But it is in the underdeveloped world that these problems reach their extreme. The case of Peru has been selected to show something of the inequality in human life chances that exists at the regional level in an underdeveloped country, and of the causal factors involved. Certain unique features will be evident, as in any national study, but we shall also be able to find further evidence of a general process expressed in the growing polarization of the space economy. Peru provides a particularly interesting case from a policy point of view, for since 1968 the country has been run by a self-styled 'revolutionary' military regime that is attempting to find a national development-strategy based on neither strictly capitalist nor socialist lines. Some commentators see the outcome of this experiment as having important implications well beyond Peru, perhaps offering a model for the underdeveloped world as a whole. Part of our objective here, and in the discussion of Peru's capital of Lima in the next chapter, is to attempt an evaluation of the effectiveness of present policies as an answer to the problem of uneven development.

Peru is a country of great physical diversity. It straddles three clearly defined ecological zones: the coastal lowlands, the *sierra* formed by the Andes mountains and the *selva* of the western end of the Amazon basin (see Figure 3.5). At the time of the 1972 census the national population was 13,568,000; today (1979) it may well have reached 16 million – an increase of about 10 million compared with the 6·2 million of 1940. Population growth has been rapid: almost 3 per cent annually in recent years, as befits a predominantly Catholic nation in which Latin pride in virility (*machismo*) is a major preoccupation. The largest city is Lima, which, with its port of Callao, has a population now probably in excess of 4 million (it was 3,318,000 in 1972). Over a quarter of the national population is now concentrated in this metropolitan core, compared with only about 10 per cent in 1940 – a dramatic example of polarized growth. Other lesser cities and towns are also expanding quite rapidly: in 1972, 43 per cent of the national population lived in places with 20,000 or more inhabitants

136

Figure 3.5. Major features of the physical and population geography of Peru. The administrative subdivisions named are departments.

137

compared with 15 per cent in 1940. This rapid urbanization has been a result of large-scale population migration, focused particularly on the Lima-Callao metropolis (see next chapter). The regional differences in population growth shown in Figure 3.5 underline the relative shift from the mountainous *sierra* country to the coast.

In its economic structure, Peru exhibits typical features of the dualism found in large areas of the underdeveloped world, and especially in ex-colonial countries. On the one hand there are modern industrial concerns concentrated in the cities, enclaves of highly capitalized mining activity, and plantations producing crops largely for industry or export. On the other hand there are the more traditional handicraft trades, a multitude of small-scale service activities and the mass of the peasants working very small plots of land (the *minifundio*, as opposed to the *latifundio* of the large landowners). The Indian descendants of the Incas form a distinctive element in the population of the *sierra*, and their relative lack of integration into the national society at large (as exemplified by the persistence of the Quechua language instead of Spanish) strengthens the modern/traditional dichotomy. The modern sector is highly focused on the Lima-Callao metropolis, which accounts for about two thirds of Peru's industrial production.

With this background, we may now proceed to examine the reality of regional differences in levels of living within Peru. The results of two different studies may be reviewed briefly. Both adopt the twenty-four departments as the spatial frame of reference. Although both the studies are now somewhat dated, the general pattern of regional variation has probably changed very little in recent years though, as we shall see, the degree of regional inequality appears to have been somewhat reduced.

The first study was undertaken by C. T. Smith (1968), using data from the 1961 census and the industrial census of 1963. Thirteen conditions were selected to assess regional income and living standards. These are: proportion of people in towns with populations over 5000; industrial establishments per 1000 population; value added by manufacturing (per capita); proportion of households with, respectively, electric light, fuels other than grass and wood for cooking, sewing machines, radios, refrigerators and piped water;

proportion of houses with concrete, timber or tile roofs; literacy; children over four years old in school; and proportion of farm units given fertilizer. The emphasis is very much on housing conditions, which reflects not only the usefulness of housing quality as a general indicator of living standards but also the amount of housing data in the Peruvian census. (In the next chapter we will see how data on housing can be used to identify variations in living standards within the Lima metropolis.)

The data on each of these conditions were expressed as department ranks, a transformation that loses some information but asks less of possibly inaccurate figures than would the use of the original data. Table 3.8 lists the sums of each department's ranks on the thirteen conditions along with a final rank-order. Top department on the sum of ranks is Callao, first on all thirteen conditions. (For the final ranking Callao and Lima are combined.) The first six departments belong to the coastal zone, while most of the lowest are predominantly *sierra* departments.

The second study is by Slater (1975), and identifies departmental variations in 'socio-economic development' in 1955. The conditions included in his index differ from those used by Smith. They are: telegrams per 10,000 population; motor vehicles per 10,000; percentage of motor vehicles in private circulation; secondary- to primary-school student ratio; percentage of primary-school students in the final two years; females in primary education as a proportion of the total; hospital beds per 10,000 people; provincial council expenditure per 10,000 population; and commercial bank savings and deposits per capita. The stress on housing by Smith is replaced by an emphasis on education as a contributor to development in Slater's analysis. Nevertheless, the two studies produce closely similar results (Table 3.8). The correlation between the two sets of rankings is 0·95 (Spearman's coefficient).

Figure 3.6 maps these two views of regional inequality. The Lima-Callao metropolitan region is well ahead of all other parts of the country, as is indicated by the gap separating first and second rank on Slater's scores. Then come four of the remaining coastal departments, separated by another marked gap on Slater's scores from the bulk of the *sierra* and *selva* departments. The departments with

139

Table 3.8. *Alternative measures of living standards or socio-economic development for departments in Peru*

Department	Smith c. 1962 sum of ranks	final rank	Slater 1955 scores	rank
Callao	13 ⎫		2·92	1
Lima	26 ⎭	1		
Ica	59	2	1·76	2
Tacna	61	3	1·06	5
Arequipa	76	4	1·11	4
Lambayeque	91	5	1·22	3
La Libertad	116	6	0·19	7
Moquegua	124	7	0·11	9
Tumbes	125	8	0·35	6
Junín	136	9	0·17	8
Piura	148	10	0·00	10
Pasco	156	11	−0·45	13
Loreto	166	12	−0·53	15
Ancash	177	13	−0·36	11
Cuzco	203	14	−0·46	14
Madre de Dios	208	15	−0·82	19
San Martín	211	16	−0·74	17
Huánuco	213	17	−0·65	16
Cajamarca	242	18	−0·83	20
Amazonas	246	19	−0·44	12
Puno	252	20	−0·84	21
Ayacucho	271	21	−1·03	22
Apurímac	275	22	−0·79	18
Huancavelica	277	23	−1·04	23

Sources: C. T. Smith, 1968, Table 1; Slater, 1975, Table 2.7.

Note: The signs of Slater's original scores have been reversed so that positive indicates a high level of development.

lowest levels of living or development tend to concentrate in the southern *sierra*. A difference between the two studies is that the *selva* tends to look better on Smith's results than on those of Slater. But the broad pattern of core-periphery contrasts is clear enough, complicated only by the coastal extensions of the more developed zone and the very low levels of living in some of the *sierra* valleys. A similar impression is gained from an analysis at the province level (Cole and Mather, 1972).

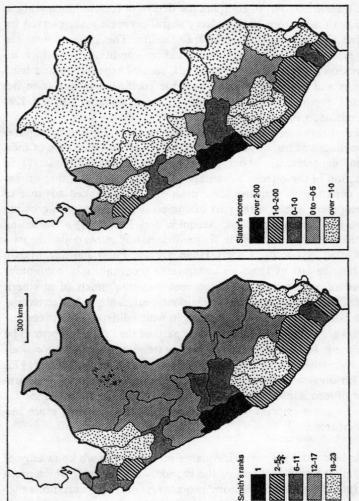

Figure 3.6. Two views of regional variations in living standards or development by departments in Peru. (Sources: C. T. Smith, 1968, Fig. 4 and Slater, 1975, Fig. 2.4.)

Slater's scores

- over 2·00
- 1·0–2·00
- 0–1·0
- 0 to –0·5
- over –1·0

Smith's ranks

- 1
- 2–5
- 6–11
- 12–17
- 18–23

300 kms

Where the Grass is Greener

Slater's study provides some evidence as to recent trends in regional inequality. Coefficients of variation were calculated for all nine measures, so as to compare the degree of regional inequality in 1955 with data from 1946. A 'very slight' decrease was observed for all but the provincial expenditure measure. The same comparison was made with 1965–6 data for the three conditions for which information is available – hospital beds, council expenditure and bank savings and deposits. In each case the coefficient of variation decreased: regional inequality is falling, though, as Slater (1975, p. 128) reminds us, it is still high.

The conclusion concerning reduced regional inequality requires some modification, in the light of the differential experience of individual departments. Slater points to the following trends: (1) a reduction in the relative advantage of Lima-Callao, as other urbanized departments improve their position; (2) a marked advance in development levels on the part of coastal departments with growing cities, i.e. Lambayeque, Ica, Arequipa and Tacna; (3) a worsening relatively if not absolutely in six predominantly *sierra* departments – Apurímac, Ayacucho, Cuzco, Huancavelica, Puno and San Martín (all but the last of these six comprise a geographically contiguous region of extreme underdevelopment covering much of southern Peru). Thus, the general level of regional inequality may be decreasing, but a polarized structure is emerging in which differences between the coastal growth zone and the poorest parts of the interior appear to be increasing. In fact, two rather opposing trends may simply be cancelling themselves out in the coefficients of variation, as Slater (1975, p. 133) suggests. This raises a practical question as to the measurement of inequality, of the type hinted at in Chapter 1: an index that may give one impression may obscure another perhaps more important trend.

Understanding regional inequality in Peru requires a knowledge of certain structural features of the economy and society, which are a product of a particular historic process replayed with variations elsewhere in Latin America. Before the arrival of the Spaniards in 1532, those parts of the Peruvian *sierra* that now exhibit the worst characteristics of underdevelopment were in fact centres of the advanced

Inca civilization, the organization of which appears to have been well attuned to local resources and ecological conditions. But the colonial era brought a quite different social and economic structure. The mass of the (Indian) population became subject to the domination of a small Spanish ruling élite, and the emphasis of the economy shifted from the satisfaction of local community needs to the support of a rich landowning class and the repatriation of wealth to Spain. The legendary gold of the Incas was the initial attraction to the colonizers, but soon an extensive plantation and ranching economy developed. Deposits of copper brought large-scale mining to the *sierra*, notably at La Oroya and Cerro de Pasco. The export orientation of the economy focused development on the coastal region, where good soils, ease of irrigation and access to markets encouraged the growth of an efficient system of extensive agriculture, as exemplified by the sugar plantations. The main function of the peasant communities of the Andes for the past four centuries has been to provide labour for the mines and agricultural estates. Those not thus employed live a subsistence existence forced on them by the general structure of the economy. The Andean communities have more recently acted as reserves of labour for the expanding economy of Lima-Callao and other coastal areas; pressure to leave the land for the city has transferred underemployment from the countryside to the metropolis.

The social consequences of such a process of economic 'development' go a long way towards explaining the degree of poverty in Peru today. As C. T. Smith (1968, p. 272) puts it:

> Export-oriented mining industries employ a relatively small proportion of the population and their effects on wages, standards of living and on the commercialization of farming appear to have been relatively small and local . . . Export-oriented pastoral farming has been associated with large estates, some of them certainly efficient and producing high-grade wool, but necessarily labour-extensive and sometimes sterilizing potential arable land in areas of peasant overcrowding.

People drawn to the mines, ranches and plantations as employees received (until recently) little protection from the extremes of exploitation, with minimal wages, harsh working conditions and often a squalid living environment. The concentration of land-ownership in very few hands had a particularly severe impact in the *sierra* where

143

'feudal forms of tenure and share cropping act as a brake on agricultural development; capital investment by many landlords is minimal and revenues are syphoned away by absentee landlords to Lima or to regional capitals' (C. T. Smith, 1968, p. 274). Thus, there developed a highly polarized society, with a small, rich, landowning and capitalist class and the mass of the people in poverty.

A typical feature of a colonial society is dependence on overseas sources of capital and economic control. Such has been the history of Peru. Independence in the political sense, achieved by Peru early in the nineteenth century, may do little if anything to alter economic dependence and its accompanying uneven pattern of development. Since independence Peru has been effectively ruled by what Fitzgerald (1976, p. 4) describes as 'an export-based oligarchy organized in large capitalist units and dependent upon close relations with foreign capital, while relying upon the military to suppress popular movements, and take power temporarily in times of crisis'. Peru thus continued to experience what is sometimes termed dependent capitalist underdevelopment – a state of unbalanced, uneven or unequal development that can be attributed largely to the country's place in the world capitalist system.

But the past decade has seen a rather dramatic change in Peruvian development, with the take-over in 1968 by the *Gobierno Revolucionario de la Fuerza Armada* or military revolutionary government. This regime has made a deliberate and concerted attempt to tackle some of the fundamental causes of uneven development. The extreme concentration of ownership of the modern sector of the economy has been broken by measures that include the expropriation of foreign-based mining companies, including American oil interests, and the conversion of the sugar estates into cooperatives. Thus the economic power of foreign capital and the domestic élite has been substantially reduced, and with it the degree of external dependency. The state has gained control of over one third of output and one fifth of the workforce in the modern productive sector. Great emphasis is now being placed on planned industrial development, in the context of geographical dispersal. This is aimed at stemming rural migration to the Lima metropolis, the disproportionate growth of which is the most obvious manifestation of the process of uneven development.

Despite brave attempts to gain domestic control of the economy, it is doubtful whether the policies of the present regime will be able to solve the basic problem of uneven development. While the expropriations may appear to be antagonistic towards capitalism, the regime is not anti-capitalist, nor is it truly revolutionary in the sense of being driven by socialist or egalitarian ideology. The fundamental difficulties still to be faced revolve around the questions of financing and planning the process of industrialization and the persistence of the traditional pattern of economic dualism.

Financing a programme of industrialization in order to reduce imports and generate employment requires a social surplus, or excess material production over the consumption requirements of the population. The present situation in Peru reveals a contradiction, or inconsistency in the functioning of the system, manifest in the new role of the state: 'although it is required to undertake the bulk of the investment programme it is not granted the bulk of mobilized surplus (i.e. savings)' (Fitzgerald, 1976, p. 55). In other words, much of the surplus remains in private hands, and may be spent on the type of luxury consumption favoured by the wealthy élite rather than on productive investment. Thus the state must borrow to finance industrialization. Borrowing from foreign sources helps the regime to avoid the issue of which groups in Peruvian society should have their income cut in order to provide for capital accumulation; part of the price is external dependency again, including the need to maintain conditions conducive to acceptable returns on overseas capital. The reforms appear to have done little to change the highly skewed distribution of income and wealth. This, together with failure to control output in the domestic manufacturing sector, means that what is produced continues to reflect the effective demand of the élite and the middle-class consumer rather than the need for capital goods to sustain further industrialization, which would be geared to the more modest needs of the mass of the people. In short, the necessary conditions for fully integrated economic planning in the modern sector have not been met.

Failure to address the problem of economic dualism is also an outcome of the limited commitment to comprehensive economic and spatial planning. The take-over of large agricultural estates in the

Where the Grass is Greener

modern, capitalist sector has certainly helped some workers, but land reforms have done little if anything to improve the lives of the majority of the peasants. The exploitive power of the landlords has been removed and some redistribution of land has been effected, but basic shortcomings of under-capitalization, low productivity and poorly developed marketing organization remain. A recent review points out that whole sectors of rural activity remain untouched by agrarian reform, and concludes (C. T. Smith, 1977, pp. 109–10):

> It is becoming all too obvious that agrarian reform in Peru can never achieve the great things that many hoped for from it. In many parts of Peru, and especially in the sierra, land reform of the large estates could never make available enough land to relieve significantly the land hunger of the small-scale peasantry ... Agrarian reform, however important it may be from a social and political point of view, is only a beginning in an economic sense.

At the root of the problem of rural poverty in the *sierra* is the economic relationship with the coastal region and especially metropolitan Lima. Gilbert (1974, pp. 231–2) points out that the *sierra* has a trading surplus in its dealings with the more prosperous coastal areas, but because most of this trade is controlled by a small number of enterprises based in Lima the profits go to banks in the metropolis or overseas, instead of being invested in the *sierra*. Another problem is that any attempt to benefit peasant agriculture by raising prices adds to the food bills of the urban population, which makes such a move difficult politically. But as long as economic dualism remains, so will the problems of rural poverty, migration to the cities and the severe pressure on the urban fabric of Lima (see next chapter), as well as the difficulties of narrow domestic markets, highly unequal income distribution and inadequacy of food supplies.

Regional disparities in level of living in Peru are thus the outcome of a complex set of interrelated conditions. C. T. Smith (1977, pp. 107–8) provides the following summary:

> problems presented by the extreme regional disparities of income in Peru ... may be viewed as a geographical consequence of the highly concentrated distribution of income in the country as a whole as between social groups, but in geographical terms, they may also be seen in differ-

146

ent ways which necessarily overlap: as a rural/urban dichotomy, and in a larger sense, as a dichotomy between Lima and the rest of the country (centre/periphery, metropolis/satellite); or as a contrast between the relative prosperity of the coastal region and parts of the central sierra on the one hand and the poverty of much of the sierra, especially in the south of the region. It has been argued that the poverty of predominantly rural areas is not merely a product of low productivity and lack of economic opportunities for development, but is also the result of a positive drain on rural income which may also be associated with a condition of rural dependency. The component elements of this 'drain' are: the result of unfavourable terms of trade as between agricultural and industrial products; high costs of marketing and distribution associated with low farm-gate prices and high profits to urban-based middlemen and carriers; the depletion of the human capital of the periphery as a result of the migration of its most skilled, educated and enterprising manpower to the centre; payments from the countryside to the towns of interest on loans and mortgages; the impact of government taxation, in so far as this results in a net flow of revenue from the country to the town or from the periphery to the centre in excess of the value of investment or provision of goods and services by central government in the periphery; and finally, the export of unrequited revenues derived from the transfer of rents and profits by absentee owners from the countryside in which they are earned to the urban centres where they are spent, saved or invested.

It is difficult to see how changes in individual elements of such a system can significantly improve its performance.

Peru may thus be sailing some very troubled water in its search for a passage between the Scylla and Charybdis of capitalism and socialism. In a careful review of development since 1968, Fitzgerald (1976, p. 2) sees the present situation as a considerable step forward, but suggests that 'in the long run further reforms will probably be necessary if Peru is not to slip back into dependent capitalist underdevelopment.' The critical question is whether the interconnected problems of dualism and the financing of economic development can be solved within the constraints on policy imposed by the present regime's ideological stance and the nature of its popular support. As Fitzgerald (1976, p. 96) points out: 'The dominance of the modern sector is bound up with the interests of the middle class, and a determined

147

attack on duality might well require a politically infeasible degree of resource reallocation.' The Peruvian experiment may well demonstrate to other parts of the Third World that there is no effective middle way between dependent capitalism with its accompanying uneven development and a fully-fledged planned economy geared with rational deliberation to the needs of the entire population. In so far as the latter course inevitably threatens the existing middle class or bourgeoisie as well as the élite, it can probably be accomplished only under some form of revolutionary socialist regime.

Socialist Countries: Where Some are More Equal than Others

The persistence of regional inequalities in the underdeveloped world and in advanced capitalist nations raises the question of the socialist alternative. If uneven development appears to be a natural outcome of the way in which a capitalist market economy works, even with substantial state intervention, then perhaps some form of socialism or communism is necessary if spatial inequality in human life chances is to be eradicated. The basic features of a socialist system are collective ownership of the means of production and central planning of the economy. This provides an element of control over the spatial arrangement of production that is not present in a free-enterprise system, so that industry and other activities can be established in peripheral or backward regions if this is considered to be in the general public interest, subject only to the capacity to meet the relatively high production costs in these locations. By controlling the surplus product, a centrally planned economy can overcome the kind of problem found in Peru and other Third World countries, where the surplus could be both larger and more effectively invested in growth-inducing activity. The process of state expropriation of the surplus under socialism may sometimes appear brutal (the treatment of the peasants in Stalin's USSR being an extreme case), but it is doubtful whether any industrial revolution has been achieved painlessly.

The principles of Marxism–Leninism that guide development in socialist societies place great stress on the reduction of inequalities among regions and especially between town and country. This is an integral part of regional policy in, for example, the USSR: 'the drawing together of town and country, the evening out of regional living standards, rationalization in the use of natural resources, and so on – are among the principles adopted for the location of socialist productive forces over the long term.' (Alayev and Khorev, 1976, p. 176.) However, references to the long term, and elsewhere to the need to improve the whole settlement system if 'living conditions and living standards of the urban and rural populations *are to be* evened out' (ibid. p. 172; my italics) stress that the removal of inequalities is still a future aspiration, sixty years after the October revolution. It is also recognized that 'privileged conditions' may be created in some districts to attract population, in the interests of national economic goals (ibid., p. 171). Eastern Siberia is a case in point: in Yakutia, where major development is taking place in association with the new Baikal–Amur Magistral stretch of the trans-Siberian railway, wages paid are up to three times the Soviet average.

There are, therefore, reasons to anticipate some geographical inequalities in living standards under socialism. The critical questions are: how do they arise (to what extent are they fortuitous or inevitable as opposed to a result of planned privilege), and just how great are the variations. Problems of data availability make the second question difficult to answer. In a perceptive examination of Russian society, the American journalist Hedrick Smith (1976) includes facts on relative costs and standards of living in various parts of the country, and on the availability of social services in rural areas compared to the cities, among the information gaps that might be explained by the reluctance of the authorities to reveal situations that could be a cause for popular discontent. However, the limited data that are available allow us to make some inferences about general patterns of regional inequality under socialism in the USSR, and to speculate as to their origin.

We shall begin by looking at variations in housing among the fifteen constituent republics of the Soviet Union. These areas vary enormously in size (Figure 3.7), like the states and major regions of the USA, and there will be considerable internal variation. But they are of special interest as territorial subdivisions because the

149

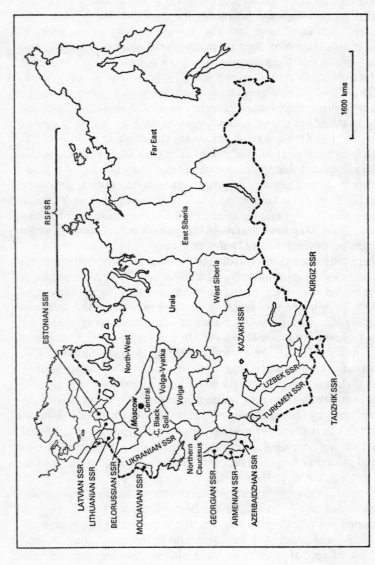

ESTONIAN SSR

LATVIAN SSR

LITHUANIAN SSR

BELORUSSIAN SSR

MOLDAVIAN SSR

UKRANIAN SSR

GEORGIAN SSR

ARMENIAN SSR

AZERBAIDZHAN SSR

North-West

Moscow

Central

Volga-Vyatka

C. Black
Soil

Volga

Northern
Caucasus

RSFSR

Urals

West Siberia

East Siberia

Far East

KAZAKH SSR

UZBEK SSR

TURKMEN SSR

KIRGIZ SSR

TADZHIK SSR

1600 kms

Figure 3.7. The republics of the USSR, with economic regions of the RSFSR.

overcoming of the relative dackwardness of some of the peripheral republics has long been an avowed aim of Soviet planning. Official statistics are probably accurate as far as they go: students of the USSR generally feel that unpalatable information is not released rather than being distorted in published data.

The provision of adequate housing has been a problem in the USSR ever since the revolution. The need to replace sub-standard dwellings and to build for the rapidly growing urban workforce has often conflicted with other claims on resources, so that limitation of living space is a widely recognized shortcoming of Soviet society. Table 3.9 lists the per capita living space (i.e. area of living rooms other than kitchen and bathroom) for urban housing in the fifteen republics for 1970 and 1974, compared with the situation in 1958. The most recent figure shows a variation from almost 10 square

Table 3.9. Variations in per capita living space in urban housing among republics of the USSR, 1958, 1970 and 1974

Republic	1958 sq. m per capita	% of USSR average	1970 sq. m per capita	% of USSR average	1974 sq. m per capita	% of USSR average
Armenia	5·3	91	6·7	87	7·0	90
Azerbaidzhan	5·7	98	6·5	85	6·5	83
Belorussia	5·8	100	7·5	97	7·8	100
Estonia	7·6	131	9·6	125	9·9	127
Georgia	6·7	116	8·5	110	8·9	114
Kazakhstan	5·3	91	6·8	88	6·9	88
Kirgizia	4·9	84	6·2	81	6·5	83
Latvia	8·4	145	9·7	126	9·8	126
Lithuania	6·6	114	7·9	103	8·5	109
Moldavia	5·5	95	7·1	92	7·6	97
RSFSR	5·7	98	7·7	100	7·9	101
Tadzhikistan	5·4	93	6·2	81	6·5	83
Turkmenia	5·7	98	6·9	90	6·8	87
Ukraine	6·4	110	8·3	108	8·6	110
Uzbekistan	5·2	90	5·7	74	5·8	74
USSR	5·8		7·7		7·8	

Source: Morton, 1974, p. 171; Bater, 1977, p. 194.
Note: figures are not available for rural housing.

151

metres per capita in Estonia and Latvia to less than 6 in Uzbekistan. For most republics there is a 'sanitary housing norm' of 9 square metres of living space, which in practice means almost 13 in aggregate space terms. All but Estonia and Lithuania are below this figure. The general pattern is of the greatest disadvantage in Soviet Central Asia followed by two of the trans-Caucasian republics. The RSFSR, covering most of the country, is on the average, while the European republics are above average except for Moldavia.

A comparison with the 1958 figures shows a general improvement in per capita housing space. At first sight, inequality has been reduced, for all but one of the republics above the average in 1958 have reduced their degree of advantage measured by percentage of the national average. But at the other end of the scale most republics have lower figures relative to the national average in 1970 and 1974 than in 1958. Uzbekistan especially shows only a small absolute improvement and a marked decline compared to the USSR average. However, too much should not be made of these relationships to the national average, for this figure is very much a reflection of the situation in the RSFSR with about 55 per cent of the total population. Morton (1974, p. 172) summarizes the situation as follows:

> Although the Soviet housing situation has substantially improved, the fact remains that the great majority of the Soviet people living in urban areas have so far not yet achieved the minimum housing standard of nine sq. m of living space set by the regime in the 1920s and that wide-ranging differences in urban housing comfort exist among various republics – even when measured by only the single variable of space. Housing conditions in rural areas are worse where by observation the level of housing and amenities (gas, water supply, sewage disposal) is much lower.

As in other aspects of life (see below) it is the urban–rural differences that are probably most severe in the USSR. In the countryside the typical dwelling is a single-storey structure, often of timber and lacking basic amenities. Villages without sanitation can be found just outside Moscow, within twenty miles of the Kremlin (reports former BBC Moscow correspondent Philip Short, 27 December 1976).

Other research into inter-republic variations suggests some consistency of geographical pattern. Schroeder (1973) has looked at differences in income and levels of living, using a variety of information on earnings and consumption that point to substantial and, in some respects, increasing gaps between republics. In 1970, Latvia and Estonia has per capita national incomes two fifths above the average for the USSR, while Tadzhikistan and Turkmenistan had less than half the national figure. Mickiewicz (1973, pp. 35–40) in a pilot study using twenty-three economic and social measures, reveals fairly stable orderings of the republics. European USSR except for Moldavia generally comes out ahead of Asian USSR except for Kazakhstan. In the Baltic republics Estonia nearly always leads, with Lithuania generally well below the other two. In the Caucasus, Azerbaidzhan consistently shows up below Georgia and Armenia.

Some indication of differences in over-all levels of output and consumption is provided by a recent Soviet study conducted for twenty-four regions (fourteen republics and ten subdivisions of the RSFSR – see Figure 3.7). Per capita GNP in the top region (Estonia) was found to be 2·38 times that in the bottom region (Tadzhikistan). For per capita national income produced, Latvia, at the top, had a figure 2·29 times that of Tadzhikistan. On the consumption side, per capita consumption of the national income was 2·07 times as high in Estonia as in Tadzhikistan; for per capita non-productive consumption fund the figure was 2·12. The fact that consumption levels are less differentiated across the country than production 'seems to be evidence of some mechanisms of levelling out of the regional differences in the consumption sphere' (Granberg and Suslov, 1976, p. 86). Each of the four indicators ranked the regions similarly, suggesting the following levels of economic development: (1) the Baltic area and North-West region of the RSFSR, at the highest level; (2) the Ukraine and East Siberia; (3) a medium level, including the Volga region, North Caucasus and Kazakhstan; (4) Belorussia, the Volga-Vyatka and Central Black Soil regions; (5) West Siberia; (6) the trans-Caucasian republics and Moldavia; (7) the republics of Central Asia. The authors consider variations in the proportion of population in employment to be a major factor in regional variations in production and consumption. Also important is the regional economic structure:

as in a capitalist country, areas with disproportionate shares of high-wage or high-productivity industries will generate relatively high levels of output per capita, and this will be reflected in consumption unless strong inter-regional redistributive measures are in force.

Cole and Harrison (1978)* list figures for retail sales per capita in 1975 for these same twenty-four regions. The range is from 492 roubles in Azerbaidzhan and 495 in Tadzhikistan to over 1000 in Estonia and Latvia (both with 1174), the Far East region of the RSFSR (1144), the North-West region (1097) and the Central region (1065). The ratio of highest to lowest region (2·39) is similar to that for the income and consumption figures reported by Granberg and Suslov. Further analysis of regional variations in the USSR can be found in Cole and German (1970).

How far inter-republic inequality has actually been reduced in recent years is the subject of a statistical study by Zwick (1976). He compared figures for 1940 with 1970, on two indicators of health services (doctors and hospital beds per capita – see also Chapter 5 below) and a number of measures of educational enrolment. In all cases, substantial decreases in the level of inter-republic inequality were found. But the process of change has affected different parts of the USSR in different ways. The trans-Caucasian republics have shown considerable improvements from an original situation of substantial disadvantage, but their levels of attainment still tend to be below average. Estonia and Latvia have lost some of their original advantage, while the RSFSR and other European republics have not suffered a relative deterioration and are in some respects even better off than before. Zwick's general conclusion is that removal of the original extreme inequality has not occurred at the expense of the most advanced (and politically privileged) republic of the RSFSR. Progress towards equality has been made, but the elimination of inter-republic differences is far from complete. Zwick stresses the role of urbanization in accounting for variations in the rate of 'modernization': because the lowest levels of living tend to be in the countryside, the socio-economic status of a republic is closely associated with the proportion of people in urban areas.

*I am grateful to Professor John Cole for the opportunity to see a pre-publication draft of this paper.

Evidence of substantial progress towards equality at a finer geo-graphical scale is provided by Cole and Harrison (1978). They have calculated Gini coefficients for the RSFSR, using figures for seventy-one subdivisions (*oblasts, krays* and Autonomous Soviet Socialist Republics). The coefficient for retail sales per capita has gone down from 36·6 in 1940 to 12·1 in 1975. For students in higher education the reduction is from 54·3 to 32·5

It is harder to make rural–urban comparisons in the USSR than to judge differences among republics. What evidence is available points to a persistence of the relative disadvantage of rural residence. Mickiewicz (1973, p. 5) suggests that 'in many ways life in the country is becoming qualitatively inferior to that in the cities at a rate that is faster than that at which the population is leaving for the cities.' In education, for example, it is pointed out that rural schools tend to have less-qualified staff and may suffer shortages of textbooks and technical equipment; rural teachers tend to be deprived relative to their urban counterparts with respect to living standards; rural children have limited occupational aspiration levels (Yanowitch, 1977, pp. 62, 69). Matthews (1976, pp. 130–33) states that: 'Many well-documented distinctions still exist between the quality of education in rural and urban schools', and that, 'Education levels are still sig-nificantly lower in the villages.' A similar situation exists in medical care, as we shall see in Chapter 5. Hedrick Smith (1976, p. 205) sug-gests that the gap in living standards between city and country is much narrower in the USA than in the USSR. He summarizes his observations as follows (H. Smith, 1976, pp. 207–8):

By any measure of living standards – income, schools, social life, wel-fare, health care, consumer goods, leisure outlets, transportation – rural people are worse off than city residents. Millions live at or below what would be the poverty level in any other industrialized nation ... From bits and pieces in the Soviet press, I sensed in rural Russia that same demoralizing, self-reinforcing combination of conditions found in American pockets of rural poverty – social stigma, poor schools, physical isolation, bad working conditions, low wages, poor morale, limited leisure, and chronic alcoholism. These are conditions that make rural poverty in Russia such a hard-core problem, passed from generation to generation, because the most able and energetic young people depart for the cities, leaving the less able and the elderly to man the farms.

If this is fair comment, then we have many of the features of the poor periphery of the advanced and underdeveloped capitalist world, without capitalism as the causal factor.

Some indication of the disadvantage of rural residents with respect to social services is provided by the American authority Bernice Madison (1975). She refers to the system of social insurance and security for collective farm workers as more recent and considerably less generous in benefits than for other employees. Child welfare services are concentrated in the larger urban centres. Vocational rehabilitation services are provided only to a limited degree in rural communities. Pensions and public assistance provision for farm workers are much more precarious than for others because the amount and duration of aid are determined by what a particular farm is able and willing to offer. Institutional care facilities are very unevenly distributed: a lower percentage of destitute, aged and disabled people from farms can enter them compared with city residents.

Understanding uneven development in the USSR requires recognition of the specific historical and geographical circumstances involved. The Soviet Union began with enormous internal variations in resource endowment, culture and level of economic achievement. For example, in 1926, less than 4 per cent of the population of Tadzhikistan were literate and in three other Asian republics the figure was well under 20 per cent. Distance exacerbated by severe winter climate makes for the isolation of some areas and the sheer physical difficulty of obtaining goods and personnel where they are needed. Mickiewicz (1973, p. 38) quotes the following summary of the problem by Vsevolod Holubnychy:

> The comparative regional endowment with natural and other 'fixed' resources, geographic location and distances from and to markets, the historically given levels of economic development and the given structure of industries, as well as the sociocultural and political conservatism on the part of the local population and leadership may all combine to hinder, if not completely prevent, the equalization and convergence of the levels of development in the short run. Time is indeed needed to develop natural resources, to expand and specialize local industries and the regional export–import relations, and to break through conservative traditions.

The emphasis on the barrier of conservatism is reminiscent of the 'modernization' argument in Western society, which views certain cultural traditions as impeding (capitalist) economic progress, as explained in the previous chapter. Regional variations in income and consumption largely reflect the degree of urbanization and industrial development, and the consequent territorial differentiation of occupational structure, just as in the West. In fact, we are beginning to sense that there may be quite a resemblance between both the reality of regional inequality and the reasons for it under capitalism and socialism, a theme to which we will return.

As a second example of geographical variations under socialism, we may look at the results of a study of Poland (Luszniewicz, 1974).* Polish scholars have attempted to derive a general level-of-living index, following the method originally developed by Drewnowski at the UN Research Institute for Social Development. The subdivisions used are the five metropolitan areas (Warszawa, Wroclaw, Poznan, Lodz and Krakow) and the seventeen *voivodships* into which the rest of the country is split up. Data were compiled for seven general conditions: food intake, occupancy of dwellings, health, education, leisure, security and surplus of current incomes. The individual variables used to measure these conditions are listed in Table 3.10. Although the concept of level of living has been modified to fit conditions and data availability in Poland, it compares closely with those proposed in other contexts earlier in this book. The general impression from this list is that what concerns people in Poland is very much the same as in other advanced industrial nations.

The results are shown in Table 3.11. For each of the seven major conditions a composite index has been derived, and these are combined into the general level-of-living index in the first column. Areas are listed in order of their score on the general index. The national capital of Warszawa is first, a clear ten points ahead of any other area. The four other provincial capitals come next, emphasizing the relative advantage of cities over the countryside. A gap of eight on the general index separates the metropolitan areas from the rest. Mapping the general index (Figure 3.8a) reveals a fairly regular

*I am grateful to Roman Chmielewski for this material.

157

Table 3.10. Conditions taken to measure level of living in Poland

1. *Food intake index*
   a. Satisfaction of calorific needs
   b. Protein intake per capita daily
   c. Percentage of non-starchy calories

2. *Occupancy of dwelling index*
   a. Quality of dwellings: percentage of dwellings with a bathroom
   b. Density of occupation: persons per room
   c. Independent use of dwellings

3. *Health index*
   a. Access to medical care: persons per hospital bed
   b. Morbidity by tuberculosis
   c. Infant death rate per 1000 live births

4. *Education index*
   a. Percentage of population aged 7–24, attending schools and colleges
   b. Performance index for schools: percentage of pupils and students completing courses
   c. Pupils per teacher

5. *Leisure index*
   a. Leisure time: hours per year
   b. Theatre and entertainment audience, per 1000 population
   c. Number of persons possessing TV set, per 1000 population

6. *Security index*
   a. Sudden mortality per 1,000,000 population
   b. Persons covered by health insurances
   c. Persons covered by retirement insurance
   d. Work-accident rate (excluding deaths)

7. *Surplus of current incomes index*
   a. Surplus of current incomes over minimum living wage
   b. Surplus of non-current incomes: number of private cars per 1000 population; number of refrigerators per 1000 households

Source: Luszniewicz, 1974.

pattern of regional variation, with relatively high levels of living in the south-western (largely industrial) areas and in the north-west, contrasting with lower levels in north-eastern central and (lowest of all) south-eastern Poland. The pattern of metropolitan peaks protruding from an undulating plain is reminiscent of that observed in the USA (Smith, 1973) and in similar studies of other capitalist countries.

Table 3.11. Index of level of living and its contributory elements in Poland, 1971

Area	General Index	Food	Occup-ancy	Health	Educ-ation	Leisure	Sec-urity	Sur-plus
Warszawa	94	91	75	75	92	67	88	35
Poznan	84	79	62	78	88	60	89	27
Krakow	84	74	67	78	86	58	84	29
Wroclaw	83	77	62	80	86	59	87	26
Lodz	83	82	65	69	89	62	87	26
Katowickie	76	73	63	75	81	48	83	24
Gdanskie	74	75	59	69	85	49	87	19
Szczecinskie	74	64	57	67	86	51	87	18
Opolskie	72	75	62	77	83	43	86	16
Wroclawskie	72	77	58	76	86	45	85	13
Zielonogorskie	70	73	60	66	87	45	82	13
Koszalinskie	70	76	57	67	85	45	86	13
Bydgoskie	69	78	53	63	85	44	85	15
Olsztynskie	68	78	55	71	85	40	86	12
Lodzkie	67	77	52	68	89	42	80	11
Bialostockie	66	81	54	66	89	39	76	11
Poznanskie	66	70	54	67	85	39	85	13
Warszawskie	65	80	51	65	87	39	78	11
Rzeszowskie	64	76	54	61	87	37	75	11
Krakowskie	63	77	54	62	85	36	75	11
Lubelskie	62	76	50	63	90	35	74	10
Kieleckie	61	74	51	67	88	37	75	10
Poland	70	76	57	68	86	44	82	17

Source: Luszniewicz, 1974, Tables 2 and 4.

Table 3.11, derived directly from the original Polish sources, suggests that the seven conditions have contributed unequally to the general index. For example, the scores on surplus of current incomes are much lower than on the other conditions. We have recalculated the seven individual indexes as standard scores and summed them, to form a new index after the fashion of those used earlier in this chapter, in which contributory elements are weighted equally. There are a few changes in ranking when compared with the original general index, but the over-all national pattern is broadly the same (Figure 3.8b).

What kind of magnitudes of inequality do these patterns imply?

Where the Grass is Greener

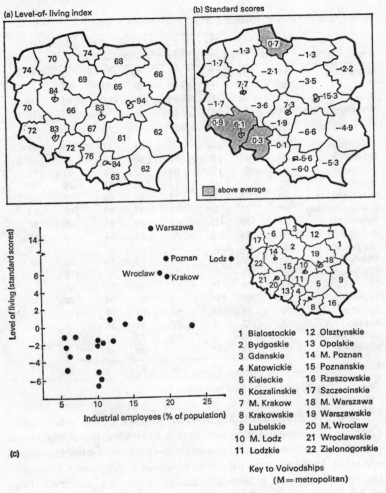

(a) Level-of-living index

(b) Standard scores

above average

(c)

Level of living (standard scores)

Warszawa

Poznan   Lodz

Wroclaw Krakow

Industrial employees (% of population)

Key to Voivodships
(M = metropolitan)

1 Bialostockie	12 Olsztynskie
2 Bydgoskie	13 Opolskie
3 Gdanskie	14 M. Poznan
4 Katowickie	15 Poznanskie
5 Kieleckie	16 Rzeszowskie
6 Koszalinskie	17 Szczecinskie
7 M. Krakow	18 M. Warszawa
8 Krakowskie	19 Warszawskie
9 Lubelskie	20 M. Wroclaw
10 M. Lodz	21 Wroclawskie
11 Lodzkie	22 Zielonogorskie

Figure 3.8. Variations in level of living in Poland, 1971. (Source of data: Luszniewicz, 1974; industrial employment from Murray, 1974, Tables 2 and 3.)

160

As we have already stressed, problems of data comparability and differences in level of areal aggregation make precise comparisons with other (e.g. non-socialist) countries impossible. But some of the extreme values give an impression of the extent of the variations identified. For example, satisfaction of calorific needs ranges from 100 per cent in the highest area to 60 per cent in the lowest, infant mortality from 13 to 60, and hours of leisure per year from 6816 to 2912. Life for the average city dweller may not be vastly different from that in Western Europe, except for possession of fewer mass-consumption goods, such as automobiles and refrigerators, and the smaller size of dwelling in Poland. In the countryside, however, the more remote areas may well resemble those of the USSR, suggesting greater town–country or core–periphery inequality than in the advanced capitalist world, though less than in underdeveloped countries. The collective provision, characteristic of the centrally planned economies of Eastern Europe, may enhance inequalities between rural and urban areas because of uneven spending on social services. Mieczkowski (1975, p. 41) provides some idea of the difference, citing the work of Michal Winiewski, a Polish expert on social consumption: 'in 1950, an inhabitant of rural areas received on the average only 10·9 per cent the social consumption of an urban dweller; that underprivileged relationship improved to a still very inferior 20 per cent by 1965.' Critics of this kind of discrimination point to the dangers of exacerbating 'class' differences between town and country people, that are inconsistent with the ideals of socialism. Differences in public expenditure of this order would be hard to find in 'class-ridden' Western Europe, even if the range of services provided is generally less comprehensive than in the communist countries.

Differences in level of living in Poland, at the *voivodship* level, can be accounted for in part by the progress of industrialization. The graph in Figure 3.8 shows a clear positive association between standard scores on level of living and proportion of the population employed in industry. Recent government policy has been directed towards the dispersal of industry from the major metropolitan centres and the Upper Silesia industrial region in the south, and the encouragement of development elsewhere. Thus the most rapid industrial growth in the 1950–70 period was in the *voivodships* of Bydgoskie,

Rzeszowskie and Lubelskie (Murray, 1974, p. 137), which are well down the level-of-living table. How far the diffusion of industry and urban development has reduced inter-regional inequality in Poland is a matter for conjecture.

A more detailed and up-to-date picture of variations in levels of development in Poland is provided in a study by Gruchman and Krasinski (1978) for the United Nations. It is based on the forty-nine *voivodships* set up in 1975 as a new administrative framework for analysis and planning. Data were compiled for a variety of indicators of regional 'socio-economic development' (see Table 3.12) and a composite indicator was derived for each *voivodship* by summing its rank on the individual measures. The geographical pattern is very similar to that illustrated in Figure 3.8. The highest levels of socio-economic development are registered by Warszawa, followed by the country's second city – Lodz. Then come Poznan, Gdansk and Wroclaw, where the main urban centres dominate the entire *voivodship*. They are closely followed by Katowice, which includes the major part of the Silesian industrial region. At the bottom end of the scale are predominantly the agricultural regions to the north-east of Warszawa and in the south-eastern corner of Poland.

The low indexes of dispersal in Table 3.12 show that there is little variation in many aspects of living and working conditions. This is particularly true of housing conditions (as measured by living space) and individual consumption – a fact that clearly reflects the outcome of central planning. However, there are significant qualitative differences in housing, such as the provision of apartments with bathrooms and hot water. And the pattern of relative equality among regions in the consumption of principal products hides differences among income groups within each region. Of the four major appliances of the modern industrial state, radios and TV sets are markedly more equally available than cars and telephones. The maximum and minimum *voivodship* figures help to highlight the extremes: the number of cars per 1000 inhabitants varies from 64 in Warszawa to 11 in the *voivodships* of Przemysl and Zamose and telephones from 126 per 1000 in the capital to 19 in Zamose, while TV ownership per 1000 ranges from 255 in Lodz to 165 in Ostroleka.

As the Polish authors of this study recognize, variations in living

Table 3.12. Indicators of regional socio-economic development in Poland, 1975

Indicators	National average	max	min	Index of dispersion*
1. Value of retail trade (1000 *zl* per capita)	23·7	32·7	17·1	1·9
2. Saving deposits (1000 *zl* per capita)	8·5	17·2	4·7	3·7
3. Electricity consumption (kwh per urban inhabitant)	300·9	379	208	1·8
4. Electricity consumption (kwh per rural household)	873·2	1184	549	1·9
5. Cars per 1000 popn	30·0	64	11	5·8
6. Housing: number of persons per room	1·2	1·0	1·4	1·4
7. TV ownership per 1000 popn	189·0	255	110	2·3
8. Radio ownership per 1000 popn	238·0	307	176	1·9
9. Telephones per 1000 popn	42·9	126	19	6·6
10. Fixed capital stock: gross value (1000 *zl* per capita)	141·5	207	82	2·5
11. Capital investment (1000 *zl* in 1975 per capita)	15·6	33·5	8·3	4·5
12. Communal water consumption per capita (cubic m)	52·2	72	13	3·9
13. Employees with higher education (% of total)	6·3	13·1	3·0	4·2
14. Expenditure on services (1000 *zl* per capita)	4·5	9·7	2·8	3·5
15. Balance of inter-regional migration per 1000 popn	—	12·8	—12·5	2·0
16. Hospital beds per 10,000 popn	66·3	132	31	3·5
17. Meat production per 100 ha of arable land (100 kg)	160·0	259	99	2·6
18. Yields of main grains per ha (100 kg)	24·8	33·6	17·8	1·9
19. Least productive land (% of total arable land)	12·6	38·7	2·3	15·9
20. Arable land per tractor	36·0	74	21	4·0
21. Railway lines (km per 100 sq. km)	8·5	23·1	2·7	8·5
22. Hard surface public roads (km per 100 sq. km)	45·6	87·6	30·2	2·7
23. Public relief and assistance in kind (*zl* per capita)	39·3	56·1	27·6	2·0

Source: Gruchman and Krasinski, 1978.
* Range divided by lower extreme value
zl = zlotys

conditions among regions are 'quite substantial'. And the differentials depicted by the quantitative indicators might well be aggravated by more qualitative measures of such things as housing conditions, promptness of medical attention and satisfaction with services. It is

163

these less tangible aspects of life that take on special importance, as economic growth under socialist planning assures the relatively equal access to the kind of material consumption associated with advanced stages of industrial development. 'With the projected much higher consumption levels of material goods and the intended reduction in the differences among regions, indicators measuring consumption and ownership of consumers' goods will lose much of their significance. Instead, stronger emphasis will have to be put on indicators more closely associated with the quality of life' (Gruchman and Krasinski, 1978, p. 161). This is just the same issue as has emerged recently in the advanced capitalist world.

As a final illustration of regional inequality in Eastern Europe, we may look briefly at some recent figures for Hungary compiled by Rudolf Andorka (1976) of the Central Statistical Office in Budapest.* The historical process of development has created a distinctive pattern of regional inequality in Hungary, which present national policy seeks to reduce. Since the modern phase of economic development, living standards in the capital, Budapest, have been markedly higher than elsewhere, while in the rest of the country the west and industrial parts of the north have tended to fare better than the southern and eastern regions. Table 3.13 lists figures for selected conditions in Budapest and Hungary's nineteen counties. Monthly income shows a range from 1867 *Ft* per month in Budapest to 1364 in Borsod-Abauj-Zemplén in 1972, a ratio of 1·36 : 1 between highest and lowest. (By way of comparison, the ratio between per capita income of the highest and lowest states in the USA, excluding Alaska, was 1·92 : 1 in 1975). The eastern part of Hungary tends to have the lowest per capita income. Car ownership follows a similar pattern, but with rather more distinct variations (the ratio of Budapest to the lowest county is 2·69 : 1). The greatest differentiation is in housing quality, as indicated by proportion of dwellings with inside water supply. The low incidence of this (by Western European standards) basic amenity, especially in the counties of the Great Plains, underlines the relatively primitive living-environment in large parts of Hungary, where

*I am grateful to Seppo Siirilä for bringing this source to my attention.

Table 3.13. Selected social indicators for Budapest and the counties of Hungary

County	Income per capita (Ft*/month) 1972	Private cars per 10,000 popn 1975	Dwellings with inside water (%) 1970	TV per 1000 popn 1974
Budapest	1867	669	84·5	263
Transdanubia				
Baranya	1576	549	38·8	220
Fejér	1617	415	30·3	224
Györ-Sopron	1638	419	36·2	226
Komárom	1565	466	52·6	239
Somogy	1547	455	25·1	209
Tolna	1556	451	18·1	214
Vas	1462	397	25·4	213
Veszprém	1543	439	38·3	216
Zala	1480	450	22·8	191
Great Plains				
Bács-Kiskun	1597	460	15·3	175
Békés	1573	316	11·3	215
Csongrád	1615	428	25·6	208
Hajdu-Bihar	1432	271	18·7	192
Pest	1560	388	19·6	206
Szabolcs-Szatmár	1456	249	7·7	178
Szolnok	1470	292	15·1	216
North				
Borsod-Abauj-Zemplén	1364	298	25·8	206
Heves	1452	401	21·4	223
Nógrád	1479	353	19·0	219
Hungary	1586	440	35·6	218

Source: Andorka, 1976.

Note: correlations between per capita income and the other conditions are as follows: private cars $r = 0·776$; dwellings with water $r = 0·713$; TV $r = 0·583$.

*Ft = forints

running water is not necessarily laid on in newly built homes. And even these figures are a substantial improvement on the recent past: the national average of dwellings with inside water supply in 1960 was only 22·5 per cent compared with the 35·6 per cent in 1970. Finally, television subscribers show a fairly even pattern of distribution with relatively little differentiation outside Budapest: the 'great cultural equalizer', as Andorka (1976, p. 14) puts it, much as in the capitalist West.

The predominant impression from the Hungarian data is the sharp distinction between Budapest and the rest of the country. Dienes (1973, p. 31) suggests that this produces what is probably a wider regional spread in per capita consumption than in Western capitalist countries. The capital has a distinctive employment structure, with only 2·7 per cent in agriculture compared with the national average of about 25 per cent, and 43 per cent in non-manual occupations. This predisposes the city to relatively high per capita income and material living standards. Otherwise, variations in county employment structure do little to explain the patterns of inequality revealed in Table 3.13. Outside Budapest there is a general regional trend overlain by long-standing town–country differences, which are still far from being eliminated. We shall see something more of Hungary in Chapter 5 when we consider variations in health care.

The persistence of regional inequalities in certain socialist countries might in part be an outcome of the particular development strategy adopted. In the USSR, for example, the initial industrialization was accomplished very much at the expense of the countryside, from which the surplus for investment was extracted with a degree of ruthlessness that matched the worst excesses of capitalist exploitation. Subsequently, the needs of the rapidly growing urban proletariat have generally been assigned higher priority than those of the peasants. But what of socialist countries where rural development has been given greater stress? China is the obvious case in point. Here the pre-eminence of agriculture in the economic structure of a country with some 800 million people to feed has given rural development a special practical and ideological importance. Industry has played a part in this, with China favouring dispersed small-scale development rather than the massive and highly concentrated plants more evident in the USSR. Another difference between China and the USSR has been the greater practical stress on what is sometimes described as

166

'developing the socialist consciousness of the masses', which includes emphasis on non-material rewards, a factor that should make for reduced inequality of living standards in so far as these arise from wage differentials. Frolic (1976, p. 151) summarizes the differences between China and the USSR as follows:

> Today the Soviet countryside lags behind the urban sector and remains a depressed area from which each new generation can hardly wait to escape. China, on the other hand, has formulated an urban policy which favours countryside over town. During the Cultural Revolution, purifying and revolutionizing values of rural life were re-emphasized ... high-school graduates are being asked to leave their homes and families to settle permanently in the countryside. Other policies designed to help uplift the countryside include increasing investment in village housing and in other amenities; upgrading local cultural and educational facilities, and giving first priority to rural youths in the new admissions policies of urban universities; inflating the value of rural produce to raise incomes; generating a measure of economic self-sufficiency through a network of small-scale factories utilizing local resources.

There have been reversals in some of these policies since Frolic wrote, following the demise of the 'gang of four' after Mao's death. But the real significance of recent events in China is hard to judge as yet, at least as far as development strategy is concerned.

The reduction of town and country differences is a fundamental aim of Chinese communism. Initially, the gap between the real income of the urban wage-earner and the average peasant widened; in the 1960s there appears to have been a reduction, but the urban worker in the 1970s is still probably better-off than those in the countryside and, in addition, is not subject to the vagaries of the weather that affect peasant incomes (Byers and Nolan, 1976, p. 66). These same authors also claim that developments in health services, especially preventive medicine, have brought about a narrowing of the gap in health levels between town and countryside and a significant fall in the rural death rate (in marked contrast to India where the more curatively oriented health services remain very unevenly distributed in favour of the cities, as is typically the case in underdeveloped countries). There has been great stress on rural community

167

self-help, with a medical role for ordinary working peasants as 'barefoot doctors' with only basic training (see Chapter 5). In education also there has been a reduction in the urban–rural gap, with the agricultural cooperative organization the focus for self-help programmes, as in health care. Ability to attract (or push) more teachers, and educated people generally, into the countryside is suggestive of different ethics from those prevailing in the USSR and underdeveloped countries. A key to China's success (if this is an appropriate evaluation) is the emphasis on objectives realistically scaled to resources available, e.g. basic preventive medicine and an emphasis on functional literacy, neither of which require the highly qualified personnel for whom country life may be anathema. But above all is the positive recognition that, in a poor and populous land, solving the problems of the rural areas is fundamental to the over-all functioning of the economy and society. There is much for the underdeveloped world to learn from China's strategy.

Nevertheless, it is generally recognized that marked spatial inequalities do exist in China. An American authority, Vogel (1976, p. 60), writes: 'The gap in standard of living between the east coast centres and the backward areas of inner China is almost as great as that between the more developed and the less developed countries'. In addition to salary differentials, 'the whole range of educational and medical facilities in the remote mountainous and frontier areas is considerably below that of the more advanced urban areas.' (Vogel, 1976, p. 72.) Despite attempts to disperse industry in the interests of more balanced regional development, the imperative of national economic growth has led to a concentration of investment in the east, especially Shanghai, Tientsin and Manchuria, and it is here that living standards are highest. The continuation of urban–rural disparities has been responsible for population migration to the cities, as in other countries.

More local differences also exist. Vogel (1976, p. 72) quotes Mao's recognition of this as follows: 'There are poor and rich brigades [subdivisions of communes], poor and rich villages . . . It is mainly differences in resources, conditions, administration, and history which result in . . . disparities.' There is even the suggestion that these differences may become entrenched and increased as a conse-

168

quence of the emerging spatial structure of the economy. Some insight into this is provided by an article in the *Guardian* by Martin Woollacott (1976). He suggests that self-reliance in agriculture is 'a recipe for grave inequality in the countryside'. The communes and lower-level production teams operate as commercial farms, selling their products for income that can be paid out in wages or set aside for investment and social services such as schools and clinics. The result is that 'a commune or production team on good land near a city market can earn, according to Western studies, up to nine times as much as a more distant one on poor mountain soil'. In the rich commune there will be individual houses or apartments, plenty of machinery, good schools and clinics, and also cash incomes. In the more distant communes people work harder but receive less by way of money and services. The capacity of the richer production teams to implement further mechanization from their surplus is likely to widen the gap still further. The parallel with uneven development under capitalism is striking. Woollacott points out that these inequalities at the local level, together with selective industrial development, generate serious disparities between provinces and regions. If the kind of figures available on income and access to education and medical services in Britain could be compiled for China, our regional disparities would 'pale by comparison', he claims. What China may be creating is thus a system of personal equality within unequal communities and regions.

The reasons for this appear to relate to the incentives required to sustain the national goal of economic growth. For all the weight given to non-material motivation in Maoist rhetoric, it seems that people in different places are being rewarded in accordance with the bourgeois ethic of 'to each according to level of output'. Societies that experiment with exhortation, coercion and material incentives seem almost inevitably to find the latter most effective as a means of stimulating production. The parallel in the USSR is the system of wage incentives designed to attract people to work in areas of harsh environment. Uneven development and a spatial differentiation of rewards is thus justified in the interests of over-all national goals, whether they be to maximize economic growth or to achieve the strategic objectives implied by some of the projects in Siberia. The question raised is how long it will take such societies to pass through this transitional phase into full communism, where bourgeois ethics of differentiation are replaced by redistribution according to need. As this will require a very specific strategy of transfer of resources from rich to poor, it may take much longer than Marx or Mao envisaged. It may well be that, once created, local and regional inequalities will be self-perpetuating, as the political power of the richer, more productive places enables them to maintain their differential claim on resources.

Both the USSR and China have vast territories and distinctive histories, which make it difficult to generalize from their experiences of socialism. Brief comments on another nation – Cuba – may be more directly relevant to the question of socialism as a development strategy for Third World nations. Before the revolution of 1959 Cuba was typical of underdeveloped countries, with a sharply dualistic economy, heavy penetration of foreign capital and a primate city (Havana) that dominated many aspects of national life. Whereas the present regime in Peru (see above) has attempted to find a middle way between capitalism and socialism to solve these kinds of problems, Cuba has adopted a more truly revolutionary strategy.

The colonial pattern of economic development in pre-revolutionary Cuba made sharp town–country differences in levels of living inevitable. Agriculture, especially sugar production, was geared to external demands rather than to local needs. Much of the land was controlled by a small élite, whose wealth stood in sharp contrast to the poverty of the agricultural workers, who were subject to the irregular labour requirements of the plantations. Most of the surplus generated in the countryside went to the urban areas, especially to Havana, and within these to a small capitalist or landowning class. Susman (1974) provides the following facts: annual per capita income of rural agricultural workers in 1957 about $(US)91 compared with the national average of $374; 9·1 per cent of rural homes with electricity in the early 1950s compared with 87 per cent of urban dwellings; one physician for every 2550 people in rural Oriente province compared with one to 420 in Havana. Within Havana itself over half the families had poverty incomes in 1951 (less than

$70 a month) while 5·4 per cent received over $500 a month. The education system also worked to the disadvantage of rural areas, with high-quality private facilities for the children of the élite, mainly in Havana, while for the poor, opportunities were restricted to the inadequate public school system.

The revolution of 1959 headed by Fidel Castro brought fundamental changes to Cuba's economy and society. Far-reaching land reforms were undertaken, and foreign-owned businesses were nationalized along with much domestic private property. A system of central planning was initiated to restructure the economy in accordance with what was viewed as the nation's needs. An important spatial aspect of Cuba's planning strategy has been to slow down the growth of Havana and reduce the high degree of centralization of the pre-revolutionary economy. New towns have been set up in the countryside and there has been very positive 'encouragement' of population dispersal. The transportation system has been much improved, with highway projects designed to achieve the spatial integration of the island's economy. Social services have been greatly expanded outside Havana, as part of the strategy of eliminating the inequalities inherited from the uneven development of the past.

What progress has actually been made? In a careful review of the situation in Cuba a dozen years after the revolution, Gordon (1976, p. 193) cites evidence of 'significant development' of rural hospitals, with a shift of emphasis towards preventive medicine and health needs in rural areas. In education, the major objective has been the elimination of illiteracy, which has required the development of facilities in the many rural areas not reached by basic education in the pre-revolutionary era. The training of teachers is designed to overcome the traditional problem of staffing rural schools. In the sphere of communications, emphasis has been placed on improving the telephone service in rural areas; as in health care, the idea is to provide basic services in all parts of the island rather than a superior service in urban areas and little or nothing in the countryside. Along with an evident reduction in inequality has come a uniformity of life typical of other socialist societies. 'Drabness perhaps best explains the Cuban environment, there exists a sameness caused both by the unavailability of a variety of consumer products and by the natural

uniformity bred among the have nots from a proletarian revolution.'
(Gordon, 1976, p. 227.) An equally-shared drabness may, of course,
be preferable to the original situation of luxury for the few and
squalor for most of the people.

Evaluations of the success or otherwise of the Cuban revolution as
a solution to the problems of uneven development in the Third World
tend to vary with the ideology of the observer. Certainly a more
equal society is being created, and the pre-revolutionary corruption
and exploitation of labour has been eliminated. However, Gordon
(1976) considers that the Cuban government could have removed
dependence on the USA and achieved its objectives in such fields as
health and education without the massive expropriations and the
'chaos' that this brought to the economy. Part of the price of Cuba's
wholehearted revolution is, of course, dependency on the USSR,
without which the island's economy would have collapsed. The
alternative path for nations like Cuba appears to be one of more
selective take-over of basic industries and perhaps a more gradual
extension of public ownership, without such a dramatic impact on
the well-to-do section of society (which, in Cuba's case, drove out
many skilled and professional people). Again, the Peruvian experiment comes to mind. So we return to the basic unresolved question
of whether something short of revolutionary socialism is capable of
creating a just society out of Third World conditions and, even if this
is the path chosen, whether the outcome will indeed be a society
characterized by regional equality of levels of living. We will return
to this issue at the end of the book, armed with the experience of
considering aspects of territorial inequality within the urban system.

4 Urban Inequality: Cities and Neighbourhoods

We live in a rapidly urbanizing world. As was suggested in the previous chapter, the spatial organization of human life is becoming increasingly focused on major metropolitan areas, both in the industrially advanced nations and in the underdeveloped world. And in socialist countries, plans to promote development in the countryside frequently run counter to the attracting power of the city. The urbanization process varies with level of economic development: in the richer nations such as the USA and the UK, there may be some intra-regional dispersal from the central parts of such cities as New York and London as the metropolis spreads out, whereas in most Third World countries (such as Peru) growth is still very much concentrated on a single dominant or primate city. But, whatever the particular manifestation, more and more people are living in cities. The quality of life of urban residents – new and old – is very much dependent on the capacity of city government to control the physical process of urbanization and to provide the various services required. And the activities of those who manage cities are themselves constrained by the broader structure of society – by how much 'intervention' is sanctioned and by the volume of resources made available for the improvement of city life, especially for those people most in need.

Clearly, it is a mistake to see the running of a city in isolation. What happens in one city cannot be divorced from life in other cities, or in the countryside whence streams of urban migration originate. Some years ago Brian Berry (1964) titled a paper on urban spatial structure, 'Cities as Systems within Systems of Cities', to stress the interrelated nature of urban-settlement patterns. In looking at inequality at the urban scale in this chapter, we will set the case studies in the broadest possible geographical context, stressing the place of cities not only in their national urban system but also in the spatial structure of society at large. The background on the cases of the USA, Great Britain and Peru, from the previous chapter, helps to provide such a context for an examination of inequality within specific cities. We will conclude with some observations on inequality in the socialist city.

The American City: Patterns, Problems and Policies

In many respects, the United States epitomizes the modern urbanized society. The sprawling American metropolis, with its expansive suburbs, shopping plazas, freeways and skyscrapers is the prototype of the emerging urban forms of Western Europe and major Third World cities. Yet beneath the surface – often literally within the shadows of the latest concrete-and-glass office block or highway interchange – substantial poverty and social deprivation still survive in the world's most affluent nation. Inequality in most, if not all, aspects of human well-being is a repetitive feature of the spatial structure of the American city, calling into question not only the managerial ability of city government but also the very nature of American society as an arrangement for the satisfaction of human needs. Nations seeking to emulate the United States, or drawn with apparent inexorability along a similar path of urban development, may see only the surface glitter; the 'other America' of the ghetto slums is easily overlooked or disregarded.

We shall begin our examination of the American city at the level of the national urban system. As Berry (1970) has shown, economic life in the United States is very much focused on major metropolitan centres, each with its own distinct sphere of influence. Lower-order cities exercise a similar if less extensive influence, perhaps coincident with the daily commuting zone. The cities are the dominant centres of business control and technological innovation. They also tend to have higher average standards of living than in the inter-metropolitan periphery, as identified by such conditions as levels of income and school years completed.

The geography of urban living standards is not a simple pattern of uniform peaks above the inter-metropolitan troughs, however. There are regional variations, very similar to those identified at the inter-state level in the previous chapter (as might be expected, in view of the fact that in many cases state conditions are largely a reflection of metropolitan conditions). A number of attempts have been made to describe inter-city variations, the most thorough being by the Mid-west Research Institute (Liu, 1975b). This closely follows the approach of the earlier inter-state study (Liu, 1973) summarized in the previous chapter. The city study covers 243 standard metropolitan statistical areas (SMSAs), i.e. cities as defined for official statistical purposes.

The criteria used by Liu are listed in Table 4.1. There are five major components, each of which is subdivided to reflect both individual and community conditions. Economic factors include such things as per capita income, wealth, poverty, income inequality and unemployment. The political component covers level of individual information (access to mass media), electoral participation and measures of the professionalism and performance of local government. The environmental component includes measures of air,

Table 4.1. Quality-of-life criteria for American cities

1. *Economic component*
   a. Individual economic well-being
   b. Community economic health

2. *Political component*
   a. Individual activities
   b. Local government

3. *Environmental component*
   a. Individual and institutional environment
   b. Natural environment

4. *Health and education component*
   a. Individual conditions
   b. Community conditions

5. *Social component*
   a. Individual development
   b. Individual equality
   c. Community living conditions

Source: Liu, 1975b, pp. 6–7.

visual and noise pollution, climate and recreation facilities. Health and education includes mortality rates, medical facilities and personnel, and school attendance. The social component is made up of measures of opportunity for self-support, individual development and choice (e.g. mobility), along with data on race and sex equality, housing conditions, community facilities and so on. Over 120 individual variables are used. For every SMSA, scores are derived for each of the five components, which are themselves aggregated into an over-all quality-of-life score.

Figure 4.1 maps performance on the over-all index, for large and medium SMSAs. Five ranked categories are recognized, though too much attention should not be given to such terms as 'outstanding' and 'adequate' (which simply represent the judgements of the research workers concerned). According to the maps, the quality of urban life deteriorates quite regularly from north-west to south-east. The generally low performance of cities in the South mirrors this region's deprived status, recognized in the previous chapter's interstate analysis. Most of the worst ('sub-standard') cities are in the South, but this category also includes New York and Philadelphia. There are no SMSAs in the bottom two categories west of the Rockies.

As with the inter-state analysis, this pattern of geographical variation is broadly confirmed by other similar if less comprehensive studies (D. M. Smith, 1973, chs. 3 and 8). Evidence that there has been little change over the past few decades is provided by an analysis undertaken by Thorndike (1939), based on data for 310 cities in 1930. He developed a scale of 'goodness' of cities, incorporating a wide range of conditions. His findings show that, as categories of cities are mapped successively from 'best' to 'worst', the concentration moves steadily south-eastwards (D. M. Smith, 1973, pp. 34–6). The general standard of urban life has improved greatly since Thorndike's study (unless we regard such contemporary problems as drug abuse as serious enough to offset higher material standards and better social services). But the basic pattern of regional variations remains. A line from Boston, Massachusetts to El Paso, Texas, still marks an important qualitative divide in standards of city life. As we observed at the state level in the previous chapter, this pattern has deep roots,

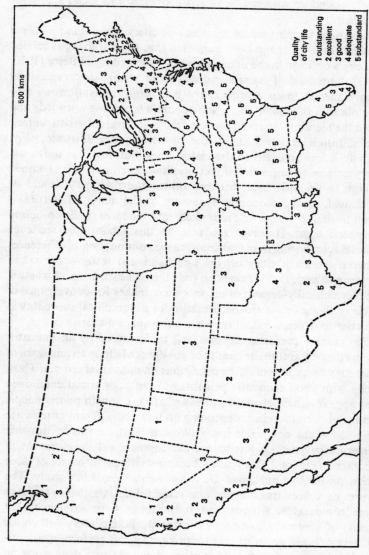

Figure 4.1. The quality of life in large and medium-sized metropolitan areas in the USA, 1970. (Source of data: Liu, 1975b, Figs. 16 and 17.)

Quality
of city life
1 outstanding
2 excellent
3 good
4 adequate
5 substandard

500 kms

closely bound up with the distinctive economic and social history of the South.

Returning to the idea of a system of cities functioning in some coherent manner, it has been suggested that level of living is related to a city's position in the urban hierarchy. According to Berry (1970, p. 43), 'impulses' of economic growth and change are transmitted from higher to lower centres in the hierarchy. Innovations tend to take place in the major cities, subsequently spreading outwards and down the hierarchy to reach successively lower levels of urban centres. The diffusion of television in the post-war years illustrates this: initially it was confined to the major cities, but now it is universal. Berry goes on to argue that if metropolitan development is sustained at high levels, differences between centre and periphery should be eliminated, as the economic dynamism of the major cities trickles down to smaller places and ultimately into the most tradition-bound peripheral areas. However, evidence for this equalization tendency is far less convincing than that showing the continuation of differences between the large cities on the one hand and lower-order urban centres and peripheral regions on the other. The question of whether the hierarchically-organized urban system makes for convergence of levels of living or for the perpetuation of geographical inequality is a matter to which we shall return in subsequent discussions.

The general 'performance' of a city, as measured by an indicator purporting to capture the quality or goodness of life, is an amalgam of what may be quite conflicting conditions on individual criteria. Thus, a city with good economic performance but poor social conditions may appear to have the same quality of life as one with poorer people but better social services, depending on how the different criteria are weighted in the composite index. We can illustrate this by drawing performance profiles, just as we did for national development in Chapter 2 (Figure 2.6). Figure 4.2 contrasts the performance of three cities, on the five quality-of-life components from Liu's study. The figures have been transformed into standard deviates, so as to make them comparable. Atlanta and Indianapolis have similar overall quality-of-life scores, just below average (0). Both do very well on the economic factor, enjoying relative prosperity, but perform substantially below average on the other components. Atlanta does worst on

178

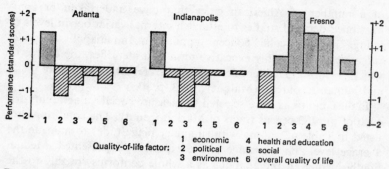

Figure 4.2. Quality-of-life profiles for three American metropolitan areas. (Source of data: Liu, 1975b.)

the political component (perhaps because of a legacy of non-participation on the part of blacks, whose *de facto* right to vote is a recent innovation in most of the South). Indianapolis does worst on the environment; it is an industrial city with no pretensions to beauty. In contrast, Fresno in California performs badly on the economic component but well on the others, especially environmental quality. These conflicting trends, which could be illustrated by many other cases, emphasize again that good performance on conventional economic criteria is not necessarily matched in other dimensions of life.

It is now time to move from the national scale of the system of cities to individual cities. We shall look briefly at the three cities featured in Figure 4.2. Each of them enables us to explore different facets of inequality in the American city – from basic patterns, to problems and how people perceive them, and on to the question of public policy and the structure of cause and effect making for inequality in city life.

We shall take Indianapolis first, to illustrate a pattern of spatial variation in human life chances typical of many American cities. Indianapolis, Indiana, is a busy industrial city in America's major manufacturing belt. The population of Marion County, which includes the city and its suburbs, is about 800,000. Indianapolis is one of a number of American cities that have undertaken or commissioned detailed studies to establish internal variations in levels of living. The particular concept applied in Indianapolis is *social vulnerability*, a suitably evocative term that identifies 'the degree to which persons are vulnerable to conditions requiring help from social and human resources' (Maloney, 1973, p. ii).

Eight conditions were selected to measure social vulnerability for each of the 183 census tracts of Marion County. The conditions are listed in Table 4.2, along with summary magnitudes to indicate the average level and the range of life experience represented. Median family income in Indianapolis as a whole conforms roughly to the national average, but the maximum and minimum figures show that the richest tract is over five times as high as the poorest tract. Proportion of families in poverty ranges from nil to over one third. The proportion of families with both parents present ranges from 98 per cent to only a little more than half. Unemployment ranges from nil to over 20 per cent. And so on, down the table. Clearly, there are very considerable differences among tracts, for all the conditions listed.

The variability of life experience in Indianapolis may be summarized by simple frequency distribution diagrams. In Figure 4.3 we illustrate just two of the social vulnerability conditions: income and the tuberculosis rate. The form of the distribution tells us something quite important, for in both cases there is a distinct skewness, i.e. the census tracts tend to bunch towards one end of the graph.

Table 4.2. Measures of social vulnerability for Indianapolis, Indiana, by census tracts

Measure	Maximum	Minimum	Mean
1. Median family income	25,943	4660	10,357
2. Families below poverty level (%)	36·5	0·0	8·7
3. Families with husband and wife (%)	98·0	56·5	83·4
4. Civilian labour force unemployed (%)	21·9	0·0	4·9
5. Houses lacking some or all plumbing (%)	36·7	0·0	4·5
6. Households with no automobile (%)	68·0	0·3	18·9
7. Ambulance runs per 1000 population	450·3	0·5	53·4
8. Tuberculosis rate per 1000 population	17·8	0·0	2·8

Source: Maloney, 1973.

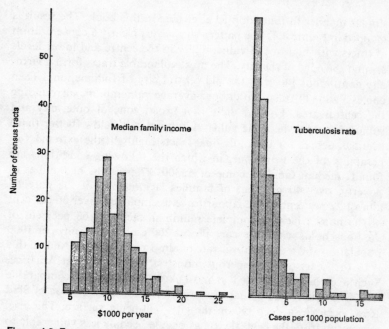

Figure 4.3. Frequency distribution of census tracts in Marion County (which includes Indianapolis), Indiana, on two social conditions. (Source of data: Maloney, 1973.)

But two distinct tendencies are revealed. The distribution of tracts on the income measure shows a 'tail' in the positive direction: in other words, there are a few tracts with very high median income while most fall within the 5000 to 15,000 range. The distribution of tuberculosis cases shows greater skewness: most tracts have very low rates but there are a few with very high incidence – a pattern typical of other severe social problems such as venereal disease and drug addiction. Diagrams such as those in Figure 4.3 help to fill in the details of inequality in distribution, hidden in summary figures of the kind in Table 4.2.

A social vulnerability index has been calculated for each of the census tracts, combining data on the eight individual conditions in a similar manner to that adopted elsewhere in this book. The result is mapped in Figure 4.4. The pattern shows very clearly a concentration of tracts with high social vulnerability in the centre and lower levels around the edge of the city. The most vulnerable tracts form a virtually continuous block in the old central city of Indianapolis. Then comes a zone of tracts with above-average vulnerability surrounding the central area. Finally, there is a broad zone of outer-city and suburban areas where the vulnerability index is below (better than) average. Scores for the individual tracts highlight the extreme vulnerability of the worst one, in which the following conditions are found: median family income of $5300, 27 per cent of families in poverty, over 40 per cent of families lacking one of the parents, almost 22 per cent of the labour force unemployed, over 36 per cent of the houses lacking complete plumbing facilities, 68 per cent of the households without a car, almost 200 ambulance runs per 1000 population and a tuberculosis rate of almost 18 per 1000. And all this is in the heart of a prosperous industrial city in affluent America. Such a picture is repeated in most American cities of comparable size. One small area, perhaps incorporating the local version of Skid Row, occupies a deep pit on the city well-being surface. The level rises away from the central city, as people become less vulnerable to social and economic ills, eventually reaching the plateaux of high well-being in the outer suburbs of smart ranch-style homes occupied by the wealthy middle classes. The worst areas of the American city tend to be occupied by blacks; in Indianapolis there is a moderately high positive correlation between social vulnerability and proportion of blacks in the tract population ($r = 0.58$).

How do the people actually involved view the problems of the American city? To find out something about this, we shall move on to the second of our selected cities: Fresno, California. Fresno is a rapidly growing city, the population having risen by about 32,000 in the 1960s to reach 166,000 in 1970. While Indianapolis has a fairly substantial black community (17 per cent of the total population), typical of northern industrial cities, Fresno has 18 per cent of its population of Mexican origin and a further 10 per cent black. These two ethnic minorities are concentrated in the south-western corner of the metropolitan area.

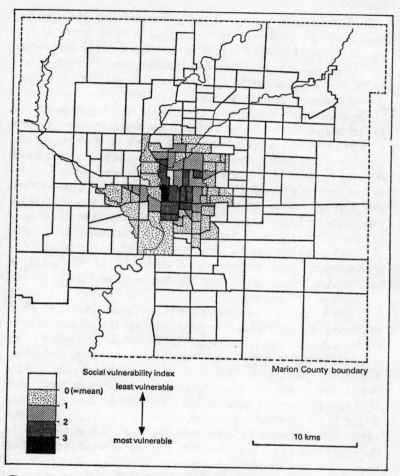

Figure 4.4. Social vulnerability in the Indianapolis metropolitan area. Index values are standard deviates. (Source: Maloney, 1973, Fig. 2.)

Where the Grass is Greener

The geographical pattern of living standards may be identified from a recent 'community profile' compiled by a city agency (City of Fresno, 1973a). Figure 4.5 highlights the worst areas on four indicators: (1) a socio-economic index incorporating median family income and school years completed; (2) a normal-family-life index (both parents present); (3) a community health index made up of the rates of illegitimacy, infant mortality, gonorrhoea, suicide and deaths due to cirrhosis of the liver (where alcohol is the probable cause); (4) proportion of adults on probation, as a measure of criminal activity. Poor conditions with respect to these measures largely coincide with the area occupied by the ethnic minorities, the south-west. That the area of low living standards or high social vulnerability should appear peripheral in Fresno rather than central (as in Indianapolis) is explained by the historical process of urban growth: the main direction of expansion has been northwards and eastwards from the city centre (CBD) leaving the area to the south and west of the railway as a predominantly poor neighbourhood attracting the 'Chicanos', or Spanish-Americans, drawn into California from Mexico by the prospects of employment.

Figure 4.5 shows the six major 'Neighbourhood Areas' into which the Fresno metropolis has been subdivided for the purpose of community analysis. Area 1, known as West Fresno, has the lowest rating on general socio-economic conditions. Areas 4 and 6 have the highest, with Area 5 third, while Areas 2 and 3 fall on the lower half of the index. McKinley Avenue, which separates the three northern areas (4, 5 and 6) from the other three, constitutes an important social divide. In the words of a recent citizen-survey report (City of Fresno, 1973b, p. 9) the people 'to some extent live in two different worlds. To the north, over 85 per cent classify themselves as White-Anglos. Less than 10 per cent are Mexican-Americans, and fewer than 2 per cent are Blacks. Over two-thirds of the respondents here report annual family incomes in excess of 10,000 dollars'. In the south, Area 1 has about 70 per cent black and over 20 per cent Mexican-American, Area 2 has a much smaller ethnic minority population but only 16 per cent of survey respondents report family incomes over $10,000, while Area 3 has a predominantly low-income population with high representation of minorities.

184

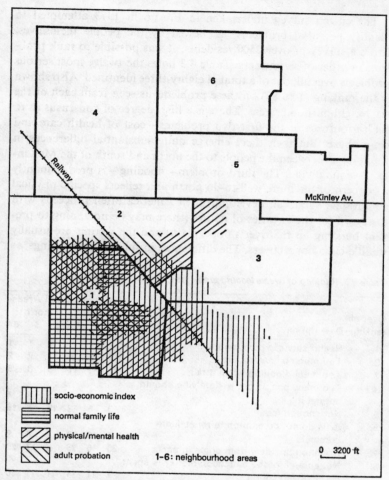

Figure 4.5. Worst areas on certain economic and social conditions in Fresno, California. (Source of data: City of Fresno, 1973a, Figs. S-15, S-16, S-18 and S-26.)

Where the Grass is Greener

The citizen survey undertaken in Fresno in 1973 attempted to identify potential problems, as viewed by the people themselves. From a survey of over 2500 residents, it was possible to rank problems in order of seriousness. Table 4.3 notes the twelve most serious problems over all, out of a total of eighty-three identified. Also shown is the ranking (1 to 83) on these problems as seen from each of the six Neighbourhood Areas. There is a high degree of consensus as to the seriousness of the first two problems – cost of health care and drug abuse. But then there emerge quite substantial differences in rankings as between the people to the north and south of the McKinley Avenue divide. The third problem – flooding – is predominantly a concern of the more well-to-do north and reflects specific physical conditions; suburban development in America often proceeds with disregard for the vagaries of nature (there may be no zoning to prevent building on the river's flood plain) and the victims are usually middle-class housebuyers. The differences in subsequent rankings, as

Table 4.3. Ranking of twelve leading problems in Fresno, California, 1973

| Over-all ranking | Description | Neighbourhood Areas | | | | | |
| | | south | | | north | | |
		1	2	3	4	5	6
1.	Health services cost too much	1	1	1	1	1	1
2.	Too much misuse of drugs	2	2	4	2	2	2
3.	Too much flooding when it rains	21	7	17	3	3	3
4.	Too many people get welfare who should not get it	29	6	3	5	4	4
5.	Not enough jobs	3	5	2	15	6	15
6.	Jails do not do enough to rehabilitate criminals	4	19	13	7	8	9
7.	Not enough safety from crime in parks	30	10	23	6	7	22
8.	Not enough of the education money is spent on basic education	7	11	14	11	17	10
9.	Not enough clean up of roadside litter, trash, old cars, lots, etc.	24	12	29	8	10	6
10.	Most places to live cost too much to buy or rent	11	3	7	9	14	19
11.	Too hard to get emergency health treatment	14	4	5	17	16	18
12.	Too much air pollution	55	24	35	4	9	5

Source: City of Fresno, 1973b, p. 19.

between Areas 1, 2 and 3 on the one hand and 4, 5 and 6 on the other, reflect the south's greater concern with such matters as job provision, neighbourhood cleanliness and access to health care. The different views of pollution are especially revealing. The preoccupation with environmental pollution in recent years has been very much a middle-class issue in America: the same may very well be true of Britain (Wood, 1974, p. 127–8). As the survey report (City of Fresno, 1973b, p. 101) puts it, 'the well-to-do citizens of the north, largely free from the pressures of day-to-day existence, illustrate a hierarchy of needs pattern by demonstrating a greater concern with environmental problems – with the quality of living once a solid economic base is assured'. The general findings of the survey of citizen opinion are summarized as follows: 'the north–south differences expressed in this study are those between the poor and insecure to the south and the affluent and secure in the north'.

Whether people in the poor areas actually view their lives as inferior to that in the rich areas was not considered in the Fresno report. However, some evidence is now emerging from studies in other cities. For example, research on personal evaluation of environmental quality in Detroit undertaken by the Survey Research Centre of the University of Michigan's Institute for Social Research shows marked differences between the inner city and the suburbs. In the entire Detroit region 35 per cent of the people interviewed claimed to be 'completely satisfied' with their neighbourhood; within the city the proportion ranged from 26 to 21 per cent, while it rose to 48 per cent completely satisfied in suburban Wayne County.

Just as there are ethnic and social-class differences in perception of problems and levels of environmental satisfaction, so there will be conflicting views as to the improvements required. In Fresno, people in the south appear to want greater job security, more training and better social services, while the more affluent residents in the northern suburbs place greater stress on other things (as reflected in Table 4.3). As a more specific illustration, we may cite some of the results of a survey undertaken in Los Angeles (Stern, 1973, p. 88). A sample of people were asked: 'If you could allocate $1 million to the Los Angeles area, to which Public Service would you allocate this money?' Police protection and public education were by far the most popular services for more spending. But police protection was chosen by less than 20 per cent of the blacks interviewed and less than 30 per cent of the 'browns' (Chicanos) compared with almost 40 per cent of the whites; education was chosen by over 40 per cent of the blacks and almost 35 per cent of the browns compared with only 30 per cent of the whites.

For further exploration of the issues raised by inequality in the American city we may now move to Atlanta, the third of our cases. Atlanta has a population of over 500,000, a little more than half of them black. The city is the major commercial centre of Georgia, home state of President Carter. Atlanta is often taken to epitomize the 'new' prosperous South, and in recent years it has spawned large office blocks, freeways and a magnificent sports stadium befitting such an image. But these symbols of affluence distract attention from the fact that severe poverty still exists, especially in the black ghetto.

The geographical pattern of differences in living standards or quality of life has been mapped by Bederman (1974). He calculated a composite quality-of-life index from measures of health, public order, housing quality, socio-economic status and population density, for each of the city's census tracts. The results are shown in Figure 4.6. There is a marked wedge of relatively low life-quality by Bederman's criteria, extending somewhat north of westwards from the city centre (CBD), and a less pronounced wedge to the east. As Figure 4.6 shows, these areas largely correspond with those of predominantly black population. Clearly, there is a process of discrimination at work here, with social problems and economic disadvantage afflicting some people in some places to a much greater extent than others.

During the past decade various programmes have been initiated in Atlanta and elsewhere, aimed at combating the problem of localized urban deprivation. Some have focused on the apparent racial dimension, others have involved attempts at urban renewal and increased spending on social facilities in the poverty areas; others have been directed towards increased mobility with respect to the location of employment opportunities. However, they all have one feature in common: failure to solve the problem. The reason for this is a failure to understand the processes at work, and a failure (or reluctance) to

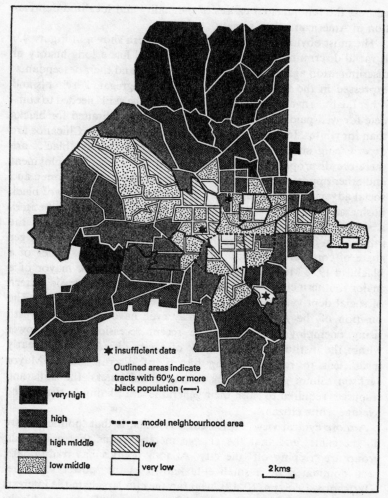

Figure 4.6. Variations in the quality of life in Atlanta, Georgia. (Source of data: Bederman, 1974, Fig. 2.)

189

address the fundamental causes of inequality and localized deprivation in American urban society.

The most obvious explanation for the pattern shown in Figure 4.6
is racial discrimination. The South in general has a long history of
discrimination against the emancipated slaves and their descendants,
expressed in the inferiority of the (usually segregated) schools and
other facilities available for blacks. Access to the skills needed to com-
pete for well-paid jobs has thus been much more limited for blacks
than for whites. In western cities (e.g. in California) the Chicanos are
experiencing similar discrimination. Atlanta's 250,000 blacks are
therefore disproportionately penalized with respect to employment
and other opportunities to earn the money needed for economic and
social advancement, though the city has a prominent group of black-
businessmen and successful professionals. 'Black power' is sometimes
advocated as the solution to problems of racial discrimination, the
implication being that political power is required to obtain a larger
share of community wealth. In Atlanta power *is* in the hands of a
black: in 1972 Maynard Jackson was elected first black mayor of a
major southern city. But the ghetto is still there and the basic pattern
of social deprivation shown in Figure 4.6 has hardly changed. The
position of the ghetto residents may even have deteriorated, with
rising unemployment, during the recent recession. Black power
within the institutional framework of a city like Atlanta is clearly
insufficient to redress a long history of discrimination. Mayor
Jackson cannot give his black 'brothers and sisters' the skills and
resources required to raise their general level of living to that of the
average white citizen.

A more cynical view, expressed in Atlanta, is that 'politicians are
all the same' and that the change merely means that a different
group are 'ripping off' the city. Atlanta politics has traditionally
been dominated by a small élite known as the 'power structure'
(Hartshorn, 1976, pp. 10–12), who ran the city largely in the interests
of the white business community. After a century of exclusion blacks
have now entered the power élite, but the economic/political system
still functions to the advantage of the well-to-do (white or black),
with little more than token regard for the needs of the poor.

Specific policies ostensibly designed to help the poor usually address symptoms of problems rather than basic causes. This is true of the much-publicized Model Cities programme and its later extensions – America's major attempt in recent years to improve the quality of life in the poorest parts of the cities. The neighbourhood 'face-lift' schemes that formed a prominent component of the Model Cities programme in many cities were quite literally superficial improvements confined to the physical fabric of the slums. Resources needed to upgrade significantly the quality of health care and other social services were not available. As a recent review puts it, 'despite marginal improvements in social services, social and physical blights remain blatantly undisturbed. . . The impact on local government has also been minimal . . . no radical changes in the distribution of influence or benefits have occurred. And since it was no less difficult or more rewarding for the poor to participate in American society, little has changed in the slums of American cities.' (Kasperson, 1977, p. 186.) The citizen participation that was supposed to assure that the preferences of the poverty-area residents themselves would be fed into the plans was often subverted by agencies not really sympathetic to the needs of ghetto residents. Thus, a government report on progress of the Model Cities programme, in general, concluded that it had 'not yet achieved legislative objectives concerning "quality of life" improvements in the disadvantaged areas'; it had not lived up to the expectations created by the early rhetoric of the programme's proponents (Norman, 1973, pp. 6, 10).

In Atlanta, the Model Cities programme was focused on a so-called Model Neighbourhood Area in the heart of the slums (Fig. 4.6). The population was almost 50,000, 68 per cent of them black. Unemployed (1973) was 15 per cent, compared with 3·4 in the city as a whole. Almost three quarters of the houses are classed as substandard. Infant mortality is 42 per 1000, or well over twice the national average. The programme in Atlanta was characterized by a strong chief executive, with little involvement on the part of a resident group that was neither cohesive nor integrated into local political processes. The government report referred to above describes the Atlanta Model Cities programme as having an enormous number of projects and sponsors that caused the staff to get 'bogged down' in preparing and negotiating contracts, etc., and points to the failure to implement an ambitious health programme because of conflict with the local medical establishment. Eventually Model Cities became so much a matter of political and social controversy that the mayor downgraded the programme (Norman, 1973, pp. 31, 33–4). Achievements of Model Cities in Atlanta have done little to change the standard of living of the target population.

At the root of the plight of Atlanta's poor, black or white, is access to employment. Atlanta has experienced a decentralization of employment similar to that in most other American cities, with firms moving to the fringe of the urban area. Physical access to these jobs from the inner city is rendered difficult by the inadequacy of public transport and lack of a car reliable enough for freeway driving. Those most in need of employment gain little from the impressive freeways of cities like Atlanta, for they are designed largely to get suburban commuters to inner-city jobs. But access to employment is not simply a matter of transportation. Bederman and Adams (1974) have shown that variations in under-employment by census tract in Atlanta cannot be explained by accessibility: the inner city is in fact the area from which accessibility to the city's job centres is greatest. Underemployment stems from other causes: 'Atlanta's critically underemployed are mainly black female heads of families, and no matter where they live in the metropolitan area they have neither the skills to qualify them for most of the new jobs being created, nor the opportunity to acquire marketable skills.' (Bederman and Adams, 1974, p. 386.) The root cause of localized poverty in Atlanta is thus to be found in the operation of the economy and its labour market. In a society where access to most sources of need satisfaction is via money, those whom private employers find not worth their hire live in poverty and social deprivation. In Atlanta, the history and culture of the American South tends to mean that these poor are, disproportionately, blacks.

Another dimension of the crisis in the American city is housing. Many inner-city families do not earn enough to pay rents which would be sufficient to enable landlords to maintain their property and still make a profit. In addition to overcrowding, this has led to the large-scale abandonment of structurally quite-adequate housing in some large cities. Castells (1977, p. 408) cites the following figures from a 1973 government publication: 100,000 housing units abandoned in New York City, 30,000 in Philadelphia, 12,000 in Baltimore and 10,000 in St Louis – and these are probably underestimates. This process is generally accompanied by a deterioration in social services and the closure of community facilities such as schools, which further depresses the quality of life for people who remain in the neighbourhood. Abandoned houses may be occupied temporarily by drug addicts and other squatters, which accelerates the process of deterioration. At the extreme, otherwise 'worthless' property may be set on fire for its insurance value. Castells (1977, p. 414) sums all this up vividly: 'Zones of New York appear as if they have been bombed. And among the ruins, the unemployed and the kids without schools sit and chat waiting to see what might turn up.' What does turn up is more likely to be opportunities for petty crime and the partial employment associated with prostitution, drug-running and gambling than the chance of escape to the 'American dream' of a comfortable suburban home, conventional family life, and the economic security to support it.

Differences between the inner city and the suburbs are exacerbated by discrimination with respect to social services. Access to health care depends on money; in the USA, doctors and medical facilities are attracted by the prospect of economic gain, not social need (see Chapter 5). Schools, which are so important for the acquisition of passports to well-paid employment, are generally much superior in the suburbs, where there is a larger tax base to support them. The allocation of resources for public services suffers from a general societal preoccupation with *individual* consumption of material goods and personal services, hence the contrast between private affluence and public squalor to which Galbraith (1958 and 1967) drew attention some years ago. Opportunities for equalization of important aspects of living standards via greater *social* consumption are thus missed, in an America primed by business interests and the mass media to suspicion of 'creeping socialism'. In fact, the provision of social services in cities is often regressive, representing a redistribution of resources from poor to rich.

Inequality in Atlanta and other American cities may be viewed as the spatial expression of a process of class polarization, closely

193

associated with the operation of the economy. The migration of industry and offices to the city fringe has been accompanied by large-scale suburban residential development. People who can afford it move out of the inner-city, while the highly mobile managerial and professional workers, attracted by new employment prospects, also look to the suburbs for places to live. Suburbanites working in the offices of the central business district can commute by car on the new freeways. Those left behind in the inner-city residential areas tend to be the poor, unskilled and relatively immobile, joined by others who are also in a weak position in the city labour market. Many of these people are recent migrants, mainly blacks from predominantly rural backgrounds. They have been displaced from the countryside by the mechanization of agriculture, and attracted to northern cities in large numbers as well as to places like Atlanta in the South. There are not enough suitable jobs outside white-collar employment in the city centre, and people who might wish to move out to the suburbs where more jobs are being created are often prevented from doing so by the operation of the market in housing and land. They can afford the low rentals for inner-city property (often of low quality) but they cannot raise the mortgages necessary for a suburban home. And many estates (or 'subdivisions') in the suburbs apply zoning regulations which require a certain size of house or flat, thus effectively excluding those with limited resources.

Thus business and the middle class or bourgeoisie are becoming increasingly settled in the suburban ring around the old central part of the city which contains the poor and the inner-city offices. The central areas are losing the tax base needed to support social services; many of the suburbs are autonomous politically and administratively, which means that they need contribute nothing to the running of the central part of the city where much of their wealth is generated. The social deprivation of the inner city, with its high crime rates (and threat to property), drug addiction and 'deviant' sub-cultures increasingly threatens the people and businesses that remain, thus accelerating the migration process. The ultimate prospect is of the inner-city poor eventually inheriting the hole in the centre of the metropolis, abandoned by everyone else, in some kind of 'doughnut city'.

194

On the other side of this fence lives President Duvalier of Haiti, in splendid isolation from the squalor of most of the rest of Port au Prince. Despite the widespread poverty of Third World countries, the élite often enjoy conspicuous affluence. Soweto (below) is probably the most equal city in the world. About a million people live in identical dwellings in this black residential area of Johannesburg, South Africa. Conditions are better than in many Third World cities but greatly inferior to those of white South Africans.

Part of Manhattan in New York, where many of the American multinational corporations have their headquarters. The Pan Am building contrasts with the traditional skyscrapers of the central business districts of cities in the USA. Below, is part of what Michael Harrington has termed the 'other America'. This home of a poor white family in Canton, Mississippi, is typical of rural poverty in the South – a timber-framed shack with, characteristically, obsolescent domestic appliances and general clutter on the front porch.

Essex Street, Colne – typical of nineteenth-century workers' houses in this former cotton-mill town on the edge of the Pennines in Lancashire. It is in this kind of community that the decline of the textile industry has had its major impact. Below, is another side to northern England, exemplified by Gateway House, Manchester, an office complex completed in the 1960s. As elsewhere in Britain, speculative commercial development abounds while the real need of the depressed regions and inner-city areas is for new industrial jobs and better housing.

Some of the squatter settlements of Pampalona Alta on the edge of Lima, Peru –
typical of the environment of millions of recent migrants to Latin American cities.
The picture shows the rudimentary dwellings, the primitive conditions for storing
water and the poor state of the streets. The well-to-do middle class in Lima enjoys a
level of affluence comparable with its counterparts in Europe and North America,
as these houses in the Corpac district indicate (below).

Contrasting styles of recreation reflect South Africa's highly unequal society. Above, whites enjoy a leisurely game of bowls near the sea-front in Durban, in a scene that evokes the era of British colonialism. Not far away, on waste land near the docks, Zulu workers perform a modern version of tribal dancing on a Sunday afternoon – almost the only opportunity for recreation in the 'white' city, where there are no facilities for blacks. The sign on the shield shows that their 'tribal' affiliation is now to the Standard Bank, their employer.

Modern apartments in a Moscow suburb. Under Soviet planning, each family will have a specific allocation of living space, with ready access to shops (on the ground floor of these blocks) and to a full range of services and recreational facilities. Privileged conditions are enjoyed by the political, artistic and academic élite in socialist countries. The single-family homes, below, are for members of the USSR Academy of Sciences in Akademgorodok, the 'academic town' set up near the city of Novosibirsk in Siberia.

A centrally planned economy is not always closely attuned to consumer demand. Queues are a familiar feature of the Soviet city: the people above are waiting to buy fresh fruit or vegetables stacked up on the pavement of a street in central Novosibirsk. The market forces of the free-enterprise system have their own perverse outcomes. The side-street in Natchez, Mississippi (below), shows how effectively the American economy produces automobiles, while failing to provide decent housing for millions of people.

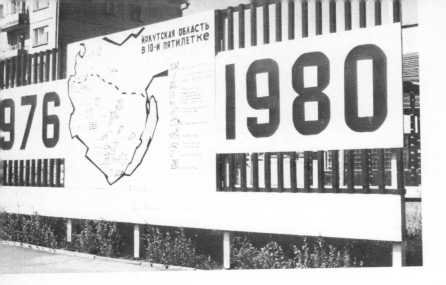

Features of the latest Five Year Plan for Irkutsk *oblast*, displayed in the centre of the new industrial city of Bratsk. Planned industrial complexes are an important element of economic-development strategy in western Siberia, as elsewhere in the USSR. The Iowa corn farmer on the other side of the fence, below, wants nothing to do with socialism, or anything else that threatens his independence. What is freedom from capitalist exploitation in Irkutsk is slavery in Iowa.

The growing socio-economic polarization of the American city clearly works to the advantage of one class of people and very much to the disadvantage of the other. However deplorable the outcome may appear, little can be done to change the forces at work. City planning is largely confined to clearing 'obsolescent' areas for new development or freeways, and to laying down bare guidelines within which various forms of land development and business activity operate. It facilitates the activities of people with property, helping them to accumulate more wealth. The urban form thus created may be quite unsuitable for the lives of most ordinary people, as they attempt to satisfy their needs. To alter the forces making for the polarization of the American city requires, at the very least, a fundamental change in the markets for labour, housing and land so that employment and residential space can be provided for those who need it *where* they need it: The prospects of such changes are very slight, as they would be contrary to the interests of those who run the system and gain from the present state of affairs. The so-called 'urban crisis' in America is not a crisis of urbanization *per se* but of the structure of American society, in which the operation of market forces within the prevailing capitalist mode of production makes gross inequality inevitable. To change the cities requires fundamental changes in national economic, social and political organization. It remains doubtful whether the conflicts generated in the modern American city will themselves lead eventually to a revolutionary change in the process of city formation, unless the existing situation becomes too much to control.

The British City: Deprivation in the Welfare State

It is often supposed that the problems of inequality in the American metropolis reflect weak city planning and poorly developed social services. Far from being an inevitable outcome of the capitalist system, localized poverty is frequently viewed as capable of almost instant elimination with appropriate physical and social planning. Yet pockets of poverty persist even in the cities of Britain, birthplace of the welfare state and of town and country planning as well as originator

195

of various innovations in urban design such as garden cities and new towns. We will look briefly at the phenomenon generally termed 'multiple deprivation' in the British city, to see what might be learned about urban inequality in general from this particular case.

The problems of the inner city have become a subject of growing concern in contemporary Britain. According to a report by the Department of the Environment (1977), almost 4 million people live in 'exceptional concentrations of poverty and deprivation' in the declining inner areas of major cities. As this figure comprises one in fourteen of the entire national population, it is questionable how 'exceptional' the situation really is. In any event, conditions in the areas referred to are obviously very serious. For example, the report refers to low-skill workers caught in a 'housing trap' in the Stockwell area of Lambeth in inner London, unable to buy their own homes, while denied access to council housing. In inner Liverpool the picture portrayed is one of physical decay, with more than a tenth of the area studied comprising vacant slum-clearance sites. In the Small Heath district of inner Birmingham, consultants found deteriorating housing, vandalism and petty crime, and in some places a high level of tension between neighbours in this racially-mixed area. Local authorities, interest groups and academics have been mounting pressure on central government for some kind of action. Almost overnight, it seems, the so-called regional problem has been replaced by 'inner-city deprivation' as the most serious manifestation of geographical inequality in Britain.

The government's formal response came in June 1977, with the publication of the White Paper *Policy for the Inner Cities* (HMSO, 1977). The nature of the problem, as outlined here, may be summarized as follows. The economic fortunes of inner-city areas have been declining, with a loss of jobs in traditional industries, affecting in particular semi-skilled and unskilled workers. New investment has not been sufficient to generate replacement employment of the type needed by local people. Despite progress with urban renewal, there still remains a great deal of poor-quality housing, set in a drab environment. The inner-city areas have high concentrations of poor people, arising partly from high unemployment but also due to low levels of earning on the part of those at work. These areas tend to become 'a refuge for those least able to cope in society', including the homeless, drug addicts and alcoholics. In some inner areas there is a 'collective' deprivation, which affects all residents, even though individually the majority may have satisfactory homes and jobs. In some cities, the deprived areas tend to coincide with ethnic-minority immigrant communities. The White Paper recognizes the need to strengthen the economies of the inner areas and the prospects of their residents, to improve the physical fabric and make the environment more attractive, to alleviate social problems, and to secure a new balance between the inner areas and the rest of the city region in terms of population and jobs.

As in the case of the American city, we will explore the problem of deprivation in urban Britain within a broad policy context. There are two alternative responses if it is decided to embark upon programmes to alleviate economic and social deprivation. One is to provide assistance directly to the *individuals* found to be in need, for example those with incomes or housing conditions falling below some clearly defined standard. There are various drawbacks to this strategy, including the possible indignity of means tests designed to judge family resources in relation to need, invasion of privacy by officialdom, and failure of many people to obtain assistance to which they are entitled but for which they are too proud or ignorant to apply. The alternative is to focus assistance on *territories* rather than on individuals, i.e. on groups of people defined by area of residence irrespective of individual circumstances. These areas of deprivation would be defined by objective social indicators and programmes would be implemented within the areas selected. The Model Cities programme in the USA, mentioned above, is a case in point. An obvious disadvantage of such area-based policies is that they can assist well-off people who happen to live in generally deprived areas, just as they can miss poor people outside the target areas. But it is generally assumed that area-based policies get closer to the local economic, social and environmental problems leading to personal deprivation than do the programmes directed towards the immediate alleviation of individual symptoms. We shall return to this judgement later, after we know something of the nature and extent of urban deprivation in Britain.

A thorough statistical examination of urban deprivation (Holter-mann, 1975) has recently been undertaken at the Department of the Environment (DOE). Deprivation is said to exist when, because of deficiencies of consumption or income in relation to needs, an individual's well-being falls below a level generally regarded as a reasonable minimum in Britain today. The DOE study made no attempt to define this minimum, but addressed the more descriptive questions of how bad conditions are in the worst areas, where the worst areas are, to what extent deprived individuals are spatially concentrated in the worst areas, and to what extent the worst areas on different conditions overlap. The spatial unit of observation is the census enumeration district (ED). There are 87,578 urban EDs in England, Scotland and Wales, with an average population of 163 households. The analysis is therefore at a very fine level of areal aggregation.

Eighteen indicators were selected from data in the 1971 Census. They are listed in Table 4.4, along with summary measures. The conditions chosen are rather heavily weighted towards housing quality and tenure, but also include level of employment and certain economic conditions. The measures of 'special needs' attempt to identify particular population groups (the old, the young and 'New Commonwealth' or black immigrants), whose presence in itself does not constitute deprivation but may aggravate conditions where they are already bad.

The 5 per cent cut-off values in Table 4.4 indicate the figures above which the worst 5 per cent of all EDs will be found. Thus for proportion of households sharing or lacking hot water, the worst 5 per cent of EDs have at least 38·2 per cent of households in this category. This criterion provides one possible definition of the worst areas on each of the eighteen indicators, and can be used to summarize broad features of the distribution of urban deprivation.

Table 4.5 shows the geographical distribution of EDs above the 5 per cent cut-off value, for four of the indicators. The figures report the proportion (%) of the worst 5 per cent of all EDs to be found in the geographical subdivision in question. Thus London 'Group A' (inner London) contains 21·8 of all Britain's EDs in the worst 5 per cent on the overcrowding criterion (cut-off 10·1 per cent – see Table

Table 4.4. Indicators of urban deprivation in Great Britain

Indicator (percentages)	Mean	Standard deviation	5% cut-off
Housing			
Households who share or lack hot water	9·7	13·6	38·2
Households who share or lack bath	14·5	20·0	58·8
Households in permanent buildings who lack bath	10·4	18·0	50·5
Households who lack inside W C	12·5	19·4	57·0
Households with more than 1·5 persons per room	2·3	4·5	10·1
Households with more than 1 person per room	8·1	8·8	25·7
Households in shared dwellings	4·7	11·8	29·1
Households not having exclusive use of all basic amenities	20·2	23·6	71·0
Employment			
Economically active males unemployed, but seeking work or sick	5·8	4·9	15·1
Economically active females unemployed, but seeking work or sick	5·1	4·1	12·3
Assets			
Households with no car	53·9	20·1	83·4
Socio-economic group			
Economically active and retired males – unskilled manual workers	8·3	10·0	27·8
Special needs			
Population aged 0–14	23·0	7·4	35·7
Pensioner households (of 1 or 2 persons with 1 or 2 persons of pensionable age)	27·2	11·9	46·8
Population born in 'New Commonwealth' with one or both parents born in N C, or born in G B with both parents born in N C	3·6	7·4	17·4
Housing tenure			
Households in accommodation rented from local authority	31·1	37·9	99·3
Households in privately rented unfurnished accommodation	17·5	19·2	57·9
Households in privately rented furnished accommodation	5·1	10·4	26·4

Source: Holtermann, 1975, Table I.

Table 4.5. Geographical distribution of worst 5 per cent of urban enumeration districts on selected indicators

	All urban EDs in Great Britain	Households overcrowded >1·5 persons per room	Households lacking exclusive use of all basic amenities	Males unemployed but seeking work or sick	Households with no car
Conurbations					
London Group A	8·6	21·8	21·7	2·9	12·9
London Group B	10·4	5·5	1·9	0·4	0·4
Tyneside	2·0	1·3	4·2	6·7	7·2
West Yorkshire	4·3	3·0	2·6	4·2	8·6
Merseyside	2·7	1·5	5·4	9·0	5·0
South-East Lancashire	5·8	1·9	9·6	6·1	8·9
West Midlands	4·8	5·6	4·7	2·8	2·9
Clydeside	4·3	37·3	13·5	23·1	25·7
Regions					
Rest of South-East	14·9	2·0	1·6	5·3	2·0
Rest of Northern	4·1	0·8	5·1	8·9	5·6
Rest of Yorks & Humber	5·0	0·2	6·8	5·0	4·7
Rest of North-West	5·4	0·6	4·0	5·0	2·7
Rest of West Midlands	4·2	0·5	1·6	0·8	0·3
East Midlands	5·0	1·0	4·9	2·3	1·9
East Anglia	2·0	0·1	0·4	1·3	0·2
South-West	5·3	0·3	0·7	1·8	0·5
Rest of Scotland	6·8	16·3	8·3	11·4	10·3
Wales	4·3	0·3	3·1	5·2	0·3

Source: Holtermann, 1975, Table II. All figures are percentages of the total in Great Britain.

Note: London Group A comprises the inner boroughs of Camden, City, Hackney, Hammersmith, Haringey, Islington, Kensington and Chelsea, Lambeth, Lewisham, Newham, Southwark, Tower Hamlets, Wandsworth and Westminster; Group B is the rest of the Greater London Council area.

4.4), 21·7 of the worst 5 per cent on lack of basic amenities, and so on. The first column shows the percentage distribution of all urban EDs, thus providing a basis for comparison of the distribution of the worst 5 per cent. If the worst EDs on any indicator were distributed geographically in proportion to all urban EDs, the percentage would be precisely as in the first column. As the other four columns show, this is not the case.

The figures in Table 4.5 show the degree of disadvantage (or advantage) of the area in question, with respect to its share of the worst 5 per cent of EDs. Thus inner London's share of worst EDs on overcrowding (21·8 pr cent) is almost three times its share of all urban EDs (8·6 per cent); inner London has far more than would be its 'fair share' in an equal distribution, or worst EDs distributed in proportion to all EDs. However, inner London is not so disadvantaged on all conditions: as the table shows, it has much less than its 'fair share' of EDs in the worst 5 per cent on male unemployment. Similar comparisons can be made with respect to other conurbations and regions. As we have seen in other cases in this book, performance on different criteria of human well-being often shows conflicting results.

But general tendencies emerge from the British data, as elsewhere. The figures for all eighteen indicators highlight the degree of deprivation in certain parts of urban Britain. As Holtermann (1975, p. 37) summarizes the situation:

> The most striking feature . . . is that Clydeside consistently has a very much more than proportionate share of the worst five per cent of EDs on nearly all kinds of deprivation, and so to a lesser extent does the rest of 'urban' Scotland. Inner London (the A boroughs) has a more than proportionate share of most types of housing deprivation . . . The other English conurbations also have disproportionately large numbers of the worst EDs on many indicators, but rarely to the same extent as Clydeside.

Urban England outside the conurbations consistently shows less than its 'fair share' of worst EDs. Within the conurbations, the core local-authority areas account for a disproportionate (larger) share of the worst EDs than their share of all EDs would warrant. Urban deprivation, as identified by the type of conditions listed in Table

201

4.4, is unevenly distributed and with a marked tendency towards concentration in specific geographical areas.

The DOE study deliberately avoids the calculation of a composite indicator of deprivation, in the manner attempted elsewhere in this book. Holtermann (1975, p. 34) considers such a measure to be misleading when so few aspects of deprivation are included, and in any event wishes to avoid the value judgements implicit in the weightings built into an aggregate indicator. Thus, a more simple approach is adopted to investigate the 'multiple' aspect of deprivation, involving the identification of overlaps among deprived areas on different conditions. Some results are presented with respect to a limited number of overlaps – among the worst areas on overcrowding, male unemployment and exclusive use of basic amenities. The conclusion is that, 'The geographical distribution of EDs with more than one kind of deprivation is, if anything, even more dominated by the conurbation, especially Clydeside and inner London, than that of individual deprivations.' (Holtermann, 1975, p. 40.)

What kind of patterns are formed by deprived areas within individual cities? One example, that of London, must be sufficient.

We will begin with a composite index (despite Holtermann's reservations), calculated for the thirty-three London boroughs. The data come from a recent country-wide study of personal social service authorities, by the Department of Health and Social Security (Imber, 1977). Ten conditions were identified as indicating need for personal social services. These are listed in Table 4.6, with the national average and figures for the best (Harrow) and worst (Islington) boroughs overall. These figures in themselves provide a vivid illustration of the degree of inequality in living standards between the inner city and outer suburbs of London.

A composite measure of the overall level of need has been derived by summing standard scores on the ten conditions for each borough. The results are shown in Figure 4.7. The higher the index in a positive direction, the greater the need. The geographical pattern is remarkably regular, with an almost continuous ring of outer boroughs in the most favourable of the four categories recognized, and a solid inner core of greatest need, broken only by the City of London.

Table 4.6. Conditions used to measure need for personal social services

Condition (percentages)	National average	Borough of Harrow	Borough of Islington
Households with more than 1 person per room	6·6	3·8	15·1
Households in privately rented furnished property	5·2	4·7	19·2
Households lacking at least one basic amenity	18·4	7·1	48·9
Pensioners living alone	24·7	19·1	33·5
Persons out of employment	4·9	3·4	6·0
Unskilled workers in the economically active popn	7·3	3·2	10·6
Married women working, with children under 5	31·3	28·5	51·4
Lone-parent families with children	9·4	7·0	17·0
Married couples with 4 or more children	4·2	2·9	4·7
Households in council rented accommodation	29·1	11·0	28·7

Source: Imber, 1977.

Note: all the conditions are expressed as percentages of the appropriate population. Data from the *Census of Population*, 1971.

This impression of regularity hides two important geographical aspects of deprivation at the intra-metropolitan level, however. One is that there can be considerable variations within territories the size of London boroughs. To illustrate this, we shall return to the results of the DOE study. As an extension of the research described above, the DOE has identified EDs with various overlap character-istics. One of these overlaps reveals areas of housing deprivation, by the following criteria (based on the judgement of the research workers):

1. Lacking bath: cut-off 12·5%
2. More than 1·5 persons per room: cut-off 4·2%
3. Lacking exclusive use of three basic amenities: cut-off 45%
4. Private rented accommodation: cut-off 30·4%

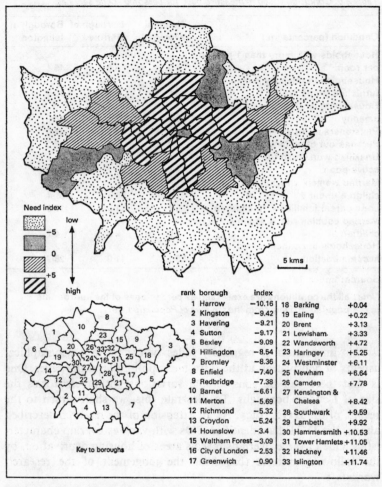

rank	borough	index			
1	Harrow	−10.16	18	Barking	+0.04
2	Kingston	−9.42	19	Ealing	+0.22
3	Havering	−9.21	20	Brent	+3.13
4	Sutton	−9.17	21	Lewisham	+3.33
5	Bexley	−9.09	22	Wandsworth	+4.72
6	Hillingdon	−8.54	23	Haringey	+5.25
7	Bromley	−8.36	24	Westminster	+6.11
8	Enfield	−7.40	25	Newham	+6.64
9	Redbridge	−7.38	26	Camden	+7.78
10	Barnet	−6.61	27	Kensington &	
11	Merton	−5.69		Chelsea	+8.42
12	Richmond	−5.32	28	Southwark	+9.59
13	Croydon	−5.24	29	Lambeth	+9.92
14	Hounslow	−3.4	30	Hammersmith	+10.53
15	Waltham Forest	−3.09	31	Tower Hamlets	+11.05
16	City of London	−2.53	32	Hackney	+11.46
17	Greenwich	−0.90	33	Islington	+11.74

Figure 4.7. Need for personal social services in Greater London boroughs, measured by a composite index. (Source of data: Imber, 1977, p. 42.)

An ED conforming to all these criteria would have at least 12·5 per cent of households without a bath, 4·2 per cent in severe overcrowding, and so on. The incidence of such EDs provides a picture of the geographical pattern of housing deprivation.

The pattern is summarized at two different spatial scales in Figure 4.8. The top map shows proportion of EDs in each London borough falling into the category of housing deprivation as defined above. The proportions range from 37·1 per cent of all EDs in a state of housing deprivation in Islington to 0·3 per cent in Barking and Merton. The map suggests the existence of a solid block of poor-housing areas occupying the inner part of Greater London, similar to but not identical with that of need in Figure 4.7. The bottom map identifies individual wards within the boroughs, in which at least half of the EDs suffer housing deprivation by the four criteria above. Now it can be seen that the pattern is, in fact, one of a scatter of deprived areas. There is one marked concentration centred on Islington in the northern part of inner London, but otherwise wards with bad housing tend to represent local pockets of poor environmental quality rather than part of a more extensive zone of contiguous wards.

The second element in the geographical complexity of the incidence of urban deprivation is the absence of a close coincidence between different criteria. This is important because implicit in the popular conception of 'multiple deprivation' is an expectation to the contrary – namely, that a certain set of social and economic problems invariably coincide. The DHSS report referred to above shows that this is not so. At a national level the need indicators by no means always correlate highly with one another; there are even a few negative associations (Imber, 1977, p. 20). A similar if less marked discrepancy exists within Greater London. Further evidence along these lines is provided by the *Social Atlas of London* (Shepherd, Westaway and Lee, 1974). In housing, households without an indoor lavatory are concentrated in the East End, especially the Borough of Newham, whereas overcrowding is found more frequently in northern and western parts of inner London (including Islington, Kensington-Chelsea and the eastern part of the Borough of Brent). Car ownership displays a pattern of concentric zones, with low levels in inner London rising to high levels in the outer suburbs.

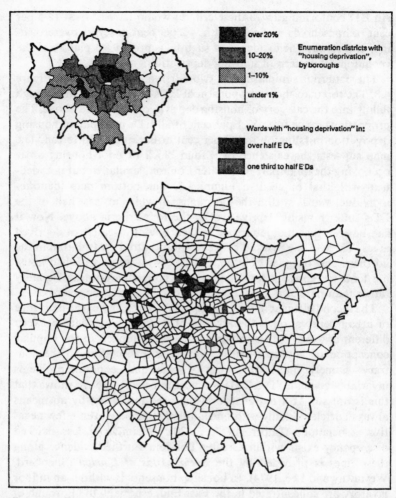

Figure 4.8. The pattern of housing deprivation in Greater London, by boroughs and by wards. (Source of data: Department of the Environment, 1976.)

As a final illustration, we may look briefly at the incidence of aspects of deprivation at the most local level – by enumeration districts. The London Borough of Tower Hamlets is, by most criteria, among the worst-off local authority areas in the country. A preliminary analysis of some possible criteria of social deprivation at the census E D level reveals relatively little overlap. Four conditions were selected, indicative of social and economic deprivation: overcrowding (proportion of households with more than 1·5 persons per room), households lacking the three basic amenities (hot water, bath and inside W C), male unemployment, and proportion of households without a car. Mapping the worst ten enumeration districts on these four measures revealed only two areas where as many as three conditions overlapped. And there were only six overlaps of two conditions. Social problems are thus less geographically coincident and more scattered in their occurrence than is often supposed. The more we disaggregate the population geographically, the more social conditions will reflect distinctive local circumstances, such as the pattern of immigrant settlement or the progress of urban renewal. In Tower Hamlets, for example, areas with people of low economic status and living in overcrowded conditions appear otherwise well housed by the criterion of possession of basic amenities, simply because they live in modern council flats. Whether these 'tower blocks' do in fact constitute good family housing is another question.

The spatial arrangement of deprived areas in London clearly does not conform to any single, simple pattern. The D O E report similar findings from a study of Merseyside. They conclude that 'the pattern of spatial association between different kinds of deprivation may vary significantly from place to place, being the outcome of a complex combination of many forces, some of which can operate anywhere while some are specific to particular places.' (Holtermann, 1975, p. 42.)

We may now return to the problem of policy, and the underlying question of cause and effect. Recent years have seen a growing emphasis on what we have termed area-based policies in Britain's urban areas. These policies necessarily involve the delimitation of target or priority areas. In London, attempts have already been made to identify 'education priority areas' and areas of 'housing stress' (Knox, 1975, pp. 14–17), on the basis of which resources are allocated in a process of 'positive discrimination'. Concepts like multiple deprivation have been viewed as a means of more broadly identifying priority areas for programmes aimed at interrelated groups of problems, after the fashion of America's Model Cities programme. The past decade has seen a succession of area-based programmes to investigate or combat inner-city deprivation in Britain, including the Inner Areas Studies, the Neighbourhood Schemes, the Community Development Projects and the Comprehensive Community Programmes.

The very number of these programmes is itself indicative of their experimental nature. Like the regional-development strategies of the 1960s, inner-city policy has been in an almost continuous state of flux with changing governments, ministers, fashions and academic wisdom. Against official claims of modest success is the reality of a continuing problem. The most severe critics of these programmes, battle-weary from work on the Community Development Projects, claim that 'despite their range and number, they have done nothing to improve the conditions of those working-class areas as measured by income levels, unemployment rates, housing conditions and so on'. (Harford, 1977, p. 99.) Clearly, something is amiss.

Confidence in the ability of area-based policies to alleviate deprivation is based on a number of beliefs as to the origins of the conditions of concern and of the impact of the particular approach adopted. Among these is the assumption that policies confined to specific 'problem' areas will catch most of the deprived individuals in society, that single problems such as poor housing and low income have a cumulative effect so that the spatial concentration and coincidence of different dimensions of deprivation reinforce each other, and that the appearance of problems in particular areas is indicative of the fact that the area (and its inhabitants) are somehow instrumental in causing the problems. If these expectations do not accord with reality, then the effectiveness of area-based policies is called into question.

The DOE investigation summarized above does in fact cast doubt on some of these beliefs. A study of the spatial distribution of deprived *individuals* shows that the degree of concentration in deprived *areas* is really quite low. Holtermann (1975, p. 39) provides figures: only 23 per cent of individuals sharing or lacking hot water actually live in the worst 5 per cent of EDs on this criterion, only 30 per cent of individuals in households without a bath live in the worst 5 per cent of EDs, and so on. For the worst 15 per cent of EDs the proportion of deprived individuals on these two criteria actually living there, are 53 per cent and 64 per cent respectively. On some criteria the proportion in the worst areas is even lower: for male unemployment it is only 16 per cent in the worst 5 per cent of EDs and 36 per cent in the worst 15 per cent; for households without a car it is 7 per cent and 21 per cent respectively. Thus policies confined to the worst *areas* will fail to help many (probably most) of the *individuals* suffering that particular aspect of deprivation. Such policies might, then, be regarded as unjust, as well as largely ineffectual.

The belief that there is some kind of local syndrome of deprivation, arising from the spatial coincidence of different problem conditions, runs counter to the observation that overlap between deprived areas on different criteria is far from complete. The evidence from London cited above is a case in point. Other local studies cast further doubt on the assumption that problem areas comprise neat amalgams of sets of similar interrelated problems. Hamnett (1976, p. 11) cites a study of the London Boroughs of Newham and Southwark by Hatch and Sherrott: 'areas suffering from multiple deprivation do not seem to form a quite separate category easily distinguished from other less deprived areas. It is more realistic to think of deprivation as multi- rather than uni-dimensional, and of deprived areas as being of different kinds containing different combinations of deprivations.' Hamnett (1976, p. 12) also cites the work of Edwards in Birmingham, where two different types of 'stress areas' could be identified, characterized on the one hand by physical decay, poor housing, overcrowding and predominantly manual occupations, and on the other by a mobile, transient population of non-family households and immigrants. Research on the American city similarly shows different combinations of problems afflicting different areas (D. M. Smith, 1973, pp. 127–32). Obviously, there are different forces at work, on different people in different places. Accepting some monolithic concept, like multiple deprivation, as the key to understanding and to

209

policy formulation obscures this fact. There may well be some clearly connected groups of problems, recognition of which is critical both to finding the origins of individual deprivation areally expressed and to the design of effective policy. But preoccupation with the areal coincidence of common sets of conditions distracts attention from the possible uniqueness of local situations. Conditions in a particular place will be a response to both local (internal) and broader (external) forces.

This leads us to the third of the beliefs underpinning area-based policies, namely that the spatial manifestation implies an areally-specific cause. At its simplest, this takes the form of an argument that the deprivation evident in a particular territory is a direct expression of some inadequacy in the people inhabiting that territory. They may be viewed as having a 'culture of poverty' in which pathological individuals or deviant groups are unable or unwilling to cope with the demands of 'normal society', or are trapped in a 'cycle of deprivation' in which individual handicaps and inadequacies are passed on from one generation to another. But these arguments tend to beg the question of how individuals, families or groups found themselves in particular deprived circumstances in specific areas in the first place. Some types of people may be led (or forced) to live in the slums or the ghetto, because of poverty or racial discrimination; they bring with them certain characteristics that place them at a disadvantage in a competitive society and reduce their residential choice. The congregation of many such people in the same area may exacerbate the original conditions of deprivation, and perhaps spawn others. But the origins lie in society at large rather than in the areas that the deprived happen to occupy.

Superficial explanations of localized deprivation, based solely on the character of the locality and its people, are now giving way to a more structural and less explicitly spatial interpretation. The key is to be found in the economic mechanisms that drive the markets for labour and housing in the kind of quasi-capitalist or 'mixed' economy that prevails in Britain. Important changes in occupational structure and the location of employment have taken place in British cities, especially the London metropolis, during the past two decades. Employment in manufacturing in the inner city has declined, with the encouragement of planners seeking to reduce congestion by dispersal from London. This appears to be creating more of a polarized occupational (and class) structure, with well-paid managerial/office/professional jobs for commuters from the suburbs and only unskilled service occupations for the local people. Something of this process at the national level was suggested in the reference to the findings of Westaway (1974a and 1974b) in the previous chapter. London's dockland is a case in point: the closure of the docks and decline of manufacturing in the East End has greatly reduced employment opportunities for local residents. Added to this is the difficulty of getting to jobs elsewhere, when car ownership is low and public transport not necessarily geared to local needs.

Low incomes, of course, place people at a disadvantage in the housing market. Unable to get either a council house or a mortgage for owner-occupancy, those in poorly paid jobs have no real choice other than looking to the less sought-after council flats or to cheap rental property. These are often in inner-city areas with unattractive environments, where a process of physical deterioration may have already set in. Such areas may also suffer from older, overcrowded schools unable to attract the best-trained teachers. Teenagers with poor education and few skills find employment prospects limited (and, increasingly, non-existent). There is delinquency and alienation, which may have racial undertones in areas where immigrant populations are concentrated. Thus, some form of cycle of deprivation may arise. But its origins must be traced to the economic mechanisms that deprive people of remunerative work and decent homes, mechanisms that operate independently of the particular geographical spaces occupied by the deprived population.

There are obvious similarities between this argument and the interpretation of inequality in the American city in the previous section of this chapter. There is evidence in the British metropolis of a tendency towards spatial polarization of the kind observed in the American city. It has gone further in the United States, largely because greater mobility (higher car ownership and more urban freeways) and less restrictive planning have given greater flexibility to urban expansion. But the trend is there nevertheless: towards replacement of the earlier pattern of vast working-class neighbourhoods and small pockets of affluence, typical of the nineteenth-century city, by more localized areas of deprivation in the inner city enclosed by the expansive middle-class suburbs and enclaves of well-to-do workers in their subsidized council houses. This spatial pattern of unequal life chance is essentially one of unequal access in the labour and housing markets, which may be exacerbated by local disadvantage with respect to access to social services, recreation facilities and other sources of need satisfaction.

In 1977, there was a basic reappraisal of British planning policy with respect to urban deprivation. After years of encouraging industry to leave the inner city for New Towns, overspill estates and (nationally) for areas of high unemployment in peripheral regions, the emphasis now is on attracting jobs back to the inner city – especially London. A major element in present government policy is the designation of areas for 'partnership' schemes between central and local government. Seven of these had been announced by the end of 1977 – three in London (Lambeth, Docklands and Hackney-Islington) and others in Liverpool, Birmingham, Manchester-Salford and Newcastle-Gateshead. Among other things, these schemes empower local authorities to make loans and declare 'industrial improvement areas', in an attempt to attract new sources of employment. These partnership schemes will get a major share of government spending on the inner-city problem, planned to rise to £125 million in 1979.

What are the prospects for the industrial revival of the inner city? Some people see the solution in the encouragement of small business, in the absence of enthusiasm for inner-city locations on the part of large firms. Inner-city areas like the East End of London have long acted as seedbeds for new enterprises. If this function can be encouraged, it only needs a few new firms to grow to make a major impact on the local unemployment problem, or so the argument goes. But against this it is pointed out that small firms find it increasingly difficult to survive, let alone prosper and expand, in an economy now dominated by large, often multinational corporations. The impact of a merger or the closure of a branch plant can wipe out in a day the equivalent of the new jobs created over the years by dozens of small firms, carefully nurtured by public funds. The key to local employment generation in the modern world is control over major manufacturing

212

corporations and service-sector institutions. In a nation like Britain some of this is in the public sector and its location can be used to promote social objectives, as in regional-development policy. But much remains in private hands – and these not always British.

The fundamental problem facing the inner city is, thus, that it is not ultimately within the power of the planners to counteract the major structural forces operating in a largely free-enterprise economy. Hence the survival of areas characterized by economic and social deprivation, not only year after year but for generations. Holland (1976a, p. 47) points out the remarkable coincidence between the present socially deprived areas of the inner London boroughs and those noted by Karl Marx in the first volume of *Capital:*

> This century-long perspective should encourage considerable scepticism of the kind of intervention now being adopted to cope with the problems of inner urban areas in both Western Europe and the United States. Local solutions will not work unless related to the wider spatial distribution of resources in the economy. And in the twentieth century, despite new policies, the capitalist firm remains largely free to determine the location of investment, jobs and incomes.

Area-based policies of social regeneration or economic revival may help some people in some places. More spending on schools where they are badly equipped and staffed can help children in these areas. Sub-standard housing can be repaired, parks created and streets cleaned up. And in Britain the welfare state can assure people of a basic minimum of social support in times of trouble. But unless fundamental changes are made in institutions, especially the labour and housing markets, it is hard to see much real impact being made on localized deprivation in Britain's urban areas. Inner-city deprivation may thus have to be accepted as one of the inevitable consequences of the maintenance of capitalism in Britain in this particular period of its historic evolution.

Lima, Peru: Inequality in the Third-World City

The world-wide phenomenon of urbanization and metropolitan growth takes on different forms in different circumstances. In the

213

underdeveloped world the focus has been very much on the primate or leading city within each nation. The rate of urban growth is such that even the most up-to-date census figures may substantially underestimate both the number of urban residents and the dominance of the primate city. Thus in Peru, Lima's 1972 census population of 3·3 million is ten times that of the nation's second city, yet today (1979) Lima may have already exceeded 4 million. Other examples of Latin America's huge primate cities are Buenos Aires, with 8·4 million (1970) or ten times Argentina's second city, and Mexico City with almost 7 million people in 1970 or almost six times Mexico's second city. Less typical, but similarly indicative of rapid urbanization, is the situation in Brazil with two major metropolises – Rio de Janeiro with 6 million in 1970 (1·8 million in 1940) and São Paulo with 4·3 million (1·3 million in 1940).

A particular manifestation of Third World urbanization is the growth of so-called squatter settlements. These are known alternatively as *barriadas* in Peru, *favelas* in Brazil, *ranchos* in Venezuela; other terms are used for similar features of African and South-East Asian cities. These settlements are usually, though not always, situated around the fringe of the city, often on land with steep slopes, or otherwise unsuitable for more conventional urban development. In so far as the inhabitants of the squatter settlements experience greatly inferior living standards to those of most other urban residents, the concentration around the fringe reverses the pattern of inner-city poverty and suburban affluence typical of cities in the advanced capitalist world. The emerging form of the Third World city, the growing prominence of squatter settlements, and the degree of inequality among different classes of people reveal quite clearly the inability of the societies concerned to cope with the process of urbanization. The existence of millions of people in squatter settlements reflects a failure of societal institutions as well as scarce resources.

We may gain some understanding of the nature and scale of the problem in general, via the specific case of Lima, Peru. This is in many respects a classic situation of pressure on the primate city. Some of the background was provided in the previous chapter: poverty in the countryside, especially in the *sierra*, has prompted large-scale migration of population, the major recipient being the

214

metropolis of Lima-Callao. Figure 4.9 shows the birthplace (by department) of people living in the provinces of Lima and Callao at the time of the 1972 census. The map emphasizes that, although neighbouring departments have contributed most to the population of Lima-Callao, migrants have been drawn from all over the country. As many as 42 per cent of the population of the two metropolitan provinces were born beyond the department of Lima and Callao, making almost 1·4 million such migrants. The migrants themselves tend to be relatively well educated compared with the national population at large, few come from the humblest or most impoverished backgrounds, and they are disproportionately from younger age groups (Gilbert, 1974, pp. 112–14; Lowder, 1970 and 1974). Thus the countryside has lost disproportionately from its more productive and energetic population; Lima gains from this process of selectivity. This accentuates qualitative differences between core and periphery in terms of population attributes, especially if the migrants can find more effective outlets for their abilities in the city than in the countryside.

Migrants to Lima do not typically find their way directly to the *barriadas*, or *pueblos jovenes* (young towns) as the Peruvian authorities now prefer to term the squatter settlements. They tend first to settle in the *tugurios*, or tenement areas of the inner city, where cheap if squalid rental accommodation is available. Then, after a few years, the family may move out, often as part of a group engaged in a carefully planned occupation of vacant land somewhere on the city's fringe. The land is parcelled out, crude shelters of matting or whatever else is available are erected, literally overnight, to be replaced gradually by more permanent structures as time and resources permit. In other instances the move to the *pueblos jovenes* is more truly spontaneous and individual, but the emergence of this pattern of settlement is generally somewhat more premeditated and organized than the superficially chaotic appearance of the areas might suggest. The process is described in more detail by Dwyer (1975, pp. 188–208) and in various accounts by Mangin and Turner (e.g. 1969). The *pueblos jovenes* almost invariably develop without such basic services as water supply, sewage disposal and electricity; it may take many years before this deficiency is rectified by city government or

215

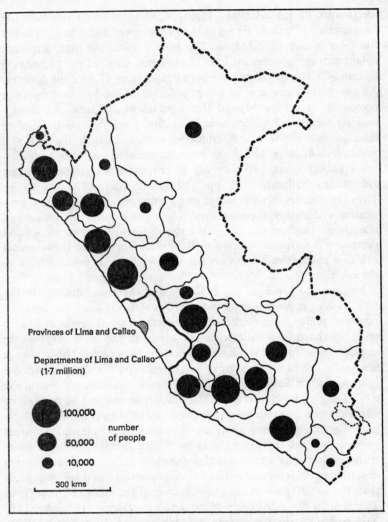

Figure 4.9. Distribution of residents of Lima and Callao provinces, Peru, by department of birth (excluding Lima and Callao), 1972. (Source of data: *Censos Nacionales de Población*, 1972.)

by the residents themselves, and most areas are still deficient with respect to utilities.

Table 4.7 summarizes the impact of population growth and the emergence of the *pueblos jovenes* over the past two decades. The 1972 census recorded over 800,000 people in the *pueblos jovenes*, or virtually a quarter of the population of the metropolis compared with less than 10 per cent in 1956. If the present (1979) population of Lima-Callao is about 4 million, the population of the *pueblos jovenes* now probably exceeds a million, or roughly the population of the entire city at the beginning of the 1950s.

The physical growth of the Lima-Callao metropolis and the distribution of *pueblos jovenes* population is illustrated in Figures 4.10 and 4.11. Three main stages can be recognized in the development of the *pueblos jovenes*, which have been responsible for perhaps four fifths of the physical expansion in recent years, nearly half of it on land not officially scheduled for development (Dwyer, 1975, p. 35). The first phase, in the mid 1950s, involved the settlement of areas quite close to central Lima and Callao and their major industrial zones. Then, towards the end of the 1950s, large-scale development began well to the north, with a series of *barriadas* growing up in the area shown on Figure 4.10 as Independencia, Comas and Carabayllo. The third phase has shifted the focus of development to the south, especially the district of Villa Maria del Triunfo, where vast settlements are spreading across the sand dunes that remind the visitor of Lima's almost desert climate. Today, the *pueblos jovenes* occupy roughly the

Table 4.7. *Population growth of metropolitan Lima-Callao and of the* pueblos jovenes, *1956–72*

	Metropolitan area number	Pueblos jovenes number	% of total
1956	1,397,000	119,886	8·6
1959	1,652,000	236,716	14·3
1961	1,845,910	316,829	17·2
1970	2,972,787	761,755	25·6
1972	3,302,523	805,117	24·4

Source: Boletin de Analisis Demografico, 1975, No. 15: *La Población del Area Metropolitana de Lima Callao*, Oficina Nacional de Estadistica y Censos; Lima, Peru.

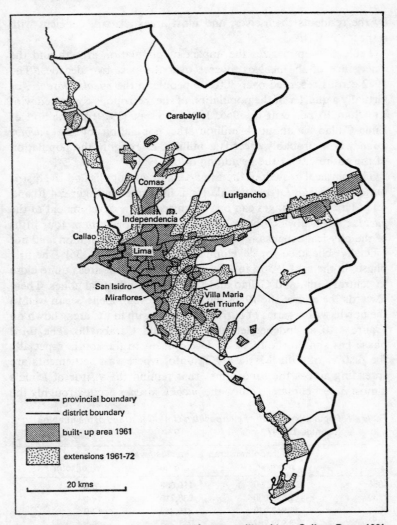

Figure 4.10. The physical expansion of metropolitan Lima-Callao, Peru, 1961–72. (Source of data: Oficina Nacional de Estadistica y Censos.)

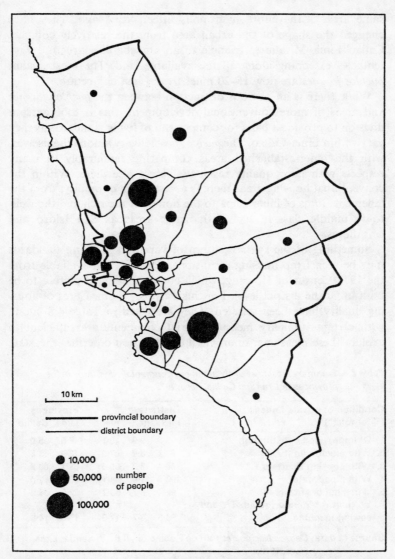

Figure 4.11. Population of *pueblos jovenes* in metropolitan Lima-Callao 1972, by districts. (Source of data: *Censos Nacionales de Población*, 1972.)

same area as the entire metropolis fifteen years ago. They have changed the shape of the urban area from the relatively compact Callao–Lima–Miraflores triangle to an amoeba-like structure with tentacles extending along all the available land. The most distant *pueblos jovenes* are now 15–20 miles from Lima city centre.

While there is an obvious distinction between the *pueblos jovenes* and areas of more conventional development, this is too coarse a division to provide a basis for comparison of living standards as they vary within Lima-Callao. The *pueblos jovenes* vary among themselves, with the older-established areas comparing favourably in many respects with poor quality residential areas elsewhere. Within the conventional housing areas there is a vast range of quality, from the tenement slums of inner Lima to the homes of the rich and the well-to-do middle class in such fashionable areas as San Isidro and Miraflores.

Something of the spatial pattern of variation in living standards may be seen from housing conditions. Statistics are available from the 1972 Census of Housing, which enable a detailed picture to be built up at the district level. For this purpose, six measures of housing quality have been selected. They are listed in Table 4.8, along with certain summary measures. Brief comments are sufficient to explain these measures. Improvised construction describes the state

Table 4.8. Summary measures of six urban environmental conditions in the provinces of Lima and Callao, Peru, 1972

Condition of private houses (% of total*)	Districts			Provinces	
	max.	min.	mean	Lima	Callao
1. Of improvised construction	25·3	0·0	6·1	7·5	5·0
2. With electric light	97·2	3·9	67·9	72·9	85·5
3. With cooking quarters	86·4	38·3	65·6	63·7	69·8
4. With piped water	100·0	1·9	58·1	60·4	62·0
5. With bath or shower	92·4	8·7	53·7	52·8	54·2
6. Without refrigerator, radio, TV and sewing machine	36·3	3·7	17·3	17·0	14·6

Source of data: *Censos Nacionales:* VII de Población, II de Vivienda; Lima, Peru, 1972.

*All data refer to occupied private houses except for condition 1 which includes all private houses. All measures are percentages of the total number of houses concerned.

of many dwellings within the *pueblos jovenes*, especially those most recently developed; the proportion of houses in this category is 7·5 per cent in Lima Province and 5·0 per cent in Callao (district average: 6·1 per cent) but it rises to over a quarter of all houses in the district of Carabayllo. Electricity is important not only for lighting but also to power domestic appliances; most dwellings in the metropolis have electricity, but many of the *pueblos jovenes* have no such service: in Carabayllo over 97 per cent of houses are without electric light. Kerosene lamps and candles are the main sources of lighting for people without electricity. Special cooking quarters (some kind of kitchen) are found in about two thirds of the houses in the metropolis, but the figure falls to half or less in districts with large concentrations of *pueblos jovenes*, such as Carabayllo, Independencia, Comas and (lowest of all) Villa Maria del Triunfo. Most dwellings without kitchens have no source of electricity and gas; occupants tend to use portable kerosene stoves, with the attendant inconvenience of having to carry the fuel into the home. About three fifths of houses in Lima-Callao have piped water, those that do not being mainly in the *pueblos jovenes*. Where piped water is lacking, people have either to carry water from a communal source or rely on deliveries by truck. The availability of a bath or shower – and also a flush lavatory – depends to a large extent on piped water. Half Lima-Callao homes have a bath or shower, but the figure falls to less than one in ten in the districts of Carabayllo and Villa Maria del Triunfo. The final measure identifies houses without any of the four 'basic' appliances of refrigerator, radio, television and sewing machine: again, Carabayllo and Villa Maria del Triunfo appear as the most deprived districts, with 34 and 36 per cent, respectively, lacking all these goods.

Figure 4.12 maps the six measures of housing quality by districts (omitting those areas of Lima and Callao provinces not part of the metropolis). Shading has been confined to the built-up areas of districts around the fringe, where settlement is restricted by relief. The maps show a distinct pattern, with high positive scores (good housing) in the districts south of central Lima and high negative scores around the metropolitan periphery where the *pueblos jovenes* are chiefly concentrated. This pattern is displayed with particular

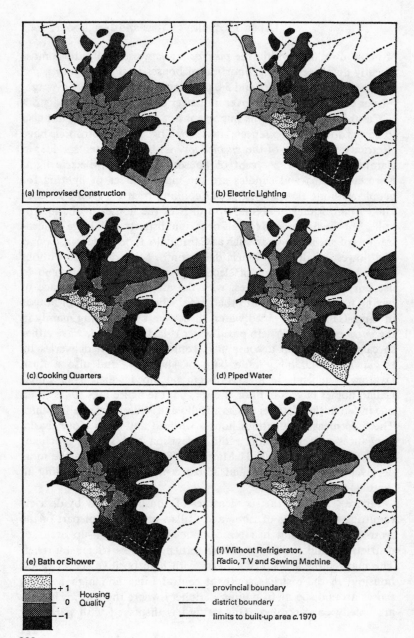

(a) Improvised Construction

(b) Electric Lighting

(c) Cooking Quarters

(d) Piped Water

(e) Bath or Shower

(f) Without Refrigerator, Radio, T V and Sewing Machine

Housing Quality
+1
0
−1

provincial boundary
district boundary
limits to built-up area c.1970

222

clarity in Figure 4.13, which shows a composite index of urban environmental quality derived from summing the standard scores on the six individual housing measures. As was suggested at the beginning of this section, the geography of living standards (as captured here by housing data) reverses the picture in the advanced capitalist world: concentric zones radiate outwards from affluent inner suburbs to the poor periphery, with the northern and southern wedges of *pueblos jovenes* occupying the lowest levels. The inner-city slums are too localized to show up on a map based on district data.

The contrasts in life quality at the extremes in Lima are hinted at by the summary figures in Table 4.8. But these are only part of the reality of the stark differences between the *pueblos jovenes* in places like Carabayllo and Villa Maria del Triunfo, on the one hand, and the well-to-do suburbs of San Isidro and Miraflores on the other. In the former there are people who are building their own homes, bit by bit, subject to the vagaries of uncertain employment and income. Basic amenities are lacking, and in the hillside settlements the heavy downpour of rain that occurs every few years is a threat to the stability of many homes. Social services are inadequate for people's needs, medical care being a particular problem because of the inconvenience of facility location in relation to the *pueblos jovenes* (Dwyer, 1975, pp. 251–2). The other side of the city is represented by the mansions of the business and military élite, and by the very considerable estates of the well-off middle class. In the eastern part of San Isidro district, for example, the Corpac area comprises acres of stylish houses that could well be the envy of affluent Europeans – elaborate, individually designed homes occupying a large part of their 500-square-metre lots, and amply supplied with servants. The bars on the windows and the presence of guard dogs provide a vivid reminder of the unequal distribution of property, rather like the white residential areas in South African cities.

Figure 4.12. Variation among districts in urban environmental quality, within metropolitan Lima-Callao, 1972. The data are expressed in standard deviates, calculated so that in each case high positive scores (and light shading) indicate the most favourable conditions. (Source of data: see Table 4.7.)

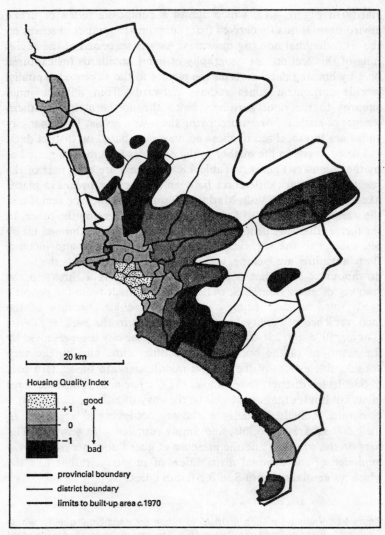

Figure 4.13. A composite index of urban environmental quality by districts in metropolitan Lima-Callao, 1972. (Source of data: see Table 4.7.)

Lima is a highly unequal city, in a highly unequal nation and society. Just how unequally income is distributed can be judged from data obtained by sample survey in 1967 (it is doubtful whether much change has taken place since then, despite the self-styled revolutionary government). It is estimated that half the income goes to the richest 13 per cent of families. Over 10 per cent goes to the richest 0·7 per cent, with incomes of over 50,000 *soles*.* At the other end of the scale, almost 20 per cent of families earned less than 1000 *soles* and, together, accounted for only 1·4 per cent of all income. Figure 4.14 shows a Lorenz curve of income distribution in Lima based on shares of twenty income groups. The Gini coefficient of 57 on the 0-to-100 scale underlines the high degree of inequality. This is the income distribution that drives the unbalanced domestic structure of private production and consumption, to which reference was made in Chapter 3.

Given the 'revolutionary' aspirations of the present regime, some serious assault on the problem of unequal income distribution might be expected. But the redistributional impact of the reforms initiated is rather modest, as was suggested in the previous chapter. A Peruvian source has estimated that only 3–4 per cent of total national income will be transferred and almost all of this will take place within the wealthiest quarter of the population; the effect of the reforms on the poorest segment of the population is virtually negligible (White, 1976, p. 61).

Within the metropolis, income redistribution can be effected on a territorial basis via local taxation. Up to 1973, each of the thirty-nine districts operated autonomously in budgetary and fiscal matters, with resources available based largely on property taxes and thus reflecting existing affluence or poverty. This fragmentation was then replaced by an integration of districts into a single provincial treasury. This provides scope for inter-area transfers of resources, but the redistributive effects appear not to have greatly benefited the poorest districts. White (1976, p. 65–6) shows net transfers during 1973–4 from five districts, including the wealthy San Isidro and Miraflores, with most benefits going to a mixture of middle- and

*Per month. (The official exchange rate in mid 1976 was 40 *soles* to the $US.)

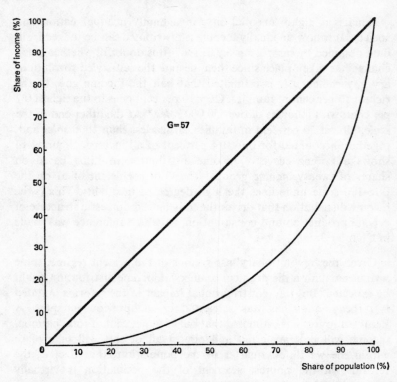

Figure 4.14. Lorenz curve of income distribution in metropolitan Lima, 1967. (Source: Gianella, 1970.)

low-income districts. But on a per capita basis some of the neediest districts (eg Independencia and Villa Maria del Triunfo) received the least, while the relatively wealthy beach districts received most. Failure to implement more radical redistribution of resources may reflect the attitudes and class affiliation of those responsible for the decision-making process in the Provincial Council of Lima. 60 per cent of the councillors reside in San Isidro and Miraflores, the two wealthiest residential districts in the metropolitan area: 'Virtually all are businessmen and professionals. Under these circumstances it seems most unlikely that the new budgetary system will reflect the

226

diverse needs of the thirty-nine districts, especially those of the *pueblos jovenes* whose preferences for public goods probably differ most from those of the majority of provincial councillors.' (White, 1976, p. 65.) The new method of resource allocation may thus be more of a symbolic gesture than a forceful mechanism for income redistribution. Obviously, more participation in decision-making by the deprived population groups will be necessary to attract much-needed funds from rich districts into the *pueblos jovenes*.

There are certain positive aspects of the contemporary urbanization process in Lima that should not be overlooked, however. While the *barriadas* may appear, at first sight, to be nothing more than squalid slums, research in the latter part of the 1960s by such scholars as Mangin and Turner (1969) revealed another aspect. The planned occupation of vacant land and the laying out of a squatter settlement requires social organization and group solidarity, as does the continuing improvement of such areas. Building a home for oneself in one's own time, with no rent or mortgage, is a convenient arrangement for people with no assets and insecurity of employment. The *pueblos jovenes* are, in fact, generally a step up from the inner slums, as was implied above. They help people with initiative but limited resources to improve their lot in life. Instead of being viewed as 'slums of despair', they might be more 'slums of hope' (Dwyer, 1975, pp. 196–8). Current urban policy in Peru is, in fact, attempting to capitalize on the positive, self-help aspects of the spontaneous settlement phenomenon, by encouraging groups of people to get together and organize their own community in areas provided with minimal public services (e.g. a central tap). Spontaneous settlement thus becomes a solution rather than a problem. Meanwhile, aid from international agencies such as the United Nations and the World Bank is helping in such fields as the servicing of existing *pueblos jovenes* and the design of low-cost housing units.

There are dangers, however, in the assumption that the better organization of spontaneous settlement might provide a solution to Third World housing problems, as exemplified in Lima. The more positive self-help element in Lima's *barriada* development may not be typical of squatter settlements in general (Dwyer, 1975, pp. 204–7). And it may not be sufficient to carry Lima itself through many more

227

years of rapid growth, driven by the dual forces of inward migration and high natural population increase, in an area with severe physical constraints in the form of shortage of land and water to sustain further growth.

But the greatest danger in accepting spontaneous settlement as a solution rather than a problem is that this risks obscuring the forces that so unequally distribute housing and other life chances. To operate on these forces might be more effective as a solution, and also more socially just. Inequality in urban environment, income, social service and so on in Lima is part and parcel of the national phenomenon of uneven development, outlined in the previous chapter. The problem of migration to Lima begins in the countryside, where people tire of the struggle to make a bare subsistence living in a system geared to the needs of external markets. In the city they find regular, well-paid work difficult to come by. They may have no choice but to join the growing 'informal sector' of small-scale and seldom full-time occupations in distribution or other services. The women may have little choice but to respond to one of the many signs advertising for a *muchacha* (maid) in a middle-class home (among other duties, they may spend their time applying shoe polish to the tyres of the master's car, as this writer has observed in the Corpac district). Not only are such jobs menial and poorly paid (though doubtless better than nothing), but they also represent an enormous amount of human labour that might otherwise be directed to tasks more closely related to the needs of the mass of the people. The fact that so many families have to live in improvised dwellings with no services is an outcome both of the labour market, which denies them adequately paid jobs, and of the distribution of wealth and income, that generates a pattern of production in which the housing needs of ordinary people have very low priority. To accept the self-help solution is to accept severe constraints on life chances for large numbers of people. Except for the fact of finite resources, these constraints are man-made – the outcome of a particular social formation and its economic structure.

The problems of Lima, with its glaring inequalities, are thus the problems of the society at large. They are urban or city problems only in so far as their manifestation is in this particular metropolis, as we have already observed of 'urban' problems in America and Britain. As McGee (1971, p. 18) says of the Third World city in general, 'cities are simply a reflection of the wider socio-economic system, and within the context of the underdeveloped world, each country has been moulded by the penetration of other socio-economic systems.' To attribute problems such as squatter settlements to 'the city' or to the process of urbanization misses the point that Lima, like all Third World cities, is part of an interconnected national and international system. Despite recent reforms, the basic forces making for inequality, set in motion under Spanish imperialism and solidified under dependent capitalism, have yet to be tackled. And, as was suggested in the discussion of regional inequality in Chapter 3, it seems most unlikely that they will be tackled except under a regime with a deep ideological commitment to the creation of a much more equal society, backed with the will and power to see the task through.

Socialist Cities: Some Sources of Inequality

The degree of inequality in cities under socialism is more difficult to identify than inter-regional differentials. As we saw in Chapter 3, some inferences can be drawn from published data at a broad level of territorial aggregation, suggestive of substantial variations in living standards among regions and between town and country. But between cities and within the city, such analyses require data that are simply not available. Thus, there is no possibility of replicating for a Soviet or Chinese city the type of studies described in earlier parts of this chapter. All we can do is make some broad suggestions as to what appears to be the situation in socialist cities, in the light of what little evidence exists. Perhaps the level of ignorance as to spatial organization in the socialist city might prompt more academic interest in this topic; it is not inconceivable that some of the more serious problems of the city in advanced capitalist nations and those of the Third World might be alleviated by some of the specific programmes adopted under socialism, even without a total socialist transformation of the economy and society.

What are the general sources of inequality within cities? Our explanations earlier in this chapter have identified a fairly clear link between the income differentials generated by the economy and its occupational-reward structure, on the one hand, and by residential choice on the other. Choice of residence, made within the constraints of income and the rent structure arising from the housing and land market, carries with it such things as environmental quality and access to social services, in so far as these vary with the socio-economic status of the neighbourhood. Under capitalism, this makes for very considerable differentiation within cities, with a clear spatial expression in the form of areas of marked deprivation and others displaying varying degrees of economic, social and environmental advantage. If the operation of the forces making for differentiation changes, so will the likely outcome. At the extreme, we might expect something approaching perfect territorial equality if all incomes are the same (and there are no stocks of wealth), if there is no urban housing market to generate differences in rent with location, and if social services and other positive (or negative) aspects of environmental quality are evenly distributed throughout a city. In the ideal socialist state, such a situation might approximate reality.

In practice, however, there are reasons to expect some inequality under socialism, both within cities and between them. The first reason is that differential rewards in different occupations at least provide the capacity for different levels of consumption, which *may* achieve a spatial expression if people of similar economic status occupy distinct neighbourhoods. Wage differentials can be quite wide in socialist economies. For example, Parkin (1971, p. 144) reports the following index of earnings for engineering and technical staff compared with 100·0 for manual workers (data for 1964): Czechoslovakia 130·3, Bulgaria 142·8, USSR 144·0, Hungary 153·3, Poland 164·9. In the USSR in 1967, monthly earnings by sectors ranged from 78 roubles in communications to 122 in science (average earnings in all sectors of the economy was 103 roubles); by branches of industry (average = 106·8 roubles) the range was from 81·3 in light industry to 195 in coal mining – an especially favoured occupation (data from Mickiewicz, 1973, p. 98). There can be even greater differentials between various grades of skills in the same industry:

230

figures compiled by Alastair McAuley of Essex University and reported in the *Sunday Times* (3 Oct. 1976) show grade VIII workers underground in the Soviet coal industry getting 3·75 times the basic rate, the same grade in ferrous metallurgy getting 2·43 times basic, and so on. These differences no doubt exist partly to attract people into particular occupations, as in a market economy. But they also reflect the degree of arduousness of certain jobs such as mining coal, and can provide compensation for living in a remote or highly industrial environment.

Some idea of the general distribution of earnings and income in the USSR is provided by McAuley (1977), using figures for 1968 – the latest available. Average monthly earnings were 112·7 roubles; 3 per cent of employees received less than 50 roubles while 5·5 per cent got more than 200. A comparison with 1956 shows a substantial decrease in inequality. Average per capita income in 1967–8 was estimated at 58 to 60 roubles per month; almost 10 per cent received less than 30 roubles while about 6 per cent received over 90. Using the ratio between the top and bottom deciles of the income distribution, McAuley suggests that the USSR has approximately the same degree of inequality as other countries in Eastern Europe. It is substantially more equal than the UK and the USA.

Before considering differences within cities it is worth speculating on the impact of wage differentials on differences among cities. As in a capitalist system, a city with an employment structure biased towards low-paid (manual or unskilled) jobs is likely to have a lower general standard of living than a city with greater per capita purchasing power, given the same cost of living. In the Soviet Union, an exclusively coal-mining town might thus be expected to have more than twice the per capita income of a light industrial town, judging from the figures quoted above. However, there is no ready source of statistics from which to make actual inter-city comparisons on general living standards.

Information on certain specific conditions is indicative of substantial difference, however. For example, figures on housing space show considerable variation among a selection of the larger cities in the USSR (Table 4.9). To some extent, more living space per capita seems to go with city size, though away from the top and bottom ends

231

Table 4.9. Per capita living space in selected major Soviet cities

City	Popn (1000s) 1974	Living space (sq. m per person) 1958	1970/71*	1974
Moscow	7632	5·0	9·1	10·0
Leningrad	4311	5·9	8·3	8·7
Kiev	1947	5·6	8·8	9·0
Tashkent	1595	4·0	5·6	5·8
Baku	1383	5·1	7·1	7·0
Kharkov	1357	5·6	8·2	8·6
Gorkiy	1283	5·1	7·5	7·7
Novosibirsk	1265	4·3	7·4	7·8
Kuybyshev	1164	4·8	7·2	7·4
Sverdlovsk	1147	5·3	7·8	7·9
Minsk	1147	4·7	7·4	7·8
Tbilisi	1006	5·7	7·6	7·8
Odessa	1002	6·0	7·6	7·7
Chelyabinsk	969	4·9	7·9	8·2
Omsk	968	—	7·3*	7·4
Dnepropetrovsk	958	—	8·0*	8·3
Donetsk	950	5·7	9·1	9·3
Kazan	946	—	6·6*	6·9
Perm	939	—	7·4*	7·5
Volgograd	900	—	7·9*	8·1
Yerevan	899	—	6·5*	6·6
Rostov	888	—	7·5*	7·6
Alma-Ata	836	—	7·2*	7·6
Saratov	834	—	7·3*	7·6
Riga	796	—	9·4*	9·5
Frunze	486	—	6·3*	6·6
Dushanbe	436	—	6·2*	6·5

Source: 1958 and 1970 figures from Morton, 1974, p. 173; 1971 and 1974 figures from Bater, 1977, p. 195.

— = no data

of the table this relationship breaks down. At the extreme, the average Muscovite enjoys almost twice the living space of his or her comrade in Tashkent (though this city's figure is depressed by the effect of the 1966 earthquake) and half as much again as in Yerevan, Frunze and Dushanbe. Where figures are available, substantial improvements since 1958 are evident, but there is a suggestion of greater inter-city inequality in 1974, especially with respect to relative improvements in Moscow. The capital, with some other major industrial cities, has clearly been favoured for investment in housing in recent years.

The picture of inter-city variations in housing conditions is complicated by regional variations, of the kind identified by republics in the previous chapter. The major difference is between the European and Asiatic regions. Morton (1974, p. 172) shows that in 1970, the capitals of the European republics (excluding Erevan and Baku) averaged 8·4 square metres of living space per person, compared with 6·5 in the capitals of the five Central Asian republics with Erevan and Baku. There are other differences in housing quality; citing a Soviet source, Bater (1977, p. 195) notes that in the eastern regions, barely 50 per cent of housing is connected to water, sewer or central heating networks, whereas in the (essentially European) west, the figure is about 70 per cent. Private housing is generally inferior to that provided by the State: 'as a rule, the smaller and more remote the urban place, the greater share of private housing and invariably the lower the level of municipal service provision ... most detached private dwellings have electricity but few are connected to water or sewage systems.'

There is other evidence to suggest some relationship between urban living standards and city size or status. For example, the best educational institutions tend to be in the major cities. A recent report in *Newsweek* (10 Oct. 1977) describes the quality of schooling in the Soviet Union as 'wildly uneven', with poor schools in rural communities contrasting with those providing 'superlative scientific training for gifted youngsters' in Moscow, Kiev, Leningrad and Novosibirsk. Matthews (1976, p. 129) points out that nearly all the schools for gifted children are in republic capitals. With respect to other social services, Madison (1975, p. 256) says of kindergartens: 'In large cities, most three-to-seven-year-olds are accommodated at first request, but in smaller cities, the situation is far from satisfactory'; extended-day programmes in schools, which help working mothers, are 'unevenly distributed, with very little being offered in rural communities'. Conditions at the lower end of the urban hierarchy, as exemplified by rural settlements in Siberia, are described thus by

233

two Soviet writers (Zaslavskaia and Liashenko, 1976, p. 66): 'in 1970, 21·8 per cent of the rural population of the province lived in villages, having as a rule only a shop, small clubhouse and medical aid station', whereas only 8·4 per cent lived in places with over 2000 inhabitants having 'complete mass service facilities'. Soviet rural-development strategy includes the amalgamation of small 'backward' hamlets into larger modern settlements with a full range of services. Equalization of service provision is, amongst other things, designed to keep people 'down on the farm' – no less of a problem under socialism than capitalism. The attraction of the big city appears universal.

A major objective of Soviet urban planning is 'to create an equitable level of consumer well-being within, and amongst, cities' (Bater, 1977, p. 190). Yet, in some respects, the existence of a hierarchy of urban centres seems instrumental in continuing differentiation. Kaiser (1977, p. 95) sees deliberation in this process:

> Consumer goods go first to Moscow, then to half a dozen other 'hero' cities, so designated for their roles in the Second World War, then down a hierarchical list on which every community is ranked. The State stores in Moscow are always supplied with fresh meat. Novosibirsk, a city of a million souls, sells no meat at all for months on end. Some meat is usually available at Novosibirsk's farmers' market, but only at high prices. There are smaller cities and towns that *never* get fresh meat in any form.

The example of fresh meat is an extreme case, given the size of the country, its climate and transport problems. (And, it might be noted in passing, that getting truly 'fresh' meat, fish and other foodstuffs is not always easy in many American cities.) But the process Kaiser describes bears some resemblance to the hierarchical-diffusion view of the functioning of the American urban system outlined earlier in this chapter.

In the USSR, the urban hierarchy is very much a reflection of the hierarchy of political control. The capitals of the republics and of lower-level units of government have the power to attract disproportionate shares of industrial investment. Huzinec (1978) has assembled evidence to suggest a polarization of industrial development in administrative centres, for economic as well as political reasons.

Accompanying this is an improvement in infrastructure and social services, to facilitate industrial expansion as well as the attraction and retention of the labour force. This can set in motion a process of circular and cumulative causation that increases budgetary disparities within the urban hierarchy: 'these cities, which are already receiving additional investment in housing, utilities, shops and so forth, because their growing industries are spending money on these things, are also favoured in the State budgets so as to enable them to build yet more housing and facilities of their own.' (Osborn, 1970, p. 229.) There is thus a distinct geographical inequality in the 'amenity surface' of the Soviet urban hierarchy, according to Huzinec. The level of living in a city is clearly related to its place in the wider economic and political formation of the urban system.

It is now time to look inside the Soviet city. Just as economic function and occupational structure may generate differences among cities, so they may be indicative of internal variation. Differences within cities may be greater the more varied the occupations (and wage levels) represented, which is likely to be a function of city size. If there is some form of residential grouping by socio-economic status, large cities in socialist societies might thus be expected to display observable territorial inequalities in living standards.

How far is this true of Moscow, Russia's largest city? A superficial acquaintance with Moscow suggests a high degree of spatial uniformity, in so far as the quality of the residential environment is concerned. Most people live in similar-sized apartments in similar apartment buildings in similar complexes, the main differences arising from their period of construction. Rents do not vary with location, thus eliminating one major source of social grouping in space in the capitalist city. In any event, rentals in the USSR take only a small fraction of income, and residential choice is greatly constrained by the allocation system in the public sector that dominates the provision of housing in the USSR. A further source of inequality in capitalist cities, differential access to social services to the disadvantage of the poor and most needy, should also fade away under Soviet socialism. For some time new residential areas in Moscow have been planned in a comprehensive manner, based on the 'microdistrict' (*mikroraion*), or neighbourhood with perhaps 5000–15,000 people, with their own services in the form of restaurants, nurseries, kindergartens, club rooms, libraries, swimming pools and so on as well as health and educational facilities. As the city continues to expand, with vast new residential complexes on its fringes, great attention is given to the need to provide everyone with reasonable access to social services, recreation and cultural facilities, via a carefully planned hierarchical system of service centres of different size (Hamilton, 1976, pp. 45–6).

In reality, Moscow displays uneven access to services and other environmental attributes, and also an element of spatial socio-economic differentiation. The failure of service development to keep up with the completion of apartment complexes has been a problem for some time: P. Hall (1966, pp. 170–71) cites the chief city architect as complaining that areas are opened up without landscaping, sports facilities or even sufficient shops, schools, nurseries or kindergartens. Hedrick Smith (1976, p. 59) suggests that many new apartment areas go without basic shops for two or three years because of failure of co-ordination between construction and commerce. A number of indicators of service and amenity provision compiled by Hamilton (1976, p. 28) show the central area to be better off than the outer ring of the metropolis. And in any hierarchical system of service provision people near the hub (the city centre) will enjoy greater overall access than those living on the fringe. To quote Cattell (1974, p. 245): 'New housing tracts without transportation, roads, sewers, telephones, retail outlets, consumer services, day-care centres, schools, and so forth provided few advantages over the traditional overcrowded housing ... As the housing tracts pushed indiscriminately farther out from the centre of the city, the network of services became increasingly far flung.' Socialist planning in a real world of resource constraints and bureaucratic inefficiency cannot entirely eliminate the effect of geographical space. However, the Soviets seem to be developing more awareness of the importance of physical accessibility as an aspect of service availability in cities (Bater, 1977; Ryan, 1978, pp. 83–4).

General environmental quality varies in Moscow, and this appears to relate to the socio-economic status of the population – at least to some extent. Hamilton (1976, p. 27) describes the areas of pre-revolutionary working-class housing around central Moscow, and now scheduled for redevelopment, displaying 'overcrowding in dilapidated houses and tenements, often without baths, narrow, often cobbled streets served by trams; cramped, sometimes obnoxious industries and occasional large factories . . . which vie for space with warehouses, a high density of shops . . . transport depots and housing; and very few open spaces or cultural amenities'. Beyond the central area there is some differentiation by wedges. The south-east is described by a Soviet geographer as having 'the worst industrial pollutant emissions, greatest smoke and the worst health and hygiene environment for the residential population in all the capital' (Y. Saushkin, quoted in Hamilton, 1976, p. 29). Other wedges have more service and research facilities than industry, and areal social differentiation is sharpened by the attraction of those areas to, for example, office workers and foreign embassy staff. For instance an increasing number of institutes of the USSR Academy of Sciences are being built in the south-western sector of the city, along Leninsky Prospekt, and this appears to be a particularly favoured residential area for scientific workers.

Some insight into residential preferences in Moscow is provided by Barbash (1977). As part of a broader study of the city's internal structure, she has identified the geographical patterns revealed by people's desire to move home, as advertised in the weekly bulletin published to facilitate the exchange of flats. Simplified maps have been prepared showing the number of announcements of the wish to move into or out of each *raion* (administrative district), standardized for size of population (Figure 4.15). In both maps, the heavier the shading the more 'desirable' the district. The pattern of wishes to move out shows higher proportions in the outer ring and especially the western sector. The second map shows the outer suburbs as most desired for inward movement, again with greatest emphasis on the western segment including the Leninsky Prospekt wedge referred to above. Thus there appears to be some kind of paradox: the districts people most want to leave are, by and large, those that others most want to enter. The reason is probably that the newer, outer suburbs seem attractive to people in other parts of the city, but those actually

237

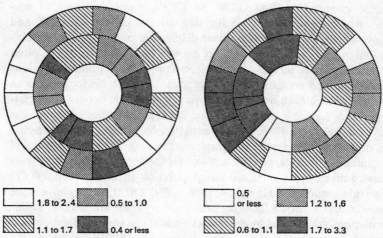

1.8 to 2.4 0.5 to 1.0

1.1 to 1.7 0.4 or less

0.5 or less 1.2 to 1.6

0.6 to 1.1 1.7 to 3.3

Persons announcing wish to move, per 10,000 inhabitants

a. Outward   b. Inward

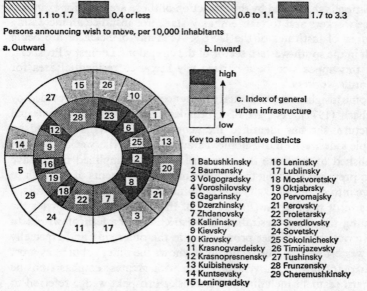

high

c. Index of general urban infrastructure

low

Key to administrative districts

1 Babushkinsky	16 Leninsky
2 Baumansky	17 Lublinsky
3 Volgogradsky	18 Moskvoretsky
4 Voroshilovsky	19 Oktjabrsky
5 Gagarinsky	20 Pervomajsky
6 Dzerzhinsky	21 Perovsky
7 Zhdanovsky	22 Proletarsky
8 Kalininsky	23 Sverdlovsky
9 Kievsky	24 Sovetsky
10 Kirovsky	25 Sokolnichesky
11 Krasnogvardeisky	26 Timirjazevsky
12 Krasnopresnensky	27 Tushinsky
13 Kuibishevsky	28 Frunzensky
14 Kuntsevsky	29 Cheremushkinsky
15 Leningradsky	

Figure 4.15. Environmental preference and quality in Moscow, c. 1972. Note that the map of *raion* boundaries has been transformed, with the shape, size and orientation of the districts changed in such a way as to make the rings and sectors more obvious; the unshaded central area does not exist in reality. (Source: Barbash, 1977.)

living there find the level of service provision and remoteness from the city centre to be a disadvantage. The grass of the metropolitan fringe is not as green as it might appear from the inner residential areas.

Something of the differentiation of the urban environment as between the inner and outer districts is summarized in Figure 4.15c. Barbash has derived a composite index of 'general urban infrastructure', reflecting such conditions as density of public transport lines, laundries, foodshops, cafés, kindergartens, public libraries, and metro stations. The higher the scores (and the heavier the shading on the map) the better off the district with respect to these kinds of services. The distinction between the well-served inner ring and the relatively deprived outer suburbs is very clearly shown. Place of residence is obviously important to the ordinary Muscovite, in so far as the everyday environment is concerned.

But the most extreme manifestations of social inequality arise from the privileged economic status of the political, intellectual and artistic élite. Hedrick Smith (1976, p. 32) identifies 'exclusive residential ghettos' occupied by the Kremlin leaders, with apartment blocks conspicuously well-constructed and maintained. One of the Stalin era's 'wedding-cake' blocks, in which distinguished ballet dancers and other artists live, is pointed out to tourists with a touch of pride. A Soviet source (Zhukov and Fyodorov, 1974, p. 7) refers to high rents for 'extra-comfortable houses in the heart of capital cities' (16·5 kopeks per square metre compared with the usual 3·5 to 4·4 kopeks) and payments of three times the normal rent for 'excess floor space'. But it also states that members of creative unions (artists, writers, journalists, architects and research workers) are allowed 20 square metres of additional floor space at the usual rate, which is virtually equivalent to the allocation for two additional people.

Membership of élite occupations in the USSR carries with it various other advantages, such as access to special shops and service facilities, described in detail by Matthews (1978). Such privileges and fringe benefits provide an important supplement to what may be quite substantial wage differentials. For example, personal inquiries in 1978 in the Siberian scientific centre of Akademgorodok revealed monthly earnings of perhaps 1400 roubles for an Academician at the top of the hierarchy of the Academy of Sciences – about ten times what a junior research worker would be paid. The Academicians have their own estate of detached or semi-detached houses, in sharp contrast to the blocks of flats for the rest of the town's population. In Moscow (and some other cities) the tendency for apartment houses to be built for particular occupational groups, such as that of the Academy of Sciences, produces an element of social segregation at the local level.

The élite also have their exclusive *dacha* (country home) communities just outside Moscow. These include the writers' colony at Peredelkino and Zhukovka which Hedrick Smith (1976, p. 39) describes as 'heart of the dacha country of the high and mighty of Soviet politics, science, culture'. If his descriptions are correct (and there is no reason to believe otherwise) the Soviet élite enjoy an environment at least as luxurious as in Britain's stockbroker belts or the country-club zone of American cities.

There is some evidence to suggest that the quality of services may vary within the large Soviet city, in relation to population characteristics. Matthews (1976, p. 130) makes the following observations about education:

> Clear distinctions can be made between the several schools in any given town or district. Sometimes such distinctions depend on individual teachers or directors and are rather ephemeral. Yet it is probable that a more permanent interrelationship exists between a school and its catchment area. One would expect the best schools to be found in the centres of large towns, where there are more amenities (and where the more influential families live).

This is not unlike the situation in Britain or the United States, except that the high-status and better-served residential areas will tend to be in the suburbs rather than the inner city.

In principle, socialism should bring every citizen equal social benefits and costs. In reality, occupational structure and social rank create some differentiation. The fact that inequality is not a more conspicuous feature of the spatial structure of cities like Moscow is largely explained by the uniformity of housing and neighbourhood quality for the mass of the people. As Musil (1968) found in Prague, land values and rents are almost irrelevant for the distribution of different socio-economic groups. But this uniformity may itself be deceptive. Relatively high earnings can enable some people to fit out their apartments with style, however limited the actual accommodation; these people may also be the car owners, and those who can afford smart restaurants and other luxuries. As has been implied above, such people may be subject to more spatial grouping than external appearances suggest. A Polish informant indicates that this is also the case in Warsaw. Another somewhat perverse feature of socialist cities such as Moscow is that poor local environmental quality cannot be compensated for via low rents, as happens to some extent in a competitive housing market. Apartment rents are basically the same, whether close to a factory, park, shopping centre or commuter railway station. This is an explicitly spatial aspect of discrimination for which equity would require some form of rental adjustment, in so far as people are constrained from freely choosing their residential location and the environment that goes with it.

Another source of inequality in housing conditions within Soviet cities is the distinction between public and private, mentioned above. Almost 30 per cent of urban housing is still privately owned, and much of this may be of poor quality when compared with modern state-financed apartments, even if the latter can suffer from a monotony of environment. The most conspicuous differences in the urban landscape are between the apartment complexes and the quarters that remain of earlier wooden houses; Irkutsk in Siberia, for example, reveals a remarkable patchwork of these older and newer residential areas, seen clearly from the air. Morton (1974, pp. 185–6) suggests that new private housing built by migrants from the countryside may lack plumbing, gas and a bath. This may be because those who build cannot afford to put in the amenities, but it is also possible that private households are discriminated against by the local authorities on ideological grounds (even though private housing has official approval as a recognized way of supplementing state provision). At the other end of the scale is the quasi-private 'cooperative' housing, in which residents can invest and become, in effect, co-owners with the state, in return for above-norm per capita living area, design and finish. Some 12 per cent of all housing built in Moscow between 1961 and 1970 was cooperative (Hamilton, 1976, p. 41). Among other things, the increasing popularity of cooperatives reflects the demand for diversity and choice, within a society characterized by growing consumerism. This, in its turn, may contribute to the development of a more heterogeneous (and unequal) pattern of environmental quality.

Some brief observations may be offered on cities elsewhere in the socialist world. In Chinese cities opportunities for variations in living standards are limited by income differentials, which may be smaller than in any other country (Byers and Nolan, 1976, pp. 75–6). Access to consumer goods is strictly limited by short supply and rationing. Housing at low rents is allocated directly by government and there are basic allowances of foodstuffs in accordance with category of work performed. Health and educational services are freely available, organized at a local-community level. Factories also perform an important 'welfare' role (as in the USSR), being responsible for the housing of many workers and providing medical care, crèches, kindergartens, primary schools and sometimes also retail and leisure facilities. The general impression is that, whatever differentiation may exist by virtue of the superior rewards of some sections of Chinese society, it is likely to be on a much smaller scale than in the USSR and even less conspicuous in the spatial structure of the city.

If the general level of living is low in Chinese cities, when compared with Western standards, this must be related to the conditions inherited from the pre-revolutionary era. The following description of Shanghai by Neville Maxwell (1974) gives some impression of the progress made in only twenty years:

> The Shanghai of the past was as bad, perhaps worse, as any of the cities exploding in the Third World today. In addition to the familiar evils of noisome slums, inhuman overcrowding, mass unemployment and massed beggars, there was also a special shamelessness in the vice, crime and ruthless exploitation which existed in old Shanghai . . .
> Shanghai today is a city transformed, even a city re-born, even if it is still overcrowded. Nevertheless there is a feeling of order, even of space.

It is brisk, clean and purposeful, a working city not an agglomeration of individuals, most of them wretched, but a huge community made up of an infinite number of small communities. It appears as a working democracy, in the sense that the people are involved, through a structure of neighbourhood and street committees, with the decisions that affect their everyday lives.

There is full employment, there are no beggars, and the look and feel of the society seem to confirm the Chinese statement that there is no prostitution. There is a network of community-run health services, with hygiene being the responsibility of neighbourhood and street groups.

Even if this observer has seen only the best of the new urban China, it clearly suggests a much more equal society than in the past. The contrast with Indian cities is striking: perhaps nowhere else is failure to control urban development in the Third World more evident than in Calcutta, where the slums make many of the *barriadas* of Latin American cities look quite attractive.

Nevertheless, there is some evidence of continuing inequality in the contemporary Chinese city. The BBC Peking correspondent, Philip Short, describes people in obvious poverty searching for scraps of wood in a rubbish pile and looking for cigarette ends in Shanghai, where shops on the main street are 'bulging' with things to be bought (BBC radio, 19 Nov. 1977), though similar contrasts could, doubtless, be found in London, New York and most Western cities. Particularly revealing is a description of Peking by Edward Luttwak of Johns Hopkins University that originally appeared in the American magazine *Commentary* and was quoted extensively by Bernard Levin in *The Times* (18 May 1977). He contrasts the broad boulevards, shopping streets, hotels and show-place factories of the tourist circuit with the narrow, unpaved alleys, shanties and small workshops which make up the 'real' Peking. The following description is suggestive of inequalities in living standards that might be associated with status in the political bureaucracy:

In the early evening, I passed a typical room, illuminated by a naked, 30-watt bulb dangling from the ceiling. About six people were preparing to go to bed; there were two beds in the room and not much space in between. The only other furniture was a decorated trunk-box and a

243

large 1930s-style radio. This was the housing of old Peking, subdivided for an expanding population.

The new housing one saw, newly built apartment blocks, seemed to be no less crowded . . . the standard three-room apartment accommodates three separate families. With its unpaved streets, its crowded alleys and its one-storey buildings, much of Peking is, in fact, village rather than city, and most of the population lives a miserably poor village life . . . But from the apartment of a diplomat friend, one could look directly into an apartment house reserved for middle-ranking cadres; they too lived in standard three-room apartments, but each housed only a single family, and instead of the naked, 30-watt bulb of ordinary folk, these apartments were well lit. More senior cadres have their own small houses with a bit of garden around, but nobody has ever seen how the top echelon lives, for their housing is hidden behind the high walls of the élite residential compound.

It is of course, difficult to generalize from the observation of visitors and journalists. People from capitalist countries, travelling in the communist world, often see what they wish to see, reinforcing their own prejudices. The undisguised glee with which the rabidly anti-communist Bernard Levin featured the description above underlines the ideological nature of much that passes for objective reporting of the communist world in the West. Until more serious *scientific* research has been done on socialist cities, it seems wise to reserve judgement on the degree of inequality that exists. This is especially true of China, with one of the world's largest but (to outsiders) least-known urban populations.

One thing seems clear, however. Socialist planning and reconstruction in some very large and very poor cities in poor countries has greatly improved the condition of the mass of the people. One city in the Western hemisphere provides striking evidence of this – Havana, Cuba. The former 'pleasure city' of Havana creates a similar impression to Shanghai. The distinguished urban specialist Jorge Hardoy describes Havana thus (quoted in Susman, 1974, p. 24):

'Touristic' Havana of pre-revolutionary decades has disappeared. In its place stands a society without unemployment or slums, with antiquated and crowded buses, but with beaches open to the people; with unpainted houses, but with an urban growth which has been ordered and controlled, once land speculation was eliminated. New parks and a green belt around Havana provide recreational facilities and permit the production of food and industrial crops. Gone are the contrasts between gaudy, well-lit neighbourhoods and dark, marginal sections, between neighbourhoods with luxurious institutions and discriminating clubs, and others with not even the most basic services, between ostentatious palaces and miserable tenements. Social classes have disappeared; schools, hospitals, and sports events are free; transportation will be free. Cuba is equalizing itself from the bottom up, and nowhere is this transformation more evident than in Havana for one who has visited the country before and after the Revolution.

The key to successful control of urban development in both China and Cuba is clearly the rural-development strategy. In both countries great stress has been placed on measures such as land redistribution and the reorganization of agricultural production, so as basically to reconstruct rural society. This serves the purpose of ensuring food supplies for the cities. But it also helps to stabilize the rural population and prevent the mass migration to the cities typical of so many Third World countries today. The message seems virtually self-evident: to combat metropolitan concentration, its distortion of the space economy, and the accompanying inequalities of human life chances requires an integrated approach to national planning in which city and countryside are viewed as interdependent parts of a whole. Until this is recognized and acted upon, there is unlikely to be any solution to the problem of the 'exploding metropolis' in the underdeveloped world. The critical issue is how many societies will face up to the basic structural changes needed to implement such a strategy, when what is involved is a revolutionary transformation of society itself.

5 Who Gets Care Where: The Case of Health Services

Geographical differences in levels of living arise in various ways, as we have seen in the previous chapters. The prevailing social and economic structure will carry with it a predisposition towards a greater or lesser degree of inequality in distribution, with specific regional, local and personal circumstances helping to generate the particular spatial patterns of advantage and deprivation. Increasingly, the condition of the individual can be seen to depend on position in some wider system, which has a specific organization in geographical space. Increasingly, people in all parts of the world are coming to rely on collective provision via social services for the satisfaction of their needs, particularly in periods of more-than-usual vulnerability, such as illness and unemployment. The availability of such services is thus very important in determining who gets what, or who gets care where, in times of special need.

In this chapter we explore various aspects of access to one selected social service – the provision of health care. Health care is perhaps the most 'basic' of all services, for on this may depend whether a newly-born child lives or dies, whether we survive illness or accident and, if we do recover, whether we retain full use of essential faculties or suffer permanent handicap. In poor nations (and certain poor parts of rich nations) human life chances are severely curtailed by the limited availability of basic health care. And even in richer nations and communities the demand for care seems constantly to outrun supply or resources available, as new problems emerge to take the place of those largely solved by the advance of medical science. Thus needs differ from place to place. In the underdeveloped world there is still a desperate shortage of doctors, hospitals and drugs, while in the more 'advanced' nations special skills and facilities are required to cope with stress-induced illness, the victims of road accidents, the

246

aged, and the growing number of children and others who survive with disabilities that would have killed them in earlier times or in more 'primitive' societies. The resources devoted to health care, typically 4–6 per cent of GNP, make it especially important for society to get the best possible value for money. Implicit in this is the imperative of ensuring that facilities and personnel are in the right places, in relation to the needs of the population. Badly located facilities can be a serious source of inefficiency in social services, just as in industrial activity.

We shall review the availability of health care at different geographical scales. The impact of health services on the lives of the people will depend on resources available and on how the provision of care is organized, which vary from nation to nation. It also depends on how the delivery system is arranged in geographical space; each nation, region and community will have its own pattern of need or demand, the full satisfaction of which may require a unique spatial response in terms of the disposition of both fixed and mobile resources. There is not room here to examine all the important issues involved, of course. All we can try to do is to show that geographical space is a relevant consideration in the provision of social services such as health care, within the constraints imposed by broader features of social and economic structure.

Some International Comparisons

Levels of health are subject to some extreme differences among nations. In Chapter 1 (Table 1·4) we found infant mortality varying from 11 deaths per 1000 live births in Sweden to 200 in Ethiopia, with even higher figures likely in some of the poorest African countries for which there is no reliable information. Life expectation varies from over 74 years in Norway and Sweden to less than 40 in Ethiopia, Burundi and similar severely underdeveloped lands. Infectious and parasitic diseases account for fewer than 10 deaths per 100,000 population in such countries as Denmark, the Netherlands, the UK, Norway and Sweden, while the rate is over 200 in many Latin American countries, and doubtless much higher in parts of Africa and South-East Asia for which figures are not available (data from UN Research Institute for Social Development). In the richest countries the leading causes of death are heart disease, cancer and strokes – predominantly illnesses of middle or old age. In the poorest nations such major killers as pneumonia, enteric diseases and birth itself, along with various parasites and infections, are more likely to afflict younger age groups.

The debilitating effect of illness and inadequate diet greatly impairs the productive capacity of people in underdeveloped countries. This, in turn, limits the generation of a surplus from which improvements in health care might be financed. Ill health is also a major source of lost production in more advanced countries: almost three quarters of working days lost in the UK result from sickness, compared with only 2 per cent from the much-publicized effect of strikes. (It is somewhat perverse that elements in British society eager to criticize trade union 'irresponsibility' towards lost production are often among the strongest advocates of the cuts in social service expenditure that weaken the ability of the NHS to keep people fit to work.) Illness must thus be seen as part of an interrelated set of conditions, national and local, which have to do with man's capacity to adjust to the environment and to use it to his advantage. Inadequate physical functioning impairs ability to meet other needs and obligations, thus compounding the initial state of deprivation.

The general level of health of a nation or community will depend on a variety of considerations. Some types of physical environment will be more unhealthy than others. Tropical climates may more readily permit the germination and spread of infectious diseases. Conditions in city slums of the traditional kind or in the squatter settlements on the fringe of Third World cities may predispose people to illnesses arising from inadequate shelter and sanitation. Even the environment of the world's most prosperous places, such as California, may induce a high incidence of stress-related illness, as people strive to succeed in a fiercely competitive society.

As health services all operate within a particular physical and social environment, it is difficult to say how much a community's health is sensitive to the level and effectiveness of the services alone. Clearly, the same level of expenditure on health care can produce

248

different results in terms of reduced mortality and morbidity, if the environmental conditions are different, and indeed if the places in question have different levels of health to begin with. It is likely to take more resources to reduce the same level of infant mortality by, say, 10 per cent in an unhealthy environment than in a healthy one. Similarly, it will cost more to reduce the rate from 20 deaths per 1000 live births to 10 than from 200 to 100, even in the same environment, because of the condition of diminishing returns. Assessment of resource effectiveness is further complicated by the fact that the same sum of money can be invested in different types of health services and with a different spatial organization, both of which can influence the result obtained.

With these reservations in mind, we may now look at some facts concerning differential availability of health care. Table 5.1 summar-

Table 5.1. Availability of physicians and hospital beds : the national extremes

	Inhabitants per physician (107 countries)		Inhabitants per hospital bed (105 countries)	
Top ten	Israel	406	Sweden	67
	USSR	420	Finland	76
	Czechoslovakia	471	Norway	78
	Hungary	507	Japan	79
	Argentina	512	Ireland	80
	Bulgaria	537	Australia	84
	Austria	542	Switzerland	87
	Italy	552	West Germany	89
	West Germany	572	East Germany	90
	Mongolia	574	USSR	91
Bottom ten	Benin	31,976	Indonesia	1388
	Malawi	38,245	Mali	1393
	Central African Rep.	38,380	Upper Volta	1673
	Mali	41,700	Niger	1844
	Burundi	56,373	Nigeria	1848
	Niger	58,202	South Korea	1893
	Rwanda	60,064	India	2022
	Chad	62,759	Mauritania	2788
	Ethiopia	73,973	Ethiopia	3011
	Upper Volta	92,827	Nepal	5538

Source: UN Research Institute for Social Development, 1976.

izes the variability of two commonly used ratios, relating to physicians and hospital beds respectively. In the best-served nations the number of persons per physician ranges from roughly 400 to 600, while in the poorest-served countries the ratios can be 100 times as high. For example, if the national population was distributed evenly among the doctors available, a Mali doctor would have to care for 100 patients for every one patient of the doctor in Israel or the USSR. The ratio of persons to hospital beds varies less extremely, but figures in the poorest nations are still twenty or thirty times those in the richest nations. This is not to say that the quality of care for all the population varies in the same proportions, however. In the richest countries, many doctors may be providing a somewhat specialized (even 'luxury') service in organ transplants or cosmetic surgery, from which relatively few people benefit. In the poor countries, benefits may be similarly unevenly distributed, even in basic care, because of the concentration of personnel and facilities in the cities and the corresponding severe shortage in the countryside.

Relationships between resources available and level of health are thus by no means clear-cut. Cross-national statistical comparisons are hazardous, as has been pointed out in earlier chapters, and especially so when questions of cause and effect arise. Nevertheless, something can be learned from limited exercises of this kind. As an example, Figure 5.1 shows the relationship between infant mortality by nations (from Table 1.4) and the ratio of population to physicians. As would be expected, there is a tendency for infant mortality to rise as persons per doctor rises, but the correlation is neither very strong nor closely linear. Above 100 infant deaths per 1000 live births the number of physicians seems to make no difference to the actual mortality figure; for example, Turkey has a slightly higher rate than Tanzania (or so the UN figures tell us) yet Tanzania has almost ten times the population per physician as Turkey. Similarly, at the lowest levels of infant mortality the population-to-physician ratio seems to account for little if any of the variation. In the middle range the figures suggest that getting infant mortality down to, say, 50 per 1000 requires at least one doctor per 2000 people. But even here there are exceptions: Jamaica's infant mortality is only 32 despite

250

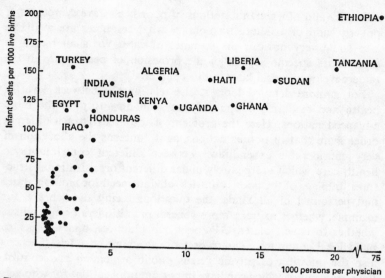

Figure 5.1. The relationship between infant mortality and population per physician by nations, 1970. The nations are as listed in Table 1.4. (Source of data: UN Research Institute for Social Development, 1976.)

its 2650 people per physician, while Sri Lanka has the figure of 53 with a population-to-physician ratio as high as 6477.

At the highest levels of infant mortality it requires relatively little by way of resources to reduce the figure substantially. For example, one authority has claimed that infant mortality in the African-occupied rural areas of the Republic of South Africa could be reduced from 350 per 1000 live births to around 70 with comparatively little effort; there may be no cheaper way of saving a life in that country than to invest in basic health care in the so-called homelands (D. M. Smith, 1977, p. 257). All that is required here and in many other poor rural areas of the Third World is rudimentary post-natal care and inoculation – though the guarantee of a sustaining diet would also help. The problem in the underdeveloped world is one of resources, as well as of organization of the provision of care. Infant mortality and other manifestations of poor health are symptoms of poverty, and of a failure to mobilize what resources are available into some very obvious programmes of care. We shall return to some more specific aspects of the provision of health care in the underdeveloped world later in this chapter.

For a more detailed look at the relationship between level of health and resources committed, we shall now turn to the more advanced nations. Here the problem of resources is of a different order from that in poorer nations, as it concerns the allocation of very considerable expenditures between different contributors to health care which are possibly under different organizational structures. In place of the poor countries' obvious need for more facilities and personnel of all kinds, the questions facing the rich are, for example, whether to train more general practitioners or specialists, whether to have isolated GPs or group practices, and whether to build local community clinics or more teaching hospitals. There is also the question of private versus public ownership and control, the resolution of which can have important implications for who gets care where.

Information from a comparative study of health care in twenty advanced nations (R. Maxwell, 1974) enables us to explore some of these issues. Table 5.2 lists selected mortality data for the non-communist nations of Europe and also for the USA and USSR. Perinatal deaths, infant mortality, mothers dying in childbirth and a measure of premature male death all distinguish among the nations in a similar manner and with a suggestion of geographical regularity. The Scandinavian countries with the Netherlands appear as the healthiest, closely followed by England and Wales and Switzerland. Then come the rest of the British Isles and the Western Europe group, followed by Germany and Austria. The three Southern European countries for the most part occupy positions towards the bottom, with high mortality rates. The USA generally does better than the Central and Southern European countries, but not as well as the four Western European countries, the British Isles and Scandinavia. Data for the USSR are not complete enough for precise comparison with the rest; on the figures shown, the USSR is fifteenth out of twenty in infant mortality and thirteenth for maternal deaths.

Figures for life expectation (not included in Table 5.2) place the USSR bottom of the list for males and equal fifteenth for females. A rough composite mortality indicator, derived by averaging each nation's rank on each of the four conditions chosen, shows Sweden first and Portugal last.

Table 5.2. Selected mortality data for twenty advanced nations

Nation	Perinatal deaths per 1000 live births	Infant deaths per 1000 live births	Maternal deaths per 100,000 live births	Male deaths aged 35–44 per 1000	Average rank (exc. USSR)
British Isles					
England and Wales	23·7	18·2	19·4	2·30	6·25
Scotland	25·6	19·6	14·4	3·20	9·25
Northern Ireland	29·2	22·9	15·4	2·80	11·0
Republic of Ireland	26·1	19·5	31·8	2·61	10·25
Scandinavia					
Sweden	16·3	11·0	10·2	2·29	1·25
Norway	20·7	12·7	14·8	2·40	4·25
Denmark	18·9	14·2	16·8	2·31	4·37
Finland	18·9	13·2	14·8	4·76	7·25
Western Europe					
Netherlands	19·6	12·7	19·4	2·10	4·0
Belgium	25·1	20·5	20·5	2·76	9·25
Luxemburg	24·7	24·9	—	3·47	12·66
France	25·4	18·2	24·9	3·65	11·37
Southern Europe					
Italy	32·4	29·6	60·6	2·80	15·5
Spain	—	20·7	37·9	2·81	13·0
Portugal	39·5	58·0	79·1	4·09	18·25
Central Europe					
West Germany	25·2	23·6	53·1	3·05	13·0
Austria	27·3	25·9	33·0	3·62	15·25
Switzerland	19·5	15·1	29·3	2·64	7·25
Other					
USA	27·1	19·8	24·5	4·07	12·75
USSR	—	24·4	32·0	—	—

Source: R. Maxwell, 1974. Most of the figures refer to 1969 except for infant mortality (1970) and are derived from World Health Organization and United Nations sources.

— = no data.

Table 5.3 shows selected indicators of national resources, level of health service and organization. GNP per capita is relevant not only to what money might be available to finance health care but also to conditions of housing, diet and environmental quality that have a

Table 5.3. Selected indicators of health care resources for twenty advanced nations

Nation	GNP per capita ($US)	Physicians per 100,000 popn	Hospital beds per 100,000 popn	Public ownership of general hospitals (%)
British Isles				
England and Wales	} 1890	123	407	} 97·5
Scotland		133	483	
Northern Ireland		133	—	
Republic of Ireland	1110	107	393	51·8
Scandinavia				
Sweden	2920	136	671	100·0
Norway	2160	138	502	93·4
Denmark	2310	144	605	91·4
Finland	1980	102	430	97·2
Western Europe				
Netherlands	1760	125	479	25·0
Belgium	2010	154	468	40·8
Luxemburg	2420	106	579	53·4
France	2460	132	450	65·0
Southern Europe				
Italy	1400	181	468	76·8
Spain	820	134	125	—
Portugal	510	87	341	36·6
Central Europe				
West Germany	2190	172	653	54·2
Austria	1470	168	600	80·7
Switzerland	2700	138	620	67·1
Other				
USA	4240	158	465	33·3
USSR	1200	238	700	100·0

Source: R. Maxwell, 1974. Data from World Bank and World Health Organization, mostly relating to 1969 or 1970.

— = no data.

bearing on level of health. Physicians and hospital beds per 100,000 people express the ratios used above in Table 5.1 on a per capita basis. Public ownership is introduced as an organizational condition that might prove relevant to national health-care performance. As the figures show, there are considerable differences among nations on all four indicators. The richest country listed (USA) has eight times the per capita GNP of the poorest (Portugal). The country with most physicians to population (USSR) has almost three times the ratio of the one with least (Portugal). Hospital beds per 100,000 people range from well over 600 in a number of countries to less than 400 in others and as low as 125 in Spain. Public ownership of general hospitals varies from complete in Sweden and the USSR to one third in the USA and a quarter in the Netherlands.

How far do these indicators find reflection in national levels of health? Figure 5.2 shows the relationships with the general mortality indicator derived from averaging ranks in Table 5.2. Mortality is quite closely related to per capita GNP – in fact somewhat closer than to the other indicators that are more clearly connected with health services, suggesting that national health may be as much a reflection of general prosperity as of the level and organization of health care. The USA stands out as a deviant case, with mortality very much higher than would be suggested by its per capita GNP. Some semblance of a positive relationship between health and number of physicians can be detected. But here there are a number of countries well supplied with doctors (over 150 per 100,000 population) but with some of the poorest performances on the mortality indicator (USA, Germany, Austria and Italy). One possible explanation is that doctors in these countries are less effective than elsewhere or that they operate with less adequate facilities and supporting personnel, but it is more likely that a higher proportion than elsewhere choose to practise lucrative specialization or to work in affluent communities where their impact on the general level of health is limited. Countries with a strong and continuing tradition of general practice seem to be able to maintain good standards of health care with fewer doctors – England's position on the graph exemplifying this. The beds-to-population ratio also shows some nations apparently well served but with lower performance than might have been

255

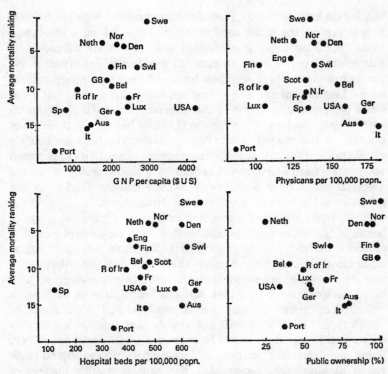

Figure 5.2. The relationship between mortality level and indicators of resource availability, personnel, facilities and organization of health care. (Source of data: R. Maxwell, 1974.)

expected (including Germany and Austria again), and some with a better performance than their relatively low number of beds would suggest.

Organization of the provision of health care clearly has a bearing on the effectiveness of resources committed. The impact of each doctor or hospital bed on mortality or other measures of health will depend on how this individual or facility fits into the over-all care delivery system. As the final graph in Figure 5.2 suggests, the highest levels of health (by the mortality criterion) tend to be in countries where there is a high degree of public ownership and control over the provision of care. The extreme cases, with complete or almost complete public ownership, are the Scandinavian countries and Great Britain. The USSR (not shown on the graph) might appear to be an exception, with total public ownership but levels of health which are poor by general European standards; however, the USSR is also a relatively poor country by the GNP per capita criterion, with a large and highly scattered population to serve, often in extremely harsh environments (we shall return to the USSR later in this chapter). The Netherlands stands out as an exception, with very good performance in a predominantly private system. The difference between the Netherlands and the USA (predominantly private and a poor performer) is probably that the former does not suffer the extremes of urban and rural deprivation found in the latter – and it is in this area that America's health problems are largely concentrated, untouched by free-enterprise medicine (see below).

Another aspect of organization related to the question of public control is *where* the personnel and facilities operate. Maldistribution of resources geographically, in relation to needs for health care, is an important source of poor *aggregate* performance, for the people who are badly serviced may contribute disproportionately to national mortality and morbidity rates. Countries with scattered rural populations require more personnel if the people are to be cared for as effectively as in highly urbanized lands. A degree of public control is required to make sure that isolated populations are served. At one extreme, this can take the form of comprehensive resource-allocation planning and manpower direction, as in the USSR, while at the other it requires at least sufficient financial incentive to attract doctors from more lucrative urban practices to country areas (and also to poor city locations). The high general levels of health in Norway and Sweden are indicative of the effectiveness of these nations' health services in meeting the needs of scattered rural populations. An extreme case from elsewhere is Australia's flying-doctor service for the people of the 'outback'.

Now that we have reached questions of spatial organization within nations, we have come to the limit of what can be learned from aggregate international comparisons. Some of the above observations are suggestive of spatial policies and their likely outcomes; for example, relatively even levels of health among territorial subdivisions of a nation require specific spatial resource-allocation strategies, that themselves require some public control. But to learn more of how spatial discrimination in access to health care arises, we need to look within nations – at some specific distributions and the forces moulding them.

Free-enterprise 'Care': The United States

The obvious place to begin a more detailed look at the delivery of health care and its distributional outcomes is the United States. As we have seen, aggregate measures of the national level of health show the American people markedly worse off than the prosperity of the country would suggest. Our crude composite mortality index places the USA thirteenth among the twenty nations in Table 5.2, below all those listed under the British Isles, Scandinavia and Western Europe. On a world scale the USA would rank even lower, because of the superior performance of Australia, New Zealand, Canada and perhaps even some Eastern European nations. Figure 5.2 suggests that, if the USA was in a position on the graph appropriate to its average mortality ranking, its GNP per capita would be less than $2000 a year instead of the actual figure of over $4000. On the individual mortality measures, the USA ranks fourteenth for perinatal deaths, tenth for infant and maternal mortality and seventeenth for males dying between the ages of 35 and 44. On life expectation, the USA, ranks eighth for females but as low as fifteenth for males.

One possible reason for the poor showing of the USA is that the resources actually devoted to health care are relatively small. But this is not so. In 1971 the USA spent 7.4 per cent of GNP on health compared with only 4.9 per cent in Britain. Since 1950 this proportion has risen by 60 per cent (from 4·6) compared with only 20 per cent in Britain (from 4·1 per cent of GNP in 1950), yet of the four conditions listed in Table 5.2 only infant mortality has improved faster in the USA than in Britain (R. Maxwell, 1974). More to the point is that care is extremely expensive in the USA compared with elsewhere, so much so that the per capita annual expenditure on health, even at the present high level, will buy only about two days of acute hospital care, including physician's fees. Part of the high cost is undoubtedly accounted for by the quality of the facilities offered in private hospitals (often including single room, television and choice of menus) and by treatment that may involve surgery or prescription of drugs beyond what is clinically necessary to cure the patient. This, in its turn, is a result of the fee-for-service system, in which private gain can easily come before the strict demands of efficient health-care practice. Very simply, the American doctor (and dentist) has a strong personal pecuniary motive for prescribing unnecessarily expensive treatment.

It may be difficult for people brought up with Britain's National Health Service to understand the extent to which the provision of medical and dental care in the United States is run on business lines. There is a set of interrelated multi-million dollar private industries focused on health, including drug manufacturing companies, hospital suppliers and insurance companies – as there is in Britain. But, in the USA, these are closely integrated financially with the hospitals and medical practices themselves. A doctor may have a financial interest in the hospital to which he refers his patients, in the store from which they buy their drugs, or in the laboratory where the blood tests are done. The American Medical Association maintains its members' monopoly by restricting entry to the profession, strictly limiting what support personnel such as nurses can do, and fighting the slightest threat to the freedom of private practice. Hence, the high salaries of American doctors. Capital is attracted to the health business, as to any other, by the prospect of good profits. Robson (1977, p. 31) cites the case of Jack C. Massey, Chairman of Kentucky Fried Chicken, who resigned to become head of the Hospital Corporation of America and commented that 'the growth potential in hospitals is unlimited; it's even better than Kentucky Fried Chicken'. As Robson remarks, the pickings are 'finger-lickin' good. In other words, health 'care' is a market commodity, like fried chicken, cigarettes or motor vehicles. Its production and distribution are organized accordingly, in response to profit-making rather than human need.

But there are two particular features of the American free-enterprise health care system that appear to account for its high in-efficiency, when outcomes are related to resources committed. These are the allocation of resources among different aspects of health care, and the geographical distribution of facilities and personnel. Both combine to put certain groups of people in certain places at a sub-stantial disadvantage with respect to access to care. And it is the inferior level of health of such people that so greatly depresses aggregate national performance indicators.

The resource allocation problem is expressed in the advanced development of certain technically sophisticated and professionally prestigious practices, while the more fundamental needs of those who lack effective demand in the medical market-place go largely ignored. The United States has achieved great success in such innovating fields as organ transplant and cosmetic surgery, yet even basic ante-natal care may not exist in some communities. Access to hospital or a physician's consulting room (appropriately termed 'office') may be effectively denied to the poor and the aged, despite public hospitals and such programmes as Medicare and Medicaid which by no means fill the gaps left by the fee-for-service system. The comparative study cited in the previous section describes the problem as follows (R. Maxwell, 1974, pp. 20–21):

> The search for prestige, money and good living has led a high pro-portion [of physicians] into specialist practice in affluent communities, leaving many areas sorely deficient in needed medical services Thus, a far higher proportion of American than of British or Swedish doctors practise surgery [25 per cent compared with 15 and 14 per cent respect-ively] – one third of them, incidentally, without certification as surgeons. Meanwhile, in the slums of New York City no primary care is available outside hospital emergency rooms; many rural areas can no longer recruit doctors for their hospitals, let alone for general practice; and even in the prosperous suburbs most people have difficulty finding a doctor outside working hours. In fact, the United States shows an inverse correlation between the geographic distribution of health care needs and resources, respectively. Affluent areas attract the most doctors, yet illness is most prevalent among the poor. In other words, the fewest resources are available to those most in need.

Under these circumstances, increasing the number of physicians available may contribute little to the general level of health, unless they work in neglected fields and in neglected places. This is the classic case of what Hart (1971) has termed the Inverse Care Law, which states: 'The availability of good medical care tends to vary inversely with the need for it in the population served. This operates more completely where medical care is most exposed to market forces and less so where it is reduced.'

The uneven geographical distribution of doctors and other health care resources in the USA is well documented (e.g. Lankford, 1974; Shannon and Dever, 1974, pp. 37–45). It is also part of day-to-day experience, even for those not actually seeking a doctor: the book on health care delivery by Shannon and Dever features on its cover a photograph of a banner across the main street of Attica, Ohio, reading 'WE NEED A DOCTOR', and this author noted a similar sign displayed continuously from 1966 to 1970 in a small Southern Illinois town. Figure 5.3 shows the situation by states. The number of physicians per 100,000 people varies from almost 250 in New York and Maryland to less than 100 in Alabama, Mississippi, Arkansas and South Dakota. The relative disadvantage of the South shows up clearly. Differences among cities are even more marked: the twenty largest metropolitan areas show a range from 321 physicians per 100,000 in Boston to 139 in Detroit (de Vise, 1973, p. 70).

The distribution of physicians bears quite a close inverse relationship to the pattern of infant mortality by states (Figure 1.5): the fewer the doctors, the more children die in infancy. The pattern of physicians is not hard to explain: in America's free-enterprise system doctors go where the money is, and there is a high positive correlation ($r=0.7$) between a state's per capita income and the physician-to-population ratio. Other factors that might influence location, such as where the doctor trained, where the best facilities are, and environmental quality, strengthen the attraction of prosperous places.

The state pattern, of course, hides more local manifestations of uneven resource allocation. One is the urban-rural difference, with rural areas consistently less well served with doctors, in addition to suffering from the relative inaccessibility of hospitals and other specialist facilities. The neglect of the health of poor blacks in the rural South is well known; the difficulty of obtaining even the basic care assured in many poorer countries (together with the inadequate

261

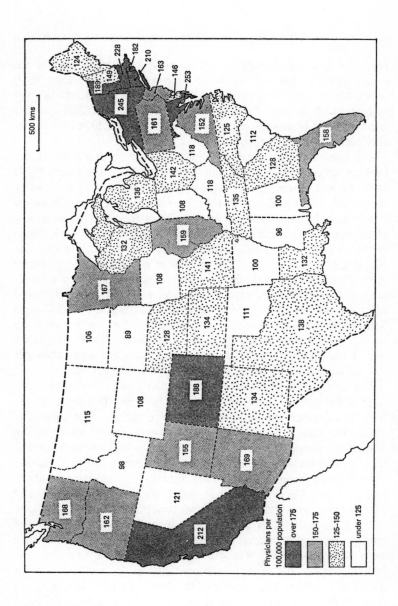

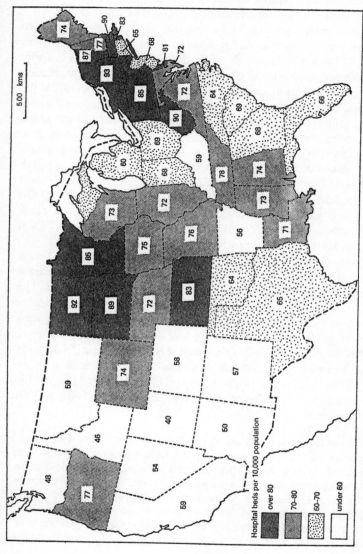

Figure 5.3. Physicians and hospital beds per capita in the United States, 1973. (Source of data: *Statistical Abstract of the United States*, USGPO.)

Hospital beds per 10,000 population

over 80
70–80
60–70
under 60

500 kms

nutrition), is expressed in mortality rates comparable with those in parts of the underdeveloped world, as we saw in Chapter 1.

But it is within the American city that inequalities in access to care are most apparent. A few specific cases (from Shannon and Dever, 1974) are sufficient to make the point. In the Los Angeles slums centred on Watts the effective ratio of physicians to population is 33 per 100,000 compared with a national figure of 158 (1970); the main source of primary care for the poor is in fact the Los Angeles County-University of Southern California Medical Center about twelve miles away, i.e. two hours by the public transport system. Washington D.C. has only 10 per cent of its physicians in the predominantly black (and poor) south-east and north-east quadrants, though they have 57 per cent of the city's population. Chicago's all-white East Garfield Park area had 212 physicians' offices in the 1930s: today there are 13 to serve 63,000 people, in what is now a black neighbourhood. Kenwood-Oakland had 110 physicians for its 28,400 white residents in 1930; today 5 physicians serve 45,400 blacks.

Three problems are interrelated in the American city. The first is that conditions of the social and physical environment generate greater need for health care in poor areas like the black ghettos. The second is that these are the areas worst served by the physicians to whom people look for primary care. The third is difficulty of physical access to public health facilities, given that real access to private facilities is barred by lack of money. The situation in Chicago is typical. In this city's 'apartheid' health service, well described by de Vise (1973), there is the single facility of Cook County Hospital for those unable to afford the private sector. As Morrill (1970, p. 170) says of this city:

> Social and economic distinctions according to race and income effectively reduce access to physicians and hospitals for the Negro and for the poor in general. Consequently, these patients must travel much further on the average than more affluent white patients: perhaps the majority travel beyond intervening opportunities not open to them (a critical matter if in urgent cases). These constraints can be overcome, given appropriate financial measures to encourage physicians to practice in or near hospitals in poor areas, in addition to the new programs to enable hospitals to care for poorer patients.

Problems of physical access may themselves be compounded by poverty, and are certainly not confined to the big city. In a smaller Florida city known to the author it could cost a $5 taxi fare to get to the hospital from the black residential area (there being no public transport) – a quarter of the prevailing weekly wage of a domestic servant at that time (1971). A quarter of the weekly wage of many white citizens could have taken them to New York.

The delivery of health care in the USA thus reveals a situation of spatial imbalance between supply and need. People most in need of care may find it hard to get locally, and when they do attend a public hospital or Medicare physician the standard of service may be inferior to that in the private sector. How this affects national aggregate performance can be explained quite simply, with the aid of a diagram (Figure 5.4). Health care typically operates under de-

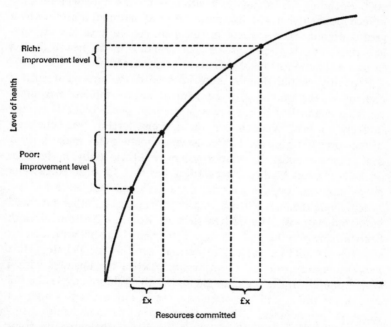

Figure 5.4. The implications of diminishing returns on the allocation of resources in pursuit of improved social service performance.

creasing returns to further expenditure, which means that the more money spent, the less the final pound, dollar or whatever, will achieve by way of reduced mortality or morbidity. Thus Figure 5.4 shows a performance indicator (e.g. infant mortality) turning down as expenditure rises: something is achieved by each addition of resources, but it is less than from the last equivalent addition. The diagram shows two communities, rich and poor, the former enjoying high health by the performance indicator while the other has a lower level. Now, suppose that the same sum of money (x) could be spent in either the poor or the rich community. The graph shows that a greater improvement in health would be achieved in the poor community. For example, 1 million spent in a poor inner-city area on basic ante-natal care might reduce infant mortality by 10 per 1000, while the same expenditure in a rich suburb might reduce the rate by only 1 per 1000. Spending the money on health care for the poor will not only reduce inequality; it will also reduce over-all national mortality by a greater amount than if spent on the rich. As we have already suggested, America's poor aggregate performance in the health field is in part a function of maldistribution of resources.

Explicitly spatial policies may be needed to implement such a change, as the quotation from Morrill above implies. Resources must be channelled to the areas of greatest need. But this is very unlikely to take place under the present largely free-enterprise system prevailing in the United States. Doctors can make a great deal of money under the present system, and their lobby, in the form of the American Medical Association, has thus far been effective in preventing the implementation of a national public-health-care system along the lines of those that exist in almost all other advanced industrial nations. Alternatives such as Britain's National Health Service (shrewdly termed 'socialized medicine' in this anti-socialist society) are seldom subject to serious scrutiny or debate. Most Americans are protected by insurance, itself a big business with a vested interest in the present system, but this seldom covers the full cost of treatment and the premiums are in any event too high for those on low incomes. Although some type of national health insurance embracing all the population has been advocated by some influential politicians (such as Edward Kennedy) it will take more than this to correct the present uneven distribution of resources. Only when health care becomes a public service and an essential part of an American citizen's rights can there be any serious attempt to create something approaching equality of access irrespective of race, class or place of residence.

Inequality in a National Health Service: Great Britain

Since 1948, health care in Britain has been available as a free public service. A private sector is still maintained for the indigenous rich and those of the middle class who can afford health insurance and choose this form of protection, along with wealthy oil sheiks and others from overseas. But, for the vast majority of the population, health care is now provided by the National Health Service. As part of the welfare state built up since the Second World War, the NHS is supposed to make care equally available to all. Health care is thus considered a public good, in the traditional economic sense of the term. Demand in the market-place is replaced by administrative procedures and professional judgement as to the distribution of health care resources, which can thus be planned with specific objectives towards equity in mind.

However, experience has shown that a system like the NHS does not guarantee equality of access to care, either absolutely or in relation to need. The initial distribution of facilities cannot be changed overnight, as vast investments of capital are involved, fixed in one place in the form of hospitals and other buildings. Personnel are potentially more mobile, but even here there are personal, professional and institutional factors making for an uneven distribution among specialities and among territories. Added to this is the fact that there is no such thing as equal access to services or facilities occupying discrete points in geographical space. Distance introduces an element of inequality or 'impurity' into the provision of public goods such as health care. Indeed, differences of physical accessibility to sources of care can be thought of as prices, exacted in the form of

267

time, effort and money expended. The NHS may be a great improvement on free-enterprise medicine, but it certainly does not offer equal treatment or distribution strictly according to need.

The question of justice in distribution of personal social services under the welfare state came to the fore about ten years ago. Davies (1968) introduced the concept of 'territorial justice' as a guide to resource allocation that would imply an areal distribution according to the needs of the population. But it was Coates and Rawstron (1971) who first used the traditional cartographic techniques of the geographer to show how far spatial variations in health care resources still exist under the NHS. They revealed the four metropolitan Regional Hospital Board Areas of South-East England to be at a distinct advantage compared with most other parts of the country, on the basis of such indicators as hospital beds per capita, reliance on junior staff or doctors from overseas, size of general practitioner lists and quality of consultants (as reflected in holders of 'merit awards', which are given in recognition of special skills and which qualify the holder for additional remuneration). The deprived areas were found to be concentrated particularly in the older industrial areas of the north and west, in parts of Greater London (despite the over-all advantage of the metropolis) and in the less prosperous farming areas.

Coates and Rawstron (1971, ch. 9) also drew attention to geographical variations in mortality, which show certain northern industrial areas in an unfavourable light. More detailed research reported in the national atlas of disease and mortality prepared by Howe (1970) draws particular attention to the high mortality rates in the industrial cities of South Wales, central Scotland, the industrial north of England and certain parts of inner London, findings that tend to accord with the pattern of resource allocation. Figure 5.5 summarizes the broad, regional pattern of health in England and Wales, as revealed by four different indicators. The general deterioration from South-East (core) to north and west (periphery) is the same as was observed in regional levels of life quality, as identified in Chapter 3 (see Figure 3.4).

An impression of the way in which health care resources are allocated geographically is provided by Rickard (1975; Buxton, 1976, pp. 39–45). He calculated the per capita expenditure for each of the

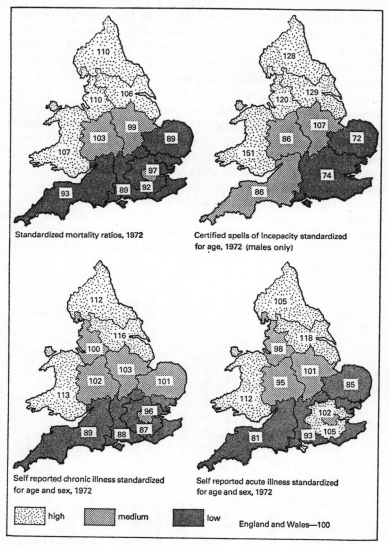

Standardized mortality ratios, 1972

Certified spells of incapacity standardized for age, 1972 (males only)

Self reported chronic illness standardized for age and sex, 1972

Self reported acute illness standardized for age and sex, 1972

high   medium   low

England and Wales—100

Figure 5.5. Regional variations in level of health in England and Wales, by four different measures, 1972. (Source of data: Department of Health and Social Security, 1976, Figure 11.2.)

269

ninety Area Health Authorities into which the Regions are sub-divided. The figures relate to current expenditure on general hospitals, psychiatric hospitals and community health services, not including the contribution of capital. The results for all services together are plotted by Regional Health Authority in Figure 5.6. At the RHA level, per capita expenditures vary from £34·16 in the SW Thames Region to £22·69 in Trent and the W Midlands. But there are very considerable differences among AHAs, often within the same Region. The AHA figures range from the exceptionally high £54·17 in Liverpool (the result of high general-hospital expenditures) to £17·14 in the Sandwell AHA of the W Midlands Region. Some RHAs reveal much greater inter-AHA variation than others, as is shown by a comparison between the Northern RHA (AHA range from £38·22 to £19·00) and Wessex (£24·65 to £26·01). But the major conclusion is that the AHA is a more significant areal unit for revealing spatial inequalities in resource allocation: the RHA figures hide the more local extremes.

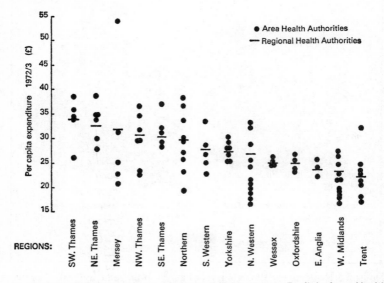

Figure 5.6. Variations in per capita expenditure among English Area Health Authorities and Regions. (Source of data: Buxton, 1976, pp. 43–5.)

The origin of the pattern of uneven resource allocation observed by Coates and Rawstron, Rickard and others is not hard to find. As Buxton (1976, p. 9) observes, 'geographical inequalities today are still very much the result of unequal distribution of incomes and charity prior to 1948.' Under the National Health Service, revenue expenditure and capital investment have tended to follow the pre-existing pattern. The essentially incremental approach of simply adding a standard growth component to the previous year's RHA budget may indeed reinforce the relative advantage of certain regions. However, some shifts in the direction of greater territorial equality can be detected. For example, the earlier extremes in size of general practice lists seem to have been eliminated; AHAs with low figures (i.e. under 2500 people per GP) are now the peripheral areas with large rural populations, whereas before the NHS was set up the South-East tended to be more favourably serviced. There is also evidence of an evening out of the distribution of consultant distinction-awards among regions during the period 1960–74 (Buxton, 1976).

The persistence of spatial inequalities in the provision of health care is a matter of great current concern in Britain. The critical question of need has long been overlooked; as Culyer (1976, p. 113) puts it: 'The ideal of equal available care for equal need could never have been implemented in the first twenty years or so of the NHS's existence for the simple reason that need had never been given operational (or even meaningful!) content, nor was there much attempt to do so.' Serious attention is now being given to the identification of local levels of need, so as to judge more effectively the extent of the disparities and the reallocation of resources required to redress them. The latest policy document to consider these issues is a report of the Resource Allocation Working Party (Department of Health and Social Security, 1976). To quote its term of reference, the Working Party was set up to 'review the arrangements for distributing NHS capital and revenue to RHAs, AHAs and Districts respectively with a view to establishing a method of securing as soon as practicable, a pattern of distribution responsive objectively, equitably and efficiently to relative need'. The findings of this study help to underline the difficulty of designing and implementing redistributive policy in social services, even with public control.

The Working Party considered the allocation of both revenue and capital expenditures. With respect to revenue, they attempted to establish a target for each RHA, based on need. The 'crude' population was recognized as being inadequate as a need criterion, because of inter-regional differences in population composition and in existing levels of health, so various adjustments were employed. Non-psychiatric in-patient services may serve as an example: first, the population of each Region was weighted to reflect differences in age/sex composition that generate different levels of utilization of health care facilities; then, the Standardized Mortality Ratio was used to reflect the unique pattern of mortality in each Region. Thus, the greater a Region's share of population groups making relatively heavy demands on facilities, and the greater its mortality rates (standardized for population composition), the greater the Region's population would be weighted. The higher the weight, the greater the need. Calculations were made for seven separate service branches: non-psychiatric in-patient care, all day- and out-patients, community health, ambulance services, mental illness in-patient care, mental handicap in-patients, and family planning. Different methods of weighting were applied in some cases because of the special nature of the service involved. Then the seven weightings were combined in proportion to the actual revenue expenditure on each of the services concerned, to give a final aggregate weighted population for each RHA. This in its turn was subject to other adjustments to reflect such factors as inter-regional patient flows and the additional cost imposed by London salary weightings of NHS employees.

The RHA population, weighted thus according to need, is compared with the crude population in Table 5.4. The ratio of these two figures (dividing need-weighted population by crude or actual population) provides a measure of the discrepancy between them: the higher the ratio, the greater the need relative to actual population. Thus, the most 'needy' RHAs – the North-West and SW Thames – have a need 9 per cent greater than their actual population suggests. Regions with ratios above unity are mainly in the north of England, but they do include two of the metropolitan (Thames) Regions. Of course, the extent of existing disparities in actual resource allocation is greater than the ratios in Table 5.4 suggest, because the most

Table 5.4. Regional population, need and resource allocation in the National
Health Service

Regions of England (RHAs)	Crude popn (1000s, 1975)	Weighted popn (1000s)	Weighted ÷ crude popn	Shortfall (−) or excess (+) of capital stock (£/cap)
Northern	3126	3183	1·02	−4·13
Yorkshire	3577	3679	1·03	−5·72
Trent	4545	4320	0·95	−7·72
East Anglian	1780	1678	0·94	+5·74
NW Thames	3475	3355	0·97	+16·28
NE Thames	3718	3719	1·00	+13·54
SE Thames	3603	3843	1·07	+0·84
SW Thames	2880	3132	1·09	+8·27
Wessex	2645	2581	0·98	−11·48
Oxford	2199	1926	0·88	+11·24
South-Western	3149	3032	0·96	−1·16
West Midlands	5178	4941	0·95	−6·75
Mersey	2499	2606	1·04	+17·53
North-Western	4078	4457	1·09	−16·54
England	46,454	46,454		

Source: Department of Health and Social Security, 1976.

needy Regions tend to get less per capita revenue than the others, even on the basis of their crude populations, as Figure 5.6 showed.

Table 5.4 also lists some results from the Working Party's calculations of need with respect to capital investment in hospitals and so on. The shortfall or excess per head of population according to need shows how unevenly the existing capital stock is distributed among RHAs. Again, the disadvantaged RHAs tend to be concentrated in the north, with the South-East relatively well off. However, Merseyside is much better off than might be expected, and Wessex markedly worse off than other southern Regions.

The resources needed to redress the disparities in regional levels of service provision are enormous. To rectify the capital shortfalls identified in Table 5.4 would cost £216 million. To equalize RHA revenue in relation to need would require very considerable reallocations within the national expenditure of about £2505 million. There are practical constraints in the way of immediate reallocation to implement equality, even if such a move was politically feasible. For example, existing facilities require a minimum flow of resources simply to ensure their continuing efficient operation, and even the most vigorous attempt at reallocation among Regions must allow for this. Thus, the Working Party's final recommendations are for limited reallocation, subject to various constraints to protect the level of service in the better-off RHAs. The time-scale for achieving equal access to health care for people at equal risk is 'eventually' (DHSS, 1976, p. 7).

Even limited reallocation of resources will have considerable impact on the operation of the health service in Regions suffering a relative reduction in funds. At times of national financial stringency and general cut-backs in social service expenditure, reallocation can be an especially painful process; it is much easier in an era of economic growth when poor areas can gain without hurting the rich. Metropolitan RHAs have already announced plans to close hospitals in the light of their probably smaller relative share of resources. For example, the North-East Thames RHA has proposed the closure of more than twenty hospitals over the next ten years, involving a loss of 4500 personnel and 4600 hospital beds, or one in seven of the Region's total.

This kind of outcome raises important questions of social justice that must be squarely faced if the equity objectives of resource reallocation are really to be achieved. By the criterion of need, the metropolitan RHAs are certainly over-provided with health care facilities, especially when compared with most of the northern Regions. But, as we have observed, there are great disparities in allocation *within* Regions – generally in the direction of fewer resources available in AHAs and Districts where need is greatest. There is serious concern at present that cut-backs in the metropolitan Regions could hurt the under-provided areas within them more than the better-off areas. Greater regional equality would thus have been achieved at the price of some increase in local inequality. In this type of problem the geographical scale becomes critical in determining whether equity objectives have in fact been met, or whether the outcomes merely give the illusion of greater equality. Much more attention has to be given to the question of precisely who will gain

274

or lose *where* from the spatial reorganization initiated by shifts in resources, if changes of the kind under way in the NHS are to achieve their avowed aims.

Resource allocation on a territorial basis is, of course, only one element in a complex web of problems currently besetting the NHS. A number of other important issues also have a bearing on who gets what sort of care where. For example, redistribution of resources to achieve greater equality is constrained by the total NHS budget. If this could be increased, services in deprived areas could be improved with less unfavourable impact elsewhere, as was suggested above. But the NHS, and social services generally, have borne the brunt of recent cuts in public spending, in the misguided belief that, in times of economic crises, the maintenance of the health of the population can be more readily sacrificed than 'productive' endeavours. The question of private practice, 'pay beds' and so on is also relevant: these relics of the old fee-for-service days not only direct resources to people and places with the money to buy private care, but also distract the attention of some of society's more influential and articulate members from what is going on in the public sector, from which most ordinary people cannot opt out. As in education, 'freedom of choice' (for those with the money) is not exercised independently of the situation of others. The role of the privately-controlled pharma-ceutical production and distribution industry is also significant: as in the USA and elsewhere, such commercial organizations have a vested interest in the consumption of drugs, which does not neces-sarily coincide with the best interests of the sick. Whatever the general merits of private enterprise and market mechanisms as regulators of supply and demand, it is difficult to see them as effective agents of resource allocation in a situation where most patients (and not a few doctors) lack the knowledge to function as discriminating consumers.

Within the NHS itself there are questions as to whether the limited resources available are being spent wisely. Doctors complain that there are too many people employed in administration and that increased bureaucratization threatens their traditional freedom of clinical judgement. Critics of the medical profession complain that there is too much stress on high-technology curative treatment: 'To

275

prolong life for short periods at great cost, to make the doctor into God, to run increasingly away from the existential need to face up to and accept death.' (de Kadt, 1976, p. 526.) Perhaps more emphasis should be placed on preventive medicine, and on a system that regards patients as people rather than as 'cases'. While issues such as these may not be strictly geographical, they form part of the context within which decisions are made on how money is spent in health care – on what, for whom and where. Geographical reallocation of public resources within the NHS may be necessary for the creation of something approaching equal access to care, but this alone will not be sufficient.

Local Imbalance of Resources and Need: Sydney, Australia

The critical requirement of any social service is, of course, that it should be in the right place when people need it. However indicative broad regional variations in level of resources committed may be, it is at the local level that availability and physical access become especially important in determining whether or not a person gets to the doctor or into hospital. It is well established that the use of health facilities is subject to a distance-decay effect, whereby the nearer a person lives to a facility the more likely he or she is to use it (assuming that there are no non-spatial barriers to access, such as income or ignorance). Thus, the precise location of facilities will have a bearing on who gets care where. And there is every reason to suspect that the location of hospitals, physicians and related services is most unlikely to be an accurate reflection of need.

The Sydney metropolitan area in Australia provides an interesting illustration of the spatial imbalance between resources and need within the city. The metropolis has a population of well over 2·5 million, with its outer suburbs now extending up to 25 miles from the centre of the City of Sydney. The urban area has expanded in an asymmetrical manner owing to the original harbour site. As so often happens, service facilities have failed to keep pace with the growth of the built-up area, so that the newer suburbs are at a marked disadvantage with respect to access to hospitals. It is not a case of under-supply of facilities, but that the expansion in the form of such things as new wards and beds takes place largely in existing hospitals. Suburban development has been confined to small 'community' hospitals with a limited range of services. As a report undertaken in 1969 put it: 'there are sufficient public hospital beds in the Sydney Metropolitan Area; but due to changes in urban development and the outward spread of residential suburbs, the hospital accommodation is largely provided where people us*d* to live'. (Quoted in Lawrence, 1972, p. 115.)

The location of hospitals in the Sydney metropolis is illustrated in Figure 5.7. They are tightly concentrated in and around the City of Sydney, which is now very much off-centre as a result of the inland pattern of urban growth. The point of maximum access to this pattern of facilities, as calculated by Freestone (1975), corresponds with one of the inner group of hospitals, whereas the optimum point (the point of minimum aggregate travel for the entire metropolitan population) is in the Borough of Strathfield seven miles west of the City of Sydney (D. M. Smith, 1977, pp. 315–19). The present location pattern is thus a source of very substantial cost to the population of the metropolis, in terms of time and travel expenditure. This affects not only patients, but also visitors, who may be deterred from giving friends and relatives their support by the distances that have to be overcome to get to hospitals. Visiting is very important to patients, especially children. Any difficulties in terms of additional time and expense will disproportionally hurt people with inflexible working hours and limited financial resources.

An initial summary of the imbalance between hospital beds and local need is provided by a tabulation prepared for the Metropolitan Hospital Survey in 1969 (Lawrence, 1972, p. 116). The City of Sydney had 3783 beds, compared with a 'theoretical requirement' of 636 according to an estimate of need, an excess of 3147. In the inner suburbs the figures were 2343 and 2180 respectively, giving an excess of 163. But in the middle ring of suburbs there were only 2765 beds compared with a needed 3700 (deficit 935), while in the outer suburban ring the difference was even greater (1659 and 3928, deficit 2269). Table 5.5 provides a more up-to-date picture, based on a different subdivision of the metropolis (see Figure 5.7), and a

Figure 5.7. The location of hospitals in the Sydney metropolitan area, with points of maximum over-all accessibility and minimum aggregate travel. (Source: hospital locations from Freestone, 1975, Fig. 3.)

Table 5.5. The imbalance between supply and need for hospital beds in metropolitan Sydney, Australia

Sector	Capacity 1971 (a)	Need 1971 (b)	difference (a–b)	Need 1980 (c)	difference (a–c)
Inner	4740	3450	+1290	3471	+1269
Southern	2381	2651	−270	2979	−598
Northern	1792	2483	+691	2743	−951
Western	1616	2493	−877	4087	−2471
Total	10,529	11,077	−548	13,280	−2751

Source: Freestone, 1975, Table 4.

Note: the figures relate to medical, surgical, gynaecological, paediatric and obstetric beds.

prediction of the situation in 1980. The 1971 figures show a surplus of beds in the inner area and also in the northern sector with its relatively well-to-do suburbs; the south has a deficit, but the greatest shortfall in relation to need is in the west where most of the low- or middle-income suburban development has taken place. Prediction of need up to 1980 shows the inner area unchanged because of its stable population, but the rapidly-growing northern sector now joins the others as a bed-deficit area.

Some of the problems that arise in attempting to correct what appears to be a maldistribution of facilities are the same as anywhere else. Hospitals cannot simply be moved, and a growth of resources is needed to implement any redistribution that is inevitably an expansion of the system. Hospitals are costly to construct and take time to plan and build: the development of a new teaching hospital near Parramatta in the western suburbs has been under discussion for years, but the first stage alone is not expected to be completed before the late 1980s (Freestone, 1975, p. 20). Major changes in service provision often have to contend with professional and bureaucratic conservatism or inertia, and this seems to have been a particular feature of Sydney. Freestone (1975, pp. 19–20) suggests that rivalry and competition between the teaching hospitals has led them to duplicate facilities and to provide a standard of care quite unrelated to real needs, similar to the specialization tendency in the

USA under which superlative care is provided for the rich, to the neglect of the poor. Professional preoccupation with prestige curative treatment as opposed to a more preventive approach is not conducive to the comprehensive planning of health care delivery required to create a better spatial balance between resources and need. As in other systems with a strong tradition of independence on the part of the medical profession, conflict can easily arise between the general societal objectives implied in redistributive planning and the narrower, more clinical approach of physicians themselves.

But the question of spatial reorganization at the intra-metropolitan level also raises the issue of efficiency as an objective that may conflict with equity in distribution – in Sydney, London or anywhere else. To provide certain highly specialized services requires some concentration of effort if the cost is not to be prohibitive. This is a simple matter of economies of scale: a minimum size of unit is needed, with a minimum caseload, to maintain specialist services in medical care, just as a minimum market size is needed to support a department store or a branch of a retail chain. Major teaching hospitals generally provide such services for entire metropolitan areas. These hospitals may form the core of an interrelated complex of laboratories, surgeries, consulting rooms and various other ancillary activities, rather like an industrial complex tied together by commercial links between buyers and sellers of materials and components. Thus, from an efficiency point of view, some highly centralized facilities are inevitable. It is sometimes argued that the optimal spatial arrangement of medical facilities in a city or region will resemble the nested hierarchy familiar to students of retail organization (Shannon and Dever, 1974, pp. 10–14). Thus there might be a major regional hospital in the metropolis offering highly specialized services as well as more routine treatment, district hospitals in regional sub-centres and perhaps in some suburban communities, and then smaller hospitals providing limited services at the local urban-community level and in the countryside. Such an arrangement may well offer the best balance between the conflicting centripetal forces driven by economies of scale and the spatial spread of care required to maximize individual access to facilities.

280

While the core feature of such a system, in the form of the major specialist or teaching hospital, seems to emerge out of the necessity for conservation of resources, the completion of the hierarchy down to the local source of care requires a much greater degree of planning and, perhaps, a willingness to sacrifice some purely economic efficiency in the interests of a more equitable distribution of care.

Before leaving this case it should be stressed (not for the first time in this chapter) that health is not simply a matter of physical access to facilities. The need for care arises from personal and environmental circumstances that may be quite unrelated to whether there is a hospital close at hand. In metropolitan Sydney, for example, the highest levels of infant mortality are in the City of Sydney itself, well situated with respect to access to hospitals but with a disproportionate share of people of low socio-economic status, as indicated by rentals, occupational structure, education and car ownership (Stilwell and Hardwick, 1973). Infant mortality in some of the western suburbs, which have the greatest deficit of hospital beds, is well above that in the inner and more affluent suburbs, but not as high as in the City itself. In a study of infant mortality in another Australian city, Melbourne, M. G. A. Wilson (1972) found variations by municipalities from 9 per 1000 to almost 27, and suggests a relationship with such conditions as housing quality, mothers at work and non-British immigrant population. The basis of differentiation is socio-economic (class with some ethnic overtones), rather than access to maternity beds. The spatial reorganization of health care delivery may promote more equal access to care, but it may have little effect on the forces making for differences in need for care.

An extreme case in Sydney may be used to underline this point. The Aboriginal population suffer severe social and economic deprivation in many Australian cities. Rather like the American Indian, they often lack formal education and job skills, find adjustment to urban life difficult, and suffer various kinds of social ostracism and discrimination. And, as with the Indian, they tend to be a source of embarrassment – a reminder of how the white settlers hurt the indigenous population, which contemporary society would like to forget. Hence, their shameful neglect in affluent

Where the Grass is Greener

America and Australia. A recent report by Dr Lou Rassaby describes something of the health conditions prevailing among Aboriginals in the inner Sydney suburb of Redfern (*The Times*, 12 Aug. 1977). More than a quarter of Sydney's Aboriginal children under five years old suffer serious malnutrition and most of them have permanent brain damage because of undernourishment. Of the 6000 Aboriginal children under five in Redfern, 64 per cent are anaemic, 60 per cent have a parasitic bowel infection, 32 per cent have at least one perforated eardrum, and 27 per cent have a condition known as lactose interference, which means that they cannot absorb food from milk because of chronic diarrhoea. These conditions are more typical of an underdeveloped African nation than of well-to-do Australia. What is more, this situation exists amid the densest concentration of health care facilities in the state, as the report points out. Redfern is, in fact, virtually on the peak of the Sydney hospital accessibility surface suggested in Figure 5.7. The problem is not necessarily that these children do not get into hospital – far from it: 20 per cent have already been in more than twice, with an average stay of 88 days. The condition of Aboriginal children is more a problem of group deprivation. By the time they get into hospital, the damage from malnutrition and related diseases may have already been done. Improving the health of deprived minorities like the Aboriginals requires providing the right kind of facilities within their local community, as part of a broader programme designed to combat the origins of their poverty.

Health Care and Underdevelopment

As was suggested earlier in this chapter, the problem of health in the underdeveloped world is one of limited resources rather than of spatial organization. Nevertheless, the location of facilities, however limited, can have a bearing on who gets health care and who does not, by virtue of difficulty of physical access. In the developed world a trip of ten or fifteen miles from the suburb to the central hospital, though inconvenient for some people and perhaps a real barrier to access for a few, can generally be undertaken quite conveniently by

282

car or public transport. In the underdeveloped world such distances are much less easily covered, so that the distance-decay effect on facility utilization is much more severe.

Some evidence from Uganda helps to emphasize this point. Jolly and King (1966) have identified the level of utilization of health care facilities as it varies with distance, giving the distance-decay relationships summarized in Figure 5.8. The graph on the left shows number of out-patient attendances per person per year by distance from the patient's home. The distance-decay curve falls away rapidly at first, then less so. It is, in fact, a linear relationship when attendances are plotted on a logarithmic scale, as the second graph shows. What this means in practice is that someone living two miles from the hospital might visit out-patients four or five times a year whereas for someone five miles away it is likely to be only once. At distances of more than ten or twelve miles utilization virtually ceases; attendances will be less than one in ten years. The third graph compares hospital utilization with attendances at dispensaries and aid posts. The former resembles that of out-patient visits. But use of aid posts, offering minimal treatment at the local level, halves with every additional mile from the facility. Very few visits will be made by people living

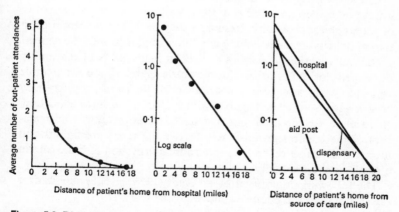

Figure 5.8. Distance decay relationships in the utilization of health care facilities in Uganda. (Source: Jolly and King, 1966, Figs. 4, 5 and 6; D. M. Smith, 1977, Fig. 11.6.)

Where the Grass is Greener

more than about five miles away; the cost of motor transport, if available, rises steeply with distance, and many patients have no choice but to walk to the post.

The impact of the location of facilities, their general scarcity and difficulties of access, means that most people are under-supplied with basic health care. In the Mityana area on the northern side of Lake Victoria, Jolly and King (1966; D. M. Smith, 1977, p. 311) show that in only a small proportion of the territory will attendance at health care facilities reach a suggested standard of 2·5 times a year, given the distance-decay effect identified in Figure 5.8. Close to the hospitals, as many as six attendances a year might be expected but in the peripheral areas people will not receive medical treatment once in six years.

A possible solution to the problem of providing care for isolated rural settlements, where permanent facilities can hardly be justified, is a mobile service. If care can be at hand when needed, it does not matter that it is not permanently fixed in the area. But mobile facilities may be too expensive for a poor country to provide. Some equivalent of Australia's flying-doctor service is quite beyond the resources of the Ugandas of this world.

Uneven distribution of facilities and the consequent under-utilization by certain sections of the community is not only a matter of geographical proximity. Resources may be highly concentrated in the capital city or metropolitan core, in accordance with the general spatial-polarization tendencies evident in many parts of the under-developed world. The urban élite may have a level of care comparable with that in the advanced industrial world; the rural periphery may be severely discriminated against with respect to resource allocation. As in more advanced nations, personal aspirations may lead members of the medical profession to favour the more prestigious and lucrative city practices to the more routine provision of basic care in a small rural community.

The following description by de Kadt (1976, p. 525) summarizes the situation in the poorer countries of the world:

In all of them, there are inequalities in the resources available for health care to different groups or areas; these inequalities are much

284

greater than those in rich countries. One of the chief reasons for this is the rural-urban imbalance in most developing countries – that is, a concentration of health care resources in the towns together with a gross neglect of the countryside. Yet from 50 to 80 per cent (or even more) of the population live in the country. Statistics of doctor-population ratios tell the same sorry tale almost everywhere: immense inequalities (often ten to one, or more) between the capital city and the rest of the country, or the major towns and the rural areas. And only a little relief is provided by the all too small number of non-professional health workers (whom the Chinese have so successfully used under the name 'barefoot doctors' [see below]). Fundamentally, of course, these inequalities are just as much related to the class structure in poor countries as they are in rich ones. Those rural-urban differences are mainly a difference in class composition between countryside and town – the élite and most of the middle class being urban. Existing power relations have produced a health care system which benefits the latter at the expense of the vast majority.

These inequalities in provision of health care are mirrored by inequalities in health, just as in Britain but to a greater extent. The capacity to improve health for the mass of the people is constrained by health care systems that are, in de Kadt's words, 'small-scale carbon copies' of those in the rich countries of the world, with their stress on high-technology curative treatment rather than on basic preventive care. As in the developed world, the nature of the system is an outcome of the ideology and professional ethics of those who run it – the doctors. They tend to be recruited from the middle classes, and may have received part of their medical education overseas in a system with health problems that differ from those at home and where there are more resources to support expensive facilities. By social background and training, the doctors tend towards a particular class affiliation, played out in practice by preference for a kind of care that favours the demands of the well-to-do rather than the needs of the poverty-stricken sick.

The distribution of resources in Peru helps to highlight on a national scale some of the problems within the underdeveloped world. Facilities and personnel tend to be concentrated in the main urban areas, especially the Lima-Callao metropolis. Figures for 1972 show a ratio of 182 physicians per 100,000 population in the capital compared with only 26 in the rest of the country: for hospital beds the ratios are 46 per 10,000 in Lima-Callao ánd 13 outside (Pan American Health Organization, 1974, pp. 67 and 77). Such differences are typical of Latin America, and of the underdeveloped world in general. Looking at the distribution of health personnel in a little more detail, a clear relationship with size of settlement emerges. Table 5.6 shows that the number of people to each physician, dentist, pharmacist, nurse and midwife increases as population decreases. The very great relative disadvantage of the smallest settlements (under 10,000 people) stands out. The hospital beds-to-population ratio falls less closely with settlement size. But perhaps the most significant fact is that the actual use of physicians falls away down the urban hierarchy: visits per capita in metropolitan Lima are more than thirteen times those made in towns of under 10,000 population. Although these figures refer to the mid 1960s, similar differences probably exist today.

Recent years have seen the beginning of health planning in Peru, and with it some reallocation of resources. Evidence compiled by Slater (1975) suggests that there has been a tendency towards greater equality of provision, at least at the department level. But some parts of the country have become relatively worse off while others have improved quite substantially. Taking figures for hospital beds per

Table 5.6. The relationship between health services and settlement size in Peru, 1964

| Population size | Population per unit of personnel | | | | | Hospital beds per 10,000 popn | Visits to physicians per capita |
	phys-icians	dent-ists	pharm-acists	nurses	mid-wives		
Metro. Lima	600	2200	2100	1000	4000	56	4·1
50,000–249,999	1200	3200	2800	2300	9600	61	3·0
25,000–49,999	1600	3300	4900	2600	8400	47	2·9
10,000–24,999	2000	5000	5100	3900	8000	49	2·2
under 10,000	17,600	45,300	63,800	37,900	72,300	6	0·3
Peru	2200	6700	6600	3600	12,800	24	1·4

Source: Hill, 1969, passim.

10,000 people, transformed into standard scores, Slater identified two contrasting sets of departments, characterized respectively by improvements and deteriorations relative to the national departmental average (Table 5.7). The first set (A) consists of three departments already near the top of the list and improving, together with Pasco which showed a steady improvement from a below-average provision in 1946. The second set (B) comprises departments with below-average bed povision where there has been a relative deterioration: of these, Puno, Huancavelica, Ayacucho and Cuzco all belong to the severely underdeveloped region in the southern part of Peru, identified in Chapter 3. This observation echoes that made concerning level of development as a whole: there is a general reduction in inequality among departments, but this hides the fact that some of the better-off are becoming even more advantaged while the relative position of the worst-off is frequently static or deteriorating.

A particular feature of recent trends in Peru has been the marked deterioration, relatively, in the metropolitan area. Lima-Callao's standard score on hospital bed provision has gone down from 3·06 (i.e. three standard deviations above the national department average)

Table 5.7. Contrasting experiences of Peruvian departments with respect to the ratio of hospital beds to population

Department	1946	1955	1965
Set A			
1. Tacna	+0·735	+0·584	+2·609
2. Moquegua	+0·681	+0·519	+1·594
3. Arequipa	+0·789	+0·974	+1·304
4. Pasco	−0·508	−0·260	+0·290
Set B			
1. Puno	−0·724	−0·909	−1·014
2. Cajamarca	−0·724	−0·974	−0·942
3. Huancavelica	−0·832	−0·974	−0·942
4. Apurímac	−0·616	−0·844	−0·870
5. Ayacucho	−0·724	−0·844	−0·797
6. San Martín	−0·454	−0·649	−0·580
7. Cuzco	−0·400	−0·519	−0·507

Source: Slater, 1975, Table 2.13.
Note: the figures are standard scores.

in 1946 to 2·47 in 1955 and 1·67 in 1965 (Slater, 1975, p. 128). From being a clear leader in 1946, by 1965 the metropolis had been relegated to second place with respect to its beds-to-population ratio, well behind the department of Tacna and only slightly higher than Moquegua and Ica. The reason for this deterioration is that the provision of services in the metropolis has simply not kept pace with the rapid rise in population.

As we have observed a number of times already, aggregate data for areas the size of Lima-Callao hide the differential experience of different groups of people in different places within the metropolis. In the case of Lima-Callao the level of health care provided for the élite and well-to-do middle class has probably not suffered from the general relative decline in hospital bed provision; indeed, the quality of care for those who receive it has probably risen with advances in medical science. Those deprived of care are in the slum communities and squatter settlements, where numbers have been so greatly swollen by migration from the countryside. A survey of the attitude of *barriada* residents has identified location of medical services as a major source of public dissatisfaction: '97 per cent felt very strongly that medical services should be closer and ranked this aspect of lack of service provision higher than the need for improvements in such physical facilities as water supply, lighting and street paving.' (Dwyer, 1975, p. 252.) For some of the *pueblos jovenes* the only source of medical care appears to be a small clinic on the main road outside the settlement itself. Yet the environmental conditions in these settlements generate a disproportionate need for care, especially in routine matters that do not require heavy financial outlays.

The provision of health care in the exploding Third World city is but one aspect of the general problem of how services can be maintained in conditions of uncontrolled urban expansion. As with the broader condition of uneven development in countries like Peru, the solution requires fundamental changes in the way society organizes the provision of sources of human need satisfaction. Setting up such facilities as aid posts and mobile clinics in the *barriadas* will obviously be of some help. But the ability to provide even modest improvements in care for the poor will remain limited as long as income, wealth and effective political power remain so unequally distributed.

Our emphasis on the geographical distribution of resources must not lead us to overlook other considerations. One is the general shortage of money that can be devoted to health care in a relatively poor country. Peru allocates only $(US)12·34 per capita to government expenditures on health compared with almost $150 in the USA and $230 in Canada (Pan American Health Organization, 1974; data for 1972). Another important fact is that poor health in Latin American countries is probably caused as much by insanitary environmental conditions as by insufficient access to medical care. But, in the last resort, all these considerations of poverty, resource starvation, poor environmental quality and shortage of care are interrelated, as parts of the general condition of underdevelopment.

So, to improve health and to more equally distribute the chance of a healthy life requires much more than better medical care. The argument is set out as follows by de Kadt (1976, p. 526):

> A peasant's child with diarrhoea and malnutrition may require antibiotics to stop the infection, but his long-term health needs will be much better served by environmental measures such as clean water and good waste disposal. He will be better off if his mother learns how to feed him properly or if his father gets more land on which to grow food or is helped to become more productive. That, in a sense, is the meaning of 'prevention is better than cure' – and it is also a lot cheaper! Whatever the impact even of preventive medicine, in general a rising standard of living and higher incomes have had a greater influence on health status than anything the health services or medical science have done: this is true as much for Britain over the last 100 years as for developing countries over the last 25 . . . in the last analysis people will *mainly* become healthier as a result of social and economic change.

He concludes: 'Health has less to do with medicine than with economics, class and politics' – an assertion for which support can be found in the USA and Britain as well as in the Third World.

The Distribution of Health Care under Socialism

As in the previous two chapters, it is helpful to look at the experience of some socialist countries. To what extent do central control and

289

absence of market-place ethics in health care make for a more even spatial distribution under socialism than in a capitalist or 'mixed' economy? As before, it is difficult to be precise about the degree of inequality that prevails under socialism, because of shortage of information. Similarly, numerical comparisons with capitalist systems are difficult, for reasons already mentioned in earlier discussions of the measurement of inequality. Nevertheless, there is evidence that the system of health care prevailing in countries such as the USSR, China and Cuba does make for a more even distribution than a system dominated by the profit motive, as exemplified in the USA. It is less easy to demonstrate superiority over a public system such as Britain's National Health Service.

At the outset, it should be recognized that the major national systems of health care developed under socialism in the USSR and China were built up from a very low and uneven level of service. Contrary to the expectation of Marx, socialism did not emerge out of the chaos of relatively mature industrial states but under what today might be considered classic conditions of underdevelopment. In pre-revolutionary Russia relatively sophisticated care was available for the élite, with little or nothing for the mass of the people; conditions in China, Cuba and (to a lesser extent, perhaps) some of the Eastern European countries after the Second World War were very much the same. The problem was therefore to construct a national system almost from scratch. In these circumstances there is more scope for implementing distributional changes quickly than in a system with substantial personnel and fixed capital, even if under central control as in Britain's NHS. Thus, experience of health care planning under socialism probably has most relevance to the underdeveloped world, though there are certainly some lessons for more advanced nations, and especially those that still rely on market mechanisms for resource allocation.

Turning first to the USSR, there are special reasons to anticipate that experience here will be highly relevant to the general problem of national development. As Field (1976, p. 237) reminds us, the reorganization of medical care was a very early priority of the Bolsheviks, coming *before* the launching of industrialization and collectivization drives. The initial improvements in the health of the population clearly assisted the general process of economic development. This runs counter to the more conventional strategy of stressing investment in physical infrastructure during early stages of development, the wisdom of which is questioned by Bryant (1969, p. 312) as follows: 'More recent evidence suggests that physical investment may not be the primary engine of development, and that investment in human resources, such as health and education, play an important role in the development process. A reasonable view is that health is an essential factor in the development process being both an instrument for and a product of development.' High priority for health care at an early stage, of course requires both the resources and (more important, perhaps) the power to allocate sufficient investment in this direction, in the face of the competing claims of more traditionally 'productive' sectors.

The situation faced by the Bolsheviks was one of very inadequate and unevenly developed health services. 'Russia was in a somewhat better position than the colonial and semicolonial countries, but lagged far behind the USA and West European countries. Many regions of Russia had no doctors at all, while in a number of outlying national areas there was one doctor per scores of thousands of people. Moreover, the few doctors who worked in the provinces lived in towns so that the rural population was practically deprived of skilled medical aid.' (Lisitsin, 1972, p. 21.) According to Field (1967, p. 27), 35 per cent of the towns had no hospital. In 1913 there were only 23,200 physicians in the USSR, – 15 per 100,000 people compared with a ratio of 157 in the USA (in 1910). The ratio of hospital beds per 10,000 people was 13 (1913) against 47 (1909) in the USA. The progress made in the USSR since 1917 is shown by the 1970 ratio of 238 physicians per 100,000 people compared with only 163 in the USA, though the Soviet definition of a doctor is broader than that in America. The bed-to-population ratio was 106 per 10,000 compared with the USA's 82 (figures from Field, 1976). The impact on level of health is indicated by a drop in infant mortality from 239 per 1000 live births in 1913 to 25 in 1970, and in general mortality from 29·1 per 1000 population to 8·2 (Lisitsin, 1972, p. 35).

Table 5.8 shows that the Soviet improvements in provision of

Table 5.8. Improvements in the provision of health services in Eastern Europe

| | Doctors per 100,000 popn | | Hospital beds per 10,000 popn | |
	c. 1936	1971	c. 1936	1971
USSR	50	245	28	111
Czechoslovakia	74	211	54	102
Hungary	112	203	53	77
Bulgaria	45	189	20	79
East Germany	73	164	99	111
Poland	37	156	22	74
Romania	na	131	na	82
Yugoslavia	37	100	18	57

Source: Mieczkowski, 1975, p. 25.

na = not available

physicians and hospital beds have been largely matched in other
Eastern European nations. However, substantial inequalities do
exist among nations, just as in the capitalist world.

Certain basic principles underlie the provision of health care in
the USSR (Field, 1976, pp. 241–2). Both public health and personal
medical care are state responsibilities and their development takes
place within the framework of a single plan (which, in turn, is part of
a broader national plan for resource allocation). Except for some
drugs, health and allied services are not subject to direct cost at
time of use, but are supported from the revenues of different levels of
government (union, republic, regional and local). Preventive medicine
is given special stress in the Soviet system. Also important from an
ideological as well as a practical point of view is the Marxist principle
of the unity of theory and practice, and the significance given to the
popular participation in work related to community health.

The spatial organization of health care comprises an intricate
hierarchy of facilities and services (Shannon and Dever, 1974, pp.
14–18). Starting at the bottom, cities, towns and rural areas are
divided into microdistricts (*uchastok*) of about 4000 people, served
by two physicians, a paediatrician and one or two nurses. Primary
care is given in an out-patients' clinic that typically serves the ten
microdistricts of a medical district (*raion*). The provision of hospitals
varies with population density; in urban areas a hospital may serve

more than one district, whereas some rural microdistricts may have their own small hospitals to ensure local in-patient services. The basic unit is the 'polyclinic', generally attached to the (district) hospital, which offers a comprehensive out-patient facility and health centre. There are specific norms for the staffing of polyclinics, as well as for other levels of provision, such as hospital beds reserved for each microdistrict and ratios of physicians with different specializations in relation to the population of different places (Field, 1967, *passim*). Above the districts in the organizational hierarchy are the regional health departments, the republics with their ministries of health and, at the top, the Ministry of Health of the USSR. Additional features that give the Soviet system spatial flexibility are the emergency medical care stations, from which ambulance services and mobile personnel operate; the *feldshers* or doctors' assistants, who provide services short of that of a fully trained physician; and mobile (e.g. airborne) services for more remote rural areas. It should also be noted that many Soviet citizens have access to medical care at their place of work, both in factories and on farms.

The prevailing distributional ethic in Soviet medicine is not one of perfect quality. On the one hand, health care is to be available and accessible to all the population, with the elimination of territorial inequalities as a major objective. The reduction of differences between town and country is important in health care planning, as in other aspects of service provision. On the other hand, it is recognized that, as long as medical services are subject to a degree of scarcity, those who perform the most important jobs are entitled to priority treatment. This is a source of inequality that will achieve geographical expression only in so far as occupational structure is subject to spatial differentiation. It is recognized that local differences in economic, demographic and health conditions may require differential treatment, rather than the rigid application of centrally determined norms for resource allocation (Hyde, 1974, pp. 182–6). In discussions with the present author in 1978, Ministry of Health officials in Moscow placed great stress on the ability to adjust local norms to take into account observed trends in morbidity and utilization of physician services.

The level of inequality in service provision by republic and region

293

of the RSFSR (see Figure 3.7) is shown in Table 5.9. For physicians or doctors, the best-served republic of Georgia has twice the ratio of the worst-off – Tadzhikistan. The highest figures of all are for the North-West and Central regions of the RSFSR, containing respec-

Table 5.9. Ratios of physicians and hospital beds to population in the USSR, by republics and regions of the RSFSR

Republic or region	Physicians 1975 no. per 100,000 popn	% of USSR ratio	Hospital beds 1974 no. per 10,000 popn	% of USSR ratio
Armenia	348	106	87	76
Azerbaidzhan	289	88	96	83
Belorussia	302	92	113	98
Estonia	368	113	114	99
Georgia	411	126	96	83
Kazakhstan	273	83	123	107
Kirgizia	244	75	109	98
Latvia	392	120	124	108
Lithuania	342	105	112	97
Moldavia	262	80	105	91
Tadzhikistan	206	63	97	84
Turkmenia	258	79	100	87
Ukraine	320	98	116	101
Uzbekistan	260	80	102	89
RSFSR:				
NorthWest	455	139	128	113
Central	459	140	127	110
Volga-Vyatka	270	83	117	102
Central Blacksoil	252	77	106	92
Volga	300	92	111	97
North Caucasus	315	96	102	87
Urals	287	88	125	109
West Siberia	312	95	129	112
East Siberia	289	88	126	110
Far East	368	113	138	120
USSR	327	100	115	100

Source of data: Cole and Harrison, 1978.

Note: physicians include doctors of all kinds.

tively the cities of Leningrad and Moscow. The range for hospital beds is less: from 124 in Latvia to 87 in Armenia. Most of the regional figures for the RSFSR are above the national average. The low over-all level of inequality is indicated by Gini coefficients of 10·9 for doctors and 5·2 for hospital beds; comparable figures for retail sales per capita and enrolment in higher education are 11·6 and 12·8 respectively. Similar inter-republic differences are evident in figures for expenditure on health protection and on the availability of paramedical personnel (Ryan, 1978, pp. 21–3, 65–6).

Cross-national comparisons are hazardous, as has already been indicated, but it is of some interest to see how inter-republic variations in the USSR compare with those at a comparable scale in the USA. As was shown earlier in this chapter (Figure 5.3), physicians per 100,000 population are subject to considerable variations among the states, from a maximum of 253 in Maryland to 89 in South Dakota. The ratio is 2·8 : 1, compared with 2·0 between the top and bottom republics in the USSR. Variations among the nine major regions of the USA are less than between states: from 198 in New England to 111 in East South Central, or a ratio of 1·8 : 1. For hospital beds the ratios of top to bottom in the USA are 93 per 10,000 to 40 (2·3 : 1) by states and 88 to 55 (1·6 : 1) by regions, compared with 1·4 : 1 in the USSR by republics. An inequality coefficient for the distribution of physicians compared to population is 8·6 (1973) for American regions and 4·2 (1968) for Soviet republics. The figures for hospital beds are 5·5 for the USA and 1·8 for the USSR. The general conclusion is that, at this broad level of territorial aggregation, there is greater inequality in the USA than in the USSR. At the more local level, inequality in access to health care is much more pronounced in the USA, for reasons that will be clear from the discussion earlier in this chapter: the USA has no equivalent to the USSR's microdistrict and district services, which embrace all the population irrespective of financial resources.

The existing inter-republic inequalities in the USSR must, of course, be seen in historical perspective. At the time of the revolution the differences were very much greater, with a ratio of 45 : 1 between the best- and worst-serviced republics on the physicians-to-population ratio and 65·5 : 1 for hospital beds. By 1940 these ratios had been reduced to 3·76 and 2·25 respectively, and there has been a steady decrease since then (Table 5.10).

The convergence of republic hospital-bed provision rates between 1913 and 1975 is shown graphically in Figure 5.9. The great disadvantage of the Asian and Caucasian republics is revealed here, with two of the Baltic republics at the other end of the scale. Dramatic improvements in the period up to 1940 pulled up the deprived republics very substantially. Estonia and Latvia have been pulled down correspondingly, but they remain the two best-served republics, just as those with the lowest bed rates tend to be those that were worst off originally.

Zwick (1976), in his general study of inter-republic inequalities referred to in Chapter 3, notes a difference between trends in hospital beds and doctors. While there has been a marked tendency towards equalization in hospital beds, as we have seen, there was no corresponding shift in the distribution of doctors. In fact, the correlation between doctors per capita by republics in 1940 and 1970 is very high: statistically, about three quarters of the variation between republics in 1970 can be accounted for by the 1940 distribution (the comparable figure for hospital beds is just over one third). 'Evidently it was easier to construct health facilities in places where they had not previously existed than to re-allocate the professional personnel to work in those installations . . . All this should not be surprising since Soviet

Table 5.10. Ratios of highest to lowest republic rates for the provision of health care in the USSR

Date	Physicians per 100,000	Hospital beds per 10,000
1913	45·00	65·50
1940	3·76	2·25
1950	3·42	1·74
1958	2·95	1·74
1963	2·41	1·48
1968	2·33	1·37
1975	2·00	1·43

Source of data: Mickiewicz, 1973, pp. 108, 112–13; 1975 figures from Cole and Harrison, 1978.

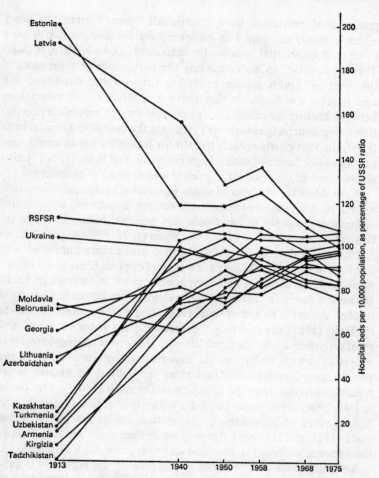

Figure 5.9. The convergence of republic ratios of hospital beds to population, expressed as percentages of USSR ratio. (Source of data: Mickiewicz, 1973, pp. 112–13.)

professional personnel have traditionally been hesitant to work either in newly developed or backward regions and most still have to be paid substantial bonuses for such duty.' (Zwick, 1976, p. 508.) This is important in understanding the persistence of differences in the level of health service provision between the cities and the countryside. Zwick shows that there is a much closer association between doctors per capita and the proportion of a republic's population living in urban areas ($r=0.75$) than is the case with hospital beds ($r=0.45$). This partly reflects the almost inevitable urban concentration of major facilities with a high proportion of doctors, but is also an outcome of the residential preferences of doctors themselves.

If considerable progress towards equalizing health care provision among republics has been achieved, success in reducing urban–rural differentials appears to have been less marked. Numerical data on this aspect are not easily found, but Ryan (1978) provides the following facts: 345 doctors per 100,000 urban inhabitants compared with 179 for the rural population; a lower level of posts filled and a higher turnover in rural areas; and out-patient consultation rates of 12–15 per person per year in large manufacturing cities but only 4 per rural dweller. An examination of some earlier figures for doctors per capita by Field (1967) showed that the greatest gaps between urban and rural provision are in the republics with the lowest aggregate on total provision, which underlines the disadvantage of rural areas in the poorest-served republics. Rural rates are subject to greater inter-republic variation than the urban rates: the ratio of highest to lowest is 1·4 : 1 for urban areas but 2·1 : 1 for rural areas. Generally, the highest rates of physicians to population are in the largest cities. Field (1967, p. 111) cites a figure of more than three and a half times the national average for Moscow and over three for Leningrad.

An illustration of differences within one of the republics is provided by Table 5.11.* The Belorussian Republic has a population of over 9 million, almost one in eight of them in the capital city of Minsk. The distribution of doctors per capita shows Minsk to be very much better served than the six *oblasts* outside. However, there has been a substantial move in the direction of equality in the 1965–73 period,

*I am grateful to John Sallnow for supplying this source, and for assistance with translation.

Table 5.11. Health services in the Belorussian SSR, 1965–73

Area	Doctors per 100,000 population			Hospital beds per 10,000 population		
	1965	1973	change (%)	1965	1973	change (%)
Oblasts						
Brest	156	216	+38	87	106	+22
Vitebsk	204	271	+33	98	118	+20
Gomel	174	234	+34	89	107	+20
Grodno	173	252	+46	94	114	+21
Minsk	156	219	+40	86	114	+33
Mogilev	178	235	+32	98	115	+34
City of Minsk	683	646	−5	100	96	−4
Belorussian SSR	218	285	+31	92	110	+20

Source: *Statistical Yearbook of Belorussian SSR 1974, Minsk*, pp. 231–2.

with large gains in the *oblasts* and a slight fall in the figure for Minsk. The ratio of advantage of Minsk over the worst-served *oblast* has fallen from 4·4 to 3·0. The provision of hospital beds shows much less difference between the city and the 'countryside', as represented by the *oblasts*. The pattern of change, very similar to that of doctors, has, in fact, reversed the position, so that Minsk now has fewer beds in relation to population than any of the *oblasts*. The negative changes in Minsk do not, of course, represent a reduction in the total number of doctors and hospital beds. The former actually increased from 5165 to 7069, and the latter from 7580 to 10,545. The fall in per capita provision is due to the rapid growth of the city, which increased its population from about 750,000 to almost 1,100,000 in the period in question. The fact that health care resources have almost matched this growth is a tribute to Soviet planning, in a world where the pace of uncontrolled urbanization tends to run well ahead of social service provision. Over all, the figures for Belorussia tend to confirm the earlier evidence that equalization between town and country in the USSR may be easier to achieve with respect to fixed capital investment (hospitals) than to personnel (e.g. doctors), despite the greater apparent mobility of the latter. How much of the equalization shown in Table 5.11 really represents dispersal into the

299

countryside is difficult to say, however; most of the improvements may be in urban areas within the *oblasts*.

Further insight into distribution at the *oblast* level may be gained from information relating to the largest of the republics – the RSFSR. Figure 5.10 maps the ratios of doctors to population by the ten regions, from Table 5.9, and shows the Gini coefficients for distribution among the *oblasts*, *krays* and Autonomous Soviet Socialist Republics (ASSRs) into which the regions are subdivided. The greatest inequality is in the two regions with highest ratios of doctors, the North-West and Central regions, which is explained largely by the concentration of doctors in Leningrad (60 per 100,000) and Moscow (65). Within the regions there is a distinct tendency for the number of doctors per capita to rise with the degree of urbanization of the population, as the graph shows (Figure 5.10b). This adds further weight to the evidence of urban–rural differences in access to medical care. However, Cole and Harrison (1978) show very substantial reductions in inequality at the level of *oblasts* (etc.) within each of the regions of the RSFSR. This is summarised in Figure 5.10c. For the most part, the Gini coefficients of inequality have been reduced in rough proportion to the original figures, i.e. the regions with relatively high inequality in 1940 remain so today. Two regions stand out with a particularly rapid movement towards equality in the distribution of doctors, however: Eastern Siberia and the Urals. The general impression is of greatest progress towards equality in the more peripheral regions. This is, no doubt, an outcome of Soviet economic-development strategy, where promotion of industrial activity in remote and inhospitable areas requires favourable conditions with respect to the provision of services.

Providing services for rural areas in a country the size of the USSR is not easy, of course, as we found in the discussion of education in a previous chapter. Field (1967, pp. 155–7) points out that 'the establishment of the network of medical institutions and services for the peasant population has lagged considerably behind that of those available to the urban population', and describes the countryside as the one major area that is still quite deficient in services. The discrepancy is conceded in Soviet literature: Lisitsin (1972, p. 86) refers to the 'gradual' disappearance of differences between town and

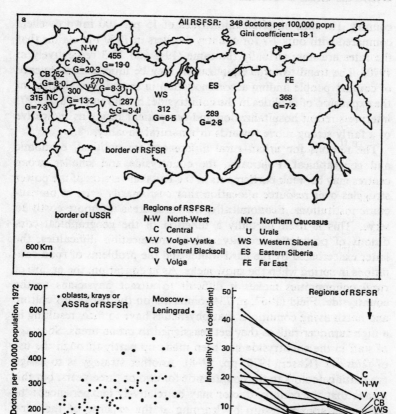

Figure 5.10. Aspects of the distribution of doctors in the RSFSR. (Sources of data: (a) and (c) Cole and Harrison, 1978; (b) *Narodnoye Khozyaystro RSFSR, Narodnoye Khozyaystro SSSR*, 1972.)

country. He cites hospitalization rates of 15 per 100 town dwellers compared with only 7·7 for country dwellers in 1950 but claims that the rates are now virtually the same (19·8 and 19·3 respectively in 1970). The trend towards equalization may be more a consequence of country people finding accommodation in town hospitals than of the expansion of facilities in the countryside, but Ryan (1978, p. 127) interprets recent hospitalization and out-patient ratios as indicative of a fairly strong move towards urban–rural equality.

The reasons for urban–rural differences are political, economic and geographical. Politically, the countryside and smaller urban centres may be weak participants in the Russian version of the power struggles over resource allocation that customarily exist in bureaucratic institutions. Economically, the rural areas are more costly to serve. This is itself partially a function of the geographical conditions of population density and communication difficulties, the latter exacerbated by the hard winter and the problems of road conditions in spring when the snow melts. As in education, the nature of rural communities makes it difficult to attract physicians to the countryside. Field (1967, p. 73) comments on the backward culture and harsh living conditions that physicians have to face, resulting in a high turnover rate as they get reassigned to urban areas. Shortage of staff in the countryside has been made up partly through the use of *feldshers* (Kaser, 1976, pp. 57–8). Another strategy is to assign graduating doctors to the countryside for two or three years, but this means that the country doctor may be relatively inexperienced: 'he serves his apprenticeship by learning at the expense of the rural population.' (Field, 1967, p. 117.) According to Ryan (1978, p. 38), the academically ablest are given the opportunity to opt for more attractive vacancies in urban areas, where career advancement is presumably easier. Thus, any attempt to truly equalize the quality of health care, as between town and country, comes up against some almost intractable human problems.

Differentiation within Soviet cities is likely to be slight, by virtue of the comprehensive network of facilities. For example, Moscow has hundreds of polyclinics serving areas with perhaps 20–50,000 inhabitants, district hospitals catering for about 300,000 people, and major specialist hospitals in each of the eight zones into which the metropolis is divided for planning purposes. The general practitioners who operate from the polyclinics are responsible for the health of those living in particular apartment houses. Distance from residence to sources of care may have a bearing on use, but the distance-decay effect should not be very great, as facilities are close to most people, often at the workplace. However, the trend towards construction of larger new polyclinics involves a centralization and spatial concentration of services, with longer trips for some patients (Ryan, 1978, pp. 83–4). Efficiency in service provision conflicts with equality in access, or, in the words of a Moscow informant, it is a question of whether to save time for the people or money for the state. As in other services, there may be a time lag in getting the full range of health care into new residential developments, thus disadvantaging people on the outer edge of large cities.

Special facilities for the political and intellectual élite exist in some cities: a number of writers (e.g. Field, 1976, p. 256; Kaser, 1976, pp. 55–6; H. Smith, 1976, p. 34) refer to the so-called Kremlin Clinic in Moscow, reserved for politicians and their families, and there are similar facilities for members of the Academy of Sciences and certain artistic companies. The general view is that these special clinics or hospitals provide a service well above average. Thus, whatever spatial differentiation may exist with respect to the socio-economic status of Moscow's population, superior medical care will comprise part of the privileges enjoyed by people at the top end of the scale.

Soviet achievements in the field of health care appear impressive to most objective observers. To the American authority Mark Field (1967, p. 202), measures of health such as infant mortality and life expectation 'indicate substantial if not dramatic improvement over the last fifty years. The Soviet regime has created a comprehensive and national system of health protection and medical services that might well serve as a blueprint for any modernizing nation.'

As a second illustration of geographical differentiation under socialism, we may look at Hungary. Before the Second World War, and its aftermath, health care in Hungary was extremely unevenly distributed: in 1938 the country enjoyed the highest over-all ratio of

Where the Grass is Greener

physicians to population in central and Eastern Europe, but 4668 of the 10,590 doctors lived in Budapest (Kaser, 1976, p. 166). This was part of the general condition of polarized development referred to in Chapter 3. Hungary is still very much dominated by its capital city which houses one in five of the country's population and is exceeded in size only by Moscow and Leningrad among Eastern European cities. A major objective of socialist planning has been to distribute health care resources more equally, and especially to reduce the disadvantage of the rural areas.

Table 5.12 shows variation in level of health (measured by infant

Table 5.12. Infant mortality and the availability of doctors in Hungary, by counties

County	Infant mortality per 1000		Doctors per 10,000 people	
	1960	1974	1960	1974
Budapest	46·1	41·8	36	48
Transdanubia				
Baranya	44·4	32·7	18	33
Fejér	44·0	30·6	10	17
Györ-Sopron	45·0	24·9	11	18
Komárom	44·8	27·2	13	18
Somogy	49·5	36·0	9	17
Tolna	37·0	43·0	9	20
Vas	39·6	24·7	12	20
Vaszprém	50·3	28·4	11	20
Zala	46·7	37·6	9	17
Great Plains				
Bács-Kiskun	61·9	33·4	9	16
Békés	46·5	36·0	8	15
Csongrád	37·9	25·1	19	31
Hajdu-Bihar	39·7	30·8	15	24
Pest	47·2	39·7	8	14
Szabolcs-Szatmár	60·1	38·5	6	12
Szolnok	38·7	23·3	9	16
North				
Borsod-Abauj-Zemplén	50·8	31·7	10	17
Heves	51·3	38·1	10	19
Nógrád	50·8	35·5	11	17
Hungary	47·6	34·3	15	24

Source: Andorka, 1976, pp. 32–3.

mortality) and medical services (doctors per capita) by counties. The infant mortality figures range from 43 per 1000 live births to about 23, roughly the range from Uruguay to West Germany, nationally (Table 1.4). Substantial improvements on the 1960 figures are evident, but these seem rather unevenly distributed. Large proportional reductions have been achieved in the highest-mortality counties, and also in some which had relatively low figures to start with. Thus, differentials between counties have changed, but the general level of inequality seems to have altered little; the ratio of highest to lowest county has actually increased slightly.

The smallest decrease in infant mortality was in Budapest. The 1974 figure of almost 42 per 1000 is, in fact, very high indeed compared not only with Western cities, but also with the USSR: Kaser (1976, p. 75) gives 1969 figures of 22 for Moscow, 21 for Leningrad and 18 for Kiev, and even Tashkent (40) is below Budapest. Andorka (1976, p. 14) notes that in Hungary infant mortality tends to be highest in the larger towns, especially Budapest, and attributes this to the higher frequency of premature births, possibly associated with abortions. In Hungary, as in the USSR, abortion is an officially recognized method of birth control, and in the peak years of the 1960s and early 1970s, abortions exceeded live births, sometimes by a substantial margin (Kaser, 1976, p. 184). Some doubt must be expressed as to the 'progressive' nature of abortion on demand, if it does indeed find reflection in infant death rates.

A glance at Table 5.12 is enough to confirm that the distribution of doctors cannot account for differences in health by county, as indicated in the infant mortality figures. With very few exceptions (the most noticeable being Budapest), doctors per capita vary little at the county level both in 1960 and in 1974. Comparing the per capita income figures from Table 3.13 also does nothing to explain how infant mortality differs among counties. Of the various conditions tabulated by Andorka, the most suggestive is dwellings which lack inside water supply: with few exceptions, as this condition improves, so does infant mortality. Thus, it seems that failure to provide basic domestic amenities may be more important as an impediment to infant survival in Hungary than the impressive progress towards equalization of incomes and the availability of doctors.

As was pointed out in Chapter 3, the county situation no doubt hides more extreme town and country differences. It is in the villages that environmental conditions are at their most primitive: not much more than 10 per cent of dwellings with piped water in 1970, only 5·4 per cent on mains sewerage, and relatively poor schools (Barta, 1975, p. 106). Kaser (1976, p. 180) cites a Ministry of Health estimate that 17 per cent of the population fails to use the social security provisions to which they are entitled, these people to be found 'mainly in remote villages and homesteads to which physicians are rarely called or which they can reach only with difficulty'. He points out that only 4000 out of a national total of almost 25,000 physicians actually practise in rural areas (yet Budapest alone has almost 10,000); in 1973, 2500 localities were without a doctor. Barta (1975, p. 107) puts the number of doctors per 100,000 population at only 75 in the villages in 1972, compared with 360 in the towns, and comments: 'The low standard of the rural health service is indicated by the lack of National Health surgeries and resident doctors in at least half of the villages of the country. The living conditions of approximately 20 per cent of the rural population are considerably aggravated by this inadequacy.' This frank admission from a Hungarian authority is indicative of the difficulties imposed by resource constraints and the geography of population distribution. As in the USSR, equalization of access to health care is far from being achieved, even when this is a major government objective.

What of the experiences of underdeveloped countries outside Europe who have taken a socialist path? One such nation is Cuba, where the post-revolutionary development of health services has been influenced by the Soviet model. There has been a major shift of emphasis from curative to preventive medicine. An important objective has been to improve the almost non-existent services in rural areas. There was only one rural hospital, with ten beds, before the revolution, but by 1966 this had been increased to 46 hospitals with 1288 beds (Gordon, 1976, p. 193). The training of medical personnel now places great stress on the basic needs of rural areas, in such fields as hygiene and epidemiology. A system of polyclinics is being built up, to act as health centres from which more serious cases can be referred to regional hospitals or speciality centres in Havana. Many more doctors have been placed in the countryside: their inclination to work there rather than in Havana having been accomplished by changes in professional ethics, in accordance with the new social consciousness required by revolutionary practice. As in the USSR, medical services are provided free of charge, with payment required for drugs, subject to certain exceptions.

Judging the performance of a fundamental change in service provision is not as easy as might appear at first sight. In Cuba, the revolution led to the emigration of over a third of the island's doctors and there was a severe shortage of resources, so that mortality rates rose initially. Improvements are more evident in the control of conditions such as diphtheria, malaria and parasitic diseases than in general and infant mortality. Great progress has been made in the rural areas, to create much more equality of access to care on a geographical basis than before. Gordon (1976, p. 199) describes the results of Cuba's health programme as 'truly impressive', saying that 'the government has successfully carried out a plan to offer the most basic preventive medical care to a significant percentage of the population.' If little progress has been made in further improving the sophisticated treatment previously enjoyed by the élite under their private system of care, the implicit redistribution of resources towards basic preventive medicine has clearly been to the advantage of the vast majority of the population.

It is worth adding a few comments on health care in China, as here again there is a great problem of equalizing services as between town and country. In devising a system geared to the needs of its vast rural population, China has tended to underplay Western standards that could be maintained only for a privileged minority, stressing preventive rather than curative medicine (Byers and Nolan, 1976, p. 66). The parallel with Cuba is clear. But in China the practice of health care has certain unique features, reminding us that socialist development-strategies aimed at equalizing access to services can differ one from another. In China, improvements in the countryside have come about by a combination of rural self-help, based on the collective organization of agriculture, and direct assistance from urban areas. Communes have built their own health centres, and organized the training of so-called 'barefoot doctors', or peasants with basic medical knowledge. Campaigns have been run to improve sanitation and eliminate common diseases. The urban areas have provided resources, contributed to the training of personnel for country practice, and transferred urban health workers to the countryside. Byers and Nolan (1976, p. 67), citing a Chinese source, report more than a million barefoot doctors, 800,000 medical workers in the countryside as part of mobile medical teams, and more than 100,000 permanently resettled from the towns. Such a shift of personnel is possible only under direction of labour or a new work ethic. How much specific direction of health workers to country locations takes place is difficult to say. But it is clear that a major contributor to the dispersal of medical personnel is a change in consciousness and motivation, which induces different personal behaviour from that typical of the medical profession in more 'advanced' societies. In India, where more traditional professional ethics prevail, an extreme shortage of doctors in rural areas is still the rule.

As in other services, it seems that 'the Chinese have employed principles particularly suited to the historical, cultural, geographical, and political conditions of the society' (Sidel, 1977, p. 194). Among these are the stress on the rural areas, decentralization, deprofessionalization and demystification of medical practice, and mass participation in the provision of health care and preventive measures. Despite the uniqueness of the Chinese experience, there are lessons for others, especially for the organization of health services in the underdeveloped world. It is significant that Western interest in Chinese medicine is so preoccupied with the *technical* curiosity of acupuncture.

What general conclusions might be justified from our comparative review of the provision of health care under different conditions and ideologies? A summary is provided by R. Maxwell (1974, p. 35), commenting on the continuum from private finance and control, to a public, centrally planned system:

At the United States end, the best medical care may equal or surpass the best available elsewhere, and medical progress is at its most rapid, but at the same time there is gross neglect of some real needs. At the other extreme the peaks and valleys of health care are levelled out; standards are more uniform and there is greater equity, but something is sacrificed by way of excellence and speed of development. Too highly centralized administration, moreover, carries with it serious risk of rigidity, inefficiency and inability to respond to local needs and conditions.

All we might add to this is the observation that 'medical progress' and 'speed of development' have meaning only in the context of specific needs and conditions in particular places. The basic preventive care offered in countries like China and Cuba under conditions of severe resource constraints certainly constitutes progress for the mass of the people, in a way that the limited extension of more sophisticated care would not. Similar developments to those observed in Russian cities would be major progress in the American city. Further advances in cosmetic surgery and organ transplants are surely not progressive anywhere, in a world where so many people still die in misery for lack of a pill, an injection or an adequate diet.

6 Patterns and Processes in Geographical Space

The purpose of this concluding chapter is to draw together the more important findings from the cases already discussed. In so doing, we hope to be able to provide a general perspective on the nature and origins of the geographical differentiation of human well-being or life chances. We shall proceed from a summary of the patterns themselves, through an attempt to identify the basic processes involved and the structure upon which they rest, to some final observations on the kind of theory and practice required to promote greater equality.

Inevitably, what is suggested will be highly generalized. The precise distribution of sources of need satisfaction in any part of the world is an outcome of specific historic and cultural circumstances as well as of broader forces making for inequality. However, the cases from which the argument is built up are representative of a wide range of real-world situations, and what can be inferred from them has a universality that transcends local, regional or national conditions.

Geographical Patterns of Inequality

Our summary of the patterns observed in earlier chapters may be brief, as ample illustrations have already been provided. What we seek here is to show that the patterns identified independently at the international, intra-national and intra-city levels slot together into a world-wide pattern with similar general features at different spatial scales.

At the international level there are enormous differences between the high material standards of living in the advanced capitalist world and the so-called Third World, with most socialist (or communist)

310

countries occupying an intermediate position. We recognize that possession of material things, such as the consumer 'durables' so effectively provided by the economies of the advanced capitalist nations, is not the ultimate criterion of living standards. We recognize that in the pursuit of even more *things* with which to fill the home or adorn the person, some of the less tangible pleasures of life are lost. We realize that, once basic survival is virtually assured, life in a more 'primitive' society may be more relaxed and in some respects more fulfilling than in the fiercely competitive societies of Western Europe and North America. But for most of the world's nations the problem of over-abundance and the contemplation of such abstractions as the quality of life must await basic improvements in material aspects of life. Thus, it seems justifiable to view standard of living in terms of such conditions as money income, quality of housing, health and education, at least for international comparisons.

Geographically, we may view the world as comprising peaks of affluence centred on the nations of Western Europe and North America, with the outliers of Australia, New Zealand and Japan (the only non-Caucasian nation in this group). Beyond the peaks, and the secondary-level heights of Eastern Europe and the USSR, the standard of living falls away rapidly, through some of the better-off Latin American countries, to reach the broad plain of the great world periphery of poor·nations. Here we find most of Africa and what in Europe is known as the Middle East, practically the whole of South-East Asia, and the poorer countries of Central and South America. Much of this poverty plain is barely above the sea-level of human survival. Some of it falls below this critical level, in the world equivalent of California's Death Valley, identified as the starvation belt in Chapter 2.

The poor periphery is by no means homogeneous. Over vast areas the standard of living varies little; millions of people in central Africa and rural India, for example, have a very similar daily experience of getting just enough to eat and a bare minimum (if anything) of rudimentary social services. But the underdeveloped, Third World countries almost all have their own peaks of high living standards occupied by the urban élite, the aristocracy and even some rural tribal chiefs. A small but powerful group can live very well, even in some of

311

the world's poorest countries, if they control most of the surplus product. And if this surplus is rapidly expanding, as, for example, in the oil-rich sheikdoms, its exclusive appropriation by a very small segment of society can generate a level of affluence for the few, comparable with that of the very richest people in the advanced capitalist world. Elsewhere, mining towns and other enclaves of foreign-owned business may constitute local peaks in the standard-of-living topography of poor nations, though those individuals actually enjoying the good life may be largely, if not exclusively, expatriate Europeans.

So, the well-being surface of the world's poor periphery will have its local peaks and troughs. The same is true of the more advanced nations, capitalist and socialist. In the United States we have observed the major cities as the peaks, surrounded by areas of lower living standards in the inter-metropolitan periphery. In smaller countries, such as Britain, the capital city may appear as the sole major peak, though not in the same extreme position of relative advantage as the primate city of the Third World. In the socialist world of Eastern Europe and the USSR the cities still appear as peaks, with a standard of living superior to that of the countryside – perhaps to a greater degree than in Western Europe. There is likely to be some differentiation among peripheral regions, in accordance with their economic role, the rewards generated and the degree of isolation. In the capitalist world the periphery will have its depressed regions of economic decline or stagnation, such as Appalachia in the USA and parts of northern England.

A graphic summary of this view of the world topography of living standards is attempted in Figure 6.1. At the centre is the world core or metropolis of the advanced capitalist world. Level of living falls away towards the periphery, as it approaches the minimum required for human survival. Whereas in profiles of the *physical* surface of the earth the vertical scale has to be exaggerated to bring out the details of topography, on the human-well-being surface the opposite is probably true: real differentials between the world core and periphery are likely to be more extreme than the diagram suggests.

Figure 6.1 offers a general representation of inequality on a world scale. At the level of individual nations, the core–periphery structure

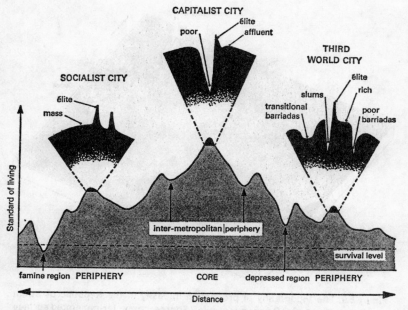

Figure 6.1. A generalized view of world inequalities in living standards.

is usually repeated, but with variations arising from the historical process of development in relation to the geography of resources. This can be illustrated by the case of South Africa. Figure 6.2 shows a three-dimensional surface representing intensity of economic activity, measured by gross domestic product generated per unit of area. Although this is not a direct indicator of level of living, the well-being of the population is closely related to the form of this surface (Board, Davies and Fair, 1970, p. 370; D. M. Smith, 1977, p. 247). The impression is one of highly polarized development. The Witwatersrand conurbation centred on Johannesburg comprises the major peak: this metropolitan core accounts for about three quarters of the total Republic GDP. The coastal cities of Durban and Cape Town show up as secondary peaks, rising above the barely undulating plain of the peripheral rural areas.

The historical pattern of resource exploitation took a distinctive

313

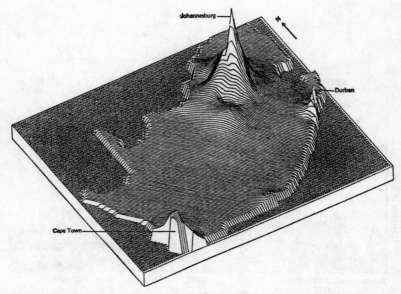

Figure 6.2. The topography of production intensity in the Republic of South
Africa: G D P per square mile. (Source: computer-generated surface
courtesy of John Browett and the Urban and Regional Research
Unit, University of the Witwatersrand.)

course in South Africa, which accounts for the particular features
illustrated. Up to the latter part of the nineteenth century, economic
activity was largely concentrated in the major ports. As in other
colonial lands, agriculture was very much geared to external markets,
and the ports grew up as commercial centres to handle trade with
Europe. The interior was largely the province of the indigenous
population and of the Boers – the Afrikaner descendants of the
original Dutch settlers, whose 'treks' took more locally oriented
European farming well inland. South Africa's spatial economic
structure might well have remained focused towards the two coastal
primate cities, had it not been for the discovery of the Witwatersrand
goldfield and other sources of precious minerals in the interior. Thus
emerged the city of Johannesburg and its various satellite towns,
along with the administrative capital of Pretoria near by. The presence
314

of gold, the technology to mine it and the availability of masses of cheap labour among the indigenous African population were enough to shift the country's economic centre of gravity from the coast to the plain of the high veld. The continuing dominance of the rural periphery by this metropolitan core is closely related to another distinctive feature of South Africa – the policy of *apartheid* – as we shall see later in this chapter.

Turning to patterns of inequality within cities, each has its unique features. Johannesburg itself is a case in point, with spatial differentiation heightened by *apartheid*. Each of the four officially recognized races (Whites, Coloured, Africans and Asians) occupies its own segregated residential 'group areas', and the fact that the races are differentiated economically by government policy makes for a peculiar geographical hierarchy of levels of living. The greatest contrasts are between the affluent white suburbs and the massive African townships making up Soweto. Soweto itself is, without doubt, the most equal city in the world, with its million or so black inhabitants living in conditions of almost total uniformity within the wider, highly unequal society of South Africa.

The *apartheid* city is an extreme case – a highly distinctive pattern, reflecting a very strange social formation. We have mentioned it at this point simply to underline the theme of uniqueness. Every city has its own particular geographical features. There will be differences in urban morphology, arising from local topography as well as history, as the rich have perhaps selected the more elevated sites for their homes while the poor have been confined to the less salubrious valley bottoms. Economic and social differentiation may take the form of wedges radiating out from the centre in one city, or something more resembling concentric zones in another. But if we look at the city world-wide, certain generalities can be detected – features highlighted by our case studies in earlier chapters.

In Figure 6.1 we have picked out three types of cities to illustrate inequality at the intra-metropolitan scale. The city of the advanced capitalist world generally shows a pattern of plateaux of suburban affluence surrounding a trough of economic and social deprivation corresponding with the inner city, or the largely black ghetto in the

315

USA. The heights of the plateaux and the depth of the trough will vary with the city – with its size and occupational diversity. Large cities will have the greatest extremes, while predominantly one-industry towns will tend towards social homogeneity except for the local managerial and professional élite. But there will be some consistency within nations: for example, the range from affluent suburbs to the slums will be greatest in the USA and least in the welfare states of Western Europe where the provision of social services and more progressive taxation reduces the extremes. Some cities may have variations on the general pattern, such as largely working-class residential areas or 'overspill' estates comprising people rehoused from the slums, to form pockets of lower level of living in parts of the suburban ring. The inner-city may have its own small and very rich enclaves. These can be relics of the pre-industrial era when the élite occupied the central area (as in London and other European cities) or they may be prestige apartments for people able to afford the convenience of city-centre living (as in some American cities).

The socio-economic topography of the Third World city generates a somewhat different profile. There will be features similar to the city of the advanced capitalist world: some inner-city slums and central élite residential areas, the latter probably more extensive than in Europe and North America where less of the pre-industrial spatial structure survives. The major difference is in the ever-increasing areas of squatter settlements around the fringe of the Third World city, and occupying vacant land within the city itself. As we observed in Lima, Peru, these *barriadas* need not be the squalid slums that are often assumed of such spontaneous settlement: some are transitional and associated with upward social mobility, as we suggest in the profile. The colonial city of the Third World may have special features such as separate enclaves for the expatriate élite. Poor, Third World cities have greater over-all extremes of living standards than is the case in richer countries. But, paradoxically, the spatial expression of these differences between rich and poor may be blunted by residential mixing on an individual or family basis. The rich have their living-in servants, and white areas of cities in South Africa and Rhodesia, for example, may have back-streets of servant dwellings between the rows of houses of the rich. Building workers and their

316

families may temporarily inhabit the shell of the home they are constructing in a well-to-do Lima suburb.

Socialist cities will have a different pattern again. They tend to be more homogeneous, though probably not to the extent suggested by the uniformity of housing. Occupational structure makes for personal differentiation of living standards, though the spatial expression of social stratification is restricted by constraints on freedom of residential choice and the fact that a specific location within the city may have less obvious benefits and penalties than in a capitalist or Third World city. This is the reverse of the situation in non-socialist cities, where economic restrictions on freedom of residential choice tend to confine the poor (or ethnic minorities) to specific areas, often compounding an initial problem of social deprivation and poor environmental quality. Although social stratification under socialism is not a well-researched subject, it would appear that in the USSR, and possibly some Eastern European countries, the political, cultural and academic élite is sufficiently substantial and differentiated from the mass of the people to have some impact on the spatial structure of the largest cities. So there will be some intra-urban peaks of affluence, however visually inconspicuous.

Obviously, there is an element of simplification in the picture that we have attempted to portray. The actual topography of human well-being, nationally, regionally and locally, is much more complex than Figure 6.1 suggests. There will be minor peaks, possibly at a number of different levels, corresponding with the urban hierarchy. There will be local plateaux and depressions, reflecting perhaps a favourable resource endowment or special privileges somehow exacted from the national distributive mechanisms.

The pattern is also subject to change. While the basic difference between core and periphery on a world scale is a fairly constant feature, intra-national variations may be more transient. Regional fortunes change, as with Appalachia and Britain's textile-manufacturing districts, so that one generation's growth areas are the pockets of poverty and industrial decline in the next. In some countries the contrasts in life chances between the primate city and the countryside are increasing; in others vigorous regional-development policy and national

317

standards of service provision may promote some move towards equalization. Within the cities, the expansive middle-class suburbs are largely a phenomenon of the last half-century, while the squatter settlements that house a rapidly growing share of Third World urban dwellers are of very recent origin. The more rigorously revolutionary communist countries, especially China, have achieved some reversals of the trend towards rapid urbanization, though the consequences for town-country differentials in living standards are hard to assess.

A final point is that the different spatial scales at which inequality can be observed are themselves interrelated. Our three levels of analysis – international, intra-national and intra-city – have been chosen largely as a matter of convenience. Nations are real political entities and cities real units of human settlement, of course. But they are connected together in obvious ways. Many cities are such because of the role that they play in the life of particular nations. Groups of nations may form associations, such as the British Commonwealth, the European Economic Community or the Warsaw Pact. Nations have bilateral relationships: colony and colonizer, importer and exporter, aid donor and recipient. Individual cities form elements in systems of cities, as we have shown. The city and countryside are closely connected, by flows of goods and, often, of migrants. Neighbourhoods in cities may be closely connected by social interaction and workforce flows; however apparently separated by race or class segregation, they function as part of a wider system. Some city subdivisions may, indeed, be more closely connected with the countryside, for example with the home areas of recent migrants, than with other parts of the city. So, our different levels of description fuse together, in a world system where few people, if any, are completely cut off from other people in other places. As we turn from patterns of inequality to analysis of process, we shall stress further this interrelatedness of human affairs as organized on the surface of the earth.

Spatial Structure and Uneven Development

Whatever its precise morphology, place on the world, national or local well-being surface matters to the individual. The chance of birth in a particular place immediately constrains life chances. If the

318

mother is already malnourished, so is the child likely to be. If the 'home' is an insanitary hut, shack or tenement apartment, with medical care inaccessible by virtue of distance or lack of money, the chances of survival and healthy growth will be diminished. Educational opportunity will vary according to place of residence. So will the opportunity to play football on grass instead of tarmac, to learn that milk really does come from a cow rather than a carton, to discover first-hand something of the ecological balance of the countryside, the beauty of painting and sculpture and the exhilaration of rock music or a symphony concert. Occupational choice is severely constrained in some places, such as agricultural villages and one-industry towns, which means that the bright child set on a professional career may lose some of his or her cultural roots as part of the price of upward mobility. Prospects for promotion are limited by the local structure of business or institutional organizations. Expectation of life has much to do with early experience, with the models formed by parents for the behaviour of their children. An environment dominated by fathers perceived as failures – unable to maintain the dignity associated with regular employment and success as a 'bread-winner' – can predispose a son to aspirations quite different from those acquired in an achievement-oriented environment, where doors can be opened a little for those unable to push for themselves. Even such apparently random events as meeting a marriage partner or making a friend – among the most important sources of personal fulfilment – are not unconnected with where people live in relation to others and with their patterns of movement as they live their daily lives. There is often a geographical element to serendipity.

But place is not the only determinant of human life chances. Nor does it necessarily dominate all other influences; indeed, some would argue that location or place *per se* is largely irrelevant and vastly overestimated in its importance by geographers. Further still, it might be argued that to focus so heavily on the effect of place obscures more fundamental sources of inequality. This point has emerged already, from a number of the cases in previous chapters. In particular, we have come to see that the manifest geographical differentiation of human life chances is very much an outcome of how the economy works – how the surplus is appropriated and distributed, how resources are allocated and how opportunities are competed for – within a specific social and political institutional framework. The task now is to see what specifically spatial aspects of economic (and social) processes might be usefully recognized, in our pursuit of general understanding of the origins of inequality. We shall confine the discussion initially to the capitalist system, because there are certain basic features of the general process of capitalist development and its spatial organization that must be recognized. Later in the chapter we shall broaden the argument to include the experience of socialism, from which there is much to be learned about the origins of inequality in geographical space.

Inequalities in living standards are the product of a distinct historical process. As the capitalist mode of production has emerged and spread its presence or influence into most parts of the world, the lives of people in different nations and regions have become inter-dependent, as we noted above. We exist in a gigantic, interconnected economic system, in which the conditions of our own existence may be much more closely governed by decisions made elsewhere, perhaps in another country, than by the actions of ourselves, our neighbours or fellow citizens. In Britain, the 'national' economic policy may be determined as much from the USA as by the British government, as American investment increases and the conditional assistance of organizations like the International Monetary Fund is sought in times of crisis. In much of the underdeveloped world, the economy responds more to the decisions of overseas businessmen and investors than to the needs or wants of the indigenous population. Similarly within many nations, local or regional affairs are controlled by outsiders, often in the capital city.

The rise of capitalism in the eighteenth and nineteenth centuries was accompanied by a great increase in geographical economic specialization. Some local specialization had existed for a long time, as particular places revealed a comparative advantage for certain types of production, by virtue of favourable climate and soils or the local availability of appropriate materials. As production for local need was steadily augmented or replaced by production for sale, the merchant emerged as an important organizing agent in economic activity. The growth of trade encouraged further specialization. The technological innovations of the Industrial Revolution in Britain made possible large-scale factory production, organized on capitalistic lines. The earlier forms of social stratification thus gave way to the class dichotomy of owners of the means of production (capital and land), on the one hand, and those who sold their labour, on the other. This was part of a general process of redefinition and specialization of individual roles, most marked in the growing division of labour, characteristic of modern occupational structures. *Geographical* division of labour was a fundamental feature of the rise of capitalism. The expansion of industry during the nineteenth century, along with developments in transportation, accentuated local and regional comparative advantage, thus making for extreme geographical specialization. Often, one narrow line of production dominated the economy of whole towns and regions, making them highly vulnerable to changes in demand or to competition from elsewhere. Thus, a shift in fashion could destroy the industrial base of a locality almost overnight, where previously there had been sufficient economic diversity to cushion a community from the decline of one activity. Similarly, development of domestic production in what had previously been profitable markets for exports could threaten the prosperity of entire regions, as is the case of Lancashire's cotton industry. This is another aspect of geographical interdependency – of the fact that the fortunes of people in one place are dependent on the actions of others elsewhere.

International expansion was an essential feature of the rise of capitalism. European nations became interested in the appropriation of wealth from overseas well before the Industrial Revolution – Spain's plundering of Peru, referred to in Chapter 3, being a case in point. Gradually, the colonies of the European powers developed as suppliers of materials for the growing textile, metal and foodstuff industries of Britain, France and elsewhere. Plantations and mines in the colonies were an important means of transferring the surplus product of cheap and foreign labour to Europe, as well as supplying the materials themselves. Overseas possessions offered opportunities for investment of profits generated by industry at home, and also markets for European industry, as an indigenous élite and the more fortunate of the new wage-labour class developed effective demand for

321

consumer goods. Thus there emerged the great world periphery of dependent nations, contributing to a steady concentration of wealth and economic power in Europe (and, later, North America) and, in return, gaining very unevenly as overseas capital selected certain places and lines of production for development.

As the world capitalist system has emerged, two conflicting tendencies have become apparent. On the one hand, modern methods of production have spread from core to periphery, thus dispersing productive capacity and opportunities to share the benefits of industrialization. On the other hand, there has developed world-wide concentration of wealth, and with it the economic and political power that accompanies control of the surplus product. The growing significance of what are variously termed multinational, international or transnational corporations is an important contemporary feature of the concentration of control. This, in its turn, has a major bearing on the persistence of unequal living standards in geographical space, as exemplified by the underdeveloped nation, the depressed region and the inner-city slum.

Hymer (1975) has drawn attention to the emergence of what may be viewed as a spatial equivalent of the control hierarchy of a large modern corporation. The top level in the hierarchy will comprise the senior-management functions of goal determination and planning. Those involved will have very well-paid, high-status jobs. The bottom level comprises the day-to-day management of the operations of the enterprise, performed by people with relatively low pay and status in comparison with those at the top level. Between them will be an intermediate level, concerned with co-ordination of the lowest-level management, within the framework laid down from above. Hymer sees the lowest or third-level functions widely distributed over the globe in accordance with the location of the manpower, markets and materials required for production. Second-level activities will tend to concentrate in larger cities. Top-level management functions are even more concentrated, in the major financial centres of the world.

As Hymer argues, the structure of income and consumption will tend to parallel the structure of status and authority. The citizens of the capital cities will have access to the best jobs, along with first

322

experience of new products and other innovations. 'Income, status authority, and consumption patterns would radiate out from these centres along a declining curve, and the existing patterns of inequality and dependency would be perpetuated.' (Hymer, 1975, p. 38.) Although this is more of a prediction of the consequences of the growing influence of North American multinationals than a description of the existing situation, it bears a strong resemblance to the world-wide core–periphery differentiation of living standards as we have observed it, and also to what our analysis in Chapter 3 suggested may be taking place in Britain.

Figure 6.3 sketches out the broad features of Hymer's 'control hierarchy' and the related pattern of living standards or human well-being. We recognize a 'home' territory, representative of the North American or European nation, with its metropolis of top-level control

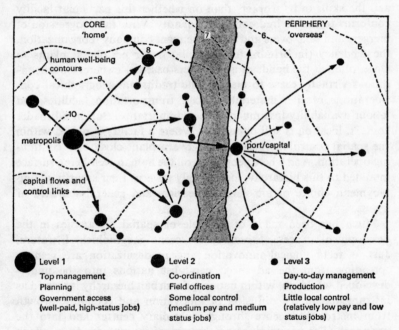

Figure 6.3. The spatial control hierarchy and patterns of human well-being, as suggested by Hymer (1975).

and its own subsidiary centres. In the 'overseas' territory representing the underdeveloped world there is the capital city (usually the major port) from which internal control is exercised, but itself subsidiary to the metropolis overseas. Most activity in the underdeveloped world is at the lowest level in the control hierarchy.

One important implication of this view of the world economy is, once again, that control over local affairs is increasingly exercised from elsewhere. At the international level, the continued operation of a branch factory or plantation of a large corporation is dependent on business strategy determined elsewhere. Similarly, within nations: textile mills in Lancashire may be closed down from the London head-office of a multi-plant firm, as happened repeatedly in the 1960s. The continued existence of a branch factory, and the jobs that it provides, may depend less on the independent profitability of the plant and the skills of its workers than on whether this particular facility conforms to the desired corporate identity. With the progression of mergers and take-overs and the subsequent company reorganization, the tendency (in Britain, for example) is for peripheral plants to close, often at the hands of new owners based elsewhere. Local conditions virtually cease to matter. The traditional geographical considerations of site, material sources, transportation facilities and labour availability lose much of their importance. But, in a broader context, location is still important. Where a facility is placed within the spatial control-hierarchy, may govern plant closure or continuing operation. And where people live on the human-well-being surface moulded to this hierarchy, increasingly governs their security of employment, choice of job, level of services and general standard of living.

Much has been made of the role of spatial hierarchies in the development process, especially in recent geographical literature. Just as technological innovation and modernization are seen as spreading from the advanced capitalist nations into the underdeveloped world, so, within nations, the urban hierarchy is viewed as instrumental in the diffusion of innovation and economic growth from metropolitan core through subsidiary centres and into the periphery. The major cities are centres of innovation, from which new ideas and products find their way progressively down through successive levels of the settlement hierarchy. This process was summarized in Chapter 4, in the discussion of the American urban system. Hierarchical diffusion of economic growth in an integrated space-economy is an important feature of the regional-development theory propagated by Friedmann (1966) and others, which has had a major influence on planning in some underdeveloped nations.

Real-world experience suggests that there may well be an element of wish-fulfilment in this view. Certainly, some innovations have been observed to flow down the hierarchy after the manner postulated by adherents of the diffusion view. But what diffuses may simply reflect the values and preferences of the metropolitan élite, which may have little bearing on the real needs of people in the countryside. And, as we have pointed out already, the spatial spread of economic growth via the dispersal of productive capacity is unlikely to be matched by an equal spread of control, or political power. Indeed, the penetration of a 'traditional' (pre-capitalist) rural economy by modern capitalist activity is likely to reduce local control; it can merely serve to advantage a few large landowners at the expense of the mass of the people, who have perhaps been forced from farming for themselves into wage labour for others. So, all that finds its way out from core to periphery is not necessarily for the good.

Another objection to the conventional view is that it disregards the role of the hierarchy in the concentration of wealth. Harvey (1973 and 1975) has drawn attention to the part played by cities in extraction of a surplus product from their hinterland. (Indeed, it is sometimes argued that the city, as a settlement form, owes its origins to the capacity to control and exploit the surrounding area.) Just as returns on investment at a world scale flow into the major centres of business and financial control, so, within nations, the major metropolis or core city attracts a disproportionate share of new wealth because it is the source of most of the investment capital.

A specific illustration of the concentration effect of hierarchical spatial structure is provided by the migration of doctors. Within nations, potential doctors are drawn, as medical students, to universities and teaching hospitals, usually in the larger cities. Once trained, doctors often prefer to practise close to their own medical school, as Coates and Rawstron (1971, ch. 10) found in Britain.

This promotes concentration in the city and also in certain regions with disproportionate shares of training facilities – South-East England, for example. Concentration also operates internationally, in the form of a 'brain drain' up the hierarchy. Doctors from the underdeveloped world come to countries like England to complete their training. Some stay on, perhaps to fill gaps left by British doctors attracted to the USA or Canada by the prospects of lucrative private practice. Thus, affluent Americans gain, in a very real sense, at the expense of the health of the Third World poor. The development gap becomes that bit wider, and more permanent.

Some insight into the process of development within a hierarchical urban system is provided by a study of capital flows in the USA, based on observed events in the Midwest during the latter part of the nineteenth century (Conzen, 1975). This is illustrated in Figure 6.4. In early stages, the urban hierarchy facilitates the spread of funds from major commercial centres to more distant investment opportunities. Later, there may be some reinvestment of capital generated locally in medium and small centres. But capital may also be attracted back *up* the hierarchy, in search of the investment opportunities of the larger centres. Returns on outside capital will, of course, make their way up the hierarchy automatically, as dividends to shareholders in the metropolis. The flow of funds in underdeveloped countries probably resembles this pattern closely, the periphery often being a high-risk area with limited scope for investment – or perceived as such by big-city businessmen.

The internal spatial structure of urbanization and economic activity is of special importance to the underdeveloped, ex-colonial world. Slater (1975) provides a graphic summary of how the space economy of a typical colonial country might have developed, based largely on African experience (Figure 6.5). The pre-colonial stage was one of largely, if not entirely, non-capitalist production, with a predominantly local orientation but some inter-regional and external trade-links. The initial era of colonial penetration (say, 1880s–1914) brings mines and plantations and the beginnings of a modern transportation system. The colonial economy is very much externally oriented towards London or whatever the overseas 'metropole' within whose sphere of influence the colony happens to be. Subsequently,

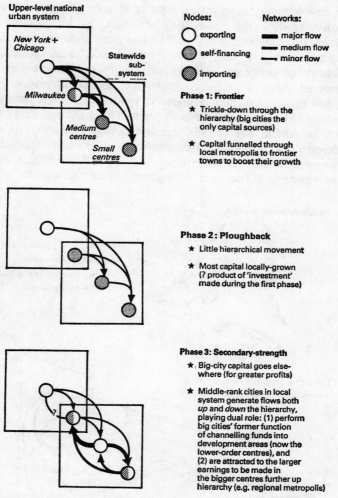

Figure 6.4. Capital flows in an urban hierarchy. (Source: based on Conzen, 1975, Fig.4.)

the new economy develops an internal structure of growing complexity, eroding the pre-existing structure, as indigenous agriculture and handicrafts decline and the population is increasingly drawn into wage labour for overseas concerns. The final stage, after political independence, sees the colonial spatial structure largely preserved. With its external orientation and concentration on a narrow range of (generally primary) products, it is geared to the needs of the consumers of North America and Europe rather than those of Africa. The colonial economies have changed little since independence, facilitating a continuation of external exploitation: what exists 'is either an inheritance from a world that is past, or the merely peripheral fragment or fragments of an international system

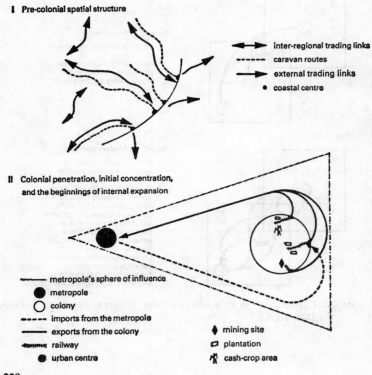

I   Pre-colonial spatial structure

<del>→</del> inter-regional trading links
------- caravan routes
——→ external trading links
● coastal centre

II   Colonial penetration, initial concentration, and the beginnings of internal expansion

——— metropole's sphere of influence
● metropole
○ colony
----- imports from the metropole
——— exports from the colony
＋＋＋＋＋ railway
● urban centre

♦ mining site
▱ plantation
⚘ cash-crop area

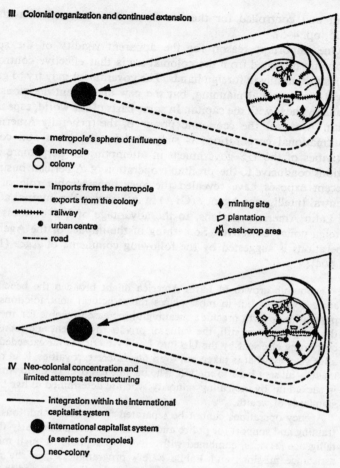

III Colonial organization and continued extension

- metropole's sphere of influence
- metropole
- colony
- imports from the metropole
- exports from the colony
- railway
- urban centre
- road
- mining site
- plantation
- cash-crop area

IV Neo-colonial concentration and limited attempts at restructuring

- integration within the international capitalist system
- international capitalist system (a series of metropoles)
- neo-colony

Figure 6.5. The evolution of a colonial space economy. (Source: based on Slater, 1975, Fig. 3.2.)

built and controlled for the benefit of non-Africans' (Davidson, 1975, pp. 4–5).

One important reason for the apparent rigidity of the space economy inherited from the colonial era is that effective control is still substantially in foreign hands. The government may try to guide events via regional planning, but the new investment decisions are made by those with the capital. In some parts of the world, especially Latin America, the economic power of the (generally American) multinational corporations is supported by the overt and covert activities of the US government in attempting to perpetuate conditions conducive to the profitable operation of American business. Recent exposés have revealed the very considerable role of the Central Intelligence Agency (CIA) in influencing the internal affairs of Latin American nations, to the advantage of US business and foreign-policy objectives. Something of the impact of the Agency's operations is suggested by the following comments of Agee (1975, p. 504):

Economic growth in Latin America might broaden the benefits in some countries but in most places the structural contradictions and population growth preclude meaningful increased income for most of the people. Worse still, the value of private investment and loans and everything else sent by the US into Latin America is far exceeded year after year by what is taken out – profits, interest, royalties, loan repayments – all sent back to the US. The income left over in Latin America is sucked up by the ruling minority who are determined to live by our standards of wealth.

Agency operations cannot be separated from these conditions. Our training and support for police and military forces, particularly the intelligence services, combined with other US support through military assistance missions and Public Safety programmes, give the ruling minorities ever stronger tools to keep themselves in power and to retain their disproportionate share of the national income. Our operations to penetrate and suppress the extreme left also serve to strengthen the ruling minorities by eliminating the main danger to their power.

American business and government are bound up with the ruling minorities in Latin America – with the rural and industrial property holders. Our interests and their interests – stability, return on investment – are the same. Meanwhile the masses of the people keep on suffering because they lack even minimal educational facilities, health-care, housing, and diet. They could have these benefits if national income were not so unevenly distributed.

(The writer of these perceptive observations has subsequently been refused permission to live in Britain and, it appears, is also *persona non grata* in a number of other European countries closely allied to the USA.) The association between the CIA and American multinational corporations is a particularly important element in the control that US capital attempts to exert over Central and South America. Among the more dramatic achievements of this alliance for underdevelopment has been the 'destabilization' of left-wing governments in Chile and the Dominican Republic.

The process of uneven development or polarized growth in Latin America was described in some detail in discussions of Peru in previous chapters. All that needs to be stressed here is that the way such a nation fits into the international pattern of economic relationships has a vital bearing on internal variations in level of living. An effective summary is provided by Gilbert (1974, p. 218) as he elaborates the point that all backward areas have not always been poor:

Regions such as the sierra of Peru were in fact supporting advanced civilizations before the onset of colonialism. Their backwardness, poverty and traditionalism, rather than being an eternal condition, has been the result of four hundred years of economic and political colonialism. Such areas are backward not because they have failed to develop but because other regions consistently expropriated capital and wealth from them. By such means, the developed nations accelerated their own growth at the expense of the poor nations of the world. Similarly, the backward regions within those poor nations have been handicapped by the transfer of their economic surplus to the more prosperous regions. The resolution of this dilemma cannot be achieved by relying on the actions of governments, who represent the most economically powerful sections of the community and whose policies lead to the benefits of growth by-passing the backward areas. The only long-term solution is to achieve a structural and revolutionary reform of government.

As we have already observed, it remains in doubt whether the halfway measures taken in Peru to overcome the problem of dependent capitalism are radical enough. If not, the alternative is revolution

331

Cuban-style, or along the paths chosen by Angola and Mozambique in southern Africa, guided by their own brand of Marxist–Leninist practice.

As a specific illustration of the role of spatial organization in the perpetuation of inequality, we may return briefly to South Africa. Over the past three decades, the ruling National Party has been implementing the policy of *apartheid*, or separate development, under which particular territories are designated for the occupancy of particular race groups. Not only are the cities subdivided racially, as was mentioned above, but the country as a whole is split up between whites and blacks (*Bantu*, or the indigenous African population). Ten so-called homelands or *Bantustans* have been set up, one for each of the major African tribal groups. These territories are supposed eventually to become independent nation states: those of the Transkei and Bophuthatswana have already achieved this in theory, though without the recognition of the United Nations.

Apartheid is widely recognized outside the Republic as a system of legalized race discrimination. But it must also be seen as an attempt at planned spatial reorganization of the national territory of South Africa, designed to maintain white control and the perpetuation of an exploitive economic system. 'White' South Africa needs the black man's labour, but does not want his vote: there are only 4·3 million Whites compared with 18·2 million Africans, 4·4 million Coloureds and 0·7 million Asians (mainly Indians). Blacks have no franchise in 'white' South Africa, which comprises almost 87 per cent of the Republic's area, even though half of them live there. Africans are expected to exercise their political 'rights' in their homeland. (Coloureds and Asians have no homeland and, thus, no place in the country's political geography.) The homelands give the semblance of a franchise to the Africans, without conceding them political power where it could threaten white control – in the cities. In addition to being subdivided among the tribes, the homeland areas are highly fragmented geographically, in accordance with the government's divide-and-rule strategy towards the black majority.

Figure 6.6 shows that the homelands form an almost complete peripheral crescent about the country's core industrial region, centred

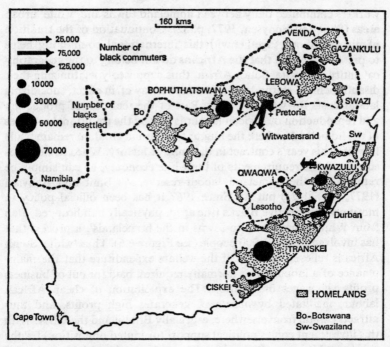

Figure 6.6. Aspects of the political economy of spatial organization in South Africa, emphasizing the functional relationship between the African 'homelands' and the white-controlled cities. (Sources: migration and commuting flows based on Board, 1976, Fig. 1 and Smit and Booysen, 1977, Fig. 10.)

on Johannesburg – the peak on the national-production surface illustrated in Figure 6.2. They function as labour reserves for the Witwatersrand and other industrial cities. Although millions of Africans are, in fact, permanent residents of townships such as Soweto, attached to the 'white' cities, the government hopes to foster an increasing reliance on migrant labour. It also encourages daily commuting from dormitory towns within the homelands, where they come close enough to a city (as, for example, where the Kwazulu homeland adjoins the city of Durban). In 1975, some 557,000 black

333

workers commuted daily between homeland towns and 'white' urban areas (Smit and Booysen, 1977, p. 32). Continuation of the tradition of migrant labour, together with this 'international' commuting, helps to preserve the idea that the Africans do not belong to the geographical entity of 'white' South Africa, thus supposedly legitimizing their disenfranchised status. It also provides a way of, in effect, subsidizing labour costs for white business. Part of the real cost of production and reproduction of African labour is met by the traditional societies of the homelands, where the migrant's wife and children remain while he works his year's contract in the mine or factory. When he becomes surplus to the requirements of the white economy, he can simply be returned to the homeland labour-reserve. As Smit and Booysen (1977, pp. 20–21) put it: 'Since 1967 it has been official policy to move non-productive Blacks (the aged, physically handicapped, etc.) from White urban areas to towns in the homelands', a process that has involved over 171,000 people (see Figure 6.6). Thus 'white' South Africa is relieved of some of the welfare expenditure that the maintenance of a labour force normally requires, paid for out of business profits via wages or taxation. The exploitation of cheap African labour, facilitated by *apartheid*, generates high profits, and thus attracts capital from elsewhere, especially Britain and the USA. With this investment comes political support (or muted opposition) for the existing white minority regime. The outcome is a highly polarized pattern of economic development within South Africa, and extreme differentiation in levels of living between core and periphery. There is more to *apartheid* than this brief account can convey (see, for example, Lemon, 1976; D. M. Smith, 1977, ch. 10), but what has been said should be sufficient to demonstrate that spatial organization is instrumental in promoting racial inequality which, in South Africa, is itself inevitably also spatial.

Turning now to the city, the case of South Africa helps to emphasize that intra-urban inequality must be understood as part of the outcome of the role that a city plays in some wider system. The Johannesburg conurbation generates most of the national wealth, and the fact that this is extracted largely from the labour of blacks necessitates the physical presence of these people in large numbers.

Hence, the unique pattern of urban inequality, referred to earlier in this chapter. As we have seen elsewhere, the process of uneven development at the national level may be behind some of the most extreme manifestations of inequality within the city. The inner slums and fringe squatter-settlements of cities like Lima represent a spatial transfer to the core of some of the poverty from the periphery. Such stark contrasts in living standards as are observed in the Third World city underline the ability of the indigenous élite, often as agents of overseas capital, to appropriate a large share of the surplus product that remains in the country in question. The city takes on a polarized spatial structure, as the wealth of the élite brings political and economic power and hence more wealth with which to build fine homes and support high-quality services. Meanwhile, the poor must be satisfied with promises and a few tokens: modern lamp standards on mud streets and a few model 'low-income' dwellings funded by the World Bank or some other international agency.

Uneven development within the city is by no means confined to the underdeveloped world, as we have shown. In the cities of advanced capitalist nations clear spatial differentiation exists. Again, this can be traced to economic processes, with a specific geographical dimension to resource allocation. An unequal initial distribution of resources generates further inequality in income distribution under the capitalist mode of production. Markets respond to the demand of those with money to spend, so the resource allocations tend to favour the rich; the economy produces what people can pay for, not what they want or need if that is not backed up by purchasing power. Wealth brings other kinds of power, economic and political, and hence the capacity to influence resource allocation more directly. Thus, the new library or swimming pool goes to a well-to-do part of town with political pull, rather than to a poorer district. The new motorway cuts through the low-income neighbourhood rather than the middle-class suburb. Such writers as Harvey (1973), Cox (1973) and Pahl (1970) have stressed the extent to which people in cities enjoy differential access to sources of well-being and proximity to nuisance. Harvey sees much of the political activity in the city as a struggle for control of the hidden mechanisms whereby public-sector resource allocation and location decisions are made, advant-

335

aging some people and disadvantaging others, according to just how much is spent on what where. As Lineberry (1974, p. 30) succinctly summarizes the issue: 'Force gives way to public policy as a device for securing and maintaining locational advantage.' While people with low incomes are generally those who lose most from this process, membership of an ethnic minority confined by custom or even law to particular parts of a city may be the passport to the worst environmental conditions. Once in a poor and perhaps socially disorganized environment, disadvantage can easily become self-perpetuating.

Part of the geographical reality of living in cities is that people exist in close proximity to each other. Activities that generate negative side-effects thus impinge on the well-being of far more people than would be the case in the countryside. Some people in some places will be especially vulnerable to the nuisance generated by others, whether it is industrial pollution, noise from a street or freeway, traffic congestion, road accidents, unruly behaviour of football crowds and drunks, or whatever. The vulnerable localities tend to be where population density is greatest or flows heaviest – in the inner city. They are usually occupied by the poor, who lack freedom of residential choice and the power or influence to exclude sources of what economists term negative externalities (nuisance inflicted by some people on others and not captured by the price mechanism). Contemporary urban society seems particularly prone to the generation of nuisance that is not somehow accounted for in user charges for goods and services. As with airport noise, referred to in Chapter 1, there seems to be no way that market pricing can compensate those who suffer from the effects of traffic, litter and other forms of pollution, via a levy on those who benefit from the activities involved. Yet these effects themselves arise out of the spatial structure that market mechanisms have helped to create.

Once again, the theme of geographical interdependence emerges. The lives of poor people in cities are as they are because they form part of a wider whole. As under *apartheid*, capitalism needs its convenient sources of cheap labour, to be taken on and laid off as market forces dictate. Even the inhabitants of Skid Row or the pit of the well-being surface play a role, for example as casual labour or source of raw material for blood banks (and sometimes medical-school dissecting rooms), as well as providing a market for alcohol and drugs. As Mandel (1962, pp. 151–2) says of the United States: 'It is enough to look at the frightful slums that fill entire districts of New York, Chicago, Detroit, San Francisco, New Orleans, and other southern towns, to realize that these victims of an inhuman society; brutalized and dehumanized by this same society, continue to constitute a terrible reproach to the richest capitalism in the world.' Harsh words, perhaps, but the plight of these people is directly related to the affluence enjoyed by others. As we suggested in Chapter 4, the contrast between rich and poor in the American city is taking on the form of a spatial class-polarization – a type of separate but unequal development.

Societal Structure and the Role of Space

The emphasis in the previous discussion has been on the processes making for inequality under capitalism. Certain features of a capitalist economy are instrumental in promoting uneven development. As we have seen, the contemporary era of capitalism in both advanced and underdeveloped countries is characterized by powerful forces of polarization or centralization. These are *spatial* processes, in the sense that they concern the disposition of man and his activities on the surface of the earth. And they have spatial consequences with respect to the differentiation of human life chances or standards of living.

But these processes themselves depend on other non-spatial ingredients of capitalist institutions and ideology. In particular, they depend on a method of organizing the satisfaction of human needs and wants which gives a primary role to individual self-interest, on the part of both producers (as profit-seekers) and consumers (as satisfaction-seekers). The institution of private property and the rights vested in ownership facilitate the operation of markets, whereby people can offer their capital, land or labour for alternative uses, selling to the highest bidder. Similarly, those who undertake production must offer their wares to the critical scrutiny of individual consumers, with the freedom to select and reject as it pleases them. The outcome

337

of perfect markets working perfectly thus generates a structure and distribution of goods, services and incomes sanctioned by the people in some equivalent of a democratic process, or so the ideology of traditional economic theory would have us believe. Thus, any inequality that results can be claimed to have the implicit approval of society. The pursuit of individual freedom or liberty, including the right to dispose of one's property as one thinks fit, is elevated almost to an ultimate end. The best of all worlds emerges from the pursuit of self-interest within a competitive framework, with, of course, a minimum of government 'interference' with free enterprise.

We do not have time here to set out all the shortcomings of this conventional view of how a capitalist economy works. But two important points must be stressed. First, the institution of private property creates great inequalities of power in the market-place, which make for inequalities in other aspects of life. Those who own capital and land (including its natural resources) control the means of production, and although they also need labour they are not compelled to employ a given number of workers at any specific level of wages. They have the flexibility to substitute capital for labour if it suits them, to 'hire and fire', to close down the plant in the face of demands for higher pay, and even to cease production altogether and live on capital. The worker, with nothing to dispose of except his or her labour, must work to survive – or such was the case until the introduction of the 'welfare state' in capitalist societies. The growing power of organized labour has gone some way towards redressing the imbalance of market-place power as between employers and workers. And in any event the crude class dichotomy recognized by Marx a century ago has given way to a more complex alignment of social groups in the modern pluralistic society. But it is still true that the advantage of an initially favourable endowment of resources in the form of capital and land enables an individual or group to maintain a position of economic, social and political advantage to which few ordinary workers can aspire, whatever their personal ability. In some societies the relics of a former aristocracy strengthen this social cleavage: Britain is a case in point, with its monarchy and House of Lords. Very simply, there is a self-perpetuating element in the class structure of capitalist societies, reflected in differential consumption possibilities or living standards. Markets are unlikely to generate a socially just distribution of income, goods and services unless the initial distribution of 'votes' in the market-place is just. In reality, the initial distribution of resources is likely to be biased very much in favour of a few people whose brain, brawn or good fortune has given them disproportionate rights over property.

The second point is more directly geographical, in that it concerns how market mechanisms are supposed to operate in a space economy. In theory, 'factors of production' (land, labour, capital and enterprise) will find their way to the use offering highest returns, as revealed by market-place competition. Thus, land under wheat will go over to barley next season if the farmer sees the latter crop offering a higher return per acre for a given expenditure of time and other resources. A worker will switch from driving a bus for the corporation to driving a truck for a haulage contractor if this pays better. And so on. It is recognized that factors of production do not flow with perfect ease from one use to another, if only because of ignorance as to alternative opportunities and the fact that neither workers nor businessmen behave with perfect, calculated economic rationality. But in the space economy, factor mobility is further constrained. In theory, labour and capital will flow from places (cities, regions, even nations) offering low returns, to those of greater opportunity. This should bring an equalization of returns to capital, labour and so on, as no further advantage could be gained from movement. But the reality is of continuing differentiation, as we have seen in the United States (Chapter 3). Capital may be highly mobile, except in its 'fixed' form as buildings, but labour may be much less free to move. People may prefer to remain in a depressed industrial area or poor, peripheral agricultural region rather than move to the uncertain opportunities of the growth area or city. Businessmen may be ignorant of opportunities in more distant locations. Thus, any tendency towards convergence of regional incomes or living standards in a competitive system is constrained by the fact that distance and relationships between places can strengthen the immobility of factors of production, and their failure to respond to the 'true' signals of the market. What may be happening in fact is that both capital and labour are overestimating the advantage of metropolitan locations, thus driving on the spatial polarization evident in so many parts of the world. Market forces themselves may reverse the centralization trend eventually, as the economic disadvantages of scale become more obvious. But the human cost in the meantime will be enormous. And ultimate reversal could leave millions living in misery in half-abandoned cities; the blighted inner areas of the American metropolis could for many be the city of the future.

Socialism would appear to have distinct advantages over capitalism as a mode of economic organization, if the objective is greater equality. The two major problems of capitalism raised in the previous paragraphs are eliminated under socialism. Some form of collective ownership of the means of production eliminates the capitalist/land-owning class with its concentration of wealth, and thus a major source of general inequality under capitalism. Central planning greatly reduces the role of markets, and the reliance on unpredictable responses of individuals to what may be largely unintelligible collections of price 'signals'. Living standards can be equalized by central dictate, that ensures resources allocation among territories such that all meet specific norms for the availability of consumer goods, services and so on. More generally, the replacement of an ideology stressing individual self-interest by one that places more emphasis on collective responsibility should ensure that the allocation of resources and the distribution of output respond to the needs of all people, not just those with effective market-place demand.

Our case studies of socialist societies, sketchy though they are, cast some doubt on the egalitarian expectations that might be aroused by the rhetoric of Marx, Lenin and Mao. It may well be true that some form of socialism is a *necessary* condition for an equal society, or one in which differentiation is generally agreed to be fair. However, socialism as actually practised is certainly not a *sufficient* condition for this kind of outcome. There are enormous difficulties in running a centrally planned economy, released from the regulation and discipline of the market-place – a matter beyond the scope of the present discussion. But there are also certain aspects of the organization of human activity in geographical space that seem to make for inequality, irrespective of mode of production and political structure.

The first consideration arises from the general nature of control in complex modern societies. We have already seen something of the spatial expression of the control hierarchy of the contemporary capitalist world, as suggested by Hymer. Something similar may well exist in the socialist world. Even putting aside simplistic notions of communist parties in other nations dancing to Moscow's tune, the Communist Party of the USSR clearly occupies a pivotal position of influence over affairs in other socialist countries. At one extreme this can take the form of direct military intervention, as in Czechoslovakia in 1968 (analogous to the United States involvement in Vietnam and the Dominican Republic). At the other, there is an ideological conformity on the part of the satellite nations, exceptions being Romania, Yugoslavia and countries more under Chinese influence. Somewhere between these positions is the economic dependence generated by financial and technical aid. On the face of it, underdeveloped nations like Cuba, Tanzania, Angola and Mozambique stand a much better chance of building decent societies without glaring inequalities under their own type of socialism, than would be the case with continuation of dependent capitalism. But how truly free they are, and can remain, to modify Marxist–Leninist doctrine to local cultural and environmental conditions remains to be seen. There could be very little to choose between dependent capitalism and dependent socialism for such countries.

Within each socialist state we can expect to find some version of the control hierarchy, with a spatial expression. There may indeed be two parallel structures: one representing the ministries running the economy and social services, the other the Communist Party. Just as under capitalism, the highest-level control functions will be exercised from the capital city. This is where the highest-status (and best-paid) jobs will be found. Secondary control will be exercised in, for example, the republic capitals in the USSR, themselves controlling and co-ordinating activity at the regional level, and so on. Just as under capitalism, places at the lower end of the control hierarchy will offer limited occupational opportunities and limited access to upper-level jobs. The skilled local manager or party official may have to move to the provincial or national capital to realize his or her full potential.

Central places in the spatial control-hierarchy will have dispro-

Where the Grass is Greener

portionate numbers of high-level business and party posts. This,
along with the tendency for the world of culture, the arts and education to concentrate spatially, will create local élites, as in Moscow,
enjoying living standards substantially better than those of the mass
of the people. Thus, some social stratification seems inevitable by
virtue of the hierarchical nature of bureaucratic organizations, and
this is likely to be reflected in differential rewards. Matthews (1978,
p. 20) claims that, 'The leadership of the Soviet Communist Party
has, from its earliest days, been profoundly élitist in its attitudes',
ensuring for itself and its closest associates privileges commensurate
with its great political responsibilities. Thus there may be a contradiction between equalitarian ideology and the functional necessity
of Soviet-style social control.

How far China and other nations, placing greater stress on non-
material incentives, have been able to prevent the emergence of a
differentiated and spatially-concentrated élite is difficult to say.
However, there is evidence that even here people in different places
enjoy different levels of living, by virtue of favourable local resource-
endowment or special incentives to promote regional development.
The central control exercised in socialist societies does permit
deliberate differentiation of territory with respect to such things as
wages and levels of service, in accordance with the wider objectives
of the national plan. As in capitalist societies, what a territory can
attract by way of these privileges may be related to the political pull
of local officials and to their place in the wider control hierarchy.

Internal politics clearly play an important part in the process of
resource allocation in the USSR. Just as in the USA a forceful
congressman can be instrumental in attracting to his district valuable
public-works projects or defence contracts, so similar forces may be
at work under socialism. Khrushchev's memoirs provide a vivid
example. Khrushchev (1977, p. 272) describes the following situation
of conflict between Voznesensky, Chairman of State Planning, and
the notorious NKVD Chief, Beria: 'He [Voznesensky] had sought
to redistribute the country's economic resources more evenly, and
this meant taking money away from certain commissariats which
enjoyed Beria's patronage. Beria had many commissariats under him,
342

and he always demanded that they receive much more than their share of funds. Beria was extremely powerful because of his closeness to Stalin.' In Khrushchev's account, Beria was the victor and the unfortunate Voznesensky was eventually shot. So much for the equalitarian ideals of socialism in practice, at least in Stalin's time.

While this may well be an extreme case, political power and patronage probably still operate significantly in the competitive bargaining for scarce resources. Bureaucratic organizations, and individuals working within them, may well be subject to the same general pattern of behaviour, irrespective of whether the prevailing socio-economic structure is capitalist or socialist. Resource allocation under both systems may often be guided by some form of incrementalism, whereby those places already well endowed by being favoured in the past get proportionally greater shares of this year's budget. The result is, at best, perpetuation of existing geographical patterns of inequality. And if the favoured places build up disproportionate political pull, inequality may be exacerbated.

Some of the inequalities in human life chances observed in capitalist systems arise from the uneven development of service provision. A socialist system has the freedom to disregard effective demand and provide services according to local need. The conflict between dispersal of facilities, in the interests of consumer access, and concentration, in the interests of functional efficiency, can be partially resolved by a planned spatial hierarchy of centralized specialist services and a more even spread of those required on a day-to-day basis. The spatial organization of health care in the USSR is a case in point. But again, we must recognize that geographical space will create inequality, even in the most carefully planned organizational structure. Unless everyone can have equal medical facilities on their own doorstep – no more and no less – some will be potentially better served than others. People in the big city will be closer to the major hospital than people in the countryside, and this could make the difference between life and death in the event of sudden illness or accident. Within the city, some people will have farther to go than others when a visit to the doctor is needed, just as some will be closer to parks, cinemas, theatres and restaurants, no

343

matter how evenly such facilities are distributed on a neighbourhood basis. Again, geographical space makes some differentiation inevitable, even in a city of people with equal personal income.

One source of inequality in access to urban services, which socialism appears to find difficult to solve, is the failure to keep up with residential development on the fringe of the metropolis. As we found in Chapter 4, there is ample evidence of this problem in the Soviet city, as exemplified by Moscow. An analogy from the capitalist world is the deficiency of health care facilities in the western suburbs of Sydney, Australia, as described in Chapter 5. The edge of the metropolis is bound to be disadvantaged with respect to centrally provided facilities, perhaps calling for some degree of dispersal as suburbs or satellite towns become steadily more remote. This is part of the geographical reality of urban growth as a universal phenomenon. But there is also an organizational dimension to the problem. The need to co-ordinate the provision of all types of services with the progress of residential development seems to stretch the capacity of city planners, especially when different branches of the bureaucracy are involved. And the tendency to centralize certain services rather than disperse them is, itself, often more a matter of organizational convenience than of necessity.

Of course, a planning society can decide its own balance of service provision. It may choose to supply little by way of specialized, centralized medical facilities, for example – accepting that people with rare diseases or physical disabilities will simply not get treated – and prefer to allocate more resources to basic services like preventive medicine. Perhaps China has gone furthest in the direction of highly decentralized basic care, offering greatest spatial equality of health care provision. One way of promoting greater equality, given some differentiation of access by virtue of a spatial hierarchy of facilities, is to remove as far as possible the necessity for the service. Effective preventive care with the onus on the individual, family unit or local community to play an active role, may thus be the most equalitarian strategy. The problem of unequal access to specialist facilities then arises only when local preventive care has proved inadequate.

A final problem revealed by our examination of socialist societies is the servicing of remote, rural areas. The provision of facilities and personnel will be relatively expensive where population is scattered, and resource constraints may tempt administrators to overlook such areas in favour of places where the same investment can yield a higher level of service or performance. This type of discrimination can be overcome if sufficient priority is given to the elimination of town–country differences. The same problem exists under capitalism, of course, even in a country as small as Britain. A conference in 1977 drew attention to low wages, bad housing, poor medical services and a threadbare education system producing 'rural deprivation' in Britain as extreme as in the inner urban areas (*New Society*, 8 Dec. 1977). And all this despite the welfare state.

At the root of this kind of problem is the question of how to get trained people to work in remote areas. It is one thing to allocate funds disproportionately to the countryside; it is quite another matter to ensure that good doctors, dentists and teachers stay in a country town or village. This appears to be a universal problem: Hyde (1974, p. 102) quotes the *Report of the Royal Commission on Medical Education* of 1968 as follows:

We have found from our enquiries that no country in the world has really succeeded in persuading recent medical graduates to serve in outlying areas where they are necessarily denied access to specialized medical facilities and the constant company of other doctors, with its important implications for maintaining professional competence and the amenities of social life which a highly educated young person normally expects.

The problem is not entirely one of geography, of remoteness from the mainstream of life. It arises because the process of professional training involves personal change – the taking on of new values, be they cultural or a set of professional ethics. These themselves stem from the nature of society. And, however much they might be related to the maintenance of professional competence, they do have a strong element of self-gratification about them. Professional people prefer a certain cultural milieu, therefore they will avoid living in places where this cannot be found.

Part of the solution to such problems involves a change in professional ethics and personal attitudes. Coercion is no solution, for it is rather unlikely that a doctor forced to practise somewhere will

345

be fully dedicated to the job. Perhaps China has approached the problem realistically, by a combination of non-material incentives associated with revolutionary zeal and a de-professionalization of the practice of medicine. Post-revolutionary Russia tried to eliminate bourgeois elements in the medical profession (Field, 1976, p. 237); the doctor in Soviet society today appears to lack both the pay differentials and the social status of his or her counterpart in the capitalist world. But still the problem of getting doctors into the countryside remains.

Earlier in this section, and elsewhere in this book, we have observed that, under capitalism, geographical inequality in levels of living is an inevitable outcome of how the economy works. Whatever the theory of the self-balancing market mechanism may suggest, inequality is an observable and predictable outcome of the capitalist system as it actually functions. Similarly, socialism, as it is actually seen to operate, is accompanied by inequality. This may not be on the extreme scale of capitalism, and especially of those Third World nations dominated by the great capitalist powers. But it is inequality nevertheless. And it stems, to a great extent, from the way in which human activity is organized in geographical space. So, socialism provides no panacea. As Friedrich Engels wrote a century ago:

> Between one country and another, one province and another and even one locality and another there will always exist a *certain* inequality in the conditions of life, which it will be possible to reduce to a minimum but never entirely remove. Alpine dwellers will always have different conditions of life from those of people living on plains.

Towards a More Equal World

Most of us would like to see a more equal world. When we talk of greater fairness, equity or justice, we generally have in mind greater equality. When governments take a hand in the process of distribution, via urban and regional planning, or the provision of social services, the avowed aim is almost invariably to assist 'underprivileged' people or places, to close the 'gulf' between rich and poor, to narrow the 'development gap', or some similarly equalizing sentiment. All this is a familiar part of contemporary political rhetoric.

Yet the evidence presented in this book is of great and continuing inequalities in living standards, as between people in different places. We now understand that the organization of modern economic activity carries with it a predisposition towards a certain spatial structure, from which inequality appears almost inevitably to arise. But, surely, more could be done to reduce inequality, even if it can never be entirely eliminated. Why has planning proved rather ineffectual in this respect, especially in the capitalist world? Unless we understand past failures, we are unlikely to do better in the future.

Planning for the promotion of equality, like any other human endeavour, depends on a particular view of how the world works. At the one extreme, this may be highly intuitive and subjective, generating an almost subconscious foundation for pragmatic decision-making based on 'gut feelings' or hunches. At the other, it may take the form of a tightly structured scientific theory, expressed as a mathematical model in which the outcome of change in the system can be predicted with a high degree of accuracy. But whatever the level of sophistication of such a view, action based upon it is unlikely to achieve the desired objectives if the view is wrong – if the subjective impressions are incorrect or if the theory rests on false premises. Such is the case with important elements of the body of knowledge upon which development planning is often based.

The practice of planning, in pursuit of equity or any other objective, involves the allocation of resources. How these allocations are made, and where, depends on some theory as to how the economic processes thus modified or set in motion will operate. In the capitalist world, this theory is generally provided by a body of knowledge known as neo-classical economics, conveyed in such textbooks as Samuelson (1973). As we saw at the beginning of the previous section of this chapter, there are some good reasons to doubt whether conventional economic analysis of this kind accurately describes how a competitive market-oriented system actually operates. Indeed, it can be argued that neo-classical economics, with its formal elegance and mathematical rigour, and almost magical self-regulating properties, performs more of an ideological than a scientific role. Its function may be seen as mystification rather than clarification: a mask for the

347

exploitive nature of capitalism, a justification for the gross inequalities that accompany such a system, and a rationale for minimizing government 'intervention'. This is a major point of the critique currently being mounted by radical economists, most of them inspired by Marx.

A detailed exploration of the deficiencies of conventional economic theory and of the possible superiority of a Marxist perspective is beyond the scope of this volume. All we shall attempt here is to elaborate one particularly important line of argument, elements of which have appeared in a number of the case studies in previous chapters. It is an argument of special relevance to spatial planning-strategy in so far as this is based on conventional economic analysis, which is usually the case. The threads thus drawn together help us towards some final observations on what it may take to create a more equal world.

We begin with the notion that the 'market-regulated' capitalist economic system is, to a significant extent, not really regulated by competitive market forces. The best-known exponent of this view is not a Marxist but J. K. Galbraith. Galbraith (1967) has suggested that much of the economic activity in the modern industrial state, as exemplified by the USA, is controlled by a 'technostructure' of upper management, quite different from the owner-operating *entrepreneur* of traditional economic theory and motivated more by the desire for long-term security than by strict profit-maximization. The security of the modern corporation is achieved, in large measure, by eliminating risk and uncertainty through control of sources of materials and markets for finished products. This implies large-scale organization, frequently in cooperation with government. Galbraith (1975) sees two distinct sectors in the new industrial state under capitalism: a 'market' system of small, dispersed firms still responsive to the interaction of supply and demand, and a 'planning' system of large corporations capable of substantial control of the market forces that should, in theory, be regulating them. The planning system incorporates certain government activities, such as defence and space exploration. These work very much in the interests of the major industrial corporations, which supply the expensive goods and technology required, but of course quite contrary to the interests of

348

the vast majority of the world's population. While the planning system prospers, the small businesses of the market system come under increasing pressure, both in the advanced capitalist world and in underdeveloped lands. Marx predicted a similar tendency for the emergence of large monopolies at the expense of the small-scale producer, as the capitalist system matures. The demise of the small business, from the street-corner grocer's shop to the independent industrial concern, will be portrayed in capitalist ideology as a consequence of government discrimination (as in Britain today) rather than as an inevitable consequence of the growing concentration of economic power.

The planning system includes the giant trans-national corporations. In previous discussions we have seen something of how their activities might be viewed as generating geographical inequalities in living standards. Galbraith (1975, p. 190) summarizes the situation as follows: 'the trans-national system internationalizes the tendency for unequal development and to unequal income that has occurred domestically as between the planning and the market systems.' The world economy is increasingly being organized by these major corporations. Association with them brings a highly selective prosperity, often achieved at the expense of people and places outside the system.

The point of all this with respect to development planning is that much of what is done to promote economic growth in underdeveloped lands or depressed regions is based on theory which neglects the role of the multinationals, or at least underestimates their influence. This theme has been elaborated at length by Stuart Holland, whose views on the regional problem were referred to in Chapter 3. On a world scale, the proposals for redistribution of wealth that regularly emanate from the United Nations Organization are quite unrelated to the momentum of the world capitalist system – driven on by the multinational corporations – which is itself a major factor in the perpetuation of the development gap. National and regional development plans, with their investment incentives to encourage private business to make the 'right' location decisions with respect to public objectives, simply do not operate at the required scale. As Holland (1976a, p. 57) remarks: 'Capital is not moving in the incremental shuffle beloved of perfect-competition theorists, but strides the world in seven-league boots, over-stepping problem regions in both developed and less-developed countries.' Looking up at this Colossus or Gulliver figure are the Lilliputian masses of the world's poor, left wondering why the promised process of industrialization has passed them by. And in those countries or regions where the feet happen to fall, leaving a lump of capital in the form of an outpost of some multinational corporation, the outcome may be very much a mixed blessing. Some people may gain from the employment generated by the firm, from related business activity and from bribes to government officials. But many may lose, as this branch of Galbraith's planning system penetrates the traditional sectors of the economy and begins to break them down. Per capita income may show an improvement. 'Development' may appear to have taken place. But the distribution of income may well have become more unequal, especially as between the 'modern' and the 'traditional' components of the economy. Theories of economic development that see industrialization via outside capital as the solution to underdevelopment neglect the *distributional* impact of the type of 'development' promoted by large foreign-owned corporations.

Similar problems arise at the regional level in developed nations. If a branch of a big-league firm comes into a depressed area, it may not be closely integrated into the rest of the local economy. Its 'multiplier' effect, whereby additional jobs are created in near-by ancillary activities, may be slight, because connections are primarily outside – with other branches of the corporation. It may indeed damage other local firms by creaming off the labour force, as we suggested in Chapter 3. It may bring in its own management and skilled workers from elsewhere, limiting local recruitment to relatively low-paid jobs. Profits leak out of the area to institutional investors and large capitalists, rather than being retained in the local economy to generate more economic activity. And when the next recession comes, or when government incentives cease, the branch may prove 'uneconomic' and close down. Impressive though the glossy new factories may look, they are frequently more unstable in an economic sense than long-established local industry.

What we suggest here is only one side of the story, of course, and ignores the benefits that can be derived in a depressed region from the infusion of outside capital by a successful business organization. We are simply pointing out that there are aspects to the process of the large corporation's economic development in the modern world, that tend to be overlooked in the design of spatial planning-strategy. The operation of multinational corporations renders many traditional development-policy instruments ineffective. There is a basic contradiction between planning by local, regional and even national territorial units, on the one hand, and the international planning of the large corporation, on the other.

What are the lessons, for planning a more equal world? One seems quite obvious. To paraphrase Holland (1976a, p. 57), the dynamism of the big-league firms can only be harnessed to the needs of problem regions and areas if governments at least understand their operation, a matter on which conventional development theory offers little assistance. A realistic theory must incorporate the analysis of Holland, Galbraith, Hymer and others who have been able to break out of the imaginary world of perfect competition. Such a theory will recognize the leading role of the major corporations within individual nations, and the supra-national scale of their operations. It will recognize the true, often parasitic, nature of the interaction of these firms with more localized, small-scale or traditional activities. It will also recognize the political power of the multinationals, capable of turning lands overseas into virtual company countries, like United Fruit's 'banana republics', akin to the company towns of the last century. No theory of development and underdevelopment, relevant to what actually happens in Latin America, South-East Asia and southern Africa, is complete without recognition of the role of big business, operating in association with the anti-socialist foreign policy of the major capitalist powers, in organizing the internal affairs of countries in which they operate.

Another necessity is to purge development theory of the (often implicit) assumption that, with minimal government guidance, a free-enterprise economy in private hands is in the best interests of the public at large. There may be some merit to the argument that a highly decentralized economy of small-scale producers in active competition could quite effectively and fairly satisfy consumer

351

preferences, via the intermediary of the market, given a 'just' distribution of wealth to begin with. But this kind of economy does not exist. The formal association between free-market capitalism working perfectly and the maximization of social welfare, still perpetuated in some economics textbooks, is irrelevant to the real world, except in so far as it is used in an ideological role to minimize 'interference' in private-business activity. In the modern world of big business and government partnership (as opposed to intervention and control), so many of the assumptions on which the conventional theory rests simply do not hold true. It should be self-evident that there is a fundamental conflict between the private pursuit of profit within the structure of the contemporary economy and the effective and equitable satisfaction of human needs. The multinational corporation serves itself, not the public interest. And there is no logical, scientific reason why the two should be coincident.

The most obvious solution is greater public control of the multinationals. One possibility is that they could be broken up, at least into elements small enough to be within the effective jurisdiction of a single national (or even regional) government. But because these corporations do operate internationally, there is no practical way of achieving this. And within individual nations, the power of big business over government, mass media and so on is such that the multinationals can be made to appear almost as benevolent guardians of the public interest. Another possibility is that these corporations could be taken into public ownership. Again, their supra-national status makes this rather difficult, but the process could at least be started at a national level. It seems utter folly to leave so much of the organization of economic activity to bodies responsible only to private shareholders, and often only nominally even to them. Nothing short of full public ownership and accountability will ensure that such organizations truly serve the interests of all the people.

Operating in a proper context of publicly controlled planning, the large-scale organization of economic activity is capable of achieving great advances in the direction of a more equal society. A major feature of socialist economic planning, as exemplified in the USSR, is the development of territorial production complexes in which various elements of a regional economy are tied together into an integrated and centrally planned system designed with the aid of mathematical models (Bandman, 1976). Such a system can be operated with the explicit objective of maximizing the living standards of the people in the territory concerned. The level of provision of goods and services in different places can be set, equally or otherwise, and implemented by planning production accordingly. All this is within the capacity of a society where the means of production are not in private hands, and where the prevailing theory of economic development recognizes the reality of the scale and degree of integration of modern industrial organization.

Whether such a system actually works according to plan is another matter. It is well known that personal motivations of management and workers, along with bureaucratic bungling, can lead to considerable imperfections in centrally planned Soviet-type economies. Equality objectives may not be met for this reason. Furthermore, we have already seen that large, hierarchically structured organizations can generate their own momentum towards uneven development, under socialism as well as capitalism. Overcoming this may require more decentralized control, popular participation at the local level, and an effective means of ensuring that the necessary central-control functions are truly responsive to local needs and preferences. In theory, the Soviet system of government provides for this. In practice, real control may be as remote as under capitalism.

The crucial question is whether sufficient decentralization to ensure something approaching territorial equality of life chances, is in fact consistent with the functioning of a centrally planned organization, whether in public or private control. If not, the alternative would appear to be a *dis*integrated economy organized on a small local scale, as in the 'back-yard blast furnace' phase of Chinese industrial development or the 'small is beautiful' movement. But then we are back to the inescapable geographical fact of unequal local resource-endowment. Dependent on the local resource-base, living standards will be unequal. And to equalize supply of resources on a territorial basis requires a central organization.

353

Where the Grass is Greener

The discussion so far has been confined to a regional and national context. Let us now relate what has emerged to the problems of the city. What we have learned from our case studies suggests, again, that planning for greater equality has been frustrated by misleading theory as to the origins of social and economic deprivation in urban areas. The argument has been effectively summarized by Townsend (1976). The explanations of poverty upon which Americans have attempted to tackle this problem rest on three principal theories: orthodox economic theory, with emphasis on deficiencies of individual ability or skill; a more sociological view, which stresses individual shortcomings or misfortunes; and the theory of the 'sub-culture of poverty', whereby poverty is seen as not only a state of economic deprivation and social disorganization but a way of life passed on from one generation to another. Policy in Britain has been guided by the same sort of views, as we saw in Chapter 4. Inner-city deprivation is seen to stem from some intrinsic characteristics of place, or of the people living in particular areas. The response has been a series of policies of positive discrimination, in which areas whose aggregate populations show poor performance on various social indicators qualify for some special government programme or allocation of resources.

As we found in Chapter 4, the assumption that the socially deprived are highly concentrated geographically is open to question. And belief in the efficacy of area-based policies rests on erroneous assumptions as to the geographical distribution of poverty, that arise from erroneous theories as to its origin. Poverty stems from the economy, rather than from the inadequacy of particular individuals or groups concentrated in particular places. The very idea of 'inadequacy' has meaning only in a specific socio-economic context.

An accurate theory of the origins of poverty requires recognition of the way in which the economy allocates resources and distributes benefits and penalties among people living in different places. This means recognition of the hidden controls exercised by, for example, big business, government and the media, which are missed in the preoccupation with drawing lines around 'problem areas' on a map. Certain institutions of the contemporary capitalist state must be

354

seen as instrumental in differentially distributing jobs, housing, good education and health care, and in promoting a lifestyle that requires the possession of various material goods or symbols of status. To quote Townsend (1976, p. 19):

> An institutional theory of poverty is, therefore, required, drawing on labour market theory, industrial location and land use theory, and housing market theory, as they relate both to the national and local occupational class structure, and social security theory as that relates to minority status but also class position. The theory would be expressed in terms of two processes: the process by which different types of resources are unequally allocated or *withheld*; and the process by which styles of living are generated, emulated and institutionalized.
>
> We are obliged to come back to the *national* system of resource allocation to explain the major part of local dispersion of income and extent of deprivation – to *nationally* determined salary and wage structures, *national* taxation, *national* social security, the conditions of the *national* housing market, the *nationwide* system of industry, commerce and transport. These provide the bricks and mortar of the class structure to be found in all communities. (My only qualification would be that these national systems must be looked at, in turn, in a wider, international context.)

The origins of deprivation manifest in the inner city are thus national rather than local. And they will be international, in so far as such features as employment prospects and the process of urban redevelopment are responsive to the activities of multinational businesses and their manipulation of capital on the world money markets. 'Inner-city deprivation' is a consequence of the workings of the international capitalist system, at its present stage of development.

This general line of argument raises questions relating not only to the theory of social deprivation, but also to geographical methodology as applied to the design of anti-poverty programmes or development planning. Figure 6.7 explains the implications, with respect to policy aimed at eliminating 'poverty areas' (regions or nations). The traditional explanations arrived at by conventional geographical analysis focus attention on superficial association, such as between inner-city poverty and race in America. The related policy response is to define the 'problem area' by some more-or-less

355

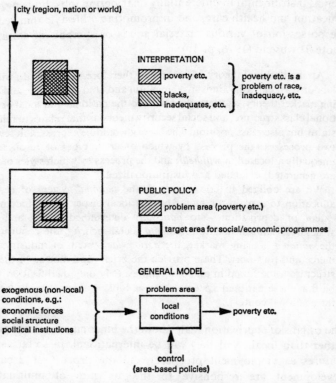

Figure 6.7. Area-based explanations and public policy for the elimination of poverty. (Source: based on Smith and Ogden, 1977, Fig. 2.)

objective measures of poverty, and then to initiate remedial programmes, such as job training, school improvements or environmental facelift, within the area thus bounded. Such an area-based policy misses the external (exogenous) conditions really responsible for poverty – for example, the operation of the market for labour, land and housing. The policy implemented thus addresses symptoms rather than causes. To assail fundamental causes threatens the entire capitalist system, of course, while the area-based palliatives keep at bay more basic structural changes.

356

We are back, once again, at the geography of control. The major decisions that affect the lives of people in cities so often originate elsewhere, in our highly interconnected world. There seems to be a need for people to have much more real control over their own destinies. This is not advocated in a narrow, individualistic sense, since we realize that the pursuit of self-interest is often at the expense of other people in other places. Indeed, the ethic of rugged individualism that epitomizes frontier-mentality free enterprise is really little more than a mask for human greed, which is itself the foundation of economic processes that generate broader inequality. What we have in mind is greater control at the local group level, the level at which living together in some form of community creates a strong commonality of interest. Surely it is right that people, brought into geographical propinquity by choice, chance or necessity, should have substantial control over the kind of lives they live, subject of course to this not hurting other groups of people elsewhere. This is true whether the people in question live in Soweto, a Lima *barriada*, a cotton town facing closure of the mill, or wherever.

In Chapter 4, reference was made to certain positive aspects of squatter settlements in the Latin American city, as exemplified by Lima. Here, a kind of local control has developed, as groups of people occupy the land, build homes, form a community and try to make a living. Such a process can be found in other parts of the Third World. For example, Hake (1977) describes a similar situation in what he calls Nairobi's 'self-help city'. By 1971 a third of Nairobi's population of half a million were living in unauthorized housing and had created 50,000 jobs for themselves outside the modern sector of the economy. Hake describes how the city's marginal residents provide not only work but also a range of welfare services for themselves. Within the existing structure of political and economic power, and the history of neglect of the poor African population in general, these developments might be regarded as progress, as in Lima. But an optimistic view of such self-help schemes carries the seeds of another, possibly misleading, theory of development: that the poor will somehow find the initiative to cope with adversity, and that all the city authorities need to do is to legitimize occupation of the land, put in a tap and sewer line, then leave things to the local people.

357

But local control within the existing (spatial) structure of society may be largely an illusion. How can squatters on the edge of a Third World city, urban blacks in South Africa or Lancashire mill workers be truly in control, as long as there are slums excluded from the mainstreams of city life, segregated settlements subject to external domination and one-industry towns vulnerable to the whims of market forces? Just as local problems may have an origin elsewhere, so true local control requires a broader liberation.

'Power to the People' is a popular slogan of contemporary revolutionary rhetoric. To achieve full liberation from an economic system and class structure that generates and perpetuates inequality may well require the type of armed struggle implied by a revolution. It is indeed difficult to point to cases where programmes of 'moderate' reform have succeeded, especially in the Third World. It is inconceivable that the whites in South Africa or the entrenched élites of many Latin American nations will voluntarily concede power to the mass of the people. The emergence of guerilla movements or 'freedom fighters' is a natural outcome.

The situation in the developed world is different. The sharp contrasts between affluence and poverty have been blunted somewhat through redistributive measures facilitated by economic prosperity and encouraged by the growing power of organized labour. There are ways in which groups of people who are sufficiently informed and articulate can exercise some control outside the formal political system, if their local interests are threatened. Pressure groups can be organized to stop a motorway, operate a nursery school, petition a local authority or run a strike. A particularly successful example of such a movement is provided by the 'green bans' that have been organized in Sydney, Australia. Faced with a city government more sympathetic to property developers than to the preservation of the environment (as is so often the case), the Builders Labourers Federation became a *de facto* countervailing power. Over the past few years they have implemented a series of bans on development projects that threaten open spaces or historic buildings. This rather unusual application of trade union power has proved very effective, as construction cannot take place without construction workers. At one time projects valued at no less than $A3000 million were held in abeyance because of green bans (Camina, 1975, p. 234). Such a case shows that direct action can be effective in a situation where the formal political structure seems not to be acting in the general public interest.

Public participation is supposed to be part and parcel of the planning process in countries like Australia, Britain and the USA, of course. How much the public actually participate depends on the administrative procedures involved, which may do more to deter the public than encourage them. Whether vested commercial interests are involved or not, planners seem to prefer to do their own job in their own way, without 'interference' from the public or their representatives. Like doctors, they value their professional expertise, and the freedom to use it in accordance with their personal judgement. The same is probably true in socialist countries. The extent of true public participation in the USSR and similar systems is difficult to judge; there will not be any battles with private developers, but the monolithic apparatus of the state may be no more sympathetic to environmental considerations, for example. The axiom that you can't fight City Hall may be as valid in the East as in the West.

The true local control to which we look depends on cohesive social groups, whether they are trade unions or neighbourhood resident associations. And these may more easily be formed in some places than others. Adversity and the desperate need for some kind of collective action obviously provide some stimulus. The way the environment is built may also help. A sense of community and belonging no doubt develops more easily where human interaction is encouraged. Planners have tried to create such conditions through the design of, for example, residential areas and New Towns. But this has frequently failed. An instructive example from the Soviet Union illustrates the problem, and leads us on to a more general issue relating to human behaviour in contemporary urban society. City planning in the USSR has, as a central feature, the creation of self-contained neighbourhoods of apartment complexes with the required services, as was pointed out in Chapter 4. These are supposed to help create the sense of collective identity that is thought essential to the development of an equalitarian communist society. While the economics of resource limitation has prevented the full provision of facilities and led to population densities higher than desired, the difficulties of these neighbourhoods seem to go deeper. Frolic (1976, p.157) explains as follows:

> Urbanologists now recognize a conflict between the values they would like to see developed in socialist society and the values that tend to emerge during urbanization, regardless of what was planned. Thus the neighbourhood unit has not been successful, in part for economic reasons, but also because of 'the values and technology of urbanization' – many people living in large industrial cities prefer anonymity and want to be mobile; they don't care to be cooped up in far-out neighbourhoods; access to cars and telephones make them establish friendships in other parts of town; the five-day work week and diversification of leisure opportunities encourages people to get away from home and neighbourhood commitments. The dilemma for Soviet planners and officials is how to come to terms with such 'modern, urban' values, while creating a new communist man whose values differ substantially. Can he become socially conscious, cooperative, and integrated into the community in a setting which generates precisely the opposite values, and which Soviet planners now admit is part of a 'universal' process?

What the Soviet planners are observing would appear to be common elements of contemporary urbanism as a way of life, elements which have been recognized in the West for decades.

Beneath the particular characteristics of urban life seen in the Soviet city, is the fact of growing material affluence. For some time, catching up with the standard of living prevailing in America and Western Europe has been a cherished ambition of Soviet society, or at least of its leaders. The most conspicuous difference between East and West is the availability of *things*, in the form of consumer goods. This is what the good life in the advanced capitalist world is all about; it is the struggle for still more things that drives the system on and makes it what it is. The Soviet Union seems, to put it crudely, to be hell-bent on apeing the rampant materialism that passes for quality of life in the West. It would not therefore be surprising if this singularly un-Marxist path led the people into individualistic and competitive modes of behaviour. The result is likely to be a more affluent society in aggregate but with greater internal inequality, just as in the West. The major difference under socialism will be the relatively uniform provision of social services. But even this can come under pressure in a society geared to private consumption, as resources are diverted from collective provision of such services as health care and education in order that every family can have the coveted car and television set. There is the further point that running a system that, literally, delivers the goods to satisfy growing materialistic aspirations, necessitates centralized planning and control. And this, as we have seen, can be a major source of inequality, personal and geographical.

Once set in motion, the process of socialist development may take on a momentum of its own, as in Marx's interpretation of capitalism. Immediately after the revolution, wholesale implementation of equalitarian measures may reform the society quite dramatically, but after a while some reversal may set in. Parkin (1971, p. 143) comments on Eastern Europe generally:

> Certain of the egalitarian tendencies of the reconstruction phase appear to have been halted, or even reversed, in later periods. This is not to say that inequalities on the Western scale began to be discernible, but rather that the impetus towards social and material levelling appears to have become noticeably weaker. This has been more so in some societies than in others; in the Soviet Union, for example, the reaction against early egalitarian measures was much sharper than it has been elsewhere in Eastern Europe. In the early 1930s Stalin launched an attack upon the equalization principles which had formed the basis of Soviet incomes policies for the first decade or so of Bolshevik rule. Stalin declared that greater material incentives and privileges had to be offered to those who were engaged on skilled work, including the newly emerging managerial and technical cadres. Without sharp income differentials, he argued, there would be no stimulus to learn the skills and assume the responsibilities required in a rapidly industrializing society.

Despite subsequent vacillations, rewards in Soviet society are still explicitly geared to the quantity and quality of work performed. The communist ideal of 'from each according to ability and to each according to need' is still a long way off. And an established society characterized by materialism and occupational class stratification will not bring it any nearer. There is an identifiable political, economic and intellectual élite, within which privilege in such realms as education and access to high-status positions carries an element of self-perpetuation, just as under capitalism. This may be explained away as a necessary aspect of the 'social division of labour' in the transition to true communism, but the evidence of the extent of inheritance of economic and social advantage compiled by Yanowitch (1977), for example, suggests a truly stratified society with a degree of stability that mitigates against change. After all, the 'transition' initiated in the Great October Revolution has now lasted more than sixty years.

Perhaps some kind of ongoing revolution, after the fashion of Mao's China, is needed, to prevent socialist development from ossifying or reverting to bourgeois values. This would involve regular infusions of revolutionary zeal to ensure that equalitarian measures actually operate in practice, so that, for example, doctors and teachers are brought into the countryside and workers into the harsh frontier territories. This could, of course, degenerate into the excesses of the 'cultural revolution'. More optimistically, it might be able to create necessary opportunities for personal re-dedication to the cause of human collective endeavour. The incentives would be of a non-material nature, arising from the satisfaction of active participation in the building of a new society. Individual aspirations would be fulfilled by contribution to the common good. The prevailing ethic would be give rather than take. This, of course, is the ethic upon which Christianity is supposedly based, but this creed seems to have had as little impact on the abolition of inequality as has true communist thought, at least as actually practised.

Ultimately, changes in human behaviour of the kind implied by the imperative of cooperation may require changes in the spatial formation of society. Perhaps geographical equality of income, services and other contributions to living standards can be achieved only in some real fusion of town and country after the Marxist ideal. We are most unlikely to plan things this way; planners (capitalist and socialist) are socialized into ways of thinking which conform to the prevailing wisdom that the magnificent metropolises of the drawing-board comprise the natural habitat of modern man. But we may eventually be forced into a more decentralized (even 'primitive') way of life by our evident failure to make a mass-consumption society based on big cities both civilized and just.

Shortages of the fuel sources needed to support ever greater levels of material production and to sustain high-energy metropolitan living may bring this reversal sooner than we expect. There are, of course, hints of a limited 'back-to-the-countryside' movement in some advanced societies. And it has been an important element in some socialist development-strategy already, as in China, Cuba, and Vietnam after the Americans had withdrawn. It is to be hoped that, if the time comes for the rest of us to follow suit, it can be done with sufficient planning and deliberation to allow us to take advantage of the opportunities presented for a new and more equal way of life, rather than letting us be pulled reluctantly into just another form of dehumanizing chaos.

The ground that we have covered in this book reveals little basis for optimism, however. Striving to become unequal seems almost to be an imperative of human existence, in a world so accustomed to competitive behaviour. There are powerful forces making for differentiation, that appear hard to resist or reverse. And however we may strive for equality, or even achieve some semblance of an equal world, the inclination for people to compare their conditions of life with those of others in other places will surely remain, as part of human curiosity. Someone, somewhere, is always likely to believe that the grass is really greener somewhere else.

Appendix

The Gini Coefficient of Inequality

The Gini coefficient measures the area between the diagonal of perfect equality and the Lorenz curve, as illustrated in Figure 1.1, and as used to portray inequality elsewhere in this book. The Gini coefficient can be calculated from the Lorenz curve by a simple graphic technique. Arbitrary divisions are taken at equal intervals along one axis; they can be at every 10 per cent, as in the accompanying version of Figure 1.1. The corresponding values on the Lorenz curve are then read off: 40, 64, 80 and so on in the illustration (to the nearest whole number). The sum of these values, designated x, is then inserted in the following equation:

$$G = \frac{x - 550}{1000 - 550}$$

The number 550 is the sum of the values giving x that would be found if the Lorenz curve corresponded with the diagonal, i.e. perfect equality or $G = 0$; it is the summation of 10, 20, 30 and so on up to 100. The number 1000 is x in conditions of the extreme of inequality where the Lorenz curve would follow the lines AC and CB; it would be the sum of ten values of 100 and the calculation of G would give unity. The calculation in the illustration produces $G = 0 \cdot 622$. The coefficient is often multiplied by 100 to give a range of 0 to 100 instead of 0 to 1. In the present case, the area between the diagonal and the Lorenz curve is 62·2 per cent of the triangle ABC.

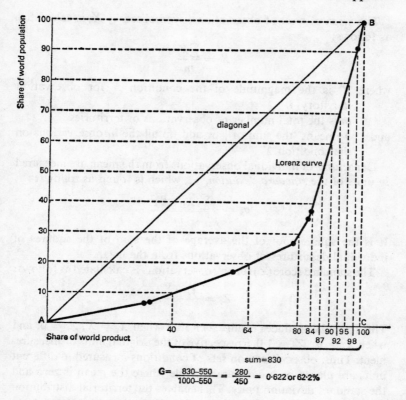

$$G = \frac{830-550}{1000-550} = \frac{280}{450} = 0.622 \text{ or } 62.2\%$$

The Derivation of Composite Social Indicators

A composite indicator of level of living, social well-being or quality of life can be derived in various ways (see D. M. Smith, 1975, ch. 5). The most versatile involves the summation of *standard scores*, otherwise known as *standard deviates*. These scores measure the departure of individual observations from the arithmetic mean (or average) of all observations, expressed in a comparable form. Technically speaking, the standard score is a linear transformation of the original data.

The *mean* of a set of observations, symbolised by $\bar{X}$, is calculated as follows:

$$\bar{X} = \frac{\sum X_i}{m}$$

where X_i is the magnitude of the condition X for observation (territory) i,

m is the total number of observations or territories

and $\sum$ means 'the sum of', or add up all the m observations on the condition X.

Departures of individual observations from the mean are measured in units of the *standard deviation*, σ_x, which is found as follows:

$$\sigma_x = \sqrt{\frac{\sum (X_i - \bar{X})^2}{m}}$$

It is the square root of the average of the sum of the squares of individual departures of observations from the mean.

The standard score (Z) for any observation i is calculated as follows:

$$Z_i = \frac{X_i - \bar{X}}{\sigma_x}$$

This formula produces results such that when $X_i = \bar{X}$, $Z_i = 0$, and when $X_i = \sigma_x$, $Z_i = 1 \cdot 0$, irrespective of the original units of measurement. Thus, observations on sets of conditions measured in different units are placed on a comparable scale where the mean is zero and the standard deviation unity. This enables the territorial distribution of such things as £s of output, number of deaths and distance from service facilities to be directly compared.

If there are n criteria of level of living (or whatever we like to call it), in a sequence that can be expressed as $1, 2, \ldots, j, \ldots, n$, then a composite index (I) can be derived for any territory i as follows:

$$I_i = \sum_{}^{n} Z_{ij}$$

where Z_{ij} is the standard score for area i on criterion j

and $\sum^{n}$ means sum all the n observations.

Repeating this calculation for all the m territories $(1, 2, \ldots, i, \ldots, m)$ gives a set of composite indicators. This is the method used in a number of the case studies in this book, e.g. regional variations in the quality of life in Britain and inter-state variations in the USA (see Chapter 3).

The various criteria $1, 2, \ldots, j, \ldots, n$ can be weighted differentially thus:

$$I_i = \sum_{}^{n} Z_{ij} W_j$$

where W_j is the weight of the jth criterion. The calculation without W implicitly weights all the critera equally, i.e. by unity. The weights can be varied geographically by W_{ij}, which is the weight of criterion j in territory i.

As an imaginary example, suppose that the following data provided observations on three conditions (X) in four regions (R), cities or nations, expressed on a per capita basis such as per 1000 population:

		Criteria		
		discos X_1	hospitals X_2	schools X_3
Regions	R_1	7	21	6
	R_2	5	8	12
	R_3	10	12	8
	R_4	6	1	4

Which region has the highest level of living by these criteria?

This can be answered by the calculation of the standard score summation. For the first criterion (discos) the standard scores are as set down below:

Region	X	$X-\overline{X}$	$(X-\overline{X})^2$	$\dfrac{X-\overline{X}}{\sigma_x} = Z$
1	7	0	0	0·00
2	5	−2	4	−1·07
3	10	3	9	1·60
4	6	−1	1	−0·53
$\sum X = 28$		$\sum(X-\overline{X})^2 = 14$		$\sum Z = 0·00$

$$m = 4 \qquad \overline{X} = 7 \qquad \sigma_x = \sqrt{\frac{\sum(X-\overline{X})^2}{m}} = \sqrt{\frac{14}{4}} = 1·87$$

Note that the sum of a set of standard scores for any criterion should be zero, subject to rounding errors in the calculation.

The full matrix of standard scores and their summation is:

	Z_1	Z_2	Z_3	ΣZ	rank order
R_1	0·00	1·48	−0·51	0·97	2
R_2	−1·07	−0·36	1·52	0·09	3
R_3	1·60	0·21	0·17	1·98	1
R_4	−0·53	−1·33	−1·18	−3·04	4

Region 3 comes out 'best' on the summation; Region 4 is 'worst'.

If we assume the differential weights of 1 for discos, 2 for hospitals and 3 for schools, the matrix and summation change as follows:

	$Z_1 W_1$	$Z_2 W_2$	$Z_3 W_3$	$\Sigma Z W$	rank order
R_1	0·00	2·96	−1·53	1·43	3
R_2	−1·07	−0·72	4·56	2·77	1
R_3	1·60	0·42	0·51	2·53	2
R_4	−0·53	−2·66	−3·54	−6·73	4

The rankings have now changed, to make Region 1 top of the league table for level of living because it is so well endowed with the highest-weighted criterion – schools. This method of weighting is substantially the same as that used in the study of British regions in Chapter 3.

Exercise: Select a small number of criteria of level of living, social well-being or the quality of life. Compile data for your own town (neighbourhood, city, region or nation) and for a set of other comparable territorial units. Calculate standard scores for each territory on each criterion, and then sum them for each territory. Differential weightings can be derived from a survey of friends or class members, and the calculation can be done again on this basis. How does your home area compare with the others? What difference do the weightings make to the results? You could also draw a level-of-living profile for your home area, as in Figures 2.6 and 4.2 earlier in the book.

Bibliography

ADELMAN, I., and MORRIS, C. T., 1967, *Society, Politics and Economic Development*, Johns Hopkins Press, Baltimore.

ADELMAN, I., and MORRIS, C. T., 1973, *Economic Growth and Social Equity in Developing Countries*, Stanford University Press, Stanford, Calif.

AGEE, P., 1975, *Inside the Company: CIA Diary*, Penguin, Harmondsworth.

AHLUWALIA, M. S., 1974, 'Income inequality: Some Dimensions of the Problem', in H. Chenery *et al.* (eds.), *Redistribution with Growth*, Oxford University Press, Oxford, 3–37.

ALAYEV, E., and KHOREV, B., 1976, 'Formation of a Unified Settlement System in the USSR', *Soviet Geographical Studies*, USSR Academy of Sciences, Moscow, 169–80.

ANDORKA, R., 1976, *Tendencies of Regional Development and Differentiation in Hungary, Measured by Social Indicators*, Central Statistical Office, Dept of Social Statistics, Budapest (mimeo).

ANDREWS, F. M., and WITHEY, S. B., 1976, *Social Indicators of Well-being in America: The Development and Measurement of Perceptual Indicators*, Plenum Press, New York.

ATKINSON, A. B., 1975, *The Economics of Inequality*, Clarendon Press, Oxford.

BANDMAN, M. K. (ed.), 1976, *Modelling of Territorial Production Complexes* (three volumes), Institute of Economics and Organization of Industrial Production, USSR Academy of Sciences – Siberian Branch, Novosibirsk.

BARBASH, N. B., 1977, 'Opyt Issledovania Faktornoi Ekologiy g. Mockvy', in Y. V. Medvedkov, *Gorodskoya sreda i puti yeye optimizatsiy*, Institut Geografii, Akademii Nauk CCCP, Moscow, 37–53.

BARTA, G., 1975, 'Changes in the Living Conditions of the Rural Population', *Review*, Hungarian Academy of Sciences, Budapest, 89–110.

BATER, J., 1977, 'Soviet Town Planning: Theory and Practice in the 1970s', *Progress in Human Geography*, 1, 177–207.

BEDERMAN, S. H., 1974, 'The Stratification of "Quality of Life" in the Black Community of Atlanta, Georgia', *Southeastern Geographer*, 14, 26–37.

BEDERMAN, S. H., and ADAMS, J. S., 1974, 'Job Accessibility and Underemployment', *Annals*, Association of American Geographers, 64, 378–86.

BENYON, H., 1973, *Working for Ford*, Penguin, Harmondsworth.

BERRY, B. J. L., 1960, 'An Inductive Approach to the Regionalization of Economic Development', in N. Ginsburg (ed.), *Essays on Geography and Economic Development*, Research Paper 62, Dept of Geography, University of Chicago, 110–19.

BERRY, B. J. L., 1964, 'Cities as Systems within Systems of Cities', *Papers and Proceedings*, Regional Science Association, 13, 147–63.

BERRY, B. J. L., 1970, 'The Geography of the United States in the Year 2000', *Transactions*, Institute of British Geographers, 51, 21–53.

BOARD, C., 1976, 'The Spatial Structure of Labour Migration', in D. M. Smith (ed.), *Separation in South Africa: People and Policies*, Occasional Paper No. 6, Dept of Geography, Queen Mary College, University of London, 63–76.

BOARD, C., DAVIES, R. J., and FAIR, T. J. D., 1970, 'The Structure of the South African Space Economy: An Integrated Approach', *Regional Studies*, 4, 367–92.

BOOMS, B. H., and HALLDORSON, J. R., 1973, 'The Politics of Redistribution: A Reformulation', *American Political Science Review*, 67, 924–33.

BROOKFIELD, H. C., 1975, *Interdependent Development*, Methuen, London.

BRYANT, J., 1969, *Health and the Developing World*, Cornell University Press, Ithaca, N.Y.

BUNGE, W., 1974, 'The Human Geography of Detroit', in R. A. Roberge (ed.), *La Crise Urbaine: A Challenge to Geographers*, University of Ottawa Press, Ottawa, 49–69.

BUXTON, M., 1976, *Health and Inequality*, Unit 13, Course D302 – Patterns of Inequality, The Open University Press, Milton Keynes.

BYERS, T., and NOLAN, P., 1976, *Inequality: India and China Compared*, Units 25–8, Course D302 – Patterns of Inequality, The Open University Press, Milton Keynes.

CAMINA, M. M., 1975, 'Public Participation – An Australian Dimension', *The Planner*, 61, 232–5.

CASTELLS, M., 1977, *The Urban Question: A Marxist Approach*, Edward Arnold, London.

CATTELL, D., 1974, 'Comprehensive Consumer Welfare Planning in the USSR', in H. W. Morton and R. L. Tökés (eds.), *Soviet Politics and Society in the 1970s*, The Free Press, New York; Collier Macmillan, London, 293–360.

CITY OF FRESNO, 1973a, *Community Profile 1973*, Management Systems Office, City of Fresno, California.

CITY OF FRESNO, 1973b, *1973 Citizen Survey*, Fresno Community Analysis Division, City of Fresno, California.

COATES, B. E., and RAWSTRON, E. M., 1971, *Regional Variations in Britain: Studies in Economic and Social Geography*, Batsford, London.

COLE, J. P., and GERMAN, F. C., 1970, *A Geography of the USSR*, Butterworth, London.

COLE, J. P., and HARRISON, M. E., 1978, *Regional Inequality in the Availability of Services and Purchasing Power in the USSR 1940–1976*, Occasional Paper No. 14, Dept of Geography, Queen Mary College, University of London.

COLE, J. P., and MATHER, P. M., 1972, 'Peru Province Level Factor Analysis', *Revista Geográfica*, 77, Dec., 7–37.

CONZEN, M. P., 1975, 'Capital Flows and the Developing Urban Hierarchy: State Bank Capital in Wisconsin, 1854–1895', *Economic Geography*, 51, 321–38.

COX, K. R., 1973, *Conflict, Power and Politics in the City: A Geographic View*, McGraw-Hill, New York.

CULYER, A. J., 1976, *Need and the National Health Service: Economics and Social Choice*, Martin Robertson, London.

DAVIDSON, B., 1975, *Can Africa Survive?*, Heinemann, London.

DAVIES, B. P., 1968, *Social Needs and Resources in Local Services*, Michael Joseph, London.

DEPARTMENT OF THE ENVIRONMENT, 1976, *Census Indicators of Urban Deprivation: Greater London*, Working Note No. 11, ECUR Division, DOE, London (mimeo).

DEPARTMENT OF THE ENVIRONMENT, 1977, *Inner Area Studies*, HMSO, London.

DEPARTMENT OF HEALTH AND SOCIAL SECURITY, 1976, *Sharing Resources for Health in England*, Report of the Resource Allocation Working Party, HMSO, London.

DICKEN, P., 1977, 'The Multiplant Business Enterprise and Geographical

Space: Some Issues in the Study of External Control and Regional Development', *Regional Studies*, 10, 401–12.

DICKEN, P., and LLOYD, P., 1976, 'Geographical Perspectives on United States Investment in the United Kingdom', *Environment and Planning, A*, 8, 685–705.

DIENES, L., 1973, 'Urban Growth and Spatial Planning in Hungary', *Tijdschrift voor Economische en Sociale Geografie*, 64, 24–38.

DONALDSON, P., 1973, *Worlds Apart: The Economic Gulf Between Nations*, Penguin, Harmondsworth.

DREWNOWSKI, J., 1974, *On Measuring and Planning the Quality of Life*, Mouton, The Hague.

DUNNING, J. H., 1972, *United States Industry in Britain, 1970–1971*, The Financial Times, London.

DWYER, D. J., 1975, *People and Housing in Third World Cities: Perspectives on the Problem of Spontaneous Settlements*, Longmans, London.

FIELD, M. G., 1967, *Soviet Socialised Medicine*, The Free Press, New York; Collier Macmillan, London.

FIELD, M. G., 1976, 'Health as a "Public Utility" or the "Maintenance of Capacity" in Soviet Society', in M. G. Field (ed.), *Social Consequences of Modernization in Communist Countries*, Johns Hopkins University Press, Baltimore and London, 234–64.

FITZGERALD, E. V. K., 1976, *The State and Economic Development: Peru since 1968*, Occasional Paper 49, Dept of Applied Economics, University of Cambridge.

FRANK, A. G., 1969, *Capitalism and Underdevelopment in Latin America*, Penguin, Harmondsworth.

FREESTONE, R., 1975, *Spatial Aspects of Health Care Provision in Sydney*, School of Geography, University of New South Wales, Kensington, N.S.W.

FRIEDMANN, J., 1966, *Regional Development Policy*, MIT Press, Cambridge, Mass.

FROLIC, B. M., 1976, 'Noncomparative Communism: Chinese and Soviet Urbanization', in M. G. Field (ed.), *Social Consequences of Modernization in Communist Societies*, Johns Hopkins University Press, Baltimore and London, 149–61.

GALBRAITH, J. K., 1958, *The Affluent Society*, Houghton Mifflin, Boston, Mass.

GALBRAITH, J. K., 1967, *The New Industrial State*, Houghton Mifflin, Boston, Mass.

GALBRAITH, J. K., 1975, *Economics and the Public Purpose*, Penguin, Harmondsworth.

GIANELLA, J., 1970, *Marginalidad en Lima Metropolitana*, Centro de Estudios y Promocion del Desarrollo, Lima, Peru.

GILBERT, A., 1974, *Latin American Development: A Geographical Perspective*, Penguin, Harmondsworth.

GORDON, M. W., 1976, *The Cuban Nationalizations: The Demise of Foreign Private Property*, William S. Hein, & Co., Inc., Buffalo, N.Y.

GOULD, P., 1969, 'Problems of Space Preference Measures and Relationships', *Geographical Analysis*, 1, 31–44.

GRANBERG, A. G., and SUSLOV, V. I., 1976, 'Use of Republican and Regional Intersectoral Balances in the Analysis of the Territorial Proportions of the National Economy of the USSR', in A. G. Granberg (ed.), *Spatial National Economic Models*, Institute of Economics and Industrial Engineering, USSR Academy of Sciences – Siberian Branch, Novosibirsk.

GRUCHMAN, B., and KRASINSKI, Z., 1978, 'Measurement of Real Progress at the Local Level: Report on the Country Case Study in Poland', *Measurement and Analysis of Progress at the Local Level*, UN Research Institute for Social Development, Geneva, 145–68.

HAKE, A., 1977, *African Metropolis: Nairobi's Self-Help City*, Sussex University Press, Brighton.

HALL, P., 1966, *The World Cities*, Weidenfeld and Nicolson, London.

HALL, T. L., 1969, *Health Manpower in Peru: A Case Study in Planning*, Johns Hopkins Press, Baltimore.

HAMILTON, F. E. I., 1976, *The Moscow City Region*, Oxford University Press, Oxford.

HAMNETT, C., 1976, *Multiple Deprivation and the Inner City*, Unit 16, Course D302 – Patterns of Inequality, The Open University Press, Milton Keynes.

HARFORD, I., 1977, 'The Inner City: Whose Urban Crisis?', *The Planner*, July, 99–101.

HART, J. T., 1971, 'The Inverse Care Law', *Lancet*, Feb.

HARTSHORN, T. A., 1976, *Metropolis in Georgia: Altanta's Rise as a Major Transactional Center*, Ballinger Publishing Co., Cambridge, Mass.

HARVEY, D., 1973, *Social Justice and the City*, Edward Arnold, London.

HARVEY, D., 1975, 'The Geography of Capital Accumulation: A Reconstruction of the Marxian Theory', *Antipode*, 7, No. 2, 9–21.

HATCH, S., and SHERROTT, R., 1973, 'Positive Discrimination and the Distribution of Deprivations', *Policy and Politics*, 1, 223–40.

HMSO, 1977, *Policy for the Inner Cities*, Cmnd 6845, HMSO, London.

HOLLAND, S., 1976a, *Capital Versus the Regions*, Macmillan, London.

HOLLAND, S., 1976b, *The Regional Problem*, Macmillan, London.

HOLTERMANN, S., 1975, 'Areas of Urban Deprivation in Great Britain: An Analysis of 1971 Census Data', *Social Trends*, 33–47.

HOWE, G. M., 1970, *A National Atlas of Disease and Mortality in the United Kingdom* (2nd edn), Thomas Nelson & Sons, London.

HOWE, G. M., 1972, *Man, Environment and Disease in Britain: A Medical Geography through the Ages*, David & Charles, Newton Abbot.

HUZINEC, G. A., 1978, 'The Impact of Industrial Decision Making upon the Soviet Urban Hierarchy', *Urban Studies*, 15 (in press).

HYDE, G., 1974, *The Soviet Health Service: A Historical and Comparative Study*, Lawrence & Wishart, London.

HYMER, S., 1975, 'The Multinational Corporation and the Law of Uneven Development', in H. Radice (ed.), *International Firms and Modern Imperialism*, Penguin, Harmondsworth, 37–62.

IMBER, V., 1977, *A Classification of the English Personal Social Service Authorities*, Dept of Health and Social Security, Statistical and Research Report Series No. 16, HMSO, London.

JOLLY, R., and KING, M., 1966, 'The Organization of Health Services', in M. King (ed.), *Medical Care in Developing Countries*, Oxford University Press, Nairobi, ch. 12.

DE KADT, E., 1976, 'Wrong Priorities in Health', *New Society*, 3 June, 525–6.

KAISER, R., 1977, *Russia: The People and the Power*, Penguin, Harmondsworth.

KASER, M., 1976, *Health Care in the Soviet Union and Eastern Europe*, Croom Helm, London.

KASPERSON, R. E., 1977, 'Participation through Centrally Planned Social Change: Lessons from American Experience on the Urban Scene', in W. R. D. Sewell and J. T. Coppock (eds.), *Public Participation in Planning*, John Wiley, London, 173–90.

KHRUSHCHEV, N. S., 1977, *Khrushchev Remembers*, Vol. 1, Penguin, Harmondsworth.

KING, M. A., 1974, 'Economic Growth and Social Development – A Statistical Investigation', *Review of Income and Wealth*, Series 20, 3, 251–72.

KNOX, P. L., 1974, 'Spatial Variations in Level of Living in England and Wales in 1961', *Transactions*, Institute of British Geographers, 62, 1–24.

Bibliography

KNOX, P. L., 1975, *Social Well-being: A Spatial Perspective*, Oxford University Press, Oxford.

LANKFORD, P. M., 1974, 'Physician Location Factors and Public Policy', *Economic Geography*, 50, 244–55.

LAWRENCE, R. J., 1972, 'Social Welfare and Urban Growth', in R. S. Parker and P. N. Troy (eds.), *The Politics of Urban Growth*, Australian National University Press, Canberra, 100–128.

LEMON, A., 1976, *Apartheid: A Geography of Separation*, Saxon House, Farnborough, Hants.

LINEBERRY, R. L., 1974, 'Mandating Urban Equality: The Distribution of Municipal Public Services', *Texas Law Review*, 53, 26–59.

LISITSIN, Y., 1972, *Health Protection in the USSR*, Progress Publishers, Moscow.

LIU, B.-C., 1973, *The Quality of Life in the United States 1970: Index, Rating, and Statistics*, Midwest Research Institute, Kansas City, Mo.

LIU, B.-C., 1974, 'Variations in the Quality of Life in the United States by State, 1970', *Review of Social Economy*, 22, 131–47.

LIU, B.-C., 1975a, 'Differential net Migration Rates and the Quality of Life', *The Review of Economics and Statistics*, 57, 329–37.

LIU, B.-C., 1975b, *Quality of Life Indicators in the U.S. Metropolitan Areas, 1970*, Midwest Research Institute, Kansas City, Mo.

LOWDER, S., 1970, 'Lima's Population Growth and the Consequences for Peru', in B. Roberts and S. Lowder (eds.), *Urban Population Growth and Migration in Latin America: Two Case Studies*, Centre for Latin American Studies, University of Liverpool, 21–34.

LOWDER, S., 1974, 'Migration and Urbanization in Peru', in B. Hoyle (ed.), *Spatial Aspects of Development*, John Wiley, London, 209–29

LUSZNIEWICZ, A., 1974, 'Koncepcja mierników poziomu życia Ludności', in J. Danecki (ed.), *Społeczne aspekty rozwoju gospodarczego*, PWN Warszawa, 205–22.

MADISON, B., 1975, 'Social Service Administration in the USSR', in D. Thursz and J. L. Vigilante (eds.), *Meeting Human Needs: An Overview of Nine Countries*, Sage Publications, Beverley Hills, Calif.

MALONEY, J. C., 1973, *Social Vulnerability in Indianapolis*, Community Service Council of Metropolitan Indianapolis, Indianapolis, Ind.

MANDEL, E., 1962, *Marxist Economic Theory*, Merlin Press, London.

MANGIN, W., and TURNER, J. F. C., 1969, 'Benavides and the Barriada Movement', in P. Oliver (ed.), *Shelter and Society*, Barrie and Jenkins, London, 127–36.

MATTHEWS, M., 1976, 'Educational Growth and the Social Structure in

375

the USSR', in M. G. Field (ed.), *Social Consequences of Modernization in Communist Countries*, Johns Hopkins University Press, Baltimore and London, 121–45.

MATTHEWS, M., 1978, *Privilege in the Soviet Union: A Study of Elite Life-Styles under Communism*, George Allen & Unwin, London.

MAXWELL, N., 1974, 'The Rebirth of Shanghai', *The Sunday Times*, 14 April 1974.

MAXWELL, R., 1974, *Health Care: The Growing Dilemma*, McKinsey & Co., Inc., New York.

MCAULEY, A., 1977, 'The Distribution of Earnings and Incomes in the Soviet Union', *Soviet Studies*, 29, 214–37.

MCDERMOTT, P. J., 1977, 'Overseas Investment and the Industrial Geography of the United Kingdom', *Area*, 9, 200–207.

MCDONALD, O., 1977, 'Multinationals, Spatial Inequality and Worker's Control', in D. B. Massey and P. W. J. Batey (eds.), *Alternative Frameworks for Analysis*, London Papers in Regional Science, 7, Pion, London, 68–85.

MCGEE, T. G., 1971, *The Urbanization Process in the Third World: Explorations in Search of a Theory*, G. Bell & Sons, London.

MCGRANAHAN, D. V., *et al.*, 1970, *Content and Measurement of Socio-Economic Development: An Empirical Inquiry*, UN Research Institute for Social Development, Geneva.

MEADOWS, D. H., *et al.*, 1972, *The Limits to Growth*, Earth Island, London.

MICKIEWICZ, E., 1973, *Handbook of Soviet Social Science Data*, The Free Press, New York; Collier Macmillan, London.

MIECZKOWSKI, B., 1975, *Personal and Social Consumption in Eastern Europe*, Praeger, New York and London.

MORRILL, R. L., EARICKSON, R. J., and REES, P., 1970, 'Factors Influencing Distances Travelled to Hospitals', *Economic Geography*, 46, 161–71.

MORTON, H. W., 1974, 'What Have the Soviet Leaders Done about the Housing Crisis?' in H. W. Morton and R. L. Tökés (eds.), *Soviet Politics and Society in the 1970s*, The Free Press, New York; Collier Macmillan, London, 163–99.

MURRAY, L. W., 1974, 'Socioeconomic Development and Industrial Location in Poland', *Antipode*, 6, No. 2, 125–41.

MUSIL, J., 1968, 'The Development of Prague's Ecological Structure', in R. E. Pahl (ed.), *Readings in Urban Sociology*, Pergamon Press, London, 212–31.

NORMAN, D., 1973, *The Model Cities Program*, Office of Community

Development, Dept of Housing and Urban Development, Washington D.C.

OECD, 1976, *Measuring Social Well-being: A Progress Report on the Development of Social Indicators*, Organization for Economic Cooperation and Development, Paris.

ONTELL, R., 1973, *The Quality of Life in San Diego*, The Urban Observatory, San Diego, Calif.

OSBORN, R., 1970, *Soviet Social Policies: Welfare, Equality and Community*, The Dorsey Press, Homewood, Ill.

PAHL, R., 1970, *Whose City?*, Longmans, London.

PAN AMERICAN HEALTH ORGANIZATION, 1974, *Health Conditions in the Americas 1969–72*, Scientific Publication No. 287, World Health Organization, Washington D.C.

PARKIN, F., 1971, *Class Inequality and Political Order*, McGibbon & Kee, London.

RICKARD, J. H., 1975, 'Per Capita Expenditure of the English Area Health Authorities' (seminar paper), Centre for Studies in Social Policy, London; reprinted in Buxton (1976), 39–45.

ROBSON, J., 1977, *Quality, Inequality and Health Care: Notes on Medicine, Capital and the State*, Marxists in Medicine, London.

ROSTOW, W. W., 1960, *The Stages of Economic Growth*, Cambridge University Press, London.

RYAN, M., 1978, *The Organization of Medical Care in the Soviet Union*, Basil Blackwell and Martin Robertson, Oxford and London.

SALIH, K., 1972, 'Judicial Relief and Differential Provision of Public Goods: A Case Analysis and Certain Prescriptions', *Discussion Paper XX, Research on Conflict in Locational Decisions*, Regional Science Dept, University of Pennsylvania.

SAMUELSON, P. A., 1973, *Economics* (9th edn), McGraw-Hill, New York.

SCHROEDER, G., 1973, 'Regional Difference in Income and Levels of Living in the USSR', in V. N. Bandera and Z. L. Melnyk (eds.), *The Soviet Economy in Regional Perspective*, Praeger, New York, 167–95.

SHANNON, G. W., and DEVER, G. E. A., 1974, *Health Care Delivery: Spatial Perspectives*, McGraw-Hill, New York.

SHEPHERD, J., WESTAWAY, J., and LEE, T., 1974, *A Social Atlas of London*, Clarendon Press, Oxford.

SIDEL, R., 1977, 'People Serving People: Human Services in the People's Republic of China', in D. Thurz and J. L. Vigilante (eds.), *Meeting Human Needs: Additional Perspectives from Thirteen Countries*, Sage Publications, Beverly Hills, Calif., 163–96.

SIK, O., 1972, *Czechoslovakia: The Bureaucratic Economy*, International Arts and Sciences Press, White Plains, New York.

SLATER, D., 1975, 'Underdevelopment and Spatial Inequality: Approaches to the Problems of Regional Planning in the Third World', *Progress in Planning*, 4, Part 2, 97–167.

SMIT, P., and BOOYSEN, J. J., 1977, *Urbanisation in the Homelands*, Monograph Series No. 3, Institute for Plural Societies, University of Pretoria.

SMITH, C. T., 1968, 'Problems of Regional Development in Peru', *Geography*, 53, 260–81.

SMITH, C. T., 1977, 'Agrarian Reform and Regional Development in Peru', in R. Miller, C. T. Smith and J. Fisher (eds.), *Social and Economic Change in Modern Peru*, Monograph Series No. 6, Centre for Latin American Studies, University of Liverpool, 87–119.

SMITH, D. M., 1971, *Industrial Location: An Economic Geographical Analysis*, John Wiley, New York.

SMITH, D. M., 1973, *The Geography of Social Well-being in the United States: An Introduction to Territorial Social Indicators*, McGraw-Hill, New York.

SMITH, D. M., 1974, *Crime Rates as Territorial Social Indicators: The Case of the United States*, Occasional Paper No. 1, Dept of Geography, Queen Mary College, University of London.

SMITH, D. M., 1975, *Patterns in Human Geography: An Introduction to Numerical Methods*, David & Charles, Newton Abbot; Penguin, Harmondsworth, 1977.

SMITH, D. M., 1977, *Human Geography: A Welfare Approach*, Edward Arnold, London.

SMITH, D. M., and OGDEN, P. E., 1977, 'Reformation and Revolution in Human Geography', in R. Lee (ed.), *Change and Tradition: Geography's New Frontiers*, Dept of Geography, Queen Mary College, University of London, 47–58.

SMITH, H., 1976, *The Russians*, The New York Times Book Co., New York.

SMITH, M. R., and SMITH, D. M., 1973, *The United States: How They Live and Work*, David & Charles, Newton Abbot.

DE SOUZA, A. R., and PORTER, P. W., 1974, *The Underdevelopment and Modernization of the Third World*, Commission on College Geography, Resource Paper 28, Association of American Geographers, Washington, D.C.

STERN, J. (ed.), 1973, *Prototype State-of-the-Region Report for Los Angeles*
378

County, School of Architecture and Urban Planning, University of California, Los Angeles.

STEVENSON, G. M., 1972, 'Noise and the Urban Environment', in T. R. Detwyler and M. G. Marcus (eds.), *Urbanization and Environment*, Duxbury Press, Belmont, Calif., 195–228.

STILWELL, F. J. B., and HARDWICK, J. M., 1973, 'Social Inequality in Australian Cities', *The Australian Quarterly*, 45, No. 4 (Dec.), 18–36.

SUSMAN, P., 1974, 'Cuban Development: from Dualism to Integration', *Antipode*, 6, No. 3, 10–29.

SUSSMAN, M., 1972, 'Family, Kinship and Bureaucracy', in A. Campbell and P. Converse (eds.), *The Human Meaning of Social Change*, Russell Sage Foundation, New York, 127–58.

TAYLOR, C. L., and HUDSON, M. C., 1972, *World Handbook of Political and Social Indicators* (2nd edn), Yale University Press, New Haven and London.

THORNDIKE, E. L., 1939, *Your City*, Harcourt, Brace & Co., New York.

TOWNSEND, P., 1976, *The Difficulties of Policies Based on the Concept of Area Deprivation*, Barnett Shine Foundation Lecture, Dept of Economics, Queen Mary College, University of London.

UNION BANK OF SWITZERLAND, 1974, *Prices and Earnings Around the Globe*, Union Bank of Switzerland, Zurich.

UNO, 1954, *Report on International Definition and Measurement of Standards of Living: Report by Committee of Experts*, United Nations, New York.

UNRISD, 1976, *Research Data Bank of Development Indicators*, United Nations Research Institute for Social Development, Geneva.

DE VISE, P., 1973, *Hospitals and Misused and Misplaced Doctors: A Locational Analysis of the Urban Health Care Crisis*, Commission on College Geography, Resource Paper 22, Association of American Geographers, Washington D.C.

VOGEL, E. F., 1976, 'The Chinese Model of Development', in M. G. Field (ed.), *Social Consequences of Modernization in Communist Societies*, Johns Hopkins University Press, Baltimore and London, 60–80.

WESTAWAY, J., 1974a, 'Contact Potential and the Occupational Structure of the British Urban System 1961–1966: An Empirical Study', *Regional Studies*, 8, 57–73.

WESTAWAY, J., 1974b, 'The Spatial Hierarchy of Business Organization and its Implications for the British Urban System', *Regional Studies*, 8, 145–55.

WHITE, A. L., 1976, 'Revolutionary Ideology and Urban Reform in Peru', *Antipode*, 8, No. 3, 59–71.

WILLIAMSON, J. G., 1965, 'Regional Inequality and the Process of National Development: A Description of the Patterns', *Economic Development and Cultural Change*, 13, 3–45.

WILSON, J. O., 1969, *Quality of Life in the United States: An Excursion into the New Frontier of Socio-Economic Indicators*, Midwest Research Institute, Kansas City, Mo.

WILSON, M. G. A., 1972, 'A Note on Infant Death in Melbourne', *Australian Paediatric Journal*, 8, 61–71.

WISNER, B., WESTGATE, K., and O'KEEFE, P., 1976, 'Poverty and Disaster', *New Society*, 19 Sept., 546–8.

WOOD, C. M., et al., 1974, *The Geography of Pollution: A Study of Greater Manchester*, Manchester University Press, Manchester.

WOOLLACOTT, M., 1976, 'China's Radical Differences', *The Guardian*, 18 Nov. 1976.

YANOWITCH, M., 1977, *Social and Economic Inequality in the Soviet Union*, Martin Robertson, London.

ZASLAVSKAIA, T. I., and LIASHENKO, L. P., 1976, 'Rural Socio-economic Development and the Migration of Rural Population', in A. H. Richmond and D. Kubat (eds.), *Internal Migration: The New World and the Third World*, Sage Publications, Beverly Hills, Calif., 64–82.

ZHUKOV, K., and FYODOROV, V., 1974, *Housing Construction in the Soviet Union*, Progress Publishers, Moscow.

ZWICK, P., 1976, 'Intrasystem Inequality and the Symmetry of Socio-economic Development in the USSR', *Comparative Politics*, 8, 501–24.

Index

Index

Index

Index

Manufacturing belt (of USA), 109
Mao Tse-tung, 167, 168, 340, 362
Market forces, 41, 120–21, 192, 195, 210–12, 261, 337–40
Marx, Karl, 42, 100, 213, 290, 338, 340, 349, 361
Marxism, 84, 101, 103, 292
Marxism–Leninism, 148–9, 332, 341
Massey, Jack C., 259
Mass media, 16
Materialism, 16, 20, 21, 95, 360, 361
Mean deviation, 27
Measurement problems, 25–33
Medical care, *see* Health
Medicare (in USA), 260, 265
Melbourne, Australia, 281
Merit (as a distributive criterion), 41, 43
Mexican Americans (Chicanos), 182, 184, 190
Mexico City, 214
Midwest Research Institute, 113, 175
Migrant labour, 333
Migration, 121, 214–15
Mining, 143, 144
Ministry of Health (of USSR), 293
Minsk, 208–300
Mississippi, 36
Mixed economy, 131, 210
Mobile facilities, 284, 293
Mobility of factors of production, 120, 339
Model Cities (in USA), 191–2, 195, 208
Modernization, 98–9, 154, 157
Monarchy, 338
Mortality, 252–3, 255–6, 268–9, 272; *see also* Infant mortality
Moscow, 66, 232–40, 298, 302–3, 342
Multinational companies, 121, 212, 322–4, 349–52
Multiple deprivation, 16, 195–213
Multiplier effect, 350

Nairobi, 357
National Health Service (NHS), 248, 266, 267–76
National Party (in South Africa), 332
Natural hazards, 80–81, 95
Need (as a distributive criterion), 42, 43
Netherlands, 76–7
Newham, London, 205, 209
Newspaper circulation, 70–71
New Towns, 212
New York City, 47, 49, 193
New York State, 113
Noise, 46–9

Norms (of service provision), 293
North Sea oil, 35
Novosibirsk, 234

O'Hare Airport, Chicago, 47
Organization for Economic Co-operation and Development, 22–4
Organ transplants, 250, 260, 309

Partnership schemes, 212
Peking, 243–4
Perception, 117–18, 186–7
Perfect competition, theory of, 120
Peru, 80–81, 331–2
    geographical features, 136–8
    health care, 285–9
    land ownership, 138, 143–4
    regional inequality, 136–48
    urban inequality, 213–29
Planning, 347–53
Poland 157–64
Polarization
    spatial, 132, 135, 211–12, 234, 284, 304
    of classes, 193–5, 337
Political power, 190, 302. 343, 358–9
Political rights, 82
Pollution, 66, 78, 187, 237, 336
Polyclinics, 293, 306–7
Poverty, theory of, 354–6
Prague, 241
Pretoria, 314
Primate cities, 132, 214
Private property, 19–20, 337–8
Production, 52, 97–8, 118
Productive forces, 97–8
Psychological well-being, 117–18
Public assistance, 29–31
Public goods, 267
Pueblos jovenes, see *Barriadas*
Purchasing power, 61–9

Queen Mary College, University of London, 125

Racial discrimination, 44–6, 119, 188, 190, 332
Racial inferiority, 96
Real income, 63
Resource Allocation Working Party (on the NHS), 271–4
Revolution, 148, 171–2, 331–2
Rhodesia, 316
Rio de Janeiro, 214
Road accidents, 78
Rostow, W., 98

384

Index